THE REPUBLICAN ERA: 1869-1901

By LEONARD D. WHITE

THE FEDERALISTS

THE JEFFERSONIANS

THE JACKSONIANS

THE REPUBLICAN ERA: 1869–1901

THE
Republican Era:
1869–1901

A STUDY IN ADMINISTRATIVE HISTORY

by Leonard D. White

UNIVERSITY OF CHICAGO

with the assistance of
Jean Schneider

THE MACMILLAN COMPANY
NEW YORK
1958

Second Printing 1958

Library of Congress catalog card number: 58–6209

To an old and
honored friend

HAROLD W. DODDS

President of Princeton University
1933–1957

PREFACE

Matthew Arnold visited the United States in 1883 and upon his return to Great Britain commented upon American institutions. "I suppose," he wrote, "I am not by nature disposed to think so much as most people do of 'institutions.' The Americans think and talk very much of their 'institutions'; I am by nature inclined . . . to regard, rather, men and their characters. But the more I saw of America, the more I found myself led to treat 'institutions' with increased respect. Until I went to the United States I had never seen a people with institutions which seemed expressly and thoroughly suited to it. I had not properly appreciated the benefits proceeding from this cause."[1]

This book, like its predecessors, *The Federalists*, *The Jeffersonians*, and *The Jacksonians*, is a study of institutions, but illuminated, it is hoped, by sketches of the men who operated them. Behind men and institutions stand the ideas and ideals of succeeding generations which bind all together into a stable whole. These I have allowed the participants to state for themselves.

One is impressed indeed with the continuity of administrative institutions, surviving the transformation of the economic structure, political convulsions, and the impact of war. Neither the Civil War nor the Spanish-American War left much impression on civil institutions; the return to normalcy was rapid and substantially complete.

Two major problems occupied the center of the administrative stage—the relation of Congress to the President and their respective roles vis-à-vis the administrative system; and the reform of the civil service. The former was an ancient dilemma; the latter, relatively novel. The former was productive of little analysis excepting Woodrow Wilson's *Congressional Government* which, as events were to

[1] Matthew Arnold, *Civilization in the United States: First and Last Impressions of America* (Boston: Cupples and Hurd, 1888), pp. 114-15.

[vii]

prove, did not foretell future trends and developments. The latter was productive of an abundant literature from Charles Francis Adams through George William Curtis, Carl Schurz, and the reformers, again to Woodrow Wilson. His prophetic essay, "The Study of Administration," was a pioneer analysis in the middle of thirty years of intellectual indifference to the problem, as he put it, how "to straighten the paths of government, to make its business less unbusinesslike, to strengthen and purify its organization, and to crown its duties with dutifulness."

This work now spans over a century of administrative history. The years from 1869 to 1901 marked the culmination of Jacksonian theory and practice, with all their strength and weakness. Federalist doctrine, long in disrepute, again made itself felt, but in a new partnership with democratic ideas. Theodore Roosevelt declared that he was both a Federalist and a Jeffersonian. Hamilton's concept of a stable, competent, and politically neutral public service was inherent in the Civil Service Act; but neither the Republican nor Democratic parties espoused Hamilton's intention to make government a positive force in society.

I am under continuing obligations to the University of Chicago Library and to the Baker Library of Dartmouth College—a generous host to visiting scholars. The National Archives and the Library of Congress have been most helpful, although their riches have hardly been touched. They invite wide ranges of monographic studies in administrative history and biography. I am also greatly indebted to the University of Chicago and to the Rockefeller Foundation for continued financial support.

To record again my heavy debt to Jean Schneider is both a duty and a pleasure. She has contributed so much to this volume, as well as to *The Federalists, The Jeffersonians,* and *The Jacksonians,* that it is just to acknowledge my obligation on the title page of *The Republican Era.*

March 15, 1957

L. D. W.

CONTENTS

CHAPTER ONE

The State of the
Administrative System

Every administrative system is the product of the moral climate, the technological capacity, and the executive talent of its generation. The federal system from Grant through McKinley was generally undistinguished. The moral climate after the Civil War was unfavorable, and only slowly improved; the technological arts useful in large-scale administration were undeveloped; executive talent tended to be drained off into railways, steel, manufacturing, and urban utilities.

Superficially, the public service seemed at a relative standstill. The influence of party was predominant, although checked by the Civil Service Act of 1883. The scene was complicated by the emergence of powerful pressure groups, notably the Grand Army of the Republic. The role of Congress in administrative affairs was excessive, and the leadership of Presidents relatively weak. The business of the departments constantly increased with the rise of population and the flow of legislation, but its effective discharge was half-paralyzed by the reluctance of Congress to provide adequate staff and by the failure of the departments to rid themselves of antiquated and time-consuming procedures. Nobody, whether in Congress or in the executive departments, seemed able to rise much above the handicraft office methods that were cumbersome even in the simpler days of the Jacksonians.

Despite such undoubted circumstances, change and progress occurred during these decades. The authority of the President, nearly wrecked by the impeachment of Andrew Johnson and the abnegation of Ulysses S. Grant, was gradually restored. The patronage system was expelled from a small but growing segment of the public service as the Civil Service Commission began its work. The doctrine of political neutrality slowly took hold against stubborn opposition. New ideals of the role and function of government were arising.

The over-all institutional framework of the federal administrative system was provided by Congress, by the President, and by the courts. These constitutional authorities established the administrative tasks, provided funds, specified procedures, supplied directives, and set limits to the operations of the system. The heart of administration, however, was in the great departments and agencies. Here the services for the benefit and control of citizens found their homes, performed their functions, and achieved their purposes. Hence the emphasis in the chapters that follow upon the policy, leadership, and operations of the executive departments and some of their major subdivisions.

An old-timer in Washington looking backward from the vantage point of the late 1890's would have found the government establishment bigger but not much different from its essential nature in 1870. There were two new departments, Justice and Agriculture. The former was not much more than the Office of the Attorney General raised to departmental status; the latter had been created in 1862 as a department under a Commissioner and was given full status in 1889. In both cases the transition meant little difference in function. There were two new commissions, the Civil Service Commission and the Interstate Commerce Commission. There were a number of new bureaus, including Labor, usually representing growth of an earlier and perhaps long-established minor activity. There were certainly many more persons on the civilian payroll: in round figures, 53,000 in 1871; 107,000 in 1881; 166,000 in 1891; and at the turn of the century, 256,000 in 1901, nearly a fivefold expansion in thirty years.[1] These figures bespoke an increase in the volume of business coincident with the growth of the country rather than the addition of new functions and activities. Mere increase in size and in the volume of business, however, brought new pressures for the improvement of administra-

[1] Figures from U.S. Bureau of the Census, *Historical Statistics of the United States, 1789-1945* (Washington: Government Printing Office, 1949), p. 294.

tive methods, reflected in repeated investigations by Congress and the gradual abandonment of much antiquated office procedure.

Washington had emerged from a country town of oil illumination and muddy streets to a city of nearly 150,000 when Hayes was inaugurated in 1877. Swamps had been drained, new streets laid out, old ones improved, and commons converted into attractive parks. Three thousand gaslights illuminated the streets at night, and in 1881 a House committee declared in favor of electricity, "the light of the future for artificial illumination."[2] Transportation was by carriage and horseback, but mule-drawn streetcars were dragged along some of the streets. Telephones were practically unknown, and it was considered a marvel when Hayes' Secretary of the Navy installed a line between his office and the navy yard three miles away.[3] Both Washington and the art of administration were in an early stage of development as the post-Civil War era began.

DOMINANCE OF LAISSEZ FAIRE

During these years there was a general, although not unchallenged, conviction of the virtue of laissez faire. This had been the prevailing temper of the people, despite Federalist doctrine to the contrary. It survived the Civil War, was congenial to the big business of the postwar years, and was proclaimed by most of the prominent men of the time.

Charles Francis Adams, Jr., dismissed the argument for public ownership of the railroads on the ground that the system of public administration was not dependable enough to bear the burden. "Government supervision among Anglo-Saxons," he wrote just as he was to become a member of the Massachusetts Railway Commission, "is apt to degenerate into jobbery. In America, particularly, the whole instinct of the people leads them to circumscribe rather than to enlarge the province of government. This policy is founded in wisdom. Government by the people is apt at all times to degenerate into government by the politicians and the caucus; and the people, if wise,

---

[2] House Report 235, 46th Cong., 3d sess., p. 1 (Feb. 14, 1881).

[3] Charles Roll, *Colonel Dick Thompson: the Persistent Whig* (Indianapolis: Indiana Historical Bureau, 1948), p. 219. The first commercial exchange was installed in 1878, the year in which Congress appropriated $150 to the Public Printer to connect his office with the Capitol (20 Stat. 207, June 20, 1878).

will keep the province of the government within reasonable limits. The spoils of victory are large enough already. . . ."[4]

Grant, in the opinion of some of his associates, was naïve in these matters. Congressman James A. Garfield helped to keep him in the straight and narrow path. Grant had considered public works expenditures to alleviate the suffering of the unemployed in 1874. Garfield wrote to his friend Hinsdale: "We had somewhat of a struggle to keep him [i.e., Grant] from drifting into that foolish notion that it was necessary to make large appropriations on public works to give employment to laborers. But the Secretary of the Treasury and I united our forces in dissuading him from the scheme, insisting that the true remedy for the finances at present was economy and retrenchment, until business restored itself."[5] Garfield declared that it was "not part of the functions of the national government to find employment for people—and if we were to appropriate a hundred millions for this purpose, we should be taxing forty millions of people to keep a few thousand employed."[6] President Cleveland concurred. "The lessons of paternalism," he declared in his second inaugural address, "ought to be unlearned and the better lesson taught that while the people should patriotically and cheerfully support their Government its functions do not include the support of the people."[7] Attitudes such as these strengthened the claims of the telegraph companies and the railroads to be let alone.[8]

Few were the voices raised against the idea that government was not a suitable means of direct service to the people. Heretical indeed must have seemed the views of Senator Roger Q. Mills of Texas who, in the midst of the lean years of the 1890's, declared: "Public works, wherever they are to be constructed, should be entered upon now, and the most liberal appropriations should be made for their con-

[4] Charles F. Adams, Jr., "Railroad Inflation," *North American Review*, CVIII (1869), 159.

[5] *Garfield-Hinsdale Letters: Correspondence between James Abram Garfield and Burke Aaron Hinsdale* (Mary L. Hinsdale, ed., Ann Arbor: University of Michigan Press, 1949), p. 300 (Dec. 8, 1874).

[6] Theodore Clarke Smith, *The Life and Letters of James Abram Garfield* (2 vols., New Haven: Yale University Press, 1925), I, 517 (Dec. 5, 1874).

[7] James D. Richardson, *A Compilation of the Messages and Papers of the Presidents, 1789-1910* (11 vols., New York: Bureau of National Literature, 1911), IX, 390 (March 4, 1893).

[8] For illustrative commentary, see Norvin Green, "The Government and the Telegraph," *North American Review*, CXXXVII (1883), 422-34; Gerrit L. Lansing, "The Railway and the State," *ibid.*, CXXXVIII (1884), 461-75.

tinuance: instead of discharging one person from government employ, two should be taken on."[9]

Great and widespread wrongs did, however, compel two radical innovations: the regulation of railroad rates and services through the Interstate Commerce Commission (1887), and the regulation of monopoly by the Sherman Antitrust Act of 1890. The latter became a responsibility primarily of the courts and the Department of Justice; the former, the task of the first of the regulatory commissions that were to multiply in the second half of the Republican era, and later. On a lesser scale the federal government was doing something for agriculture and for public health. Through the Geological Survey an interest was shown in natural resources, and in 1864 the postal money order system was established. On the whole, and with the exception of railroad and monopoly regulation, the federal government was serving the people in few areas not occupied at earlier dates. The states and the cities were diversifying and expanding their functions, but not the general government.

A corollary of federal laissez faire was a certain indifference to affairs conducted at Washington. This result was noted by a Pennsylvania independent, Isaac Wayne MacVeagh, who was a leader for civil service reform, Attorney General in Garfield's Cabinet, and ambassador to Italy in Cleveland's administration.[10] Commenting on the apparent political apathy prior to the national election of 1884, he wrote in the *Century Magazine*: "the truth, however, will be found to be that the average American citizen cares very little about politics at present, because the government under which he lives touches his life very rarely, and only at points of very little importance to him. From his rising up until his lying down, the vast aggregate of his interests and his activities are entirely beyond its scope, and there is hardly any serious interest of his life which is affected by it."[11] Republicans and Democrats joined hands to maintain this underlying tradition.

OFFICE SEEKING

The passion for office that characterized the Jacksonian period did not diminish in the post-Civil War decades. Presidents, Secretaries,

[9] Roger Q. Mills, "The Wilson Bill," *ibid.*, CLVIII (1894), 241.
[10] *Dictionary of American Biography*, XII, 170.
[11] Wayne MacVeagh, "The Next Presidency," *Century Magazine*, XXVII (1883-84), 670.

and lesser appointing officers were harassed under Republican and Democratic administrations alike. Civil service reform brought some relief, notably in the post offices and customs service, but it also induced even greater pressure on the available patronage positions. The evidence on this aspect of the public service is abundant. No President or department head failed to complain privately about the loss of time, distraction from the public business, and personal discomfort flowing from the never-ending importunity for office. President Garfield noted in his journal: "My day is frittered away by the personal seeking of people, when it ought to be given to the great problems which concern the whole country. Four years of this kind of intellectual dissipation may cripple me for the remainder of my life."[12] To his wife he wrote on May 29, 1877: "I had hardly arrived [in Washington] before the door-bell began to ring and the old stream of office-seekers began to pour in. They had scented my coming and were lying in wait for me like vultures for a wounded bison. All day long it has been a steeple chase, I fleeing and they pursuing."[13] When Grant was inaugurated, Garfield was an observer; he said then: "The rush for office is absolutely appalling; it would almost seem that the adult population of the United States had moved on the works of the government and were determined to carry every position by storm."[14]

Little improvement came with time. Secretary of the Interior Lucius Q. C. Lamar (1885-88) wrote: "I eat my breakfast and dinner and supper always in the company of some two or three eager and hungry applicants for office; go to bed with their importunities in my ears; and . . . I have no time to say my prayers. . . . I expect you think that I am in a bitter mood this morning, but I am not; only in a jocose one after an engagement with eight office seekers before breakfast."[15]

The Spanish-American War required thousands of civilian and military appointments, and great was the clamor for favors. Secretary of the Navy John D. Long confided to his journal: "Senator Penrose

---

[12] Theodore C. Smith, *Life and Letters of James A. Garfield*, II, 1151-52 (June 13, 1881).

[13] *Ibid.*, II, 654.

[14] *Ibid.*, I, 446 (March 27, 1869).

[15] Edward Mayes, *Lucius Q. C. Lamar* (Nashville, Tenn: Publishing House of Methodist Episcopal Church, South, 1895), pp. 480-81.

comes in, and we come near striking fire about a little twopenny appointment of shipkeeper at $2.00 a day at the Philadelphia Navy Yard. Representative Butler wants it, and Penrose wants it. It is like a fight of wolves over a carcass. Shameful and disgraceful picture: that a Senator of the United States should be running his legs off, wasting his time, when great questions are at stake, about this carrion of patronage—which very patronage only hurts, instead of helping his political prospects."[16] The War Department was surrounded. Secretary Alger wrote, "Great and constant was the pressure for appointments. Applicants, by mail and in person, would beg, appeal, and demand commissions. Before breakfast, and even after midnight, they besieged the Secretary's residence with a determination superb in its inflexibility."[17]

The causes which induced this continuous passion for office were numerous and complex. Some were obvious: the pressure from rising politicians pushing their individual fortunes, from Senators and Congressmen safeguarding their hold on their states and districts, from failures in the business world seeking peace in the security of government office. States demanded recognition; the machine sought its own interests; and faction fought hostile faction through the patronage. The Grand Army of the Republic had to be satisfied. Campaign contributors looked hopefully for appointment to the diplomatic corps, and the less influential to a consulship.

Even good-natured friendship was involved. The poet, James Russell Lowell, wrote to Attorney General Ebenezer R. Hoar, "Don't laugh—but the office I am most interested about is our Post Office in Old Cambridge. The present incumbent *ought* to be kept in and if you can properly say a word to Mr. Creswell, I hope you will. . . ."[18]

Office seeking was also built into the governmental system. An able political scientist, Henry J. Ford, observed a half century ago:

. . . . Office seekers apparently regard themselves as a privileged class with a right of personal access to the President, and any appearances of

[16] Lawrence Shaw Mayo, ed., *America of Yesterday, as Reflected in the Journal of John Davis Long* (Boston: Atlantic Monthly Press, 1923), p. 156 (Jan. 26, 1898).

[17] Russell A. Alger, *The Spanish-American War* (New York: Harper and Brothers, 1901), p. 30.

[18] Moorfield Storey and Edward W. Emerson, *Ebenezer Rockwood Hoar* (Boston: Houghton Mifflin, 1911), p. 174 (March 29, 1869).

aloofness or reserve on his part give sharp offense. The exceptional force of such claims of privilege in the United States may be attributed to the participation which members of Congress have acquired in the appointment power. The system thus created imposes upon the President the duties of an employment agent and at the same time engages Congressmen in continual occupation as office brokers. The President cannot deny himself to Congressmen, since he is dependent upon their favor for opportunity to get legislative consideration for his measures.[19]

DECLINE AND RECOVERY IN MORAL STANDARDS

If Americans could take satisfaction in their material gains after the Civil War, they could have no pride in prevailing moral standards, public or private. The decline during the prewar period from the austere standards of the Federalists and the Jeffersonians had been substantial, and the trend was not lessened by the confusion and laxness of the Civil War period itself. The depth of degradation was reached during Grant's eight years in the White House, years in which one scandal after another rocked the nation. Thoughtful contemporaries were deeply disturbed.

Among them was Edwin L. Godkin, editor of the *Nation* and the *New York Evening Post*. Born in Ireland of English parents and trained in both British and American law, he was a penetrating and constructive critic of American public life. Devoted to democracy, he was at times discouraged about its prospects but to its inner strength he gave constant support, notably to the cause of civil service reform.[20] In 1868 Godkin declared, "We are, at present, witnessing in the immorality which pervades the commercial world, and taints nearly every branch of business, the results of the decline of habit as a social force, before mental and moral culture has reached a sufficiently advanced stage to take its place. Every man at present may be said literally to live by his wits; hardly anybody lives by tradition, or authority, or under the dominion of habits acquired in youth. The result is a kind of moral anarchy. . . ."[21]

---

[19] Henry Jones Ford, *The Cleveland Era: a Chronicle of the New Order in Politics* (New Haven: Yale University Press, 1919), pp. 59-60.

[20] *Dictionary of American Biography*, VII, 347.

[21] E. L. Godkin, "Commercial Immorality and Political Corruption," *North American Review*, CVII (1868), 252-53. His best known works were *Problems of Modern Democracy* (New York: C. Scribner's Sons, 1896), and *Unforeseen Tendencies of Democracy* (Boston: Houghton Mifflin, 1898).

The scientist, Simon Newcomb, wrote in 1873, "Admitted corruption is not the only bad feature of our politics. The decay in the public sense of delicacy and propriety is equally striking. . . . By the sense of delicacy and propriety we mean that instinct which revolts not merely at the thought of breaches of the statute law, but at the idea of any act which can give rise to a reasonable suspicion of selfish, sinister, or improper motives."[22]

The most impressive summary of moral decline in official circles came from the lips of George F. Hoar, then a member of the House and later a distinguished member of the Senate.

My own public life has been a very brief and insignificant one, extending little beyond the duration of a single term of senatorial office. But in that brief period I have seen five judges of a high court of the United States driven from office by threat of impeachment for corruption or maladministration. I have heard the taunt, from friendliest lips, that when the United States presented herself in the East to take part with the civilized world in generous competition in the arts of life, the only product of her institutions in which she surpassed all others beyond question was her corruption. I have seen in the State of the Union foremost in power and wealth four judges of her courts impeached for corruption, and the political administration of her chief city become a disgrace and a by-word throughout the world. I have seen the chairman of the Committee on Military Affairs in the House, now a distinguished member of this court, rise in his place and demand the expulsion of four of his associates for making sale of their official privilege of selecting the youths to be educated at our great military school. When the greatest railroad of the world, binding together the continent and uniting the two great seas which wash our shores, was finished, I have seen our national triumph and exultation turned to bitterness and shame by the unanimous reports of three committees of Congress—two of the House and one here—that every step of that mighty enterprise had been taken in fraud. I have heard in highest places the shameless doctrine avowed by men grown old in public office that the true way by which power should be gained in the Republic is to bribe the people with the offices created for their service, and the true end for which it should be used when gained is the promotion of selfish ambition and the gratification of personal revenge. I have heard that

[22] Simon Newcomb, "The Session," *North American Review*, CXVII (1873), 200.

suspicion haunts the footsteps of the trusted companions of the President.[23]

Yet in the midst of these scenes of betrayal labored some of the ablest and most trustworthy public officials in the history of the Republic: men like Hamilton Fish, Secretary of State (1869-77); Benjamin Bristow, Secretary of the Treasury (1874-76); Jacob D. Cox and Carl Schurz, Secretaries of the Interior (1869-70, 1877-81). Nor should these names obscure those of secondary rank of equal integrity and ability—men such as William Hunter and A. A. Adee, whose collective service in the State Department (mostly as First, Second, or Third Assistant Secretary) spanned nearly a century; Sumner I. Kimball, superintendent of the Lifesaving Service; and Francis A. Walker, who created the modern foundations of the census.[24] Men of quality such as these became the prevalent type with Hayes, and by the end of the century the public had come to expect decency and honor in the executive branch.

THE PARTY SYSTEM

Various reasons were advanced to explain this moral decline. Many found the cause in the perversion of the party system. There was no doubt that party was not what the reformers thought appropriate, and no doubt that party was a heavy handicap to good administration.

National elections from 1868 to 1900 were fought on very few "issues," so far as matters of state were involved. The four elections immediately following the close of the Civil War (1868-80) centered on the loyalty issue—the Democrats were responsible for secession and hence untrustworthy, the Republicans had saved the Union. Garfield was the last of the northern generals to go to the White House, although both Harrison and McKinley had served in the army with distinction. The ensuing four elections (1884-96) were dominated by civil service reform, tariff, and currency issues, the latter reflecting the distress of western farmers and eastern laborers and the

---

[23] *Congressional Record*, 44th Cong., 1st sess., part 7, p. 63 (May 6, 1876), proceedings of Senate in trial of William W. Belknap, late Secretary of War. Hoar was present as one of the managers on the part of the House of Representatives. Reprinted in Frederick H. Gillett, *George Frisbie Hoar* (Boston: Houghton Mifflin, 1934), p. 68.

[24] Biographical sketches of these personalities, except Hunter, are in the *Dictionary of American Biography*.

debtor class generally. Greenback and Populist parties entered the stage and threatened the cohesion of both parties, particularly of the Democrats. The election of 1900 involved a new issue, hitherto unknown to American history, imperialism.

Both parties faced constant difficulty in maintaining a united front. The Republican problem was factional rather than doctrinal—Liberal Republicans with Greeley broke off against Grant in 1872; the Conkling wing (the Stalwarts) fought Hayes and Garfield; Blaine and Conkling were factional enemies. The Democratic problem was both factional and doctrinal, and during the 1890's the latter split the party into the Cleveland gold wing and the Bryan silver wing. After 1896 Republican ascendancy, based on a protective tariff and "sound money," was assured until the G.O.P. itself fell into factional disruption in 1912.

Party organization steadily became stronger during the postwar years, despite the disturbing effect of faction. Both parties were national, although the strength of the Democratic party was in the South and the Republicans maintained there only a shadow office-holding cadre. Organization was complete in both parties—city and county committees and periodic local conventions, state committees which possessed much influence, and the two national committees. Vitality rested in the city and county committees but much power lay in the state leadership. Party structure was confederate, not unitary; the national committee (composed of state leaders) could not direct the state committees and the latter did not undertake to dictate to local committees on city and county nominations. Local delegations to state conventions, however, might be eagerly sought (or even bought) by state leaders desiring to control these bodies; and aspirants for the presidency had to exert what influence they could to secure friendly state delegations to the national conventions.

The currency which regulated the flow of goods and services in these far-flung organizations was principally patronage, contracts, and "recognition." The amount of patronage was enormous—theoretically, before 1883, the whole public service, federal, state, and local. The necessity of carrying on the public business compelled acceptance, even during the height of the spoils system, of a central career service corps; but the bulk of the public service was available to stimulate party exertion and to pay party obligations. Contracts for supplies and services fulfilled the same purpose with another segment of the population. Leaders might be content with recognition and with power.

These were the years of the professional politicians, whose emergence, indeed, had been a characteristic feature of the Jacksonian period. Their number, activity, force, and influence now gained recognition and both acceptance and condemnation—mainly the latter. Theodore Roosevelt, one of the most successful of professional politicians, wrote in 1886: "it may be accepted as a fact, however unpleasant, that if steady work and much attention to detail are required, ordinary citizens, to whom participation in politics is merely a disagreeable duty, will always be beaten by the organized army of politicians to whom it is both duty, business, and pleasure, and who are knit together and to outsiders by their social relations."[25] Roosevelt regretted this fact and urged the short ballot to make less necessary the intervening services of the professional politician. Another practical politician, Frederic T. Greenhalge, governor of Massachusetts, held similar views. Observing that the "practical politician" was the necessary outcome of practical politics and should therefore be well understood, he continued:

He is loyal, diligent, indefatigable in the support of his party and its candidates. The genuine practical politician never bolts the ticket, and he never forgets or forgives the man who does. He is versed in all the learning of political mechanism; he knows just when a caucus is to be held; what States hold elections in any particular year; what majorities were given at this or that election; what "out" there is in any candidate. . . .

The type of practical politician now under consideration is a "professional," living for politics and living out of politics. He does much political work, but only on the *quid pro quo* principle. "The laborer is worthy of his hire," he says with great gusto, for he loves to defend his position by scriptural quotations. He must be "recognized," and he is eager to point out to the raw recruit also that for everything *he* does, *he* must be "recognized." . . .

But with all his faults, his follies, his amusing characteristics, it must be remembered that he is a *constant force*. He never lets anything go by default. He is, indeed, a machine, tireless, fearless, conscienceless, and remorseless—at least in his own sphere of action.[26]

[25] Theodore Roosevelt, "Machine Politics in New York City," *Century Magazine*, XXXIII (1886-87), 82.
[26] F. T. Greenhalge, "Practical Politics," *North American Review*, CLXII (1896), 154, 156.

To the reformers the state of the party was calamitous, a constant menace to decent government and to the safety of the Republic. Their attitude was sufficiently stated by the civil service reform leader and able New York lawyer, Dorman B. Eaton.

The facts referred to make it plain that political parties, as we now have them, are by no means what they should be; that is, convenient agencies for combining and expressing on a grand scale and with a true freedom the real views and interests of the people. They are very generally regarded as highly complicated organizations through which politicians are enabled to make themselves a great power for their own benefit and for coercing and baffling the people. We need not stop to consider how disastrous it is to the purity and dignity of all political and official life, to have, in the whole domain of politics, the largest and highest expression of national sentiment thus weighed down and suppressed by a vast selfish organization, pretending to act for the common good and in the spirit of patriotism. The specific evils thus produced are not confined to the long and alarming array of abuses and corruptions which have been more and more in recent years charged against party managers and their vicious methods. These evils have developed a vicious antagonism, on the part of great numbers of worthy people, toward all parties, as being needless, even if they be not dangerous, enemies of the State. . . .[27]

The decline in public esteem of the party system was alarming. "The degradation which has come upon the words 'politics' and 'politician,' in their American use," it was noted, "marks a degeneration in political methods which deserves the attention of every lover of his country. 'Politics' has become simply the work of managing a party for its own advantage, or that of its leaders; and the term 'politician' is applied only to the campaign director, the local committee-man, the appointment-broker—in short, to men who manage parties and distribute the public offices."[28]

In campaigns waged around "the bloody shirt," a high degree of analysis and penetration was hardly necessary, and the rank-and-file party workers did what was needed in arousing an emotional enthusiasm for victory. To explain the soundness of a tariff schedule or the free coinage of silver they were hardly prepared, and these momentous issues were settled at the polling booths by majorities which the

[27] Dorman B. Eaton, "Parties and Independents," *ibid.*, CXLIV (1887), 550.
[28] "The Real Nature of Politics," unsigned article in *Century Magazine*, XXXV (1887-88), 647.

reformers believed ignorant, led by ignorant political workers. What was worse, they had to be paid for their labors—in jobs, contracts, and recognition.

Moral decline and the rise of an ever-present, nationally organized political machine were two of the major conditions weighing upon the character and effectiveness of the public service during the years from Grant through McKinley. That the situation greatly improved in this period was evident, but the hand of the past still lay heavy on the present. The trend was in the direction thought wise by the reformers, and by the still small band of professional political scientists who were now beginning to analyze, criticize, and forecast the shape of things to come.

NATIONAL OPTIMISM

Despite recurrent depressions and hard times, the climate of opinion was generally optimistic. The Union had been saved, slavery had been erased, big business was weaving its magic, the West was revealing its great riches, population was increasing, the country was at peace unvexed by international rivalry or colonial ambitions.

Improvements in the manner of life were recorded by many observers. Even as the curtain rose on the postwar years, James A. Garfield, then an able member of Congress, declared:

We are so involved in the events and movements of society, that we do not stop to realize—what is undeniably true—that, during the last forty years, all modern societies have entered upon a period of change, more marked, more pervading, more radical, than any that has occurred during the last three hundred years. . . . Imagine, if you can, what would happen if to-morrow morning the railway locomotive, and its corollary, the telegraph, were blotted from the earth. At first thought, it would seem impossible to get on at all with the feeble substitutes that we should be compelled to adopt in place of these great forces. . . . But were this calamity to happen, we should simply be placed where we were forty-three years ago.[29]

At the same time Garfield remarked on the consequences of better means of communication.

. . . . Distance, estrangement, isolation, have been overcome by the recent amazing growth in the means of intercommunication. For political

[29] *The Works of James Abram Garfield* (Burke A. Hinsdale, ed., 2 vols., Boston: James R. Osgood and Co., 1882-83), II, 55-56 (July 2, 1873).

and industrial purposes, California and Massachusetts are nearer neighbors to-day than were Philadelphia and Boston in the days of the Revolution. The people of all our thirty-seven States know more of each other's affairs than the Vermonter knew of the Virginian fifty years ago. It was distance, isolation, ignorance of separate parts, that broke the cohesive force of the great empires of antiquity. Public affairs are now more public, and private less private, than in former ages. The railroad, the telegraph, and the press have virtually brought our citizens, with their opinions and industries, face to face; and they live almost in each other's sight. The leading political, social, and industrial events of this day will be reported and discussed at more than two millions of American breakfast-tables to-morrow morning. Public opinion is kept in constant exercise and training. It keeps itself constantly in hand,—ready to approve, condemn, and command. It may be wrong; it may be tyrannical; but it is all-pervading, and constitutes more than ever before a strong bond of nationality.[30]

The expanding strength, vitality, and productive capacity of the nation during McKinley's long public life was noted again and again, among others by the eminent economist David A. Wells. This Yankee genius began his career in the field of science, but during the Civil War became interested in the currency problem, revenue policy, and the tariff. At the close of the War he became chairman of the National Revenue Commission and Special Commissioner of Revenue. He quickly established the Bureau of Statistics with another noted economist, Francis A. Walker, at its head. A friend of Lincoln, Garfield, and Cleveland, Wells was a convinced advocate of laissez faire, free trade, and sound money.[31] In 1871 he wrote: "We are a nation of forty millions, unsurpassed in intelligence, indomitable in will, fertile in expedient. . . . We have a thousand million acres of fertile land as yet unoccupied. We have an annual immigration of 350,000, mainly persons who have passed the age of childhood, ready to occupy, to produce, to consume, and pay taxes, and whose annual money value to the country cannot be estimated at less than $300,000,000. . . . We have more coal, the source of motive-power, than is possessed by all other countries together."[32]

Ulysses S. Grant, returning from the Pacific Coast to New York City over the Northern Pacific Railway in 1883, wrote to his niece:

[30] *Ibid.*, II, 49-50 (July 2, 1873).
[31] *Dictionary of American Biography*, XIX, 637.
[32] David A. Wells, "The Meaning of Revenue Reform," *North American Review*, CXIII (1871), 113-14.

"I was not prepared to see so rich a country or one so rapidly developing. Across the continent where but a few years ago the Indian held undisputed sway, there is now a continuous settlement, and every ten or fifteen miles a town or city, each with spires of the school house and the church."[33] In 1895 the noted statistician, Michael G. Mulhall, declared:

In conclusion, I have only to repeat what I said at the commencement, that the United States in 1895 possess by far the greatest productive power in the world; that this power has more than trebled since 1860, rising from thirty-nine to one hundred and twenty-nine milliards of foottons daily; that the intellectual progress of the nation is attended to in a more liberal manner than in Europe, and that the accumulation of wealth averages $7,000,000 daily. These simple facts tell us what a wonderful country has sprung up beyond the Atlantic in a single century, and furnish a scathing commentary on the books written by English travellers only fifty years ago. Englishmen of to-day have more correct views, and regard with honest pride and kindly good-will the descendants of the Pilgrim Fathers, while the rest of mankind marks with wonder and admiration the onward march of the Great Republic.[34]

The state of the economy periodically challenged these optimistic views. The people were harassed by recurrent depressions. They were alarmed by the rise of organized labor and by the violence of capital-labor conflict. They feared the power of the railroad corporations. They lacked confidence in many leading politicians, federal, state, and local, and suspected their relations with moneyed interests. There were prophets of gloom as well as of light.

It was against this variegated pattern of optimism and doubt, of success and failure, of material expansion and laissez faire that the country turned from war to peace. No one discerned that the vast administrative experiences of the Civil War had applications in time of peace. The military and civilian apparatus, needed to recruit, equip, arm, train, and transport a million men, was dismantled. The country seemed ready to return to the standards of Buchanan's administration. Events soon proved that new circumstances would

[33] *Letters of Ulysses S. Grant to His Father and His Youngest Sister, 1857-78* (Jesse Grant Cramer, ed., New York: G. P. Putnam's Sons, 1912), p. 154 (Sept. 27, 1883).
[34] Michael G. Mulhall, "Power and Wealth of the United States," *North American Review*, CLX (1895), 650.

necessitate new adjustments in official life, both in high quarters and in low.

TWO MAJOR ADMINISTRATIVE ISSUES

During the thirty years from Grant to McKinley, two great controversies dominated the *administrative* scene. One involved the rejuvenation of executive power and leadership after the impeachment of President Andrew Johnson and the surrender of President Ulysses S. Grant to the Senate. The second was concerned with the bitter struggle for civil service reform, a battle that had an important if indirect bearing on the fortunes of executive power, on the nature of political parties, and on the standards of public morality.

The presidency had fallen to its lowest state when by a single vote Andrew Johnson escaped conviction on impeachment. Congress rose to a vindictive crescendo of power in this affair, and retained primacy for a decade before it was challenged by Hayes and his successors. The problem of the location of effective power was perceived in 1876 by the gifted American sociologist, William Graham Sumner, who in one of his early papers wrote: "The opinion seems to be gaining ground that, for fear of power, we have eliminated both efficiency and responsibility. . . . It has been observed that the discipline or coercion which we dread for national purposes and under constitutional forms appears with the vigor of a military despotism in party; and that the conception of loyalty, for which we can find no proper object in our system, is fully developed in the party."[35] During Grant's administration power was securely in the hands of a Senate oligarchy, including among others Roscoe Conkling and James G. Blaine. The influence of the President was restored in the controversy between Conkling and Hayes, and subsequently between Conkling and Garfield. The particular issue was control of federal appointments in New York State; the victor was the President. Cleveland did much to restore the symbolism as well as the fact of executive power, but a divided party in his second term destroyed any possibility of executive leadership. The President, moreover, consistently lacked the institutional support that was essential for the effective use of executive authority. Despite these handicaps the curve of presidential

[35] William G. Sumner, "Politics in America, 1776-1876," *North American Review*, CXXII (1876), 81, 82-83.

leadership was upward and considerable groundwork was laid for the marked developments that were to take place with Theodore Roosevelt and Woodrow Wilson.

The great conflict over civil service reform was a major domestic issue for two decades, as party politicians resisted the reformers in their demand for a radical change in the patronage system. This system was already old and to many it appeared the natural order in a republic. It seemed to be one means by which the people ruled— or at least participated in the art of government. It had the merit of serving as a school of citizenship and was the federal equivalent of the direct election of hundreds of thousands of officeholders in state and local government. Its consequences were nevertheless disastrous. It rendered the public services unstable, ignorant, clumsy, expensive, partisan, and at times corrupt. It attracted the politically adventurous, not the administratively competent. It divided the responsibility of officeholders between their official superiors and their party leaders. It facilitated a class of helots bound to support their feudal masters with party work, party assessments, and absolute loyalty on pain of excommunication.

The small but able band of reformers, George William Curtis, Dorman B. Eaton, Carl Schurz, William D. Foulke, and others, fought an uphill battle against bitter opposition. They suffered scorn and contumely, of which the following passage may serve as an example.

The Indiana Civil Service Reform Association is composed (if indeed such a clique existed at all) of Republican moral lepers, who, if capable of distinguishing between the truth and a lie, always chose the lie, just as a buzzard prefers carrion to fresh meat. The representatives of this aggregation of Republican ulcers, warts, tumors, sties, and fistulas pretended to investigate affairs at the Insane Asylum. They did not investigate, they were incapable of investigating. Their purpose was to manufacture and publish a lying report. They constituted the dregs of partisan malice. Each one of them was a moving, crawling, breathing pestilence. . . . [36]

Against such appalling malice the reformers spoke in the measured eloquence of George William Curtis and in the lively columns of

[36] *Sentinel* (August 24, 1887), reprinted in William Dudley Foulke, *Fighting the Spoilsmen: Reminiscences of the Civil Service Reform Movement* (New York: G. P. Putnam's Sons, 1919), p. 29.

the *Nation*. The National Civil Service Reform League, organized in 1881, was a mere handful of men with an insignificant annual budget, but they were strengthened by their cause, which they conceived as no less than the rescue of the Republic from the mass bribery of the spoils system. They won a temporary victory in 1871, and a permanent if partial victory in 1883.

Improvements in administration to the close of McKinley's first term were limited in scope. Such as they were they enabled the government to keep up with its current tasks but with recurrent arrearages. New tasks arising at the close of the nineteenth century and within the first decade of the twentieth—the management of colonial possessions overseas, the regulation of business, the conservation of national resources, the construction of the Panama Canal—induced a radical reconstruction of the administrative system.

Although there were drama and excitement in the controversies over the role of the President, the reform of the civil service, the veto power, and the regulation of railroads and monopolies, for thirty years there was relative stagnation in the art of administration. When William McKinley took the oath of office for the second time on March 4, 1901, he and the Republican party were committed to well-understood national *policies*. They were committed to no pattern of administrative organization, because they neither had one, nor were expected by the country to have one beyond honesty and economy. The thirty-odd years from 1869 to 1901 had produced almost no interest in administration other than reform. The following thirty years, however, were decades of unparalleled progress in developing both the theory and the practice of the art of administration.

CHAPTER TWO

The Struggle for Power:
President and Congress

When General Ulysses S. Grant entered the White House the office of President was at a low ebb in power and prestige. The events of the next thirty years involved a series of hard fought battles between Presidents and Congress, the net result of which was to restore in part the constitutional, political, and administrative balance between the two branches of government. The equilibrium that was attained under President McKinley did not, however, promise the end of the struggle for power nor its eventual outcome. It was a personal achievement of a high order, but it rested on no institutional foundations. The theory of the presidency set forth by post-Civil War Republican leaders, based firmly on Whig doctrine, remained ascendant, and was unchallenged—as theory—by any Republican President from Grant through McKinley.[1]

THE REPUBLICAN THEORY OF THE PRESIDENCY

The period was not one devoted to theoretical exposition by men in public life; but, nevertheless, from John Sherman, Senator, Cabinet member, and aspirant to the White House, we can draw a clear statement of doctrine implicitly accepted by many of his fellow

[1] The events narrated in this chapter are an oft-told tale. In addition to the biographies of the principal figures, see Woodrow Wilson, *Congressional Government: A Study in American Politics* (Boston: Houghton Mifflin, 1885); Wilfred E. Binkley, *President and Congress* (New York: Alfred A. Knopf, 1947); Joseph P. Harris, *The Advice and Consent of the Senate* (Berkeley: University of California Press, 1953).

Republicans. In his *Recollections*, he wrote: "The executive department of a republic like ours should be subordinate to the legislative department. The President should obey and enforce the laws, leaving to the people the duty of correcting any errors committed by their representatives in Congress."[2] Going beyond this declaration of executive subordination, he asserted that the President ought not even to be master of his own administrative household.

The impression prevailed that the President [Grant] regarded these heads of departments, invested by law with specific and independent duties, as mere subordinates, whose functions he might assume. This is not the true theory of our government. The President is intrusted by the constitution and laws with important powers, and so by law are the heads of departments. The President has no more right to control or exercise the powers conferred by law upon them than they have to control him in the discharge of his duties. It is especially the custom of Congress to intrust to the Secretary of the Treasury specific powers over the currency, the public debt and the collection of the revenue. If he violates or neglects his duty he is subject to removal by the President, or impeachment by the House of Representatives, but the President cannot exercise or control the discretion reposed by law in the Secretary of the Treasury, or in any head or subordinate of any department of the government. This limitation of the power of the President, and the distribution of power among the departments, is an essential requisite of a republican government. . . .[3]

The Radical Republicans acted on these principles. In response to Lincoln's proclamation of July 8, 1864, on his pocket veto of the Wade–Davis reconstruction bill, Senator Benjamin F. Wade and Representative Henry W. Davis issued their famous manifesto, in which it was stated: "The supporters of the administration are responsible to the country for its conduct; and it is their right and duty to check the encroachments of the executive on the authority of Congress, and to require it to confine itself to its proper sphere. . . . [the President] must understand . . . that the authority of Congress is paramount, and must be respected . . . and that, if he wishes our support, he must confine himself to his executive duties—to obey and execute, not to make the laws—to suppress by arms

[2] John Sherman, *Recollections of Forty Years in the House, Senate and Cabinet* (2 vols., Chicago: Werner Co., 1895), I, 447.
[3] *Ibid.*, I, 449-50.

armed rebellion, and leave political reorganization to the Congress."[4]
The implacable Thaddeus Stevens, according to Gideon Welles,
declared: "Congress was the supreme department of the Government
and must be recognized as the supreme power. Members of Congress
must be permitted to exercise executive duties. The legislative department must control the action of the Government, prescribe its
policy, its measures, and dictate appointments to the executive, or
subordinate, department."[5]

This language had been put to the test in the conflict between
President Johnson and the Radical Republicans in Congress. The
President was tactless, obstinate, and strong-willed; the Radicals were
determined to reduce presidential authority from its wartime peak.
Events followed each other in swift succession. Johnson kept Lincoln's
Cabinet, refused to call a special session, and proceeded during the
spring and summer of 1865 to push forward Lincoln's plan for reconstruction of the southern states. Congressional Republicans were
infuriated as they helplessly witnessed the progress of executive reconstruction on terms which they deemed unacceptable. They seized
their opportunity as soon as the regular session opened in December
1865. They voted to continue the Freedmen's Bureau, a bill which
Johnson vetoed as unconstitutional in time of peace.[6] They enacted
a Civil Rights Bill which Johnson vetoed as an aggression against the
states; Congress passed both bills over his veto.[7] This show of congressional strength demonstrated where the master power in the
government lay and ended Johnson's capacity as a leader.

The election of 1866 resulted in an overwhelming victory for the
Radical Republicans. In firm control of both Houses in 1867 they
passed the Reconstruction Act, undoing what Lincoln and Johnson
had wrought and thus certified that reconstruction was to be a
legislative, not an executive, responsibility.[8] They forbade the President and the Secretary of War to issue army orders and instructions
except through the General of the Army (Grant), established the

----

[4] *New York Tribune*, August 5, 1864, reprinted in Henry Winter Davis,
Speeches and Addresses (New York: Harper and Brothers, 1867), pp. 416, 425.
[5] *Diary of Gideon Welles* (3 vols., Boston: Houghton Mifflin Co., 1911), II,
426.
[6] 14 Stat. 173 (July 16, 1866).
[7] 14 Stat. 27 (April 9, 1866).
[8] 15 Stat. 2 (March 23, 1867).

headquarters of the General of the Army in Washington, and prohibited the President from removing the General, or suspending him, relieving him from his command, or assigning him to duty elsewhere than at headquarters except at his own request, without the prior approval of the Senate.[9] These provisions were tacked on as riders to the annual army appropriation bill.

Congress then undermined the President's authority over the civilian departments by the Tenure of Office Act (noted below), disregard of which was to lead to Johnson's impeachment.[10] The legislators protected their own position by requiring the next Congress to reconvene immediately after the adjournment of the previous one, thus avoiding the usual interval when it was not in session.[11]

The degradation of the presidency came to its climax in Johnson's impeachment in 1868. Its failure by a single vote in the Senate did not restore either Johnson or the office of Chief Executive to a semblance of authority. The remainder of Johnson's term was a relatively quiet deadlock between the legislative and executive branches.

The shadow of Johnson's impeachment and the presence of congressional aggression hung over succeeding administrations, finally dissolving during Cleveland's first term. Grant yielded a quick deference to Republican leaders in House and Senate, notably the latter. He considered himself a "purely administrative officer."[12] He had already mortgaged his future as President when he mingled with the congressional group that had sought to impeach Johnson. Henry Adams summed up Grant's executive philosophy in 1870:

. . . His own idea of his duties as President was always openly and consistently expressed, and may perhaps be best described as that of the commander of an army in time of peace. He was to watch over the faithful administration of the government; to see that the taxes were honestly collected; that the disbursements were honestly made; that economy was strictly enforced; that the laws were everywhere obeyed, good and bad alike; and as it was the duty of every military commander to obey the civil authority without question, so it was the duty of the President to

9 14 Stat. 485 (March 2, 1867).
10 14 Stat. 430 (March 2, 1867).
11 14 Stat. 378 (Jan. 22, 1867).
12 Speech of acceptance of the Republican nomination (May 29, 1868) in *American Annual Cylopaedia* . . . 1868 (New York: D. Appleton and Co., 1869), p. 745.

follow without hesitation the wishes of the people as expressed by Congress.[13]

After Grant's retirement, he was reported by the journalist John R. Young to have said:

... An Executive must consider Congress. A government machine must run, and an Executive depends on Congress. The members have their rights as well as himself. If he wants to get along with Congress, have the government go smoothly, and secure wholesome legislation, he must be in sympathy with Congress. It has become the habit of Congressmen to share with the Executive in the responsibility of appointments. It is unjust to say that this habit is necessarily corrupt. It is simply a custom that has grown up, a fact that cannot be ignored. The President very rarely appoints, he merely registers the appointments of members of Congress. In a country as vast as ours the advice of Congressmen as to persons to be appointed is useful, and generally for the best interests of the country. . . .[14]

Grant's idea of the executive office fitted perfectly with the conceptions of the powerful men who dominated the Senate. "The most eminent Senators," wrote Senator Hoar, "Sumner, Conkling, Sherman, Edmunds, Carpenter, Frelinghuysen, Simon Cameron, Anthony, Logan—would have received as a personal affront a private message from the White House expressing a desire that they should adopt any course in the discharge of their legislative duties that they did not approve. If they visited the White House, it was to give, not to receive advice."[15] John Sherman confirmed this opinion. "He [Grant] consulted but few of the Senators or Members, and they were known as his personal friends. Mr. Conkling, by his imperious will, gained a strong influence over the President. . . ."[16] It was Conkling's attack on Senator Hoar's brother, Judge Ebenezer R. Hoar, then Attorney General, that laid the groundwork for his summary removal by Grant.

After eight years of Grant as President, Henry Adams seemed to have been prophetically correct when he wrote in 1869, "The mere repeal of the Tenure-of-Office Bill cannot at once restore its prestige

[13] Henry Adams, "The Session," North American Review, CXI (1870), 33-34.
[14] John Russell Young, Around the World with General Grant (2 vols., New York: American News Company, 1879), II, 265-66.
[15] George F. Hoar, Autobiography of Seventy Years (2 vols., New York: Charles Scribner's Sons, 1903), II, 46.
[16] John Sherman, Recollections, I, 474.

[i.e., the presidency], or wrest from Congress the initiative which Congress is now accustomed to exercise. The Senate has no idea of abandoning its control of power. . . ."[17]

Hayes' *theory* of the presidency was Whig in its origin; his *practice* was almost the opposite. He defied the Senate leadership in his Cabinet appointments and, as we shall see in due course, he stoutly defended the executive office against aggression by both the House and the Senate. A full decade of executive deterioration was abruptly terminated, and the foundation laid for the dramatic triumph of President Garfield over Senators Roscoe Conkling and Thomas C. Platt. Calm ensued during the more than three years of President Arthur's occupancy of the White House—a calm in which Congress, nevertheless, remained the dominant partner. Arthur was not one to revise either executive theory or practice. These were the years when the young but observant Woodrow Wilson was writing his *Congressional Government*, and James Bryce was explaining why great men are not chosen Presidents.

Grover Cleveland possessed a strong and stubborn personality and engaged in more than one conflict with Congress. He and his fellow Democrats failed to state a systematic theory of the presidential office, and Cleveland's incidental comments on the subject are less than precise. He stood firmly on the doctrine of separation of powers. "It should be remembered that the office of President is essentially executive in its nature," he declared in his letter accepting his nomination.[18] At the end of his first year in the White House he was quoted as saying, "I believe the most important benefit that I can confer on the country by my Presidency is to insist upon the entire independence of the Executive and legislative branches of the government, and to compel the members of the legislative branch to see that they have responsibilities of their own. . . ."[19] This language did not bespeak executive leadership of Congress.

During Cleveland's second term, his party split over monetary

[17] Henry Adams, "The Session," *North American Review*, CVIII (1869), 615.
[18] August 18, 1884, in *The Public Papers of Grover Cleveland, Twenty-second President of the United States* (Washington: Government Printing Office, 1889), p. 3.
[19] *New York Herald*, Jan. 5, 1886, p. 4. Quoted in Thomas Payne, "The Administrative Theory and Practice of Grover Cleveland," unpublished doctoral dissertation, University of Chicago, 1951, p. 282.

policy; he lost control of Congress to the Republicans; and his influence and that of his office waned. Benjamin Harrison had done nothing to restore it between Cleveland's first and second administrations.

The institutional foundations of the presidential office were unchanged during the years it was held by President William McKinley, but the climate of executive–congressional relations cleared abruptly. An irresponsible House fell under the control of Speaker Thomas B. Reed; a cooperative Senate joined hands with a popular long-time member of the House of Representatives now at the other end of Pennsylvania Avenue; and the tact and discretion of the President carried the day without the need for a display of power. Binkley concluded that not "since the presidency of Jefferson had there been achieved such an integration of the political branches of the federal government and such consequent coherence and sense of direction in its functioning."[20]

During the years from 1869 to 1901 the President was slowly beginning to free himself from a special subjection to Congress induced by the patronage system, a dependence going far beyond the relatively small number of presidential offices. Henry Adams had observed the culmination of this subjection in 1870, writing "The success of any executive measure must now be bought by the use of the public patronage in influencing the action of legislators."[21] James A. Garfield confirmed this view in 1877, declaring that the patronage system invaded the independence of the executive and made him less responsible for the character of his appointments, while at the same time impairing the efficiency of the legislative branch.[22]

Hayes considered congressional demands for patronage not only a great evil, but also a usurpation of executive prerogatives.[23] Jacob D. Cox, Secretary of the Interior for a short period under Grant,

[20] Wilfred E. Binkley, *President and Congress*, p. 187. Quotations from this book reprinted by permission of the publisher, Alfred A. Knopf.

[21] Henry Adams, "The Session," *North American Review*, CXI (1870), 58.

[22] James A. Garfield, "A Century of Progress," *Atlantic Monthly*, XL (1877), 61.

[23] *Diary and Letters of Rutherford Birchard Hayes* (5 vols., Charles Richard Williams, ed., Ohio State Archaeological and Historical Society, 1922-26), III, 611 (July 12, 1880).

wrote: "The experience of President Hayes proved that an administration which seeks to abolish the spoils system must expect to lose that appearance of leadership in legislation which has been sustained by the farming out of patronage. The appearance was in the main a sham. . . . In ordinary affairs a President who will not so purchase help will find his recommendations treated with slight respect, or even ostentatiously overruled."[24]

Perhaps nothing caused so many small irritations to so many members of the House and Senate as their failure to have their way in the thousands of small appointments that were required across the country from year to year. John Sherman declared in 1871, "The position in which the President is now placed with regard to Congress is a constant source of irritation. Members of Congress, especially of the House of Representatives, claim the right to dictate local appointments, and if their wishes are not yielded to in every case it creates at once a cause of quarrel, which finds its outlet in some legislation or other. In the Senate, perhaps, that is not so much so; but even here we cannot deny that the power claimed by Senators and members to interfere in appointments does create a constant state of irritation between the legislative and executive departments of the Government."[25]

The patronage was an open sore, constantly poisoning the sources of executive–legislative cooperation. As the number of positions in the competitive service increased, the volume of dissatisfaction tended to decrease, but at the turn of the century the improvement was not pronounced. Senator George F. Hoar was able, nevertheless, to corroborate the shift in influence, writing in his *Autobiography*, "The reform of the civil service has doubtless shorn the office of Senator of a good deal of power."[26] Conversely, it tended to add authority to the office of the Chief Executive.

We may now turn to examine the period from 1869 to 1901 from the point of view of the principal administrative (and political) issues that were involved in the struggle for power between Congress and the Executive. They were primarily five: the controversy over

[24] Jacob D. Cox, "The Hayes Administration," *Atlantic Monthly*, LXXI (1893), 831.
[25] *Congressional Globe*, 41st Cong., 3d sess., p. 293 (Jan. 4, 1871).
[26] George F. Hoar, *Autobiography*, II, 46.

the power to remove, precipitated by the Tenure of Office Act of 1867; the battle over executive independence in making nominations to the Senate, involving the New York customhouse and its political overlord, Senator Conkling; the struggle against legislative coercion of executive decision by riders to appropriation acts; the veto power; and the less precisely marked problem of the location of policy leadership, whether executive or legislative.

THE REMOVAL POWER

The Great Debate in the first Congress had determined by a narrow majority that the right to remove an officer appointed by and with the consent of the Senate was vested exclusively in the President as an integral part of the executive power. The Whigs had challenged this interpretation but Daniel Webster had conceded that it was settled by construction, by precedent, and by law. Premonitions of a determination to unsettle this reading of the Constitution were visible during the Lincoln administration. In the National Bank Act Congress established the office of Comptroller of the Currency with a five-year term and authorized his removal only with the consent of the Senate.[27] In 1864 the President was required to submit to Congress reasons for the removal of consular clerks.[28] These were incidents, the underlying import of which was not fully apparent.

There could, however, be no doubt about the intention of the Tenure of Office Act of 1867. It was designed to transfer control of the public service from the President to the Senate, and thus to strike a vital blow both to executive power and to the capacity of a President to maintain a coordinate position with the legislative branch. That it was a reversal of the great decision of 1789 and of the unbroken theory and practice of seven decades meant nothing to the foes of Andrew Johnson and to the advocates of legislative supremacy.

The act required the approval of the Senate for the removal of heads of departments and other officials for whose appointments the advice and consent of the Senate was necessary. During a recess of the Senate, the President was authorized to suspend any such officer for misconduct in office, crime, incapacity, or legal disqualifica-

[27] 12 Stat. 665 (Feb. 25, 1863).
[28] 13 Stat. 137, sec. 2 (June 20, 1864).

tion, and to make a temporary appointment. He was required to report the evidence and reasons for suspension within twenty days of the opening of the next session. If the Senate refused to accept the reasons and to concur in the suspension, the officer resumed his duties, presidential displeasure or lack of confidence notwithstanding. Severe penalties were attached to any violation of these requirements.[29] Removal of Secretary of War Stanton in defiance of the Tenure of Office Act was the principal charge in the impeachment indictment of President Johnson.

The Tenure of Office Act was directed against a particular President; it probably never represented a settled conviction of the House of Representatives; and before the end of Johnson's administration the House had already approved its repeal. It was an obvious handicap to official housecleaning with a new administration in the offing, but the Senate declined to join with the House by giving up its recently won powers. For the remainder of Johnson's term, he dealt with removals under the traditional interpretation of the Constitution while the Senate in principle stood on the new doctrine. The President had the upper hand, for if the Senate refused to accept his reasons for removal and to recognize his nominations, they cut themselves off from any influence on high-level appointments. In practice the Senate did not insist, except by indirection, upon approving the causes for removal. As Carl R. Fish put it, "The battle was over. Both sides had spent their ammunition, and the administration went out amid desultory firing along the outposts."[30]

Grant promptly asked for repeal of the Tenure of Office Act. The House concurred,[31] but the Senate refused. The outcome was a compromise amendment that took the teeth out of the act by lifting the obligation of the President to report the evidence and reasons for suspension to the Senate. The Senate retained its recognized authority

---

[29] 14 Stat. 430 (March 2, 1867).

[30] Carl Russell Fish, *The Civil Service and the Patronage* (Cambridge: Harvard University Press, 1904), pp. 200, 201.

[31] It is of some interest to note that James A. Garfield refused to vote for repeal: "never by my vote shall Congress give up the constitutional principle and allow to any one man, be he an angel from Heaven, the absolute and sole control of appointments to and removals from office in this country." Theodore Clarke Smith, *The Life and Letters of James Abram Garfield*, I, 444 (March 26, 1869).

to advise and consent to a successor nominee, but lost its power to compel retention of a suspended officer.[32] Grant accepted this compromise. As Cleveland noted, much later, "President Grant did not deem it necessary afterward to renew his recommendation for its repeal, and . . . at no time since its enactment has its existence been permitted to embarrass executive action prior to the inauguration of a President politically opposed to the majority of the Senate," i.e., himself.[33]

The Republican party controlled the Senate throughout Cleveland's first administration, and new embarrassments quickly arose. Suspensions of presidential officeholders began promptly after March 4, 1885, accompanied by nominations of Democratic partisans. Senate committees as promptly asked for the reasons for suspension, indicating, as Cleveland wrote, that the Senate "even in the face of the repeal of the statutory provision giving it the right to pass upon suspensions by the President was still inclined to insist, directly or indirectly, upon that right."[34]

The issue came to a head in the case of the district attorney of the southern district of Alabama, George M. Duskin. The Senate Judiciary Committee asked the Attorney General for documents and papers; the Attorney General evaded. The Senate then required him to furnish the papers; he declined at the direction of the President. Cleveland thereupon addressed a special message to the Senate in which he declared that the papers bearing on Duskin's suspension were private papers; that the President had a right to suspend in the absence of any papers; and that the Senate had no right "by the aid of any documents whatever, or in any way save through the judicial process of trial on impeachment, to review or reverse the acts of the Executive in the suspension, during the recess of the Senate, of Federal officials." The Senate, he declared, assumed the right "to sit in judgment upon the exercise of my exclusive discretion and Executive function, for which I am solely responsible to the people. . . ." He concluded his message on a defiant note: "Neither the discontent of party friends, nor the allurements constantly offered of confirmations of appointees conditioned upon the avowal that suspensions

---

[32] 16 Stat. 6 (April 5, 1869).
[33] Grover Cleveland, *Presidential Problems* (New York: Century Co., 1904), p. 37.
[34] *Ibid.*, pp. 46-47.

have been made on party grounds alone, nor the threat proposed in the resolutions now before the Senate that no confirmations will be made unless the demands of that body be complied with, are sufficient to discourage or deter me from following in the way which I am convinced leads to better government for the people."[35]

The President was on strong ground. The Senate fortunately discovered a means of retreat. It appeared that during the controversy Duskin's term had expired, the issue of suspension automatically dissolved, and Duskin's successor was quickly confirmed. Both Republican and Democratic Senators took advantage of the occasion to repeal the Tenure of Office Act.[36] Congress thus formally receded from the attempt to control presidential discretion in suspending or removing officials in the executive branch. Its withdrawal was important symbolically, however innocuous the act had been since its amendment in 1869. "Thus," wrote Cleveland long after the event, "was an unpleasant controversy happily followed by an expurgation of the last pretense of statutory sanction to an encroachment upon constitutional Executive prerogatives, and thus was a time-honored interpretation of the Constitution restored to us."[37]

CONGRESSIONAL CONTROL OF NOMINATIONS

During the years from 1830 to 1860 members of Congress, especially the Senators, had pushed their claim to the right to be consulted by the President on nominations to office in their states or districts. Strong Presidents like Jackson and Polk had resisted the principle of the claim while recognizing the practical virtue of consultation; weak Presidents had submitted without, however, admitting the right. Lincoln had stated the claim in 1849 as a Whig Congressman from Illinois and had tacitly recognized it in practice while President. The claim to be heard easily shaded off into the assertion of a right to name the candidate.

In the case of presidential appointees, the Senate possessed a sanction in the constitutional right to advise and consent, and on the basis of this right gradually emerged the practice of senatorial cour-

---

[35] James D. Richardson, *Messages*, VIII, 375, at 379, 381, 383 (March 1, 1886).

[36] 24 Stat. 500 (March 3, 1887).

[37] Grover Cleveland, *Presidential Problems*, p. 76. For a contemporary view see Dorman B. Eaton, "The President and the Senate," *North American Review*, CXLII (1886), 572.

tesy. A Senator of the majority party who on the floor of the Senate expressed his personal opposition to a nominee (a citizen of his state or an aspirant to a federal office situated in his state) was entitled to the support of his fellow Senators in refusing confirmation.[38] Before the Civil War practice was far from precise, but the influence of Senators, and in lesser measure of Representatives, was substantial. The issue came to focus in a hot controversy during the administrations of Hayes and Garfield.

The position at the opening of the Hayes administration had been aptly described by Congressman Garfield. "During the last twenty-five years, it has been understood, by the Congress and the people, that offices are to be obtained by the aid of senators and representatives, who thus become the dispensers, sometimes the brokers of patronage." The Tenure of Office Act, he wrote, "has virtually resulted in the usurpation, by the senate, of a large share of the appointing power . . . has resulted in seriously crippling the just powers of the executive, and has placed in the hands of senators and representatives a power most corrupting and dangerous."[39]

President Hayes first affronted the Senate oligarchy in his nominations of department heads. Powerful Senators had expected to be consulted. They were not. Hayes made his own choices, determined to appoint "1. A *new* Cabinet—no member of the Present [i.e., Grant's]. 2. No Presidential candidates. 3 No appointment to 'take care' of anybody."[40] The Senate oligarchy promptly accepted the challenge, declined to confirm as a matter of courtesy, and sent the nominations to committees, not even excepting their fellow Senator, John Sherman. A storm of public indignation swept across the country and shortly thereafter the Senate confirmed all the nominations. "For the first time since the Civil War," Binkley wrote, "the Senate had been vanquished on a clear-cut issue between it and the President. The upper House had passed its zenith."[41]

[38] Joseph P. Harris, *The Advice and Consent of the Senate, passim.*
[39] James A. Garfield, "A Century of Progress," *Atlantic Monthly*, XL (1877), 61.
[40] Rutherford B. Hayes, *Diary and Letters*, III, 419 (Feb. 19, 1877).
[41] Wilfred E. Binkley, *President and Congress*, p. 155. Hayes noted after the death of Conkling that, until the announcement of his Cabinet, Conkling had been profuse in his admiration, but that he then became hostile. "We never spoke with each other afterwards." Hayes, *Diary and Letters*, IV, 385 (April 19, 1888).

The great battle, however, was yet to come.[42] The New York customhouse was a political power plant for Senator Conkling. Its collector, Chester A. Arthur, and its naval officer, Alonzo B. Cornell, were prominent members of the New York Republican organization, and the large staff of subordinate personnel was active in the state machine. Despite these political facts, the notoriously lax and corrupt administration of the customhouse was investigated at the direction of Hayes by an able commission headed by the grandson of the first Chief Justice, a successful New York merchant, John Jay. Following the report of the Jay Commission, Hayes asked for the resignation of Arthur and Cornell. They refused to resign. Hayes then sent the names of their successors to the Senate for confirmation, nominations which were greeted with derisive laughter and referred to the Committee on Commerce, of which Senator Conkling was chairman. The committee reported adversely, and the nominations were rejected. They were again rejected in the subsequent regular session. Hayes commented in his diary, "In the language of the press, 'Senator Conkling has won a great victory over the Administration.' My New York nominations were rejected thirty-one to twenty-five. But the end is not yet. I am right and I shall not give up the contest."[43]

After Congress had adjourned in the summer of 1878, Hayes summarily dismissed Arthur and Cornell, made recess appointments, and in December again sent in his nominations for these vacant posts. Conkling held up action for two months, but finally defeated himself by his unrestrained attacks on the President. The Senate voted to confirm on February 3, 1879.

The issue in controversy was misunderstood by no one. In his diary for December 9, 1877, Hayes wrote, "Mr. Conkling insists that no officer shall be appointed in New York without his consent, obtained previously to the nomination."[44] The Senator from New York would not have denied this statement. The resounding victory of the President seemed to settle the question, but the battle was not yet over.

In 1880 Hayes' nomination for collector of the port of San Francisco was rejected. "The California Senators," Hayes noted, "opposed him

[42] Venila Lovina Shores, *The Hayes-Conkling Controversy, 1877-1879* (Northampton, Mass: Smith College Studies in History, IV [1919], 215-79).
[43] Hayes, *Diary and Letters*, III, 454 (Dec. 12, 1877).
[44] *Ibid.*, III, 453 (Dec. 9, 1877).

and under the doctrine called Senatorial courtesy they succeeded in rallying against him a majority of both parties. . . . The object is evidently to reestablish the usage, so that the next President will not venture to question it."[45] Toward the end of his term, Hayes summed up the course of this struggle for power in the following terms.

The end I have chiefly aimed at has been to break down congressional patronage, and especially Senatorial patronage. The contest has been a bitter one. It has exposed me to attack, opposition, misconstruction, and the actual hatred of powerful men. But I have had great success. No member of either house now attempts even to dictate appointments. My sole right to make appointments is tacitly conceded. It has seemed to me that as Executive I could advance the reform of the civil service in no way so effectively as by rescuing the power of appointing to office from the congressional leaders. I began with selecting a Cabinet in opposition to their wishes, and I have gone on in that path steadily until now I am filling the important places of collector of the port and postmaster at Philadelphia almost without a suggestion even from Senators or Representatives! . . .[46]

President Garfield decided to force the issue immediately after his accession. Although he recognized the Conkling wing of the New York Republicans generously, he also determined to recognize the Independents in a conspicuous manner, and thus announce his own freedom in making nominations. To this end he submitted the name of Judge William H. Robertson, a factional opponent of Conkling and a friend of Blaine, as collector of the port of New York. "This," wrote Garfield to his friend Hinsdale, "brings on the contest at once and will settle the question whether the President is registering clerk of the Senate or the Executive of the Nation. It is probable that the contest will be sharp and bitter but I prefer to have the fight ended now. . . . Summed up in a single sentence this is the question: shall the principal port of entry in which more than 90% of all our customs duties are collected be under the direct control of the Administration or under the local control of a factional Senator."[47]

The dramatic conclusion of this battle is well known. In the face of defeat Conkling and Platt resigned their seats in the Senate and

[45] *Ibid.*, III, 585 (Feb. 7, 1880).
[46] *Ibid.*, III, 612-13 (July 14, 1880).
[47] *Garfield-Hinsdale Letters*, p. 489 (April 4, 1881).

returned to Albany for vindication by reelection.[48] The New York Assembly repudiated their one-time Senators; Conkling never resumed public office; and the victory of the President was, in this case, complete. Robertson was unanimously confirmed. The influence of Senators in suggesting persons for presidential consideration still remained substantial,[49] but their claim to govern executive discretion was denied.

COERCION BY RIDERS

Aggression on executive power by the Senate was matched during Hayes' administration by aggression on the part of the House through riders to appropriation bills. The Democrats were determined to defeat the reconstruction measures requiring test oaths for jury service and authorizing the use of federal armed forces to protect voters at the polls. During Hayes' first Congress (the Forty-fifth) the Republicans had control of the Senate, and the Democratic majority in the House could do no more than force a special session of the Forty-sixth Congress on March 18, 1879, by blocking the annual appropriations for the army. In the new Congress they held a majority in both Houses, but not enough votes to pass legislation over a veto. They were thus barred from direct legislative repeal of the contested statutes and consequently decided to force the hand of the President by means of riders to appropriation bills.

Riders—i.e., substantive legislation tacked onto appropriation bills—were an old practice, but (so Garfield stated) now for the first time a congressional majority asserted its right to stop supplies unless "redress of grievance" was secured by executive acceptance of an obnoxious proviso.[50] Senator Allen G. Thurman of Ohio, supporting the rider, declared that the issue involved the rights, the privileges, the powers, and the duties of the two branches of Congress and of the President: "It is the question whether or no the House of Represent-

---

[48] For a popular account of this affair, see Donald Barr Chidsey, *The Gentleman from New York: a Life of Roscoe Conkling* (New Haven: Yale University Press, 1935), pp. 329-56.

[49] Hayes himself confirmed this. "How to get the requisite information to appoint postmasters without practically giving it to the Members of Congress, is one of the questions." *Diary and Letters*, III, 515 (Dec. 17, 1878).

[50] *Garfield-Hinsdale Letters*, pp. 403-404 (April 9, 1879).

atives has the right to say 'We will grant supplies only upon condition that grievances are redressed.' "[51]

Hayes was fully alert to the situation and firmly set to protect
executive authority. In his diary for March 18, 1879 (the opening day
of the special session), he wrote, "An important struggle then begins.
The Democrats will attempt by coercion of the President to secure
a repeal of legislation which I deem wise and important. This is to
place the Executive 'under the coercive dictation' of a bare majority
of the two houses of Congress. . . . It is a 'measure of coercion,' a
revolutionary measure. . . . No precedent shall be established with my
consent to a measure which is tantamount to coercion of the Executive."[52] If repeal of the test oath and of the use of federal troops at
elections was attached as riders, he wrote that he would not even
consider the merits of bills so presented.[53] This was the precise situation with which he was soon confronted.

The special session convened on March 18, 1879, and within about
a month Congress passed the deadlocked army appropriation bill
with a rider which, among other objects, prohibited federal civil officers (i.e., marshals) from employing either federal troops or armed
civilians to keep peace at the polls where congressional elections were
held. Hayes vetoed the appropriation act, first, because he believed
the federal government should retain authority to use force if necessary to protect congressional elections; second, because of the coercive
effect of the rider. On this point he declared in his veto message,
"The new doctrine, if maintained, will result in a consolidation of
unchecked and despotic power in the House of Representatives. A
bare majority of the House will become the Government. The Executive will no longer be what the framers of the Constitution intended
—an equal and independent branch of the Government. It is clearly
the constitutional duty of the President to exercise his discretion and
judgment upon all bills presented to him without constraint or duress
from any other branch of the Government."[54]

Defeated in their first endeavor, the House Democrats turned to a
second expedient, a bill preventing the use of federal authority at

[51] Quoted by Garfield (May 20, 1879), *ibid.*, pp. 415-16.
[52] Hayes, *Diary and Letters*, III, 529.
[53] *Ibid.*, III, 530-31 (March 21, 1879).
[54] Richardson, *Messages*, VII, 523, 531 (April 29, 1879).

elections except on application of the state. Hayes promptly vetoed this bill, on the ground that the federal government ought not to be dependent on the states to afford protection to its own elections. "In my judgment," he told Congress, "this is an abandonment of its obligations by the National Government—a subordination of national authority and an intrusion of State supervision over national duties which amounts, in spirit and tendency, to State supremacy."[55]

The House then tried again, attaching a less obnoxious rider to the general appropriation bill, the purport of which was to reduce the marshals' authority over elections to the innocuous duty of observing and inspecting. Hayes directed his third veto against this plan.[56] Time was running out, but the House made still another effort, attaching a rider to the judicial appropriation bill, prohibiting the use of any money to pay marshals and their deputies for election work, but leaving the laws on the books. The President launched his fourth veto against this scheme, notifying Congress that the bill neither revoked federal protection to citizens at the polls, nor relieved the marshal of his lawful obligations, nor altered the duty of the President to see that the law was faithfully executed.[57]

The Democrats made a final effort at the very close of the special session, making it easier for the President to acquiesce in their will by removing the payment of marshals from the judiciary bill (which was approved) and by passing a second bill for the marshals' appropriations with a rider allowing compensation for election expenses for the current year (1879-80) but denying it subsequently. The fifth veto killed this bill.[58] Congress then adjourned, and the marshals were left with no appropriation.

The struggle was resumed in the succeeding regular session, the marshals carrying on in faith and hope. In May 1880, Congress enacted a deficiency bill, including funds for the marshals and also the now familiar rider. Hayes stood his ground and again lectured the legislative branch. "The objection to the bill . . . is that it gives a marked and deliberate sanction . . . to the questionable and, as I am clearly of opinion, the dangerous practice of tacking upon ap-

---

[55] *Ibid.*, VII, 532, 536 (May 12, 1879).
[56] *Ibid.*, VII, 536 (May 29, 1879).
[57] *Ibid.*, VII, 541, 543 (June 23, 1879).
[58] *Ibid.*, VII, 545 (June 30, 1879).

propriation bills general and permanent legislation. This practice
opens a wide door to hasty, inconsiderate, and sinister legislation.
It invites attacks upon the independence and constitutional powers
of the Executive by providing an easy and effective way of constrain-
ing Executive discretion."[59]

Six vetoes did not exhaust the Democratic majority. A new scheme
was invented, providing that deputy marshals on election duty should
be appointed annually by the circuit courts of the United States
and that the marshals should not be liable for any of their acts. The
rider problem was not involved in this bill, but a simple problem of
administration sufficed for Hayes' seventh veto. "The so-called deputy
marshals," he notified Congress, ". . . have no executive head. The
marshal can neither appoint nor remove them. He can not control
them, and he is not responsible for them."[60] Thus ended the "pistol
shots" of the Chief Executive and thus terminated the efforts of the
Forty-sixth Congress to repeal the reconstruction statutes.

The net result was a clean-cut victory for the President and a
powerful precedent against congressional encroachment on the executive power by means of appropriation riders. The action was defensive
and protective, but it was important. Congress was forced to enact
the long-delayed appropriation acts without imposing its will on the
President; the integrity of the veto power was sustained; and the
popularity of an unpopular President was repaired.

The object of the Democrats had not been primarily to curtail
executive authority as a matter of theory or principle; they aimed at
ending federal interference in southern elections. They were forced,
however, to the rider expedient, because they lacked the power to
pass a bill ending such interference over the head of the President.
Their theoretical inheritance supported executive power, and had
they been successful in this encounter it was not certain that the
long-run consequences would have been those feared by Hayes. Cleveland was soon to remind Democrats that *their* executive was independent also and able to use the veto power. However this may be,
the courage and stubbornness of Hayes halted this House aggression
on executive power. The Senate lost prestige in the Conkling affair;
the House lost prestige in the battle of the riders; the executive
gained in both cases.

[59] *Ibid.*, VII, 591, 592 (May 4, 1880).
[60] *Ibid.*, VII, 592, 597 (June 15, 1880).

THE VETO POWER

The great debate over the proper use of the veto power was not renewed during the postwar years. The Whig view that it was intended only for highly exceptional cases primarily involving constitutional issues or an apparent encroachment on executive powers had been finally laid to rest by President Polk. Neither Republicans nor Democrats resumed the discussion.

President Cleveland used the veto freely to kill objectionable private pension acts; others followed the general pattern of early Presidents. Grant vetoed forty-three bills, nearly thirty of which were private relief and pension enactments; Hayes vetoed twelve; Arthur only four. In his first term Cleveland vetoed about three times as many as all his predecessors, three hundred and one; most of them had no general significance. Harrison vetoed nineteen; Cleveland in his second term, forty-four; and McKinley only five.[61]

That Presidents considered themselves entitled to veto on grounds of policy difference with Congress was illustrated in some striking cases. Hayes' veto of seven successive bills carrying riders was a battle both over substantive policy and over a threatened encroachment by the House of Representatives on executive authority. Three Presidents vetoed Chinese immigration acts (Hayes, Arthur, and Cleveland); Hayes vetoed a currency bill favoring the coinage of silver. No one disputed the propriety of such policy vetoes.[62]

There was occasional discussion during the 1880's of the item veto for the Chief Executive. President Arthur recommended it to the attention of Congress in 1882.[63] A contributor to the *Century Magazine* argued in its favor in 1886,[64] but the proposal did not strike fire. A locality-minded Congress, jealous of its position, could hardly be

[61] Figures through Cleveland's first administration from Edward Campbell Mason, *The Veto Power: Its Origin, Development and Function in the Government of the United States* (2d ed., Boston: Ginn and Co., 1891), Appendix A; others compiled from Richardson, *Messages*, Vols. IX, X.

[62] The practice of sending pending bills as a matter of routine to the Attorney General and to the department concerned for advice on signature was described by President Benjamin Harrison, *This Country of Ours* (New York: Charles Scribner's Sons, 1897), p. 128.

[63] Richardson, *Messages*, VIII, 138 (Dec. 4, 1882).

[64] Unsigned article, "Appropriations and the Veto," *Century Magazine*, XXXIII (1886-87), 320-21.

expected to expose appropriation bills and rivers and harbors bills to an executive item veto.

Presidents lost no public esteem by standing out against Congress in the use of the veto power. In the *American Commonwealth* James Bryce wrote: "So far from exciting the displeasure of the people by resisting the will of their representatives, a President generally gains popularity by the bold use of his veto power. It conveys the impression of firmness; it shows that he has a view and does not fear to give effect to it. The nation, which has often good grounds for distrusting Congress . . . looks to the man of its choice to keep Congress in order. . . ."[65]

We may conclude, therefore, that the nature of the veto power was no longer in dispute between Congress and the Chief Executive. It might be used freely or rarely, and its application to particular measures might be hotly contested, but the right to veto on grounds of constitutionality, encroachment, or mere differences in policy and judgment was unquestioned.

POLICY LEADERSHIP

The relative position of the Chief Executive and Congress was revealed not only in the dramatic events surrounding the Tenure of Office Act, the demands of the Senate leadership to dictate nominations, and the effort of the House to constrain the President by appropriation riders. It appeared also in the capacity of the President to provide guidance in public policy and to bend an often factious Congress to his will.

Such a capacity depends on circumstances often beyond the control of Chief Executives. A politically hostile Congress, in either one or both Houses, almost certainly denies the possibility of executive leadership. There were eight such instances out of sixteen Congresses in the period under review. A faction-ridden majority or a party split on issues weakens any leadership. Cleveland could not possibly have given leadership to the silver Democrats during his second term. The capacity of either House to be led is also important. The Senate in the days of Conkling, Sumner, and Sherman was a constellation of independent principalities, not a disciplined organization, and the

[65] James Bryce, *The American Commonwealth* (3d ed., 2 vols., New York: Macmillan Co., 1893-95), I, 59.

House during the 1880's was an irresponsible and leaderless body finally to be rescued from its ineptitude by a powerful Speaker. The urgency of the times exerts its influence; leadership is relatively easy in years of crisis, difficult in years dominated by secondary issues. The degree of consensus among the people, or its absence, profoundly affects the range of effective leadership at any time. When the mind of the country has settled, Congress and President must concur.

The personal qualities of Presidents also count heavily, both in their immediate relations to Senators and Representatives and in their ability to appeal to the country. Grant could not make an effective public speech and fell under the influence of the reactionary wing of the Republican party. His immense popularity in 1869 waned, and by the end of his first term a large section of the party refused to accept his second nomination. Hayes was under the cloud of a disputed election throughout his term and only fitfully gained a measure of esteem. In his diary for March 1, 1878, he wrote, "I am not liked as a President, by the politicians in office, in the press, or in Congress."[66] Garfield confirmed this opinion, writing that Hayes' "defenders were comparatively few."[67] The issue of Garfield's personal influence was not put to a test; his successor, Arthur, was handicapped by memory of his part in the New York customhouse affair. Cleveland was respected for his uncompromising integrity but he stirred little personal affection. Harrison was cold and aristocratic, having little hold on public sentiment. Of all these Presidents, William McKinley was the only one who captured the affection of the public and Congress alike.

These generalities are illustrated in the course of policy leadership from Grant to William McKinley. From 1869 to 1877 the initiative and control of policy were generally in the Senate, to a lesser degree in the committees of the House. Henry Adams commented on this fact with his usual trenchant phrase.

. . . . So far as the President's initiative was concerned, the President and his Cabinet might equally well have departed separately or together to distant lands. Their recommendations were uniformly disregarded. Mr. Sumner, at the head of the Senate, rode rough-shod over their reconstruction policy and utterly overthrew it, in spite of the feeble resistance of the

[66] Hayes, *Diary and Letters*, III, 463.
[67] Quoted in Theodore C. Smith, *Life and Letters of James A. Garfield*, II, 659.

House. Mr. Conkling then ousted Mr. Sumner from his saddle, and headed the Senate in an attack upon the Executive as represented by Judge Hoar, the avowed *casus belli* being the fact that the Attorney-General's manners were unsatisfactory to the Senate. But Mr. Conkling's most brilliant triumph was over the Census bill. Here he had a threefold victory, and it would be hard to say which of the three afforded him the keenest gratification. Single-handed he attacked Mr. Sumner, the House, and the Executive, and routed them all in disastrous confusion.[68]

Hayes faced not only an arrogant group of Republican Senators but, as already noted, a Congress in which the Democrats controlled the House and after 1879 both the House and the Senate. He moved effectively where he could stand on his authority as Chief Executive, but the possibility of constructive policy leadership did not exist. He successfully defended the presidential office against aggression—and this was in itself of historic importance—but beyond this he could not go.

Garfield possessed a detailed knowledge of government and a capacity for leadership which in all probability would have enabled him to dominate his first Congress; the second (under Arthur) fell to Democratic control in the House. Congress would neither accept executive leadership nor provide its own. Binkley notes that Arthur's third message contained eight important policy recommendations of which only one was enacted by Congress.[69] This was the time when Bryce wrote that a President's wishes had not necessarily any more effect on Congress than an article in a prominent party newspaper.

Cleveland's rugged and uncompromising personality was not suited to leadership any more than his theoretical adherence to the doctrine of separation of powers. He fought Congressmen on private pension bills and then vetoed an act which they thought corrected the evils of which he complained. He was relatively indifferent to party lines; in his first term he demoralized the party with his demand for tariff revision, and in his second broke his party in two by his stand on monetary policy.

Harrison was equally unsuited for policy leadership but for different

---

[68] Henry Adams, "The Session," *North American Review*, CXI (1870), 41. This was the census bill designed to take patronage from the marshals and the Senators, for which Garfield had fought in the House.

[69] Wilfred E. Binkley, *President and Congress*, p. 177.

reasons. He had been in the Senate and fought with other Republicans to resuscitate the Senate's power to challenge the President's reasons for suspending subordinate executive officers. He subscribed to the then dominant Republican theory of the primacy of Congress. Binkley concluded, "It would hardly be an exaggeration to say that the Republican party organization ran the government."[70]

Presidential leadership in policy was, however, restored when William McKinley entered the White House. His party dominated both House and Senate; he was on friendly terms with party leaders; he had dignity, tact, and persuasiveness; he had had long experience in the House and understood the necessity for party organization. At the same time he had independence and strength of character. Senator Hoar declared that, with the possible exception of Jackson, no President had established such influence over the members of the Senate as McKinley.[71] The testimony of Elihu Root confirmed this view. "He was a man of great power because he was absolutely indifferent to credit. His great desire was to 'get it done.' He cared nothing about the credit, but McKinley *always had his way*. He understood the art of administration with a minimum of interference. . . . He had vast influence with Congress. He led them by the power of affectionate esteem, not by fear. . . . Hanna was a strong and vigorous man, but McKinley was the controlling spirit of the two."[72]

At the close of the century the prospects of the presidency therefore seemed bright, but the recollection of thirty years' conflict between the legislative and executive branches could not support much optimism for continuously effective policy leadership in the White House. A politically divided Congress, a factious party, a succession of Presidents less skillful than McKinley—these and other probabilities could readily cause reversion. Such contingencies, however, were not to happen, and a new energy in the White House was to be sustained for two decades.

While Presidents were failing to develop a theory of the presidency to defy that of the Radical Republicans and their spiritual predecessors, the Whigs, others were performing this task for them. Henry

[70] *Ibid.*, p. 182.
[71] George F. Hoar, *Autobiography*, II, 47.
[72] Quoted in Charles S. Olcott, *The Life of William McKinley* (2 vols., Boston: Houghton Mifflin Co., 1916), II, 346-47.

Adams observed in 1870 that a President was less a commander of an army in time of peace than he was a commander of a ship at sea. "He must have a helm to grasp, a course to steer, a port to seek; he must sooner or later be convinced that a perpetual calm is as little to his purpose as a perpetual hurricane, and that without headway the ship can arrive nowhere."[73]

James Bryce also forecast a stronger role for the Chief Executive. "The weakness of Congress," he wrote, "is the strength of the President. Though it cannot be said that his office has risen in power or dignity since 1789, there are reasons for believing that it may reach a higher point than it has occupied at any time since the Civil War. The tendency everywhere in America to concentrate power and responsibility in one man is unmistakable."[74] Others were thinking in the same direction, but they were to guide the future generation, not their own.

[73] Henry Adams, "The Session," *North American Review*, CXI (1870), 34.
[74] James Bryce, *American Commonwealth* (3d ed.), II, 846.

CHAPTER THREE

The Struggle for Power:
Congress and Administration

Congress was always predisposed to engage in the affairs of the executive branch, fortified by its underlying powers to legislate, to appropriate, and to investigate. The theory of separation of powers had long been a commingling of power in practice, Congress usually being the aggressor although not always successful. After the Civil War the center of gravity of the governmental system rested on the whole with the legislative branch, despite stout resistance on the part of Presidents Hayes, Garfield, and Cleveland. It would naturally follow that the impact of Congress on administration would be stronger than in other times.

This assumption was verified by events. Both House and Senate were deeply involved in matters primarily administrative in character. Patronage deals with Presidents and heads of departments flourished on a greater scale than ever; appropriations committees toiled over the detail of constantly more voluminous estimates; investigations were frequent and partisan; members surged in and out of executive offices on constituents' business; and in several fields Congress acted in effect as an appeal body to review the decisions of official agencies in particular cases. The consequences were bad both for Congress and for administration.

To reduce a complex, shifting, and varied scene to some degree of order, it will be convenient to proceed by commenting on the dominant position of Congress and the decline of its character and capacity for action until the days of Speaker Reed; and then to observe

Congress acting in its major role respecting the administrative system: the control of funds. In the next chapter the relationship of Congress to administration can be considered in four other important but secondary aspects: administration by legislation, the pressure of constituents' business upon Congressmen, the appellate functions discharged by Congress and its committees, all leading Congress into the labyrinth of review of a mass of individual cases; and congressional efforts to improve administrative management.

THE DOMINANCE OF CONGRESS

That Congress in 1869 had become the dominant partner in the executive–legislative team was obvious from what has already been written about the presidency. The inherent conflict between the two branches that John Adams had perceived came to full fruition with a domineering Senate and an aggressive House. For a time the country seemed to accept such an outcome with approval, however much the government floundered. There were no novel *theories* of representative government to support the supremacy of the elected assembly; what had been said by Jefferson in his day and by the Whigs in theirs seemed sufficient in a period when problems of foreign relations were relatively innocuous and when drift was congenial to a laissez faire philosophy.

The interest of the people and of statesmen was in Congress and politics, not in administration. It was not until 1887 that Woodrow Wilson introduced the country to the idea of administration, and he was obliged to record that up to his own day all the political writers had argued and dogmatized about the nature of the state and the seat of sovereignty. "The other question, how law should be administered with enlightenment, with equity, with speed, and without friction, was put aside as 'practical detail' which clerks could arrange after doctors had agreed upon principles."[1] The shadow of the Civil War hung long over the recurrent elections; spoils were fought for perennially; big business entered the lists for its own advantages; the battle against corruption stirred deep emotions; organized labor induced alarm; depressions and falling prices held the stage for many years. Politics was noisy, exhilarating, compelling, and dominant;

---

[1] Woodrow Wilson, "The Study of Administration," *Political Science Quarterly,* II (1887), 197-222 at 198-99.

administration was hardly perceived except in terms of the punishment of knaves.

The predominance of Congress and the derogation of the Executive appeared not only in the course of events to which reference has already been made but in the underlying assumptions of many thoughtful commentators on the contemporary scene during the 1870's and 1880's. Two of them may speak for others. In 1870 Gamaliel Bradford proposed that Cabinet members should have the right and duty to appear before the House and its committees to explain and defend their respective programs. He recognized that a fundamental difference of opinion between the House and a Secretary might involve the latter's resignation, although he argued that this need not follow. Nowhere in his proposal was there the slightest indication that the policy of the Secretary was, or was expected to be, in any way related to the policy of the President. The executive branch was tacitly understood to be a cluster of department heads, each asking for appropriations and legislation to meet the needs of his agency, each directly responsible to the proper committee of Congress, and each bowing to the decision of the people at the biennial elections in case of a stubborn dispute with Congress. The President was a mere onlooker. Bradford found no place for him in this pattern of congressional supremacy and did not even mention the consequences on the presidential office that might flow from the confrontation of department heads by Congress and its powerful committees.[2]

What Bradford had assumed as an implicit major premise became explicit in the early writing of Woodrow Wilson. In the preface to *Congressional Government* he described Congress as "the central and predominant power of the system." He declared that "there is always a centre of power," and asked his readers "where in this system is that centre?" He left no doubt as to the answer.

. . . unquestionably, the predominant and controlling force, the centre and source of all motive and of all regulative power, is Congress. All niceties of constitutional restriction and even many broad principles of constitutional limitation have been overridden, and a thoroughly organized system of congressional control set up which gives a very rude negative to some theories of balance and some schemes for distributed power, but

[2] Gamaliel Bradford, "Congressional Reform," *North American Review*, CXI (1870), 330-51.

which suits well with convenience, and does violence to none of the principles of self-government contained in the Constitution.[3]

Thus Wilson wrote off the presidency as an unimportant nonentity,
and confirmed in scholarly analysis the supremacy of Congress without recollecting the records of such Chief Executives as Jefferson, Jackson, Polk, and Abraham Lincoln.

THE DECLINE OF CONGRESSIONAL COMPETENCE

The position of Congress as the center of power in the federal government compelled appraisal of its competence to discharge the responsibilities of power. The answer was disconcerting. Effective states-
manship, wherever its location may be, requires concentration of
decision-making authority, steadiness of long-range goals, a national
outlook, a capacity to reach timely decisions, a sense of responsibility,
and an organization designed to facilitate action by securing adequate
information, opportunity for open discussion, and certainty in ultimate
conclusion. That Congress was incompetent in all these matters was
a frequent complaint until Speaker Thomas B. Reed finally brought
order and discipline into its affairs.

The temper of the constant, if ineffectual, criticism is well reflected
in the views of Gamaliel Bradford, who declared:

. . . . Yet if we look at the manner of conducting business in Congress,
the time consumed in personal contests among members, the hetero-
geneous bills and resolutions introduced at random by any member, and
quietly referred to committees; if we consider that the real measures to be
acted upon are discussed and prepared in secret committees subject to the
tremendous pressure of private interests, which govern not only the
manner of treatment, but the subjects themselves to be treated; and, further, that the measures thus elaborated are reported to Congress without
any official explanation of the theory and arguments upon which they are
based, or of their relation to the general plan of legislation; that debate is
suppressed or amounts only to a mere form; and that, after lying in abey-
ance during most of the session, these bills are hurried through at last by a
general party vote, and because something must be done;—under these
circumstances, what hope or prospect is there of any intelligent, comprehensive, and systematic treatment of the great problems which we have
just now mentioned?[4]

[3] Woodrow Wilson, *Congressional Government*, pp. xiii, 10-11.
[4] Gamaliel Bradford, "Congressional Reform," *North American Review*, CXI
(1870), 331.

These generalities were reduced to particulars by persons both within and without congressional halls. After eight years in the House, George Frisbie Hoar declared in 1879 that the House was losing its freedom of debate, of amendment, and even of knowledge of what it was doing. The contest over important measures was a struggle to decide, not whether they should be discussed, but whether they should be brought to a vote. "There is nowhere responsibility for securing due attention to important measures, and no authority to decide between their different claims."[5] James A. Garfield confirmed this opinion in the field of appropriations.[6]

Party oscillation in Congress. The massive Republican predominance in the legislative branch, an aftermath of the Civil War, disappeared when the Democrats captured the House in the mid-term election of 1874. From this moment until Republican ascendancy was reestablished in 1896, party tides uneasily and rapidly shifted back and forth. For two decades there were only three Congresses in which the same party had effective control of both Houses at the same time, and only two in which the majority party held the presidency as well. These unsettled conditions not only were unfavorable to executive leadership, they also were conducive to conflict between the Senate and the House, and to irresponsibility on the part of both.

In Hayes' first Congress the Democrats held the House, the Republicans the Senate; in his second, the Democrats controlled both. Garfield had a comfortable majority in the House but an evenly balanced Senate; Arthur's Congress was split, the Democrats having a heavy House majority while the Senate was in precarious Republican control. Cleveland faced a Republican Senate during the whole of his first term. Harrison had a House majority in his first Congress, but a Senate that showed a Republican margin of only two votes; in his second he lost the House in an overwhelming Democratic landslide. Cleveland had a Republican Senate and a Republican House in his two final years. Not even the Democratic–Whig years had revealed such political instability.

That the government was weakened during these years by such an

---

[5] George F. Hoar, "The Conduct of Business in Congress," *North American Review*, CXXVIII (1879), 133-34.

[6] James A. Garfield, "National Appropriations and Misappropriations," *ibid.*, CXXVIII (1879), 572-86.

absence of consensus was obvious. Conflict of opinion in a legislative body is natural and healthy, but the absence of an effective majority at times approached stalemate and sterility. Congressman James A. Garfield wrote in 1877, "Congress has always been and must always be the theatre of contending opinions; the forum where the opposing forces of political philosophy meet to measure their strength; where the public good must meet the assaults of local and sectional interests; in a word, the appointed place where the nation seeks to utter its thought and register its will."[7] But for twenty years the country seemed to have no decisive will, as party majorities fluctuated now in this direction, now in that.

The committee system. The congressional committee system was a fundamental weak point. Chairmen became such by the seniority rule; their power was almost absolute within their jurisdictions. Leadership and responsibility were dissolved among nearly fifty competing chairmen in the House and a somewhat lesser number in the Senate. The Speaker (before Reed) was a relatively unimportant partisan, whose control of proceedings could be, and on occasion was defied by the minority or even by a single member. The rules under which the House and its committees operated were an unknown jungle, and considerable business was pushed forward by unanimous agreement to suspend the rules, thus returning to a sort of simple state of nature.

These matters were boldly described by Woodrow Wilson in 1885.[8] There were in Congress, he wrote, no authoritative leaders who were the recognized spokesmen of their parties.

     . . . . Power is nowhere concentrated; it is rather deliberately and of set policy scattered amongst many small chiefs. It is divided up, as it were, into forty-seven seignories, in each of which a Standing Committee is the court-baron and its chairman lord-proprietor. These petty barons . . . may at will exercise an almost despotic sway within their own shires, and may sometimes threaten to convulse even the realm itself; but both their mutual jealousies and their brief and restricted opportunities forbid their combining, and each is very far from the office of common leader.[9]

     [7] James A. Garfield, "A Century of Progress," *Atlantic Monthly*, XL (1877), 60.
     [8] They had already been noted and decried by Congressman James A. Garfield, "A Century of Progress," *Atlantic Monthly*, XL (1877), 62.
     [9] Woodrow Wilson, *Congressional Government*, p. 92.

"It is impossible," he stated, "to discover any unity or method in the disconnected and therefore unsystematic, confused, and desultory action of the House, or any common purpose in the measures which its Committees from time to time recommend."[10]

The quorum problem. The problem which finally produced a crisis and the emergence of some degree of order and responsibility turned on obstruction either by filibuster or by refusing to answer a roll call to establish a quorum. Lacking a quorum the House could not proceed. No less a person than John Quincy Adams established the precedent, in 1832, by which a member could sit silently in his seat, refusing to vote or respond on a roll call.[11] During the speakership of John G. Carlisle (1883-1889), when a few members reduced the proceedings of the House to quorum roll calls for eight consecutive days, he held that a yea and nay vote must answer every shout of "no quorum."[12]

The 51st Congress opened on December 2, 1889, and elected Thomas B. Reed Speaker. The reported Republican membership of 170 was only five more than a quorum, and, according to Republican leaders, they could count on only 168; the Democrats numbered 160. The majority intended to make procedural reforms to consolidate their position, but these turned on establishing and holding a quorum. On January 29, 1890, the Democrats raised the familiar question of no quorum; Reed ordered the clerk to record as present the names of some forty members present but refusing to vote; and three days of pandemonium with intervals of serious debate ensued. At the end the Speaker was sustained; the "disappearing quorum" itself disappeared; new rules to prevent obstruction were soon accepted; and, after twenty years and more of irresolution, leadership again took hold in the House.[13]

Moral decline. Damage had been done, however, to the reputation of Congress that was not easily repaired. The moral tone of Congress

[10] *Ibid.*, p. 61.

[11] DeAlva Stanwood Alexander, *History and Procedure of the House of Representatives* (Boston: Houghton Mifflin Co., 1916), pp. 158 *et seq.*

[12] *Ibid.*, p. 164; James A. Barnes, *John G. Carlisle: Financial Statesman* (New York: Dodd, Mead and Co., 1931), p. 154.

[13] *Congressional Record*, 51st Cong., 1st sess., pp. 949 ff. (Jan. 29, 1890). For a detailed account of this affair, see William A. Robinson, *Thomas B. Reed, Parliamentarian* (New York: Dodd, Mead and Co., 1930), ch. 10, and O. O. Stealey, *Twenty Years in the Press Gallery* (New York: author, 1906), chs. 13-15. See also

had been lowered during the eight years of Grant's administration—
a matter touched upon elsewhere. The intellectual level of Congress
had suffered, despite the presence of some able men like Garfield in
the House and Sherman and Hoar in the Senate. The public standing
of both House and Senate had retrogressed as Conkling overreached
himself and as the Democrats were forced to retreat on the issue of
"riders." The quality of public discussion and enlightenment deteriorated as small men gave way to obstreperous partisanship and to
local rather than national enterprises. Drift and confusion in Congress
led the country to expect little in leadership and to fear much in un-
dercover manipulation by strong interests.

In 1869 Henry Adams declared that "as a class" Congressmen were
not venal, adding that perhaps not more than one member in ten of
the 40th Congress had ever accepted money. However, he denounced
the rings that, without decency or shame, controlled legislation in Congress, and the party organizations.[14] A year later he concluded that the
system of government that sufficed in 1820 had been outgrown.

> . . . . The government does not govern; Congress is inefficient, and
> shows itself more and more incompetent, as at present constituted, to
> wield the enormous powers that are forced upon it, while the Executive,
> in its full enjoyment of theoretical independence, is practically deprived
> of its necessary strength by the jealousy of the Legislature. Without re-
> sponsibility, direct, incessant, and continuous, no government is practi-
> cable over forty millions of people and an entire continent, and no
> responsibility exists at Washington. . . .[15]

Three years later the scientist Simon Newcomb was even more deeply
concerned. "The public," he wrote, "know or believe the legislatures
of one third of the States of the Union, perhaps we might say one
half, to be more or less corrupt, many of them thoroughly corrupt. . . . The consequence is, that charges of corruption against one
third of the Senate will not be received with incredulity, but will be
looked upon as things not at all improbable, however difficult it may

---

DeAlva S. Alexander, *History and Procedure of the House of Representatives*;
Hubert Bruce Fuller, *The Speakers of the House* (Boston: Little, Brown, and
Co., 1909). For the opposing views of Speakers Reed and Carlisle, see "The
Limitations of the Speakership," *North American Review*, CL (1890), 382-99.

[14] Henry Adams, "The Session," *North American Review*, CVIII (1869), 617.

[15] Henry Adams, "The Session," *ibid.*, CXI (1870), 60.

be to prove them. In this very opinion, apart from all evidence to sustain it, we have a loss of public confidence in the Senate which should alarm every thinking man."[16]

Others were less temperate than Adams. In 1874 David A. Wasson asserted, "No parliamentary body within the limits of civilization is less trusted and respected by the nation at large than the American Congress by the American people. From no national legislature is less expected; the best hope of the people is to be spared, not served; to escape without injury, and be no worse off at the close of a session than at its opening, is thought a piece of luck. . . ."[17] A more balanced view was summed up by Wilson in 1885: "These, then, are the conditions of public life which make the House of Representatives what it is, a disintegrate mass of jarring elements, and the Senate what it is, a small, select, and leisurely House of Representatives."[18]

These adverse comments must be balanced by recognition of the presence in both Houses of men of character, ability, and independence, whose steady devotion to duty enabled Congress to discharge its minimum obligations. Garfield well represented this group. Having been criticized by some of his constituents, he replied in an open letter setting out his theory of the relations of a representative to his district. "I believe," he wrote, "a representative should get all the light on every matter of public importance that his position enables him to and then speak and vote in such a manner as will, in his judgment, enhance the best interests of his constituents and the whole country. If the constituency, in reviewing the action of their representative, find him deficient in ability, judgment or integrity they have always the remedy of choosing another in his place. But while he is in office his course should be guided by his own judgments, based upon the suggestions of his constituents and all other obtainable information. On no other ground could I have accepted the office I now hold, on no other ground could I continue to hold it."[19] This was in 1865. In 1872, after longer service in the House, he confided to his diary, "It is a terrible thing to live in fear of their constituents

---

[16] Simon Newcomb, "The Session," *ibid.*, CXVII (1873), 199.

[17] D. A. Wasson, "The Modern Type of Oppression," *ibid.*, CXIX (1874), 281.

[18] Woodrow Wilson, *Congressional Government*, p. 210.

[19] Theodore C. Smith, *Life and Letters of James A. Garfield*, I, 382 (April 7, 1865).

to the extent which many members do. I would rather be defeated every day in the year, than suffer such fear."[20]

Whatever the deficiences of Congress in the eyes of its contemporaries (and onlookers are inclined to be more harsh than later commentators), there was no doubt that the two Houses exerted a powerful and continuous influence upon the conduct of administration. One of the strongest congressional levers was the control of appropriations and expenditures.

APPROPRIATION CONTROL OF ADMINISTRATIVE OPERATIONS

Whatever the exact form of the appropriation acts, they exert a dominant influence on the conduct of administration. The governmental functions to be performed are specified for the most part by substantive legislation, but the means of execution and the level of operations, as well as a multitude of requirements as to how money can be spent, are fixed in the appropriation acts. They may be couched in general terms and contain large lump-sum items, or they may spell out in minute detail how many clerks may be employed at what salaries, how much can be spent for postage stamps, and what may be authorized under the head of contingencies. In the former case considerable discretion is left to mangement for the most efficient use of available funds, but congressional control is correspondingly curtailed. In the latter case executive discretion is hedged about, but congressional influence is enlarged.

A long struggle had ensued from the beginning of the Republic over this phase of legislative oversight of the various departments and establishments.[21] The net outcome down to the Civil War was a form of appropriation act for the executive offices that was designed to permit little discretion to bureau chiefs, except that both the army and navy supply bills were so drawn as to leave large sums

[20] James A. Garfield, Diary (Feb. 19, 1872) in Manuscript Division, Library of Congress.

[21] Lucius Wilmerding, Jr., The Spending Power: a History of the Efforts of Congress to Control Expenditures (New Haven: Yale University Press, 1943); Leonard D. White, The Federalists: a Study in Administrative History (New York: Macmillan Co., 1948), ch. 26; The Jeffersonians: a Study in Administrative History, 1801-1829 (New York: Macmillan Co., 1951), ch. 8; The Jacksonians: a Study in Administrative History, 1829-1861 (New York: Macmillan Co., 1954), ch. 7.

available for discretionary application. This marked dichotomy prevailed also in the post-Civil War decades.

During these years Congress appropriated in eight or ten major
supply bills and in a considerable number of small special enactments.
The principal bills for the fiscal year ending June 30, 1871, were these:
legislative, executive, and judicial, carrying funds for officers and employees of the three great branches of government, including the
civilian side of the War and Navy Departments; the consular and
diplomatic services; the army, with funds for the uniformed forces
and for army supply; fortifications; the navy; the Indian department
(now a bureau in Interior), providing for annuities and other payments to Indian tribes; pensions; post office; and rivers and harbors.
As will be noted in a later section, the scrutiny of these bills exclusively by a single House Committee on Appropriations eventually
broke down, and many of them came to the House through other
and competing committees.

The act making appropriations for the legislative, executive, and
judicial departments for the fiscal year 1871 covered twenty-one
pages and represented the high-water mark of congressional dictation by itemization.[22] The application of these funds left little
discretion to Secretaries and bureau chiefs, and so far as personnel
was concerned, practically none.

A typical office appropriation was that for the first auditor. It
divided a sum of $58,280 among the staff to the last dollar: the first
auditor, $3,000; the chief clerk, $2,000; three clerks of class four,
ten clerks of class three, ten clerks of class two, and thirteen clerks
of class one; one messenger and one assistant messenger at $720; and
one laborer.[23] Office after office had specified for it the exact number
of clerks and other employees to which it was entitled, and the precise pay for each one since there was a fixed salary scale for the four
clerical classes. Thus Congress absolutely controlled the civil establishment in number, in pay, and in allocation of personnel to the respective agencies and their subdivisions.

The legislative branch was almost equally meticulous with respect
to appropriations for other than personal service in the civilian
agencies. Items such as the following for the Department of Agri-

[22] 16 Stat. 230 (July 12, 1870).
[23] *Ibid.*, at 237.

culture were common: for keep of horses, $1,500; for agricultural and scientific periodicals, $250; for philosophical apparatus, $250; for the collection of minerals and ores, $100.[24]

This major appropriation act may be taken as representing the congressional ideal. Congress knew for what the taxpayers' money was being spent; the spending agencies were put in the position of having to justify in particular each small object of expenditure; variation was made difficult; audit was made easy and exacting; and the sense of congressional power was magnified. Wherever possible this was the pattern imposed by the legislative branch.

As already intimated, this pattern broke down to a considerable degree in the army and navy, but not for the armed forces' civil establishments. The naval establishment at Boston, for example, was specified in the navy appropriation act for the fiscal year 1871 as if it were a Treasury office: every officer and employee and the salaries thereof were carefully itemized down to the gatekeeper and the detective at the yard.[25]

Naval operations could not, however, be so precisely foreseen. The Bureau of Construction and Repair retained a number of substantial lump-sum appropriations: for the preservation of ironclad vessels, $150,000; for materials by contract, $1,000,000; for labor in navy yards and on foreign stations, $2,000,000; for the general maintenance of the navy, $800,000.[26] The Bureau, under the direction of the Secretary, obviously had a relatively free hand in the disposition of these resources.

The army was in the same position, although some of the large sums appropriated permitted only limited discretion. Thus a single item of $12,935,390 for the pay of the army conveyed little freedom, since the number of officers and men, and the pay of each rank and of the enlisted men were specified by law.[27] On the other hand, an item of $4,500,000 for the regular supplies of the quartermaster department was granted without an itemized breakdown. There was also a single authorization of $800,000 for the general and incidental expenses of

---

[24] *Ibid.*, at 246.
[25] 16 Stat. 321 (July 15, 1870).
[26] *Ibid.*, at 325.
[27] 16 Stat. 315 (July 15, 1870).

the quartermaster department and for the proper and authorized expenses for the movement and operation of the army.[28]

The nature of other appropriation acts may be briefly identified. Pensions was lump sum, including one item for over $19,000,000;[29] post office was lump sum, including an item for the transportation of the mail inland of over $13,000,000 and an item for miscellaneous payments of $850,000;[30] rivers and harbors was itemized by each project;[31] fortifications specified each project, but with a contingency item of $150,000.[32]

It is apparent, therefore, that Congress was not able to cling steadfastly to its ideal of closely itemized appropriation acts. The conduct of administration is not predictable in many of its branches, and where urgency was potential, discretion was accepted. Lump-sum items, however, were not blind appropriations. They rested on itemized estimates, which were subject to congressional scrutiny and required departmental justification.

Examination of the form of appropriation acts in the 1890's revealed no substantial change in congressional practice. The legislative, executive, and judicial appropriation act was highly itemized, the civil establishment throughout was carefully controlled, the army and the navy retained lump sums for their basic operations. Other appropriation acts followed the pattern of their predecessors.

The conclusion derived from evidence such as this is that Congress prized the authority to specify the objects and amounts for which public funds could be expended; that it was prepared to curtail executive discretion in the use of appropriations so far as possible; that control of establishments and pay rates for both civilian and uniformed personnel was complete; that Congress did not trust the executive departments further than necessary, but that the exigencies of administration left much leeway in army and navy financial transactions and operations. This historic means of congressional control of administrative agencies was thus in full force and effect after as well as before the Civil War.

[28] *Ibid.*, at 316.
[29] 16 Stat. 221 (July 11, 1870).
[30] 16 Stat. 227 (July 11, 1870).
[31] 16 Stat. 223 (July 11, 1870).
[32] 16 Stat. 222 (July 11, 1870).

RESTRICTIONS ON THE SPENDING POWER

The Civil War had brought about a de facto suspension of earlier statutory limitations on executive discretion in spending funds. Appropriations for various objects were freely mingled; funds were transferred without much regard to the purposes for which they had been intended; unexpended balances (if any) were put to use rather than covered into the Treasury. Lucius Wilmerding reported that an appropriation for the extension of the Treasury building was used, in the amount of about $69,000, to buy furniture. There had been, in his words, a "complete collapse of the system of specific appropriation. Law and practice once more stood in opposition, the one prescribing the extreme of rigor, the other permitting the extreme of laxity."[33]

Congress had no intention of allowing such a gap between theory and practice to continue, and in a series of enactments at the close of the war sought to bring the departments again under control. Senator John Sherman, soon to become Secretary of the Treasury, was the Albert Gallatin of his day.

Transfers. The first move was to prevent the transfer of funds from one object to another, and from one fiscal year to its successor, an executive discretion highly prized by the spending agencies and on the whole retained in normal times despite much early congressional displeasure. Congress was now emphatic and uncompromising. In an 1868 deficiency act it repealed authority to transfer funds from one branch of expenditure to another and forbade the use of funds appropriated for one purpose to be used for any other.[34] The consequent inconvenience to the agencies was glossed over, although Senator Sherman commented on it: "It may create a great deal of trouble in the management of the Departments not to have the power to transfer from one head of appropriation to another, and within certain limits that power is right enough; but still, as I know it has been abused, and cases have been brought to my attention where the abuse has been gross and scandalous, I am rather inclined to think we had better cut up the whole system. . . ."[35] This was done.

[33] Lucius Wilmerding, Jr., *The Spending Power*, pp. 116, 117. Quotations from this book reprinted by permission of the publisher, Yale University Press.

[34] 15 Stat. 35, sec. 2 (Feb. 12, 1868).

[35] *Congressional Globe*, 40th Cong., 2d sess., pp. 561-62 (Jan. 16, 1868).

Balances. A second move was to recapture unexpended Civil War balances, amounting in 1868 to over $156,000,000 and constituting a free fund to which the departments could resort to supplement their annual appropriations. This object was attained in 1870 by legislation authorizing the Secretary of the Treasury to cover into the surplus fund any balances of appropriations remaining unexpended, or not required for pending charges for two fiscal years, without the consent of the agency head—but with specific exceptions.[36] The teeth of this enactment were promptly drawn by the Attorney General,[37] but its purpose was finally achieved by further legislation in 1874.[38]

Advance obligations. A third drive was to prevent administrative officers from obligating the government for more than the funds appropriated. In 1868 Congress forbade contracts for any public improvement beyond the amount in the Treasury appropriated for the specific purpose. Personal responsibility for violation was imposed.[39] In 1870 Congress prohibited any expenditure or contracts for sums in excess of appropriations for the fiscal year.[40] In 1872 it shut off an incidental source of agency supply by requiring that proceeds of sales of old stores or other public property should be covered into the Treasury and be withdrawn only by subsequent appropriation.[41]

Deficiencies. With this series of enactments the ability of the departments to mingle appropriations and to hold in reserve ancient balances was terminated. They had one escape, the creation of deficiencies. Because of the urgencies of administration, deficiencies now became the order of the day, and put before Congress a new problem of official control. In spirit, if not in letter, an agency deficiency could arise only in violation of the act of 1870, but Congress itself acquiesced in its nonobservance.

The issue was put in December 1879 when the Postmaster General asked for a deficiency appropriation of $1,700,000 to meet existing commitments for star-route mail transportation. The Post Office Department had, it was true, not spent money in excess of its current

---

[36] 16 Stat. 230, secs. 5-6 (July 12, 1870).
[37] 13 *Official Opinions of the Attorneys General of the United States* 289 (July 27, 1870).
[38] 18 Stat. 85, sec. 5 (June 20, 1874).
[39] 15 Stat. 171, sec. 3 (July 25, 1868).
[40] 16 Stat. 230, sec. 7 (July 12, 1870).
[41] 17 Stat. 61, sec. 5 (May 8, 1872).

appropriation, but had made commitments that would exhaust its funds in April 1880. Its defense was that, if a deficiency act were not forthcoming, it could cancel its contracts and cease to deliver the mail! Representative James H. Blount of Georgia asked his colleagues if "there ever was such audacity on the part of any departmental officer in time of peace and in the absence of any public exigency," but there was no alternative to a deficiency appropriation.[42]

Deficiencies were, indeed, the only escape from an overrigorous system of appropriation. Wilmerding concluded that from 1880 to 1905 agency disregard of congressional appropriations became habitual and finally came to be taken as a matter of course.[43] Year after year the Commissioners of the District of Columbia estimated the annual cost of fuel for the schools at $45,000; year after year they put in a deficiency bill for $30,000. "The deficiency was as automatic as the original estimate."[44] James A. Garfield exposed one of the reasons—the political virtue of underappropriation. "One of the vicious party devices too often resorted to for avoiding responsibility for extravagance in appropriations is to cut down the annual bills below the actual amount necessary to carry on the government, announce to the country that a great reduction has been made in the interest of economy, and, after the elections are over, make up the necessary amounts by deficiency bills."[45] The disintegration of the House fiscal committees facilitated such irresponsibility.

The cure for the deficiency disease was not hit upon until 1905 with the invention of monthly or other allotments[46] and did not become effective until the establishment of an executive agency to police the allotments—the Bureau of the Budget.[47]

THE COMMITTEE ON APPROPRIATIONS

The legislation noted in the preceding paragraphs set some outer limits on executive discretion in expenditure but had no relation to the amount of money sought by the executive branch or allowed by the legislative. The relations between the Appropriations Committees of

[42] Lucius Wilmerding, Jr., *The Spending Power*, pp. 137-39.
[43] *Ibid.*, p. 140.
[44] *Ibid.*, p. 142.
[45] James A. Garfield, *Works*, II, 750 (June 1879).
[46] 33 Stat. 1214, sec. 4 (March 3, 1905).
[47] 42 Stat. 20 (June 10, 1921).

the House and Senate on the one hand, and the departments and agencies on the other, in the annual consideration of the supply bills had always been one of the central aspects of congressional control over expenditure levels and objects, and by necessary connection over executive policy and procedures. Unfortunately most of these relations went unrecorded.

Until 1865 the House, which will be the center of attention here rather than the Senate, was well organized to speak with a single voice in financial matters. The Ways and Means Committee was responsible for reporting both revenue bills and appropriation measures. The burden became so great that in 1865 a new, independent Appropriations Committee was established, thus dividing responsibility for revenue and appropriations. The Appropriations Committee quickly became very powerful, and by 1880 was in such effective control of the House that rebellion broke out. The chairmanship of the Appropriations Committee, which may be considered the pivot around which revolved the fiscal relations of the executive and legislative branches, was held by three men of stature during most of the period from Grant to McKinley—James A. Garfield (1871-75), Samuel J. Randall (1875-77, 1883-87), and Joseph G. Cannon (1889-91, 1895-1901). By tacit recognition this was no post for a novice or a mere partisan.

Committee leadership: Garfield. Garfield's diary and writings present a philosophy of congressional action through the Appropriations Committee and a wealth of operating detail that amply illustrate the powerful impact of Congress upon administration. In 1872 he wrote in his diary:

It has occurred for the first time to me that while the work of the Com. of Ways and Means looks out towards the industries of the people as the particular subject of contemplation, that of the Com. of Appropriations looks inward upon the machinery of the Govt. and reviews in detail all its various functions. Every monied transaction of the Govt. has usually to be brought in close review in making appropriations and here is soonest discovered the decay or overgrowth of any part of the fabric.[48]

After brief experience on the Appropriations Committee he noted, "I am every day amazed with the steady encroachment of all the De-

[48] James A. Garfield, Diary (Nov. 27, 1872), in Manuscript Division, Library of Congress.

partments of the Government upon the money in the Treasury. There is a constant demand everywhere. The Com. on Appropriations is the natural antagonist of all the Departments in this regard. We need an expert in the employ of the Committee to examine all the accounts."[49] Suspicion of departmental estimates was a deep-seated conviction of Congressmen. A decade later Representative Joseph C. S. Blackburn of Kentucky remarked:

> . . . . We all know that when the heads of Departments come to make estimates for their maintenance they are usually submitted upon the idea that the Committee on Appropriations will cut them down. They know by precedents that Congresses, both Republican and Democratic, have been disposed to a greater or less extent to shave and reduce the estimates of the Departments. Consequently, when a Secretary or head of a Department makes his estimate, he justly puts in a liberal estimate or allowance for the reduction which he expects to be made. We know that when an appropriations committee comes to deal with the estimates, they deal with them with that fact firmly fastened in their minds.[50]

Garfield was determined to find out where the dollars went. "Committee Meeting, a dozen pages more of the bill gone over. Secy Boutwell before the Committee, to explain his estimates. . . . Worked on Legislative Bill four hours, besides three hours with the Committee."[51] "Called on Secy Boutwell and discussed some points in the Legislative and Judicial Appropriation Bill."[52] "In Comm. . . . heard General Liggett Com'r of Patents in favor of establishing an Official Gazette in the Patent Office."[53] "At 11 o'clock went with Mrs. Garfield to visit the Columbia Hospital, with a view to ascertaining how much Congress ought to appropriate for maintaining it."[54] "Am studying up the subject of lighthouses, also of the fish culture. Every day shows new elements in the great interests and forces that comprise the Govt. of the United States."[55]

Garfield operated far above either the characteristic parsimony

[49] *Ibid.*, (Dec. 9, 1872).
[50] *Congressional Record*, 47th Cong., 1st sess., pp. 5703-4 (July 6, 1882).
[51] James A. Garfield, Diary (Jan. 12, 1872).
[52] *Ibid.*, (Jan. 16, 1872).
[53] *Ibid.*, (Feb. 21, 1872).
[54] *Ibid.*, (March 2, 1872).
[55] *Ibid.*, (March 21, 1872).

or generous extravagance of many members. His budget speech of 1874 was statesmanlike in its tenor. "The Committee on Appropriations," he declared, "are seeking earnestly to reduce the expenditures of the government; but they reject the doctrine that they should at all hazards reduce the expenditures to the level of the revenues, however small those revenues may be. They have attempted rather to ascertain what are the real and vital necessities of the government, —to find what amount of money will suffice to meet all its honest obligations, to carry on all its necessary and essential functions, and to keep alive those public enterprises which the country desires its government to undertake and accomplish. When the amount of expenses necessary to meet these objects is ascertained, that amount should be appropriated; and ways and means for procuring that amount should be provided."[56]

At the close of the first session of the 43d Congress, he again addressed the House to remind it of the magnitude of the fiscal task performed by the Appropriations Committee.

I presume that not all gentlemen have thought sufficiently upon this subject to appreciate the difficulty of scaling down without injuring the efficiency of so vast and complicated a machine as the government of the United States. It is a vast Colossus, whose every motion depends upon the expenditure of money,—a vast machine, the motive power of which is money; and the appropriations made by Congress determine and limit the activity of every function from the highest to the lowest. I say that few people have considered how difficult it is to take such an organization and scale it down about ten per cent, and still preserve its necessary working force unimpaired. We might by an unwise reduction cripple some one function, and thus block the operations of a whole department, but I believe that this Congress has made its reductions so carefully that no serious injury will follow.[57]

Garfield was a man endowed with great capacity for work, a robust physical constitution, and a conscientious sense of duty to be performed. He took seriously his responsibility as chairman of the Appropriations Committee. A friend reported a conversation with him soon after he accepted this post. "No wheel, no shaft, no rivet in our

[56] James A. Garfield, *Works*, II, 97 (March 5, 1874).
[57] *Ibid.*, II, 130 (June 23, 1874).

governmental machinery performs its function without money," he said. "If I find out where every dollar goes, and how it is used, I shall understand the apparatus thoroughly, and know if there are useless or defective parts."[58]

Shortly after leaving the chairmanship Garfield recorded on the floor of the House his sympathy for his successor and the committee. "I know," he said, "how hard that task is; I know how much of local pressure is brought to bear upon them from every quarter from interested parties who desire to swell appropriations; and I know, moreover, that every executive department tends to enlarge the field of expenditure within its jurisdiction, so that it is the business of that committee to resist pressure from all sides,—pressure from the Administration, pressure from this House, and pressure from their friends outside, who are always asking for more."[59]

Dispersion of leadership. Unfortunately for fixing responsibility, the central review of estimates by a single House committee broke down in 1879-1880.[60] The task had become immense subsequent to an amendment of the rules allowing substantive riders to the appropriation act if they reduced the amounts in question. The Appropriations Committee had therefore the task, unwelcome to many of its members, of considering various policy matters as well as finance. As it was a privileged committee, with the right to the floor for its bills in precedence over other business, such riders occupied a favored position and tended to increase in number. Finally it was alleged that the Appropriations Committee in substance had gradually become the arbiter of what legislation could even be considered by the House, either by taking the floor to displace measures thought objectionable or by pushing forward riders to appropriation bills that it favored.

[58] E. V. Smalley, "Characteristics of President Garfield," *Century Illustrated Monthly Magazine,* XXIII (1881-82), 168.

[59] James A. Garfield, *Works,* II, 274-75 (Feb. 7, 1876).

[60] Garfield sensed the danger of divided responsibility and in 1879 warned the country against the impending change. "It is of the first importance that one strong, intelligent committee should have supervision of the whole work of drafting and putting in shape the bills for the appropriation of public money. That committee ought, every year, to present to Congress and the country a general and connected view of what we may fairly call our budget, showing, not only the aggregate of expenditures, but the general distribution of revenue to the several objects to be supported." James A. Garfield, *Works,* II, 752 (June 1879).

It was said of Chairman Samuel J. Randall that from 1883 to 1885 he was able practically to dictate both appropriations and general legislation.[61] It was obvious that a genuine problem of internal control of congressional business had developed. John G. Carlisle's biographer noted that decentralization was the only way by which the growing autocracy in the management of the House could be abolished; "but the greater the amount of decentralization, the greater the possibility of extravagance. No committee would ask for a modest sum when its neighbor might request a handsome appropriation."[62]

The jealousy of other committees and the resistance of members of the House to the dominance of the Appropriations Committee, plus the mere magnitude of its task, caused the first break in 1879 when the Committee on Commerce secured independent management of the rivers and harbors bill. An attempt to restore unity in 1880 failed and the process of dispersion continued. In 1880 the Appropriations Committee lost control of the agriculture appropriation bill; in 1885 it lost jurisdiction over the army, navy, Indian affairs, and foreign affairs bills.

Such a disintegration of fiscal control was fatal to balancing income and outgo. More relevant for present purposes, it tended to establish mutual reciprocal relations between executive agencies and committee chairmen that at times seemed to reverse the traditional standing of the legislative and executive branches. ". . . the spending committees," Wilmerding concluded, "having intimate and for the most part cordial relations each with a particular department, launched out into an unrestrained competition for appropriations, the one striving to surpass the other in securing greater recognition and more money for its special charge. In these circumstances it is not surprising that executive dereliction passed almost unnoticed and that the department heads and bureau chiefs came to look upon themselves rather than upon Congress as the ultimate arbiters of expenditures."[63]

While Congressmen continued to sharpen their axes against particular items, the proper function of an appropriations committee so ably described by Garfield disappeared.[64] Congress retained ultimate fiscal authority but acted disjointedly, declining to exercise its power in terms of long-range considerations or on grounds of principle.

CONGRESS, THE EXECUTIVE BRANCH, AND PUBLIC EXPENDITURE

The end of the Civil War marked the transition from emergency fiscal freedom on the part of the executive branch to renewed efforts on the part of Congress to retrench and reassert its constitutional authority over the level of expenditure and its objects. A stubborn contest had been waged since the days of the Federalists to construct a workable plan of congressional control or, conversely, to retain executive freedom to use funds irrespective of legislative restrictions. The outcome of the contest had been indecisive, but Congress had failed to achieve the close control that Gallatin had deemed essential. The defense departments in particular had maintained that a navy scouring the seven seas, or an army posted over a continent, could not be administered within the amateur limitations imposed by a relatively uninformed legislative branch. The Civil War had for the time being swept congressional restrictions on the spending power into the dustbin despite the efforts of the Committee on the Conduct of the War.

Whatever the constitutional pretensions of Congress over appropriations, its record in the years from 1869 to 1901 did not suggest a high sense of responsibility on its part. A Democratic Congress refused to pass the great appropriation bills under Hayes in order to compel removal of federal troops from southern polling places. An unreasonable parsimony often controlled Congress when faced with the major supply bills, and departmental operations were often seriously handicapped by lack of adequate resources. On the other hand, Congress was openhanded in authorizing large sums for local improvements, until the annual rivers and harbors bill became a public scandal. Executive leadership was almost, if not indeed entirely, lacking. The President was not consulted on the preparation of the estimates; he was not consulted except sporadically on their dispo-

---

[64] Lauros G. McConachie, *Congressional Committees* (New York: Thomas Y. Crowell and Co., 1898). For a subsequent debate on the same issue see *Congressional Record*, 49th Cong., 1st sess., pp. 39-238 (Dec. 9-19, 1885), especially remarks of Representative John D. Long, pp. 182-83.

sition by the committees handling appropriations; and the Secretary of the Treasury was merely a compiler, not a minister of finance. To make matters worse, the volume of fiscal business dispersed responsibility among a number of appropriations committees to the point that coordination and unity were illusory. The Budget and Accounting Act of 1921 was finally to move in the direction of both executive and legislative responsibility in fiscal programs.

CHAPTER FOUR

Congress and Departmental Business

Congress was busy not merely with its major constitutional and legislative responsibilities affecting the administrative system: conferring powers and duties, determining organization, reviewing estimates and making appropriations. Members were involved in hundreds of particulars that were settled by statute rather than by executive action; they swarmed in and out of the departments on constituents' business; they heard appeals from official decisions; and by repeated investigations they sought to remedy waste and delay. These matters reflected not so much the struggle between Congress and the President as the restless concern of Congressmen with the needs of private citizens and their dissatisfaction with official operations.

ADMINISTRATION BY LEGISLATION

For the purpose of the following analysis, it will be assumed that the essential nature of the legislative function is to enact rules of general application, whether establishing private rights or specifying administrative procedures. Thus legislation creates rights to a military pension and prescribes the conditions on which an administrative agency shall authorize payments to a given individual. It will be assumed also that the essential function of administration is to apply the general rule to the particular case. Both assumptions leave much unsaid, but they may serve as bench marks in considering to what extent Congress passed beyond its central duties in effect to enter the field of administration.

The statute book of any session of Congress provides an abundance of raw material to demonstrate the thesis that the legislative branch was constantly making decisions of individual application, both with respect to personal rights, such as pensions and patents, and with regard to administrative operations. Whether this was an appropriate course for Congress to pursue is beyond the range of a historical narrative, but it may be remarked in passing that much congressional intervention was in the interest of equity and fairness, as the hard cases went from administrative denial to legislative permission. Much of it was necessitated by the ineptness of the general rule or administrative obligation imposed by statute. Some of it was mere favoritism.

For the purpose of analysis the *Statutes at Large* for 1869–71 provide illustrative material. The corresponding volumes for 1879–81 or 1889–91 would reveal similar data, although the Civil Service Act of 1883 introduced general procedures for subordinate appointments that diminished Congressmen's importunities in this area. It is unnecessary to spread the evidence of thirty years on the record; that of Grant's administration is typical and adequate.

In substance Congress made many orders of individual application. It authorized the Secretary of the Treasury to change the name of the steam yacht *Fanny*;[1] it enabled J. H. Schnell to enter a section of public land in California for a tea colony;[2] it gave permission to Robert C. Schenck, United States minister to Great Britain, to employ a private amanuensis;[3] and by formal enactment Congress directed the repair of the enclosure of the cemetery at Harpers Ferry.[4] In this class of cases fall several categories whose numbers run into the hundreds: relief acts, private pension legislation, the removal of political disabilities after the close of the Civil War, and closing the accounts of accountable officers in disagreement with the auditors.

The structure of the field services was set by Congress, specifying the number and boundaries of local offices, laying out mail routes,[5] and confirming the abandonment or relocation of land offices.[6] There was little, if any, administrative discretion in these matters—a prece-

[1] 16 Stat. 385 (July 1, 1870).
[2] 16 Stat. 432 (Feb. 27, 1871).
[3] 16 Stat. 590 (Jan. 11, 1871).
[4] 16 Stat. 592 (Jan. 25, 1871).
[5] 16 Stat. 69 (March 5, 1870).
[6] 16 Stat. 64 (Feb. 5, 1870).

dent reaching back to the original establishment of customs districts
and ports of entry.

Both legislation and appropriation language contained instructions
concerning the internal methods of agency operation. Thus Congress
required all purchases of wood and coal to be inspected, weighed, and
certified by some employee appointed in each department or division
thereof.[7] Departments had only limited authority over real property
and were obliged to go to the legislature for permission to make even
modest changes. In 1869 Congress passed a resolution authorizing removal of the public stables from the Capitol grounds,[8] and another
disapproving a contract for leasing the customhouse block in San
Francisco.[9]

Congress was also led into much executive detail in managing the
affairs of the District of Columbia. Two or three illustrations must
suffice. In 1870 the city of Washington was authorized to set apart
certain streets as parks,[10] to reduce the width of an alley in square
number 376,[11] and to pave Pennsylvania Avenue.[12]

Examination of legislation subsequent to 1869–70 revealed a steady
output of special and private legislation and of resolutions, the nature
of which was essentially administrative. The lawmaking process was
put to use in the individual case, to this extent supplanting the normal
exercise of administrative action. The situation was not peculiar to
this period, but the mass of private and special legislation was greater.
No line of rational distinction had been formulated by Congress
between its central function and that of administration.

CONSTITUENTS' BUSINESS

More than ever Congressmen were plagued by the necessity of
performing errands for their constituents. Representative James A.
Garfield in the course of two months (April-May 1870) had requests
to search for a miscarried letter, to secure favorable action on pension
claims, to get a decision allowing a patent extension, to obtain payment of a claim, to find jobs, to determine whether a baggage man

[7] 16 Stat. 229 (July 11, 1870).
[8] 16 Stat. 51 (March 23, 1869).
[9] 16 Stat. 367 (Dec. 22, 1869).
[10] 16 Stat. 82 (April 6, 1870).
[11] 16 Stat. 148 (June 1, 1870).
[12] 16 Stat. 196 (July 8, 1870).

had been fairly appointed, and to write a book review.[13] On January 24, 1870, he wrote a constituent, "I do not know whether it will be possible to secure passes, on the Pacific Railroad, or not, but I have written Mr. Oakes Ames, one of the leading managers of that road, enclosing your letter, and requesting him to give you some favor in that direction if consistent with their arrangements."[14]

For a solid year Garfield was in and out of the departments either finding a place for the young son of a constituent or seeking to restore him to his position, once secured. "I help this man with reluctance," he wrote in his diary, "for I think he was opposed to me last year. I ought perhaps to tell him so but I concluded to let it pass and help his boy, as the father has not helped me."[15] His diary for December 14, 1872, recorded that he had spent four hours among the departments on other people's business. "I do not know that I have ever been more weary of this sort of vicarious suffering than I am tonight. The great crowd of people that come upon me for one thing or another draw heavily upon my vital forces and go far toward exhausting the large measure of strength which I possess."[16]

When Rutherford B. Hayes was in Congress, he too was active on the affairs of his constituents, notably adjusting war claims of Ohio citizens. His biographer reported that he once had seven hundred such war claims on his hands and "spent his time running to the departments and answering letters from soldiers."[17] Lesser figures had no smaller share of such trouble. John L. Thomas, a member of the 39th Congress (1865–67) and subsequently collector of the port of Baltimore, gave testimony in 1882 before the Senate Civil Service Committee. "I know when I was in Congress two-thirds of my time was occupied either in going around the departments as a claim agent for somebody or in looking out for a place for somebody. This not only was self-degrading, but it degraded the Congressman even in the estimation of his constituents when he could not succeed in getting for them what they wanted him to get."[18]

[13] Garfield Papers, Letters Received, in Manuscript Division, Library of Congress.
[14] Garfield Papers, Letters Sent, in Manuscript Division, Library of Congress.
[15] Theodore C. Smith, *Life and Letters of James A. Garfield*, II, 726.
[16] *Ibid.* II, 726-27.
[17] H. J. Eckenrode, *Rutherford B. Hayes: Statesman of Reunion* (New York: Dodd, Mead and Company, 1930), p. 82.
[18] Senate Report 576, 47th Cong., 1st sess., p. 186 (May 15, 1882).

Representative Roswell G. Horr of Michigan gave a graphic description of the labors of a Congressman for his constituents.

. . . . I think it is safe to say that each member of this House receives fifty letters each week; many receive more. . . . Growing out of these letters will be found during each week a large number of errands, a vast amount of what is called department work. One-quarter of them, perhaps, will be from soldiers asking aid in their pension cases, and each soldier is clear in his own mind that the member can help his case out if he will only make it a special case and give it special attention; and each one of them will request that you shall call personally at the Pension Department and urge his particular case forward. And no one can blame these soldiers for such requests. The delay in their cases has been so great that they feel as if some such action must be taken to give them relief.

Another man writes you to look up some matter in reference to a land patent. Another says his homestead claim should be looked after and he wants you to learn and let him know why he does not receive his full title. Another has invented some machine and the department have declared his discovery to be already supplemented by some former inventor, and have refused his patent. He would like you to go through the Patent Office and look over the patent laws and see if great injustice has not been done in his case. Another has a son or brother in the Regular Army whom he would like to have discharged. Another has a recreant son whom he would like to get into the Regular Army or Navy. Another wants you to drop into the Treasury Department and see about some claims of his; perhaps a fine or penalty has been assessed against him; as he thinks, unjustly. Another has had his boat tied up and he wants her released. Another would like to have you go to the Post-Office Department and see if extra clerk hire cannot be allowed his office. Another wants a new post-route established, and now and then some strange, singular man will seek an appointment as postmaster of some town. Another would like to have you call at the Navy Department and see if his boy cannot get into the school at Annapolis or on some training ship. . . . In conformity with these requests you are liable to be called upon, perhaps several times in one week, by these applicants *in personam*, and they will require you to go at once and exert your enormous powers.[19]

The life of a Congressman was made miserable by this kind of business, but he could not escape. The life of the departments was also rendered oppressive, since Congressmen had to receive answers

[19] House Report, 466, 47th Cong., 1st sess., pp. 2-3 (Feb. 16, 1882).

promptly. The normal order of affairs was interrupted; clerks were called off their work; conferences had to be held, facts gathered, and letters drafted. The loss of time in the government bureaus as a consequence of congressional inquiries was a constant source of complaint—however subdued.

APPELLATE FUNCTIONS OF CONGRESS

For many reasons Congress had always found difficulty in distinguishing its policy function from the management of detail and the decision of individual cases. That it was the grand inquest of the nation had been recognized from the early days of the Republic, and the function of investigation and correction easily shaded over from the general to the particular. The settlement of claims provided a typical illustration; it was the House and Senate Claims Committees that for decades made the final recommendations for settlement, and Congress that gave formal assent.

Pressure on Congress to review and correct alleged errors on the part of executive agents was heavy and persistent. So far as legal claims passing through the auditors' and comptrollers' offices were concerned, Congress was strict in refusing to intervene. Other types of claims and appeals were pressed upon its attention with varying results. Four examples will illustrate the pattern: appeals on personnel matters, pensions, pecuniary claims, and patents. In a period when administrative doctrine was almost unknown and when personal politics was in command, it was relatively easy to transfer such administrative decisions from the executive to the legislative branch.

Personnel actions. Garfield's diary gave hints of congressional interference, not to secure appointments, which was standard practice, but to control official decisions with respect to the fortunes of individual clerks and employees. In 1870 he wrote to a worried postal clerk in Cleveland, "I shall be glad to take care that no harm befalls you."[20] On May 7, 1872, he went to the Treasury "to get Mrs. Reed promoted," and on November 18, 1872, he had to go again: "Got Mrs. Reed restored to her place. . . ."[21]

These were incidents occurring well before the advent of civil

[20] Garfield Papers, Letters Sent (Jan. 7, 1870), in Manuscript Division, Library of Congress.

[21] James A. Garfield, Diary, in Manuscript Division, Library of Congress.

service reform. What of the years that followed it? The auditor for the Post Office, Henry A. Castle, gave testimony on custom at the close of the century. "The clerks in all Departments here apparently rely more on their Representative or Senatorial influence," he informed a Senate committee, "than they do on their efficiency in retaining their positions or securing promotions. In the St. Paul post-office there are 200 employees. Although I was there nearly five years, I did not make a single promotion or reduction on political grounds, and I was not requested to do so in a half dozen cases. I have been here a month, and I have had at least 100 requests from Senators and Representatives to promote their friends." Castle did not welcome this interference and declared that a false sentiment prevailed in the capital city. To this remark, Senator Stephen B. Elkins replied, "It is human nature. A clerk wants to better his position if he can. I do not blame him if it is fair. If he has any Senatorial influence, he wants to invoke it." Castle retorted that the fair way was to get ahead on merit. "Take a bureau officer, and before he has been in office twenty-four hours he has requests from a dozen Senators to push up their friends. I call that a false system."[22]

The testimony of Auditor Castle was confirmed by the Commissioner of Pensions, H. Clay Evans. Asked by Senator Henry Cabot Lodge whether the *inefficient* clerks had much influence, he replied, "Inefficient clerks have the most influence. They are engaged in getting influence." To which he added, "It is very natural for a Department officer or a Bureau officer to respect, as far as practicable, the wishes of the Senators and Representatives."[23]

Much evidence of this nature runs through the records of the years from 1869 to 1901.[24] The interest and activity of Congress in the 1870's covered both employment policy and its individual application. The Civil Service Act of 1883 marked a change in policy,

[22] Senate Report 659, 55th Cong., 2d sess., p. 309 (June 19, 1897).

[23] *Ibid.*, p. 406 (Dec. 20, 1897).

[24] In the armed forces, however, Congress was more reluctant to intervene, at least as a body. Note the report of a Senate committee in 1870 on a petition of two naval officers to be restored to the active list. The committee declared that it would not review the evidence heard by the naval retirement boards, noted that cases were becoming numerous where navy officers petitioned for advancement in rank by congressional action, and concluded that good discipline would not be served by congressional interference. Senate Report 105, 41st Cong., 2d sess., p. 1 (April 15, 1870).

the logical consequence of which was a diminution of congressional influence in the particular application. Logic, however, bowed before the dictates of human nature. Weak characters among the clerks sought protection from the powerful as small people had turned to the great from time immemorial, and the great cherished both the exercise of power and its augmentation.

Pensions. Congress became both an information agency and a court of appeals for pensioners and pension claimants after the close of the Civil War. The general pension law of 1862 established rights to pensions for injury in the armed forces, fixed fees, and sought to safeguard against fraud.[25] The decision of the Commissioner of Pensions was presumably final so far as the executive branch was concerned, but constituents who failed here often went to their Congressmen for relief.

The volume of correspondence between the Pension Bureau and members of Congress was immense. In 1880 it was reported as amounting to nearly 40,000 written and personal inquiries; in 1888 it had more than doubled (94,000 items); and in 1891 it reached a peak of 154,817 congressional calls for information on the condition of cases, an average of over 500 for each working day.[26] The burden upon both Congressmen and the Bureau was heavy, but the former were reluctant to provide additional clerks and the latter struggled as best it could.

While Congress set up a general system of pensions in 1862, it could not close the door to appeals for special acts to deal with equitable cases excluded from the general rules. They appeared promptly and eventually became a source of scandal. One or two early illustrations will indicate their nature. The initiative usually came from the disappointed applicant; his Congressman introduced a special pension bill, which was referred to the House and/or Senate Committee on Pensions: it made a report and on "pension day" each House acted, usually to confirm the recommendation of the Pension Committee. Thus in 1870 the Senate committee reported that the application of William Erwin had been rejected at the Pension Office, but that it believed he had made out a good case and

[25] 12 Stat. 566 (July 14, 1862); see below, ch. 10.
[26] Commissioner of Pensions, *Annual Reports, passim.*

recommended favorable action.[27] The widow of George Donahue had
been denied a pension because of inadequate proof of Donahue's
death on the battlefield. The committee had no doubt of the
casualty on the basis of the evidence at hand and reported a special
bill.[28] The official interpretation of the Pension Act was occasionally
reversed in substance by congressional enactment of special laws,
and the amount of pension sometimes raised above the normal figures.

The number of cases in which Congress acted in effect as an appeal
body tended to increase. In the 40th Congress (1867–69) there were
275, and for some years this represented a maximum figure. The
number doubled in the 48th Congress (1883–85) to 598, rose to 856
in the 49th Congress (1885–87), 1,015 in the 50th (1887–89), and
achieved a peak in the 51st (1889–91) with 1,388 special acts either
allowing pensions or increasing the amount.[29]

That Congress could not act intelligently or according to rule in
such an appellate capacity was clear. Senator John R. McPherson
criticized the procedure in 1888: "The bills are introduced in great
numbers (I myself have introduced 200), and they are then referred
to the Pension Committee. This committee divides the bills equally
among its members, and each one is supposed to examine a certain
number of bills. Instead of giving each bill a careful investigation, I
know, as a matter of fact, that in many cases the Senators have merely
turned over the batch to their secretaries, and have instructed these
clerks to look into the matter."[30] Passage of private pension bills was
by general consent. Usually no quorum was present on "pension day."
The proceedings were perfunctory and swift. President Cleveland
took formal note of this failure of Congress in one of his pension
veto messages. "In speaking of the promiscuous and ill-advised grants
of pensions which have lately been presented to me for approval, I
have spoken of their 'apparent Congressional sanction' in recognition
of the fact that a large proportion of these bills have never been
submitted to a majority of either branch of Congress, but are the
result of nominal sessions . . . attended by a small minority of the

[27] Senate Report 273, 41st Cong., 3d sess., p. 2 (Dec. 20, 1870).
[28] Senate Report 314, 41st Cong., 3d sess., p. 1 (Jan. 26, 1871).
[29] Commissioner of Pensions, *Annual Report*, 1917, p. 42.
[30] Quoted from the *New York Times*, Nov. 6, 1888, in William H. Glasson,
Federal Military Pensions in the United States (New York: Oxford University
Press, 1918), p. 276.

members of the respective Houses of the legislative branch of Government."[31]

The passage of a certain number of private pension acts, indeed, became a perquisite of Senators and Representatives to be used according to the dictates of influence, acquaintance, or political expediency.[32] Cleveland sought to curtail this congressional irresponsibility by vetoing a large number of such acts, but the net result was mainly to turn the veterans' lobby against him. The *National Tribune*, with a wide circulation among pensioners, declared: "An unprecedented number of these [private pension acts] have been presented to Mr. Cleveland for his signature, and he has found in them a boundless field for ridicule, cheap wit, sarcasm, satire, and vituperation of the unfortunates who were so indiscreet as to go into the army and lose their health or lives. . . . *The President has been amusing himself for years writing vetoes. The veterans now have a chance to use their hands at vetoing. Let them improve the opportunity.*"[33]

The character of the objectionable pension acts may be surmised from some of President Cleveland's comments. William Bishop entered military service with a substitute's bounty in March 1865, and after an attack of the measles and three days' active service was mustered out. Cleveland vetoed his claim with this satiric observation: "Fifteen years after this brilliant service and this terrific encounter with the measles, and on the 20th day of June, 1880, the claimant discovered that his attack of the measles had some relation to his army enrollment and that this disease had 'settled in his eyes, also affecting his spinal column.' "[34] A veteran's widow, Mary A. Van Etten, secured congressional approval for a pension based on the allegation that her husband had contracted rheumatism during his army service and consequently was unable to swim to safety in a buggy accident that occurred in 1875. Cleveland vetoed the widow's relief.[35]

William H. Hester convinced Congress of the virtue of his claim for a pension because in 1869 sand blew in his eyes resulting in nearly

[31] Richardson, *Messages*, VIII, 437 (June 21, 1886).
[32] William H. Glasson, *Federal Military Pensions in the United States*, p. 276.
[33] September 27, 1888. Quoted in *ibid.*, p. 278, n. 2.
[34] Richardson, *Messages*, VIII, 443 (June 23, 1886).
[35] *Ibid.*, VIII, 444 (June 23, 1886).

total blindness. Cleveland noted that even the House committee admitted that the claim was largely supported by perjury and forgery on the part of "three rogues and scoundrels" who acted for the claimant. The President vetoed the bill, believing it "to be a fraud from beginning to end."[36] Another claimant urged that while riding his cavalry horse he was thrown forward on the horn of his saddle, causing a rupture in his right side—Cleveland sarcastically wrote in his veto message, "The number of instances in which those of our soldiers who rode horses during the war were injured by being thrown forward upon their saddles indicate that those saddles were very dangerous contrivances. . . . there is not a particle of merit in this claim. . . ."[37]

That appeals from veterans to mitigate the hard cases under the general pension law were difficult for Congressmen to resist is obvious enough. Fortified by the political influence of the Grand Army of the Republic, an ingrained impatience with official delay and caution broke the boundaries of the administrative system and resulted in direct action by Congress on appeal from members' constituents. In some cases the private pension acts resulted in justice; in others they commanded respect for the quality of mercy; in still others they were brazen frauds which an administrative agency could not have tolerated. For better or for worse, however, this was an area of governmental action in which Congress reached over into the executive branch and dealt with the individual case—a function in its nature peculiarly administrative.

Claims. For many decades Congress had been the only body to hear and determine claims other than those of a legal character. It had suffered with growing impatience the weight of this burden, and established the Court of Claims in 1855 to relieve it of such responsibility. The remedy, however, was only partial, and after the Civil War masses of equitable claims piled up on the dockets of Senate and House committees. The appellate function of Congress in claims cases was at times a relationship between it and individual citizens rather than between it and a government agency. In other cases, however, an official body would have reached a decision that was alleged either to be in error or to violate the canons of equity.

[36] *Ibid.*, VIII, 667 (May 19, 1888).
[37] *Ibid.*, VIII, 439 (June 22, 1886).

Here Congress acted as an organ of review of the administrative decision of the executive branch, at the instance of a dissatisfied citizen.

Congress had always been reluctant to refer to the Court of Claims issues for which there was no legal means of ascertaining the amount of damages, or which involved purely questions of judgment and discretion, or the decision of which could be regarded as a matter of liberality or benevolence. These were not appropriate for judicial inquiry, were in the last analysis political (but not partisan) in nature, and involved discretion that Congress preferred to retain despite the burden of their consideration.

The volume of claims cases before Congress was substantial. The docket of the House Committee on Claims in the 46th Congress contained 1,048 cases.[38] It was estimated in 1886 that 1,800 cases would come before the committee during the session, some involving trivial amounts while others ran into hundreds of thousands of dollars. Many of these claims, the House committee reported, had been before almost every Congress for a quarter of a century. In the previous Congress the House Committee on Claims received 913 cases, of which 163 were reported out, but only 12 passed Congress and became law.[39]

That this type of appellate function was wretchedly performed was fully and repeatedly acknowledged by the Claims Committees. The House Committee on Claims declared in 1886, "Congress should relieve itself from this judicial work, which it is ever making the pretense of doing, but never completes."[40] The same committee had described its handicaps in 1882. Upon receiving a claim it was referred to a subcommittee, usually of one. This member had before him only *ex parte* evidence, had no means of securing other evidence, and little basis for reaching a judgment.[41] Moreover the procedure was intolerably slow. The Claims Committee did not conceal its opinion that to push a claim through Congress was "a work of so much delay, trouble, doubt, and expense, that such a claim, however valid, honest, and unquestioned, is almost worthless. . . . In session

---

[38] House Report 69, 47th Cong., 1st sess., p. 3 (Jan. 26, 1882).
[39] House Report 562, 49th Cong., 1st sess., pp. 1, 2 (Feb. 16, 1886).
[40] *Ibid.*, p. 3
[41] House Report 69, 47th Cong., 1st sess., p. 2 (Jan. 26, 1882).

after session, and in Congress after Congress, and year after year, claimants clamor for payment; grow old in the struggle for it, and they and their heirs after them continue to besiege Congress in the usually vain hope that at last they may receive their honest dues."[42]

Congress did not succeed in withdrawing from this appellate function, however badly it was performed. It did, however, alleviate somewhat its position. The Bowman Act of 1883 authorized any congressional committee considering a claim to transmit the papers to the Court of Claims to ascertain the facts and report them to the committee but without entering judgment. This procedure enabled a harassed Congressman to secure something more than a mere *ex parte* presentation. The executive agencies were also authorized to refer to the Court of Claims for a finding on both fact and law, but without a determination. Reports of the Court of Claims to Congress were continued from one Congress to the next, thus predisposing to an ultimate decision.[43]

The Bowman Act was one step forward. The succeeding Tucker Act of 1887 marked a second advance by extending to the federal district and circuit courts the jurisdiction of the Court of Claims— thus avoiding a potential bottleneck—and by lifting the statute of limitations for claims vesting before the passage of the act.[44] The function of the courts, however, was still to find the facts, not to make a decision on the claim.

Beyond doubt this was a useful asset to Congress. The great roadblocks still existed, however. Congress was under a constitutional obligation to receive petitions, and it felt a proper concern to do justice on equitable grounds to citizens who had suffered damage at the hands of government. Petitions, worthy and unworthy, continued to pour in and to clog the work of the Committees on Claims and the substantive committees.[45] Time for their consideration failed

---

[42] *Ibid.*, p. 3.

[43] 22 Stat. 485 (March 3, 1883).

[44] 24 Stat. 505 (March 3, 1887).

[45] Cf. the remarks of Representative William Warner of Missouri. "The accumulation of private claims has been so great within the last twenty-five years as to burden several of the committees of Congress and to retard action upon a great proportion of the claims referred, at the same time compelling members, elected to participate in the examination and discussion of national subjects, to devote their time to the investigation of these private claims." *Congressional Record*, 49th Cong., 1st sess., p. 2495 (March 19, 1886).

both in the committees and on the floor of the House. The problem remained unsolved as this period drew to a close.

Patents. The technicalities of patent rights were such as to discourage Congress from entertaining petitions to reverse the decisions of the Commissioner of Patents. The courts were available to settle claims among private parties, and provision was made for appeals from the decisions of the Commissioner of Patents to the Supreme Court of the District of Columbia, replaced, after 1893, by the Court of Appeals.[46] Issues of legal right were consequently generally barred from congressional committee rooms. The rule was stated, for example, in 1870:

> But the committee [Senate Committee on Patents], without expressing an opinion upon the question whether the Commissioner of Patents did, as the petitioner alleges, err in his construction of the legal effect of the assignment aforesaid, are of opinion that it would not be good policy for Congress to constitute itself a tribunal for the revision and reversal of the action of the Commissioner of Patents for alleged errors in his official judgment and action, except it might be in a case involving some extraordinary and controlling reason for it. . . .[47]

There were other classes of cases in which the issues were not legal but equitable, cases in which the law itself, correctly applied by the Patent Office, caused hardship or injustice. Courts could not amend the law and the Patent Commissioner could not disregard it. The only recourse was the right to petition Congress, and it was frequently put to use, to the benefit of claimants. A few cases illustrate the circumstances in which congressional committees were prepared to correct injustice.

A patent holder was denied his request for an extension because of a defective application. He declared that the omissions were inadvertent and not intended to deceive. The Patent Commissioner was not impressed but the Senate Patent Committee thought the patentee should have the privilege of correcting his papers.[48] Benevolence played its part in other cases. The indigent widow of a patentee was refused extension of an expired patent. The Senate Committee on Patents was satisfied that an extension would inure to the benefit

---

[46] 16 Stat. 198, sec. 49 (July 8, 1870); 27 Stat. 434, sec. 9 (Feb. 9, 1893).
[47] Senate Report 53, 41st Cong., 2d sess., p. 3 (Feb. 25, 1870).
[48] Senate Report 307, 41st Cong., 3d sess., p. 1 (Jan. 23, 1871).

of the widow and her three minor children, and "as an act of justice" recommended passage of a special bill.[49]

In another class of cases Congress lifted the statute of limitations to enable claimants to appear before the Court of Claims in patent cases. Benevolence and equity were often controlling considerations. Mrs. Mary K. Berdan, the widow of a Civil War general who had invented some small arms improvements that had been adopted by the government, petitioned Congress for permission to present a claim before the Court of Claims in 1898, a quarter-century after General Berdan had allowed the use of his invention. The claim was outlawed by the passage of time, but the House Patent Committee reported "that equitably the Government ought to be stopped from pleading the statute of limitations on the facts of this case, and that equity, justice, and the honor of the nation alike demand the removal of the statute bar. . . ."[50]

The Berdans case was one of a numerous group in which claims were pressed upon Congress for compensation for the use of a patent by the government. The unauthorized use of a patent was in the nature of a tort, and as the Court of Claims could not entertain tort cases, the only recourse was to Congress. Such a reference was subject to grave criticism, well stated in 1882 by the House Committee on Patents. The committee reported:

Congress is not well adapted to the careful and patient examination of the intricate and perplexing questions of law and of fact which frequently arise in this class of cases. It is certainly the most expensive tribunal that could be adopted for their determination, and, in the judgment of your committee, the decision of these questions clearly belongs to the judicial rather than to the legislative department of the government. In attempting to deal with these questions the time of Congress is largely and needlessly employed, to the detriment and delay of important legislative business; and it is feared that in its hurry to dispose of this class of cases, its decisions have not always been uniform or equitable.[51]

The committee recommended that the jurisdiction of the Court of Claims be clarified so as to enable such cases to be heard by it; but

---

[49] Senate Report 484, 42d Cong., 3d sess., p. 1 (Feb. 22, 1873).
[50] House Report 540, 55th Cong., 2d sess., pp. 1-5 (Feb. 24, 1898).
[51] House Report 591, 47th Cong., 1st sess., p. 1 (March 1, 1882).

Congress was characteristically unwilling to allow tort liability to be adjudicated in the federal courts.

Congress was faced with a hard dilemma in dealing with the particular decisions of the federal agencies. The underlying policy was to have the individual case determined by the executive in accordance with law, and thus to avoid the necessity of reference to the legislative body. But the individual citizen had the constitutional right to petition Congress for redress of grievances, and executive error, partiality, or abuse of power was a long-recognized source of grievance. Moreover the correct application of the law might and at times did result in obvious injustice that neither courts nor administrative agencies could correct. A system of escape clauses has to exist in all governments through which the forces of equity and fairness can perform their good works by tempering the rigor of the laws, easing the hard cases, and allowing the play of benevolence. The problem was ancient, and in the earliest years had been recognized by Congress by granting the Secretary of the Treasury the power to remit customs fines and forfeitures. The role of Congress in acting as an appeal agency in personnel actions, claims, pensions, and patents was consequently not unusual, and in one form or another has always been an element in the American administrative system.

The function was, nevertheless, difficult to hold within bounds. Pressure for additional exceptions or wider benevolence grew with every case. New rules might be supposed to emerge inductively within Congress by way of repeated decisions, but unlike an administrative agency where consistency is normal, Congress was a body of fluctuating membership and moods in which consistency was relatively unlikely. Equity seemed at times equivalent to caprice. The volume of appellate business induced inordinate delay and consequently the substantial denial of justice, despite the conscientious labors of committee members. Both House and Senate consumed time on individual cases that in principle could better have been devoted to larger matters. The committee members most immediately concerned were cognizant of all this, but were less than successful in persuading Congress to install better procedures. The reluctance of Congress was due in part to constitutional principle, for the right of petition was sacred in a republican government. It was also due in part to the temper and quality of many Congressmen.

Perhaps to an exceptional degree from 1870 to 1900 the interests of members were local rather than national, and perhaps also their talents were best molded to the particular rather than to the general. Setting aside the tariff, the monetary problem, and civil service reform, the bulk of congressional business was in fact particular in its nature, and indeed the tariff was discovered to be a local issue. Patronage was local and individual, too, although the issue of reform was general. The mass of business for constituents drained away time and energy from men who had capacity for statecraft, and there were only a few like Garfield who could toil for his constituents until he was weary to the bone and at the same time could find energy for study, reflection, and the refinement of broad issues of public policy.

CONGRESS AND ADMINISTRATIVE MANAGEMENT

During these years members of Congress and congressional committees were thus participating directly in the administrative process. They also sought to improve official procedures by a series of investigations originating in a desire to expedite affairs, clear up huge arrearages, simplify practice, and reduce the number of clerks. They were relatively unsuccessful, but the sequence of congressional reports opened a new chapter in administrative history.

Congress was persistently dissatisfied with the conduct of administration by the executive departments, driven by constant complaints of constituents who were outraged by delay, confusion, error, and lack of known responsibility. Congressmen were unwilling to admit that a substantial share of the difficulty lay in the patronage system and were diligent in searching for other causes to account for official laxness and departmental arrearages. Their investigations provided much raw material for the study of administration, but from our present point of view they are important because they reveal the incapacity of Congress to think in terms other than those of detail. For twenty years members of Congress acted as amateur organization and methods analysts, but they failed to rise to higher levels.

The substance of these observations is evident in the long succession of congressional inquiries and reports beginning with a Joint Select Committee on Retrenchment (1869–71), Senator James W. Patterson, chairman. There followed a Senate committee of which the former Secretary of the Treasury, George S. Boutwell, was chairman

(1875–76); replies to a Senate resolution of June 15, 1880, requesting department heads to report desirable changes in the laws to achieve economy and efficiency; the Cockrell Committee (1887–89); and the Dockery-Cockrell Joint Commission of 1893–95. These were efforts to improve administration, not to investigate error or wrongdoing, and reveal a Congress cognizant of poor administration and willing to seek remedies.[52] The incompetence of Congress during these years to consider the problem in general terms was revealed in the charters of these successive committees, in their methods of procedure, and in the content of their reports. To these matters we turn for brief summary.

Senator Patterson's Joint Select Committee on Retrenchment had no staff and proceeded by taking evidence bearing on the various matters submitted to it by Congress. Their nature spoke of economy, not of administrative reform: offices that could be abolished, salaries that could be reduced, persons unnecessarily employed, expenses that could be curtailed, and loopholes in methods of accountability.[53] The customs service was especially under scrutiny, and the committee took testimony in New York and San Francisco, uncovering much evidence of fraud and abuses. Hopefully the committee noted that it was the "fixed purpose" of the Grant administration to remove these evils.[54] The attention of the committee was focused upon particular problems: the smuggling of goods en route from New York to San Francisco, the lease of government real estate in San Francisco, the Alaska fur trade, and the sale of a revenue cutter. Although invited to make recommendations on the reform of the civil service, the committee refrained from this unpleasant task. Senator Patterson could hardly have been expected to interest himself in broader matters of administration. He was a Dartmouth professor, a rural representative in the New Hampshire General Court, a member of Congress for two terms (1863–67), and a one-term Senator whose involvement in

[52] For full citations, see Gustavus A. Weber, *Organized Efforts for the Improvement of Methods of Administration in the United States* (New York: D. Appleton and Co., 1919).

[53] Senate Report 47, 41st Cong., 2d sess. (Feb. 21, 1870).

[54] Senate Report 380, 41st Cong., 3d sess., p. 6 (March 3, 1871). In the previous Congress, the Retrenchment Committee had recommended a root-and-branch reform of the consular service, one of many reports over the decades that finally bore fruit under the care of President Theodore Roosevelt. Senate Report 154, 40th Cong., 2d sess. (July 2, 1868).

the Crédit Mobilier brought upon him a recommendation for expulsion a few days before his term ended.[55] He had had no executive experience.

The Senate Committee of 1875–76 had more promising leadership. Its chairman, George S. Boutwell, had been governor of Massachusetts, Commissioner of Internal Revenue (1862-63), and Secretary of the Treasury (1869–73). He had been a member of the House of Representatives (1863–69) and a prominent figure among the Radical Republicans. The committee procedure was more sophisticated than that of its predecessor. Boutwell arranged a personal conference with department and bureau heads to secure their observations and then submitted to each of them a "tailor-made" set of questions. The official replies gave the data from which the committee worked.[56] The advantages and limitations of such a method are obvious.

The duty of the committee was to examine the several branches of the civil service "with a view to the re-organization of the Departments," a phrase that carried a connotation much less than a later generation was to understand. The committee discharged its responsibility by asking a few general questions on arrearages, the need for additional hours of work, the grading of clerks, and the desirability of noncompetitive examinations by an independent board; and by asking a multitude of particular questions appropriate to each agency. Did the General Land Office need a law officer; should a shorthand writer be assigned to assist a principal patent examiner; should handcopying in the Treasury be discontinued; should there be inspection of the lifesaving stations? Such questions were multiplied indefinitely. The Boutwell Committee succeeded no better than its predecessor, the Patterson Committee, in advancing the art of administration. Its purpose appears to have been more constructive, but it quickly became lost in details that overshadowed any likelihood of a deeply ranging inquiry.

In 1880 the Senate took another tack in its investigating functions by means of a resolution (June 15, 1880) asking the several departments to report what changes in the laws would promote efficiency or economy, what additional safeguards to disbursements and improvements in the accounting system could be suggested, and what

---

[55] *Dictionary of American Biography,* XIV, 303.
[56] Senate Report 289, 44th Cong., 1st sess. (April 27, 1876).

changes in the clerical force would be in the public interest. The replies from the Attorney General, the Secretary of State, and the War Department suggested either a remarkable complacency with status quo or an unwillingness to expose their shortcomings to a critical Congress. Attorney General Charles Devens declared, "I am unable to suggest any change in the present system which it is desirable to make by legislation."[57] Secretary of State Evarts could report only his need to vary the salaries of his clerks.[58] The Secretary of War merely transmitted the reports of his military subordinates, most of whom wanted more clerks. The judge advocate general stated that the business of his bureau was conducted "efficiently, simply, and economically," and recommended no material change.[59] The chief signal officer reported, "I have no suggestions to make";[60] the inspector general and the chief of engineers were of the same mind.[61]

The Post Office Department was more responsive, so far as its problems were concerned. They were particular: protection of postmasters from suit by patentholders for use of articles furnished by the Department, clarification of the power to withhold mail from delivery, new rules for contracts with railroad carriers, an appropriation for publication of the opinions of the assistant attorney general for the post office.[62] Although the Senate resolution suggested, if none too clearly, the concept of management in broad terms, the agencies failed to respond in this frame of reference. The committee recommendations, like those of its predecessors, were concerned with immediate practical detail. They revealed no sense of management in general or of system. The conclusion to be drawn was that this type of procedure was not likely to be productive of ideas other than those parochial in their application.

Complaints about delay continued to mount, and arrearages in some agencies grew greater and greater. Bureau chiefs nagged Congress for more clerks, but Congressmen suspected that what was needed was better management. Another Senate committee was set

[57] Senate Ex. Doc. 1, 46th Cong., 3d sess., p. 1 (Dec. 1, 1880).
[58] Senate Ex. Doc. 53, 46th Cong., 3d sess., p. 2 (Feb. 18, 1881).
[59] Senate Ex. Doc. 20, 46th Cong., 3d sess., p. 2 (July 10, 1880).
[60] *Ibid.*, p. 5 (Dec. 22, 1880).
[61] *Ibid.*, p. 6.
[62] Senate Ex. Doc. 16, 46th Cong., 3d sess., *passim* (Jan. 5, 1881).

up in 1887 "to inquire into and examine the methods of business and work in the Executive Departments."[63] Its chairman was the popular Senator from Missouri, Francis M. Cockrell, successor to Carl Schurz in 1875 and reelected without a break until 1905. In 1904 he was nominated for the presidency by Champ Clark and William Jennings Bryan. After leaving the Senate, Theodore Roosevelt appointed him to the Interstate Commerce Commission.[64]

The Cockrell Committee decided to get the facts on the methods of handling the public affairs. It required each department to state the business methods of the Secretary's Office and of each division of each bureau. The committee demanded a report on one or more principal business matters showing its course in detail from beginning to end.[65] Over one hundred printed pages were needed to satisfy this single thirst for data. The committee also asked for a statement of the business pending in each division of each bureau on January 1, 1884, the amount received and disposed of for each succeeding year up to March 1, 1887, and remaining on hand on that date. It required the average number of employees in each division, the average amount of work performed by them, and the amount of business transacted by the best and the poorest employee in each division.[66] The committee broke new ground by calling for statements of the organization of the departments showing the number of employees in each division, the number of field offices, the number of public buildings, the organization of the Coast and Geodetic Survey and other field agencies, "all stated so as to give correctly and concisely a bird's-eye view of your Department proper, and all branches of its service."

Senator Cockrell asked for facts on an imperial scale. He received facts in such quantity that they stifled the capacity of the committee,

---

[63] Senate Report 507, 50th Cong., 1st sess., Part 1, p. 1 (March 3, 1887).

[64] *Dictionary of American Biography*, IV, 257.

[65] Senate Report 507, 50th Cong., 1st sess., Part 2, p. 1.

[66] *Ibid.*, Part 2, p. 2, for one example. This administratively naïve request was either ignored or rebutted by the agencies. The second auditor reported that he could not express in figures the work of the most and the least efficient. *Ibid.*, Part 2, p. 206. The chief of the middle division of the Bureau of Pensions replied: "As a rule, the one who accomplishes most does not do his work as well as those who accomplish less. One who accomplishes least, as shown by the data, may be of more value to the Bureau than some who appear to have accomplished more." *Ibid.*, Part 2, Department of Interior, p. 150.

which had no staff, to analyze and digest them. The committee was swamped with facts; the time and cost involved in collecting them cannot even be estimated. Arrearages and delays must have been compounded.

The sprawling, disorderly, and unsystematic report of the committee does not reveal any more than its predecessors an awareness of administration above the level of office management and the operations that a later generation would designate organization and methods. The report had much to say about unnecessary forms and duplication, arrearages, the accumulation of useless papers, office methods, excessive employment of copyists (the typewriter was just coming into use), and laxness in operations. These were well-justified criticisms, but the committee was less successful in prescribing general remedies.

Agency heads were nearly unanimous in believing that their difficulties were due to an inadequate clerical force. The Cockrell Committee declared that the remedy was not an increase in the number of clerks, but greater efficiency. It had one general panacea, to increase the hours of work; but this found little favor in the agencies.

The Cockrell Committee, faced with the mountain of documentation called forth at its command, hit upon another significant innovation. It decided that progress could best be made in two of the largest agencies, Treasury and War, by establishing departmental committees to consider and revise the methods of business. Two such agency committees were set up, and their reports were printed in a supplementary Cockrell Committee document.[67] So far as has been observed, this is the first intimation that Congress was not a suitable body to induce administrative reorganization, and that the task might best be done within the agencies themselves.[68]

Complaints of delay and inefficiency continued, and in 1893 Congress established a Joint Commission popularly known as the Dockery Commission, to continue the search for a remedy.[69] The commission comprised three members of the House and Senate respectively; the chairman was Alexander M. Dockery of Missouri, and Senator Cock-

[67] Senate Report 3, 51st Cong., special sess. (March 28, 1889).
[68] The Cockrell Committee persuaded the Senate to establish a standing committee on the organization, conduct, and expenditures of the executive departments, but apparently it was never active. *Ibid.*, p. 45.
[69] 27 Stat. 681 (March 3, 1893).

rell was a member. Dockery was a practising physician who turned to banking, became mayor of Gallatin, Missouri, a Democratic member of Congress from 1883 to 1899 and of the House Appropriations Committee for ten years. He was accordingly well placed to know both the strength and the weakness of the administrative machine. Upon leaving the House he was elected governor of Missouri (1900–1905) and from 1913 to 1921 was Third Assistant Postmaster General.[70]

The task of the Dockery Commission was the now familiar one: to inquire into and examine the laws organizing the departments, their methods of conducting business, the degree of efficiency of their employees, and whether reductions of force were possible without injury to the public service. The commission made a notable contribution to method; it was authorized to employ not over three experts and to secure detail of employees from the executive offices. The commission in fact employed three leaders in the field of accounting: Joseph W. Reinhart, just elected president of the Atchison, Topeka, and Santa Fe Railroad after an exceptional career as a railroad accountant and reorganizer;[71] Charles W. Haskins, one of the leaders of the then "modern" science of accountancy and a pioneer in its practice in New York City;[72] and Elijah W. Sells, a railroad accountant who was also one of the foremost men in this field.[73] The two latter founded the firm of Haskins and Sells shortly after completing their work for the commission.

The background of the experts prophesied the character of the work of the Dockery-Cockrell group. There was a primary interest in the organization and practice of the government for accounting and fiscal control. The experts, however, developed the first systematic presentation of the anatomy of the federal administration as a whole in two extensive compilations: a listing of all the laws creating departments, agencies, and their subdivisions, fixing salaries and regulating the employment of clerks;[74] and a tabular statement showing the number and titles of offices, bureaus, and divisions with the num-

[70] *National Cyclopaedia of American Biography*, XX, 44.
[71] *Ibid.*, VI, 395.
[72] *Ibid.*, IX, 514; William G. Jordan and others, *Charles Waldo Haskins: an American Pioneer in Accountancy* (New York: Prentice Hall, 1923).
[73] *National Cyclopaedia of American Biography*, XIII, 594.
[74] House Report 49, 53d Cong., 1st sess., pp. 1-175 (Sept. 30, 1893).

ber and status of their employees.[75] These elaborate compilations provided valuable basic data.

The Dockery Commission found that arrearages had generally been brought under control, a testimony to the usefulness of Senator Cockrell's committee. It discovered additional means of simplification and elimination of useless work, and its recommendations resulted in considerable new legislation to help clear the administrative decks.[76] The commission in 1895 estimated that it had effected a reduction of 251 clerks earning yearly salaries of over $360,000 and the elimination of other expenditures amounting to $246,000.[77]

What did this commission have to say of the art of administration? It added little, if anything, to the meager store of recorded doctrine, despite the range and detail of its inquiries. Its primary objective was economy; its focus of attention was on particulars, especially those concerned with accounting; its recommendations favored specific remedies for specific situations and gave no hint of generalities that might guide practitioners to the solution of related problems. The experts knew much about railroad organization, but they transferred little of their expertness in this field to their study of government. Their major contribution in methodology was the systematic listing of statutes and the census of the administrative offices.

The Dockery Joint Commission was the last of the congressional committees to investigate the operation of the executive departments with a view to economy and efficiency. There is deep significance in the fact that during the twenty years between the Patterson investigation and the Dockery-Cockrell study, no President had taken the initiative to activate executive studies for the improvement of administration. They seemed, as in a sense they were, more remote from the administrative system than Congress; they displayed no responsibility for systematic inquiry into the methods of its public business; they had no plans for its improvement; they watched aloof while Congress groped for better organization and procedures. Congress was inept, and it may be argued was ill-constituted for the enterprise.

[75] House Report 88, 53d Cong., 1st sess., pp. 1-207 (Oct. 9, 1893). This statement was a development of one feature of the Cockrell report.

[76] A list of these enactments is available in Gustavus A. Weber, *Organized Efforts for the Improvement of Methods of Administration in the United States*, pp. 68-71.

[77] House Report 2000, 53d Cong., 3d sess., p. 30 (March 2, 1895).

Nevertheless it was Congress that kept the initiative, and in this series of investigations political motivation was not predominant. Congress wanted economy; it needed to reduce delay in handling constituents' problems in the Pension Office, the General Land Office, and elsewhere; and it hoped also to eliminate wasted effort and official laxity so as to reduce expenditures. It was under constituents' pressure to act. The President was not. The success of Congress in improving detail while it failed in modernizing the system suggested that the larger task was perhaps appropriate for executive rather than legislative action.

In any event, after 1901 the initiative passed to President Theodore Roosevelt and remained in the hands of his successors, notably President William H. Taft. The charge made by Roosevelt to Charles Hallam Keep, Assistant Secretary of the Treasury, begins to reflect an awareness of something beyond specific practice of individual agencies. The President was rising above particulars as well as stating his own convictions about administration when he told the Keep Committee that salaries should be commensurate with the character and market value of the service performed, and uniform across departmental lines; that government supplies should be standardized, and purchased through a central purchasing office; that fiscal restrictions should not interfere with executive discretion; that comparative costs should be ascertained; and that there should be interdepartmental cooperation in the use of expert or technical knowledge. With his customary vigor Roosevelt declared that "the existence of any method, standard, custom or practice is no reason for its continuance when a better is offered."[78]

The work of the Keep Committee and of President Taft's Commission on Economy and Efficiency belongs to a later period. They are the visible symbols not only of a transfer of initiative for administrative reform from the legislative to the executive branch, but also of the tipping of the constitutional balance from Congress to the President of the United States. This shift was momentous and was not reversed.

[78] Theodore Roosevelt, *The Letters of Theodore Roosevelt* (8 vols., Elting E. Morison, ed., Cambridge, Mass.: Harvard University Press, 1951-54), IV, 1201-2 (June 2, 1905). Quotations from *The Letters of Theodore Roosevelt* reprinted by permission of the publisher, Harvard University Press.

CHAPTER FIVE

The President and Departmental Business

That the President was the constitutional head and center of the administrative organization had long been settled doctrine, although the establishment of the Interstate Commerce Commission in 1887 raised a novel issue of its relationship to the Chief Executive. That Secretaries should take the counsel and direction of the President in all important matters of departmental business was equally well settled practice. That the President should exercise an initiating and creative influence with respect to the administrative system was, however, foreign both to doctrine and to practice until Theodore Roosevelt entered the White House. Presidents were immersed in the particulars of administration—the prisoners of a system that they had neither created nor fashioned. To this observation one exception must be entered. The President did give form and substance to the new civil service regime, and it was at this point that Cleveland and his successors exercised leadership and influence upon the general plan of administration.

Presidents were very busy men. The daily grist of matters administrative, intermixed with varying political and partisan ingredients, occupied a major share of presidential time. Masses of trivial affairs continued to rise to the President's desk, and no Chief Executive appears to have thought about relief from this traditional but heavy burden. With the possible exception of Chester A. Arthur, Presidents worked hard, for long hours, and with no sense of recovery from pressure. President Garfield recorded in his diary of June 6, 1881, after an absence of three days, "The stream of callers which was damned up by my absence became a torrent and swept away my day." Two days later he wrote, "My day in the office was very like its predecessors. Once or twice I felt like crying out in the agony of my soul against the greed for office and its consumption of my time."[1] Cleveland, one of the most dutiful of Presidents, toiled through the night far into the early morning hours with his secretary. Nevertheless, the great mass of executive business was, and had to be, concluded at the departmental or bureau levels.

Woodrow Wilson was only partially justified in reducing the administrative role of the President to a mere servant of Congress. "Almost all distinctively executive functions are specifically bestowed upon the heads of departments," wrote the future President in his *Congressional Government*. "No President, however earnest and industrious, can keep the Navy in a state of creditable efficiency if he have a corrupt or incapable Secretary in the Navy Department . . . and the Secretary of State may do as much mischief behind his back as can the Secretary of the Treasury. He might master the details and so control the administration of some one of the departments, but he can scarcely oversee them all with any degree of strictness. His knowledge of what they have done or are doing comes, of course, from the Secretaries themselves. . . ."[2] He then declared: "In so far as the President is an executive officer he is the servant of Congress; and the members of the Cabinet, being confined to executive functions, are altogether the servants of Congress."[3]

Wilson was so impressed with congressional dominance at this time that he failed to grasp either the wide play of discretion vested in the President by the Constitution and by statute, or the necessary range of independent executive judgment in the normal operations of government. He concluded: "The business of the President, occasionally great, is usually not much above routine. Most of the time it is *mere* administration, mere obedience of directions from the masters of policy, the Standing Committees. Except in so far as his power of veto constitutes him a part of the legislature, the President might, not inconveniently, be a permanent officer; the first official of a carefully

[1] Theodore C. Smith, *Life and Letters of James A. Garfield*, II, 1151.
[2] Woodrow Wilson, *Congressional Government*, pp. 260-61.
[3] *Ibid.*, p. 266.

graded and impartially regulated civil service system, through whose sure series of merit-promotions the youngest clerk might rise even to the chief magistracy."[4] This fantasy was truly a product of the ivory tower!

Presidents usually take a special interest in and responsibility for the work of the State Department. Grant, on the whole, was an exception. Hamilton Fish, his Secretary of State, was an outstanding figure who held the initiative in diplomatic affairs for eight years. It was Grant, however, who personally engineered the ill-fated treaty for the annexation of San Domingo. Cleveland and Richard Olney made a cooperative team, but Cleveland was actively and personally involved in all matters of primary importance. Harrison selected James G. Blaine for the State Department, but the Secretary had long passed his prime and Harrison was in fact his own foreign officer. The same situation prevailed as between McKinley and John Sherman who, in tacit recognition of the fact, resigned as war was declared with Spain.

Blaine recorded his acceptance of presidential direction in an exchange of letters with Harrison. "The Foreign Affairs," he wrote, "are in their inception and management exclusively Executive and nothing decisive can be done in that important field except with the President's personal knowledge and official approval. So entirely confidential has the relation of the Secretary to the President been held, that questions relating to Foreign Affairs are brought to the attention of other members of the Cabinet by the Secretary of State *only* as directed by the President."[5]

THE PRESIDENT AND APPOINTMENTS

Two aspects of administration normally require personal consideration by chief executives: appointments and other personnel matters, and the annual estimates of expenditures. During the years from Grant through McKinley appointments occupied an excessive share of presidential time, but the estimates remained beyond their ken. The time consumed by applicants, by members of Congress introducing appli-

---

[4] *Ibid.*, p. 254.

[5] *The Correspondence between Benjamin Harrison and James G. Blaine, 1882-1893* (Albert T. Volwiler, ed., Philadelphia: American Philosophical Society, 1940), p. 49 (Jan. 21, 1889).

cants, and in reading applicants' files and weighing relative claims was immense.

The situation can be illustrated by instances from the experience of Hayes and Cleveland. In his diary for December 17, 1878, Hayes wrote, "Last night I took up the papers in the Lebanon, Ohio, case. There were eight competitors. Three women—two, widows of officers. Three or four of the men were well qualified and well supported by the people. I appointed a crippled private soldier. He was getting a smaller pension than the ladies received—poor, honest, moral, and religious, with requisite business qualifications."[6] This was merely one of thousands of post offices, any of which presumably had as valid a claim on presidential time as Lebanon, Ohio.

The pressure for appointments in Cleveland's second term quickly became unbearable, and in order to protect his time the President had to issue the following executive order.

It has become apparent after two months' experience that the rules heretofore promulgated regulating interviews with the President have wholly failed in their operation. The time which under these rules was set apart for the reception of Senators and Representatives has been almost entirely spent in listening to applications for office, which have been bewildering in volume, perplexing and exhausting in their iteration, and impossible of remembrance.

A due regard for public duty, which must be neglected if present conditions continue, and an observance of the limitations placed upon human endurance oblige me to decline from and after this date all personal interviews with those seeking appointments to office, except as I on my own motion may especially invite them. The same considerations make it impossible for me to receive those who merely desire to pay their respects except on the days and during the hours especially designated for that purpose.

I earnestly request Senators and Representatives to aid me in securing for them uninterrupted interviews by declining to introduce their constituents and friends when visiting the Executive Mansion during the hours designated for their reception. Applicants for office will only prejudice their prospects by repeated importunity and by remaining in Washington to await results.[7]

---

[6] Rutherford B. Hayes, *Diary and Letters*, III, 515-16.
[7] Richardson, *Messages*, IX, 399-400 (May 8, 1893).

Personal attention to appointments was, nevertheless, an inescap-able executive duty. It was important politically and it was essential administratively, for both political and administrative success could be ruined by mistakes in selection for office, high and low. The task was burdensome and often frustrating, but it was a central aspect of the executive power.

After 1883 Presidents had a new and general responsibility for personnel administration, viz., approval of the rules of the Civil Serv-ice Commission and extension of the merit system. The executive orders from 1883 to 1901 were, in fact, almost wholly devoted to these matters; and beyond the rules and extension of the merit sys-tem was consideration by the Chief Executive of many bitterly con-troversial individual cases. Presidents, as will be noted in more detail later, stood in an unhappy position, watched incessantly by the civil service reformers and hounded by masses of office seekers. The merit system was, nevertheless, a definite presidential responsibility. The act of 1871 put in the hands of the President the power to make rules for admission to the civil service, and the Pendleton Act of 1883 re-quired his approval of the rules of the Civil Service Commission. In a new sense of the term, he became the head of the civil service.

ESTIMATES AND EXPENDITURES

The nature of the presidency as a central management office during these years is sharply revealed in the prevailing practices with respect to estimates, appropriations, and expenditures. An executive who in-tends to stand effectively at the summit of the official hierarchy, to direct its broad movements, to instill his own spirit into its activities, and to supervise its operations, can find no surer means than control of finance. Such a principle was neither understood nor accepted from Grant to McKinley. Presidents had little, if anything, to do with the level or content of the estimates, with the amount or objects of congressional appropriation, or with the actual use of the funds an-nually made available. They were consequently unable to exert one powerful influence on the conduct of administration, and in fact stood by inertly while bureau chiefs and appropriation committees settled the main outlines of administrative policy and operations. In all this there was nothing new, but the separation of the President from the budget-making process became more and more anomalous with the increasing complexity of the administrative machine.

The estimates were prepared by the bureaus. They were compiled usually by the chief clerk of the appropriate Secretary's office, but the record does not suggest that department heads systematically reviewed or revised them. On the other hand, the policies of the Secretaries had a strong influence on major expenditures, as, for example, William C. Whitney's insistence on building a new fleet of ironclads. The basic operational estimates, however, were bureau figures first and last.

The departmental estimates were combined in the Treasury into a single document generally known as the Book of Estimates. The Treasury did not review or revise them; the bureau figures went untouched to the House Appropriations Committee. No evidence has been discovered to indicate that the President was consulted at any stage on the general level of expenditures or on particular objects. His approval, however, would presumably have been secured for any substantial change, or for important new policy to be reflected in the figures. Likewise no evidence has been seen to suggest that Presidents took any part in the regular deficiency bills that came to play a considerable share in financing the government agencies.

The absence of evidence conforms to the fact that no President during this period had institutional support or personal assistance to aid him in revising agency expenditure plans. The same comment holds true for department heads. Lacking such assistance, it would have been physically impossible for them to examine estimates thoroughly or systematically. So far as agency heads were concerned, moreover, they usually had too brief an experience to warrant their intrusion into the fiscal mysteries of the great bureaus.

The only leverage on the estimates that appears to have been available to Presidents was the opportunity in the annual messages to advise Congress on the virtues of economy. A comparison of Grant's and McKinley's efforts at this point will suggest how feeble they were, and how feebly they developed over a quarter-century. In four of Grant's annual messages he made no reference whatever to the estimates. In his second he mentioned the over-all figures, with neither endorsement nor disapproval. In his third he reported, "I have not given the estimates for the support of the Government . . . because all these figures are contained in the accompanying reports or in those presented directly to Congress. These estimates have my approval."[8] Two years later he recommended economy and reductions in appropriations for public buildings, river and harbor improvements, and fortifications. He did not state that he had examined agency estimates for these purposes or suggest any particulars.[9] His final reference to the estimates occurred in his sixth annual message, in which he merely remarked that they did not differ materially from those of the preceding year.[10] Otherwise Grant was silent.

McKinley's four annual messages were equally barren. In his first he expressed a general opinion that the estimates would admit a decrease in expenditures without injury to the public service, and suggested that appropriations be kept within receipts.[11] His second and third messages made no reference to the estimates. His fourth again praised economy, but made no recommendations with respect to the pending estimates.[12] All this was perfectly consistent with the then prevailing process of making estimates and securing appropriations—a process that began with the bureaus, continued with the Appropriations Committee or Committees, and ended with Congress. The President was not a party.

Evidence of the same order is found in Garfield's diary while he was chairman of the Appropriations Committee. He was constantly occupied with Secretaries and bureau chiefs, but not with the President. Study of his diary for 1872 and 1873 revealed only two references to Grant in connection with estimates. The President consulted with him on December 18, 1872, to express his interest in appropriations for the Vienna Exposition and the Texan Frontier Commission.[13] On December 15, 1873, the Appropriations Committee adopted a resolution requesting Grant to cause the estimates to be revised.[14] Garfield may not, of course, have mentioned other conferences on appropriation problems, but so far as his diary discloses, it appears that

---

[8] Richardson, *Messages*, VII, 153 (Dec. 4, 1871).
[9] *Ibid.*, VII, 243 (Dec. 1, 1873).
[10] *Ibid.*, VII, 295 (Dec. 7, 1874).
[11] *Ibid.*, X, 50 (Dec. 6, 1897).
[12] *Ibid.*, X, 232 (Dec. 3, 1900).
[13] James A. Garfield, Diary (Dec. 18, 1872), in Manuscript Division, Library of Congress.
[14] *Ibid.*

the President was not in command of the agency estimates or appropriations, nor as a rule consulted with regard to them.

THE PRESIDENT AND THE CABINET

Presidents maintained diverse relations with their Cabinets and with individual members, depending on personal, political, administrative, and other considerations. Cabinet meetings were regularly scheduled and most, if not all, major questions of policy, tactics, and administration came up for discussion, as well as the perennial problems of patronage. The predominance of the President and the merely advisory capacity of the Cabinet members were never questioned or challenged and were occasionally affirmed. On April 22, 1874, Grant vetoed a currency bill, and subsequently told a newspaper correspondent: "When the Cabinet met, my message was written. I did not intend asking the advice of the Cabinet, as I knew a majority would oppose the veto. I never allowed the Cabinet to interfere when my mind was made up, and on this question it was inflexibly made up."[15]

Cleveland's biographer wrote that in his Cabinet meetings "there were no set speeches, and no votes were taken, the President's theory being that in a cabinet there are many voices, but one vote. Each member was free to express his views; but when the illumination of frank comment and informal discussion was over, it was the President who must make the decision."[16]

Procedure in McKinley's Cabinet was recorded by Secretary of the Navy John D. Long. "There was, of course, never a set speech; there was no parliamentary procedure, and never a formal vote. Nobody ever 'addressed the chair' or stood upon his feet. Matters were discussed in a conversational way. When the President had arrived at a result, he nodded to each member in succession, saying, 'You agree?' until the last one had assented, and then wound the matter up by saying, 'You all agree.' Rarely was there any non-consent. . . ."[17]

There is scanty documentation concerning the type of matter considered by the Cabinet. President Harrison declared: "Our habit was

[15] John R. Young, *Around the World with General Grant*, II, 154.
[16] Robert McElroy, *Grover Cleveland: The Man and the Statesman* (2 vols., New York: Harper and Brothers, 1923), I, 115.
[17] John D. Long, *The New American Navy* (2 vols., New York: Outlook Co., 1903), II, 142.

only to discuss matters of general interest at Cabinet meetings, or such as affected more than one department."[18] Such evidence as is available does not suggest that problems of departmental administration were prominent in these meetings. Each agency managed its own affairs and its administrative problems were discussed privately with the President. Harrison noted: "My plan was to give to each of the Departments a stated day when the Secy would come with his papers and a full consultation would be had as to appointments and as to important matters of business. . . . All matters of large concern were brought to my attention, and were settled in the conferences I have referred to, or in the Cabinet meeting."[19]

Presidents apparently did not prepare agenda for Cabinet meetings, but depended upon department heads to bring matters to their attention. McKinley's Secretary of the Treasury, Lyman J. Gage, wrote what was probably a characteristic description of these conferences: "Twice a week, for about an hour, I met the President and all other Secretaries in formal sessions of the Cabinet. Each member reported the doings or proposed doings of his department, and responded to the President's questions."[20] A President could thus keep himself informed and could make decisions on matters brought to his notice, but the procedure left the initiative with the Secretaries.

THE PRESIDENT'S OFFICE

The personal assistance authorized for the President by Congress amply demonstrated that the President was not expected to play a creative role in the administrative system. In 1871 Grant was allowed a private secretary, a stenographer, a couple of executive clerks, a steward and a messenger, the whole appropriation amounting to $13,800. He was also allowed a secretary to sign patents for public lands at a salary of $1,500.[21] The patent secretary sat at a desk in the Interior Department, and to all intents and purposes the President had exactly one person competent to assist him in his official work. Grant pieced out by putting Generals Porter, Babcock, and Comstock on General Sherman's staff from which they were assigned to the

---

[18] *Harrison–Blaine Correspondence*, p. 301 (May 22, 1893).
[19] *Ibid.*, p. 301.
[20] *Memoirs of Lyman J. Gage* (New York: House of Field, Inc., 1937), p. 108.
[21] 16 Stat. 475 at 480 (March 3, 1871).

White House as private secretaries. He appointed a son of Stephen A. Douglas, Robert Martin Douglas, as assistant private secretary.[22] Generals Badeau and Dent also became aides to the President, a group that caused Senator Sumner to fulminate against a military ring.[23]

The status of private secretary to the President was low for some years. Grant's military "secretaries" did not command public confidence. Hayes had to make repeated offers before reaching an unsatisfactory solution. General Manning F. Force considered the appointment beneath his dignity and William Henry Smith did not think it worth accepting. Hayes finally persuaded his friend, William K. Rogers, to accept: "a gentle, impractical, scholarly soul, a dignified gentleman who fumbled a bit in public affairs."[24] President Hayes also had the services of an assistant secretary who could take dictation. The slow retreat of the letter copyist from the federal scene is illustrated by President Harrison's experience. He dictated his correspondence to his stenographer, Everard F. Tibbott. The latter then usually wrote out in longhand the letter to be sent, but also made a typed copy for the files.[25]

The President's office made an apparent gain during the McKinley administration, but the increase of staff was only partly the kind the President needed. By the appropriation act of 1901 Congress authorized a secretary and two assistant secretaries, two executive clerks and four clerks, two of whom were telegraphers, as well as numerous doorkeepers and messengers.[26] McKinley thus had authority to hire a personal civilian staff about equivalent to that which Grant had secured by detail from the army.

Perceptive Presidents recognized the need for high-level aides long before Congress was ready to respond. After his election Garfield

[22] William B. Hesseltine, *Ulysses S. Grant: Politician* (New York: Dodd, Mead and Co., 1935), p. 149.

[23] Charles Sumner, *Republicanism vs. Grantism* (Washington: Rives and Bailey, 1872).

[24] H. J. Eckenrode, *Rutherford B. Hayes*, p. 322. Force, the son of the archivist and historian Peter Force, had a distinguished military career, and at the time was judge of the superior court of Cincinnati. *Dictionary of American Biography*, VI, 511. Smith, an old friend of Hayes, was a journalist who had been secretary to an Ohio governor and secretary of state of Ohio. Hayes appointed him collector of the port of Chicago. *Ibid.*, XVII, 364.

[25] *Harrison–Blaine Correspondence*, Preface, p. ix.

[26] 31 Stat. 960 at 972 (March 3, 1901).

wrote a friend, "I am more at a loss to find just the man for Private
Secretary than for any place I shall have to fill. The man who holds
that place can do very much to make or mar the success of an administration. The position ought to be held in higher estimation than
Secretary of State."[27] He tried to secure John Hay, but without success. Hay replied: "The contact with the greed and selfishness of
office-seekers and bull-dozing Congressmen is unspeakably repulsive.
The constant contact with envy, meanness, ignorance, and the swinish
selfishness which ignorance breeds needs a stronger heart and a more
obedient nervous system than I can boast."[28]

Cleveland was equally alert to the need for help, other than clerical.
Speaking of William L. Wilson, he said as he took his way to Washington for his second term, "I would appoint him [if I could] Assistant
to the President, with a salary of $10,000 a year. As the executive
office is now organized it can deal, with a fair amount of efficiency,
with the routine affairs of Government; but if the President has any
great policy in mind or on hand he has no one to help him work it
out. . . . I have even half a notion to offer him the place anyhow
and pay him out of my own pocket."[29] Presidents needed help, but
neither they nor Congress understood clearly the kind of help that
was needed if a President was really to be the chief executive. Indeed
it was not certain that anyone intended a President to play such a
role.

How did Presidents spend their days? One occupant of the White
House has left an account of his time (Hayes), and there is a good
description of the workday of another (Arthur). About a year after
his inauguration Hayes wrote in his diary the following passage.

I rise at about 7 A.M.; write until breakfast, about 8:30 A.M. After breakfast, prayers—i.e., the reading of a chapter in the Bible, each one present
reading a verse in turn, and all kneeling repeat the Lord's Prayer; then,
usually, write and arrange business until 10 A.M. From 10 to 12 in the
Cabinet Room, the Members of Congress having the preference of all
visitors except Cabinet ministers. Callers "to pay respects" are usually

[27] Theodore C. Smith, *Life and Letters of James A. Garfield*, II, 1069-70 (Dec.
7, 1880).

[28] *Ibid.*, II, 1071 (Dec. 25, 1880).

[29] George F. Parker, *Recollections of Grover Cleveland* (New York: Century
Co., 1911), p. 183.

permitted to come in to shake hands whenever the number reaches about a half dozen waiting. Twelve to 2 P.M., on Tuesdays and Fridays, are Cabinet hours. On other days that time is given to miscellaneous business callers.

At 2 P.M. lunch. I commonly invite to that—cup of tea and biscuit and butter with cold meat—any gentleman I wish to have more conference with than is practicable in hours given to miscellaneous business. After lunch the correspondence of the day, well briefed, and each letter in an envelope, is examined. By this time it is 3:30 P.M., and I then drive an hour and a half. Returning I glance over the business and correspondence again, take a fifteen or twenty minutes' nap, and get ready to dine at 6 P.M.

After dinner, callers on important business, or on appointment previously made, occupy me until 10:30 to 11:30 P.M., when I go to bed, and am tired enough to sleep pretty well unless too much worried to throw off the vexations of the day—a thing which fortunately I generally can do by a little effort.[30]

The official day of President Arthur was described by his biographer, George F. Howe.

When Congress was in session, Arthur tried to establish a methodical procedure for every week. He usually rose after nine o'clock, ate a "continental breakfast" while dressing, and went directly to his office. Mondays were kept free from callers on all but the most urgent business, but on every other week day, from ten to twelve o'clock, he received members of Congress, usually in connection with appointments. On Tuesdays and Fridays he went from these consultations to meet his Cabinet at noon; on Wednesdays, Thursdays and Saturdays, he received general callers from noon to one o'clock, before his light lunch, and then attacked the mail. During the afternoons, callers came by appointment until four or five o'clock, after which he went for a drive or, in the latter part of his term, a horseback ride, returning for a family dinner at seven.

Such a program was constantly invaded by special demands—dedication ceremonies, short trips to New York or down the Potomac, state dinners or receptions, and the hospitalities outside the White House which Arthur somewhat freely accepted. To compensate for the interruptions, he often resumed work in the late evening and spent the hours till two or three o'clock reading reports or consulting with political advisers. Quite as often, when business was not pressing, he spent his evenings with per-

[30] Rutherford B. Hayes, *Diary and Letters*, III, 469-70 (March 18, 1878).

sonal friends, concluding with a delectable midnight supper in the private dining room he had redecorated to suit himself.[31]

The life of a chief executive was not an easy one. What did Presidents say about the presidency? Most of them were glad to exchange the honor for the peace and freedom of private life. Grant declared that he was weary of office—"I never wanted to get out of a place as much as I did to get out of the Presidency."[32] Hayes confided to his diary in 1879 that Mrs. Hayes agreed with him in saying, "Well, I am heartily tired of this life of bondage, responsibility, and toil. I wish it was at an end."[33] And as his term drew to a close, he wrote again:

. . . . We have upon the whole enjoyed our four years here. But the responsibility, the embarrassments, the heart-breaking sufferings which we can't relieve, the ever-present danger of scandals and crimes among those we are compelled to trust, and a thousand other drawbacks to our satisfaction and enjoyment by which we are constantly surrounded, leave us no place for regret upon retiring from this conspicuous scene to the freedom, independence, and safety of our obscure and happy home in the pleasant grove at Fremont.[34]

When Cleveland faced his first term he wrote a friend, "I look upon the four years next to come as a dreadful self-inflicted penance for the good of my country. I can see no pleasure in it and no satisfaction, only a hope that I may be of service to my people."[35] And four years later he wrote, "You cannot imagine the relief which has come to me with the termination of my official term."[36] Such sentiments had been privately expressed by many of Cleveland's predecessors.

TWO PROPOSED RESTRICTIONS ON EXECUTIVE STATUS

No President accepted John Sherman's doctrinaire theory that the Chief Executive could not control the discretion reposed by law in any head or subordinate of any government agency. No department

[31] George Frederick Howe, *Chester A. Arthur: a Quarter-Century of Machine Politics* (New York: Dodd, Mead and Co., 1934), p. 173.
[32] John R. Young, *Around the World with General Grant*, II, 453.
[33] Hayes, *Diary and Letters*, III, 557 (June 6, 1879).
[34] *Ibid.*, III, 637 (Jan. 16, 1881).
[35] *Letters of Grover Cleveland, 1850-1908* (Allan Nevins, ed., Boston: Houghton Mifflin Co., 1933), p. 48 (Nov. 13, 1884).
[36] *Ibid.*, p. 203 (April 13, 1889).

head undertook to assert such independence after Andrew Johnson left the White House. The executive power was the constitutional possession of the President, and it carried with it the practical authority to see that the laws were enforced. The President, in short, was the constitutional head of the administrative system.

The concentration of political, military, and administrative authority was sufficient, however, after Lincoln's demonstration of its true nature, to stir up recommendations for its limitation, notably by proposals for a single-term amendment to the Constitution, and more subtly for attendance of Cabinet members upon Congress. While neither of these matters was pressed, they have interest by revealing what some responsible contemporaries thought of the presidential office. They also throw further light on the struggle for power between the legislative and executive branches.

The single term. The argument for a single-term executive was put in different ways. Horace Greeley asserted that eligibility for a second term was the main source of a corrupt misalliance between the executive and legislative branches. "The President appoints at their bidding; they legislate in subservience to his will, often in opposition to their own convictions."[37] Reform in Greeley's opinion was dependent upon denying the temptations of a reelection. Rutherford B. Hayes formally renounced any intention of seeking a second term in his acceptance of the nomination for President.

> . . . The declaration of principles by the Cincinnati Convention makes no announcement in favor of a single Presidential term. I do not assume to add to that declaration; but believing that the restoration of the civil service to the system established by Washington and followed by the early Presidents can be best accomplished by an Executive who is under no temptation to use the patronage of his office to promote his own re-election, I desire to perform what I regard as a duty in now stating my inflexible purpose, if elected, not to be a candidate for election to a second term.[38]

Cleveland also favored a single-term limitation.

According to Jacob D. Cox, the results of Hayes' abnegation were

---

[37] Letter to Carl Schurz in *Speeches, Correspondence and Political Papers of Carl Schurz* (6 vols., Frederic Bancroft, ed., New York: G. P. Putnam's Sons, 1913), II, 391 (July 8, 1872).

[38] Rutherford B. Hayes, *Letters and Messages together with Letter of Acceptance and Inaugural Address* (Washington, 1881), p. 6 (July 8, 1876).

good. His administration, wrote Cox, "ran on from day to day in a wholesome independence and vigor. . . . Its recommendations were known to be honest, and not warped by cunning policy."[39] Cox advocated a single six-year term. General Grant's apparent willingness to be considered for a third term was not put to the test, but had he taken the Republican nomination of 1880 the two-term tradition would doubtless have been a handicap to his success. The issue faded from the scene after 1880; Cleveland served a second term, McKinley was reelected, and it remained for Theodore Roosevelt to run afoul of old tradition in his defeat for an additional term in the election of 1912.

Historically the status of the presidential office had been fortified by eligibility for a second term, and would probably have been reduced by a single-term limitation. The capacity for political or administrative leadership of an executive whose official demise is known to occur on a given date is substantially less than that of one who may continue to command power.

Cabinet seats in Congress. The issue of allowing department heads to sit in the legislative branch was raised by Congressman George H. Pendleton in 1864 and the reform was championed, among others, by James A. Garfield. "I want this joint resolution passed," he told the House, "to readjust the relations between the executive and legislative departments, and to readjust them so that there shall be greater responsibility to the legislative branch than there now is, and that that responsibility shall be made to rest with greater weight upon the shoulders of the executive authority."[40] He also argued that such a seat in Congress would call out higher talent both executive and parliamentary, but his primary object was to make department heads more responsible to Congress—that is, less responsible to the President.

Jacob D. Cox, recently Secretary of the Interior, advocated the measure in 1871 in terms which again suggested that the President had little to do with government. "A great advantage," he wrote, " . . . would be found in the necessity . . . for the Cabinet to be in the proper sense of the word a ministry, with a definite and avowed policy on public measures of importance. The tendency in our govern-

[39] Jacob D. Cox, "The Hayes Administration," *Atlantic Monthly*, LXXI (1893), 831.

[40] James A. Garfield, *Works*, I, 71 (Jan. 26, 1865).

ment has been strongly in the direction of bureaucracy, each department, to use one of Mr. Lincoln's sayings concerning them, 'running its own machine,' with little or no attempt at harmony or cooperation. . . . There is no legitimate and regular method provided by which the Cabinet shall exert its influence as a whole, unless it be supposed that the annual message of the President furnishes such a channel of influence. But no one familiar with our public affairs for the past dozen years will pretend that the message has any such significance. . . ."[41] Cox recognized that giving congressional status to department heads would probably result in their selection from the two Houses; but this consequence he approved.

The proposal earned its most formal and weighty support in 1881 from a Senate committee containing such well-known names as George H. Pendleton, chairman, W. B. Allison, J. G. Blaine, John J. Ingalls, and O. H. Platt: predominantly the "Stalwart" wing of the Republican party.[42] The bill favored by the committee was in harmony with old Whig doctrine, much of which the Republicans had inherited. Beyond this antecedent, it was also useful in the struggle then at its zenith between Congress and the President and doubtless reflected the intent of the "old guard" to keep the latter in check. For some of the committee members it may also have represented an action to delay civil service reform.

The report recommended that department heads be entitled to occupy seats on the floor of the House and the Senate with the right to participate in debate on matters affecting their respective departments, and that they be required to attend twice a week to give information. The bill was defended on constitutional grounds and as a means of better cooperation between the departments and Congress. Possible consequences upon the executive branch were not overlooked but were minimized.

It has been objected that the introduction of the heads of departments on the floor would impair the influence of the executive power; that it would bring them and Congress in closer relations and thus lessen their dependence on the President, and, to that extent, deprive him of his constitutional power and relieve him of his constitutional responsibility.

[41] Jacob D. Cox, "Civil-Service Reform," *North American Review*, CXII (1871), 112-13.
[42] Senate Report 837, 46th Cong., 3d sess. (Feb. 4, 1881).

It would be enough to say, in answer to this objection, that no power exists anywhere to diminish the duties or powers or responsibilities imposed by the Constitution upon the President. The committee ventures again to repeat that the effect of the bill does not seek to—and will not—aggrandize or impair the executive power as defined in the Constitution and vested in the President.[43]

This venture, like its predecessors, came to naught, and little was heard of the plan for many years. It was nevertheless to find intelligent support in a later era.

So far as has been noted, no President expressed an opinion on this modification of the executive branch, whether from indifference or prudence it is impossible to say. Garfield's endorsement came while he was in the House. It would be curious to know what were his views when he became President. In any event, either a single term or Cabinet seats in Congress would have upset the balance of power and, of special relevance here, would have weakened the President's effective participation in departmental business by increasing the authority of Congress and its committees. Constitutional status and operating control are not necessarily identical.

These were not years of institutional change in the relation of Presidents to the administrative system. Patterns of relationship and responsibility had been well set initially by the Federalists, confirmed by the Jeffersonians, and corroborated by the Jacksonians. The contrast with the three decades that opened in 1901 was startling. The position of the Chief Executive vis-à-vis administration in 1930 was something far different from that which prevailed from the Civil War to the close of the century.

Except for the new responsibility of the Chief Executive for the civil service, Presidents took the administrative system as it had developed by law, by departmental regulation, and by custom. They were at the head of the machine, but the machine had power of self-propulsion and power to preserve its own shape and motion. The established course of the public business went on its appointed way, for the most part without requiring or inviting the collaboration of the man who sat in the White House.

[43] *Ibid.*, pp. 6-7.

CHAPTER SIX

The Treasury Department

In a period when the major political problems were also financial in their bearing, the Treasury was inevitably the most important among its sister agencies. The intrinsic nature of its normal functions, quite apart from the great issues of resumption of specie payment, management of the huge war debt, currency policy, and the controversial question of the tariff, was enough to guarantee its primacy during years in which foreign relations were relatively quiescent. The status of the Treasury was also emphasized because of its size and the importance of its staff for purposes of patronage. In 1873 its total employment numbered just over 4,000.[1] In the days of Secretary Lyman J. Gage, McKinley's head of the Treasury Department, the force numbered more than 24,000.[2]

The leadership role of the Treasury was the theme of Henry Adams in 1870. Writing in the *North American Review* he declared:

The official importance of the Secretary of the Treasury can hardly be over-estimated. Not only is his mere political power in the exercise of patronage far greater than that of any other cabinet officer, but in matters of policy almost every conceivable proposition of foreign or domestic interest sooner or later involves financial considerations and requires an opinion from a financial stand-point. Hence in the English system the head of administration commonly occupies the post of premier lord of the Treasury. In the American form of government the head of the Treasury is also the post of real authority, rivalling that of the President itself, and almost too powerful for harmony or subordination. . . .[3]

[1] Figure derived from the *United States Treasury Register*, 1873, pp. 205-48.
[2] Lyman J. Gage, *Memoirs*, p. 108.
[3] Henry Brooks Adams, "The Session," *North American Review*, CXI (1870), 35.

However accurate this analysis, and with full recognition of the importance of the Treasury portfolio, Adams overestimated its weight. No Secretary challenged the President; all remained in harmony with the fiscal policy which, to be sure, emanated from Treasury circles but had to be validated by the approval of the Chief Executive. Cleveland made his own fiscal policy; his Secretaries followed his lead.

Throughout this period, also, the Treasury was something less than a finance ministry, in that (1) it did not control the estimates, and (2) it did not inspect the course of agency administration, although it did audit and settle agency expenditures. The difference is important. In one case, the Treasury serves as a central agency of administration with authority to require explanations of official inadequacy, laxness, or waste; in the other, regularity of fiscal papers is the primary consideration. Treasury in fact had no more standing in the administration of the Interior Department than Interior had in the collection of the revenue.

The roll of Secretaries of the Treasury contained the names of a few outstanding men, but they and their less distinguished colleagues were almost completely absorbed in fiscal rather than administrative problems. From 1869 to 1901 there were fourteen Secretaries, one of whom (William Windom) served twice. The best known was John Sherman, who held office under Hayes from 1877 to 1881, and whose long membership in the U.S. Senate and activity in the affairs of the Republican party made his name memorable to his generation. Sherman and John G. Carlisle, Cleveland's Treasury chief during his second term, three times Speaker of the House, fall in the category of outstanding political leaders.

Two Secretaries were more or less professionally bred to their task: Charles S. Fairchild, trained in law and one-time attorney general of the state of New York, who acted as Assistant Secretary of the Treasury under Cleveland from 1885 to 1887 and as Secretary from 1887 to 1889; and Lyman J. Gage, a banker by profession and, at the time of his appointment by McKinley, president of the First National Bank of Chicago and one-time president of the American Bankers Association.

Of the other Secretaries it may be stated that they had been politically active both in state and national affairs, attaining recognition within the party if not full stature as leaders in public affairs. Grant's second Treasury head, William A. Richardson, left his post under a cloud, a matter reported elsewhere. His able successor, Benjamin H. Bristow, was practically forced out of the Treasury by the hostility of the President arising from Bristow's prosecution of the Whiskey Ring. This episode is also dealt with elsewhere. In short, important though the Treasury was, whether from the point of view of politics and patronage, finance, or the public economy, its head posed no threat to the Chief Executive.

TREASURY ORGANIZATION

Treasury, like its sister departments, enjoyed a relatively stable internal organization in the period under review. There was substantially no discussion of change except in the auditing offices, which were reorganized in 1894.[4]

The essential feature of this enactment was to substitute the system of single auditing for the double audit that had been introduced by Alexander Hamilton. Under this historic system accounts were first examined by an auditor and then submitted for settlement to either the first or second comptroller. The act of 1894 placed the final settlement in the auditors' offices, but with an appeal to the comptroller. His function became principally one to determine the construction of statutes. As a part of the reorganization the office of second comptroller was abolished, leaving all appeals to go to a single authority. The technical aspects of the audit and settlement of accounts were not modified by this legislation.

A second aspect of Treasury organization concerned the range and depth of senatorial confirmation of Treasury executives. Congress was unusually exacting in requiring the advice and consent of the Senate not only for top-level officials but for some occupying quite subordinate posts.

It would be expected that the Senate would confirm such appointments as that of the Assistant Secretary of the Treasury, and it was

---

[4] 28 Stat. 162 at 205-11 (July 31, 1894). The accounting system had been so regulated as to minimize the possibility of loss. Secretary John Sherman reported in 1879 that "the financial transactions of the Government during the past two years, aggregating $3,354,345.53, have been adjusted without question, with the exception of a few small balances now in the process of collection, of which it is believed the Government will eventually lose less than $13,000. . . ." Secretary of the Treasury, *Annual Report*, 1879, p. xliv.

traditional that confirmation was required for the collectors of customs and the collectors of internal revenue. Comptrollers and auditors had also always been subject to confirmation although, prior to 1885, these positions had not been affected by partisan removal. Congress went beyond these limits to require confirmation also of deputy comptrollers and deputy auditors who, in a later period, would have fallen into a class often exempt from Senate action. The Commissioner of Customs functioned as a comptroller and fell under the rule that required confirmation. The Commissioner of Internal Revenue was, however, primarily an administrative officer but, with the Comptroller of the Currency and the register, had to pass Senate scrutiny and approval.

More surprising was the necessity for Senate confirmation of distinctly subordinate officers in various branches of the Treasury. Thus the superintendents of the local mints, the melters, the coiners, and assayers had to be approved by the upper House. In the customhouses the assistant collector, the general appraisers, appraisers, and assistant appraisers, and the special examiners of drugs, medicines, and chemicals fell under the same rule. Officers in the Revenue Marine Service and the supervising inspectors of steam vessels likewise required Senate confirmation. The list is not complete, but it suggests that the Senate intended to keep an eye on Treasury personnel to a somewhat exceptional degree. The consequences attendant upon a change of administration were to destroy continuity at levels where stability would have seemed desirable.

The long years of Republican supremacy (1861–1885) had tended to stabilize the directing personnel of the Treasury Department, notably in the auditing services. This situation was abruptly altered with Democratic success in 1885, followed by a Republican President in 1889, and a second Democratic administration in 1893. Given the general tradition of officeholding as it existed in the post-Civil War period, it was perhaps too much to expect continuity even among the comptrollers and auditors. In any event, massive changes occurred in 1885, in 1889, in 1893, and in 1897.[5] The office of first comptroller was promptly vacated when Cleveland became President; his nominee

[5] Data from the *Official Register of the United States*. In 1885 the incoming Democratic Secretary of the Interior, Lucius Q. C. Lamar, promptly removed every bureau chief in his organization. Edward Mayes, *Lucius Q. C. Lamar*, pp. 473-74.

was as promptly replaced by Harrison. The same fate successively befell the second comptroller. These were the officials who directed and controlled the whole auditing system.

There were during these years six auditors, each the head of a considerable office. None of the six survived the Democratic transition in 1885, and none of the Democratic appointees survived the return of the Republicans in 1889.

Both comptrollers and auditors were assisted by deputies, second in rank, and even more normally associated with the concept of permanent tenure. The incoming Democratic administration in 1885 replaced both the first and second deputy comptrollers; the new Republican administration in 1889 replaced one and continued the other.

The day-by-day business of the comptrollers' and auditors' staffs was directed by division chiefs, four or more in each auditor's office. They too were swept out of office in 1885, and their successors again replaced in 1889. There were four division chiefs serving the first comptroller; all went early in the Cleveland administration, and these incumbents in turn were dismissed by the Republicans in 1889. The process of change was somewhat less precipitous in the auditors' offices, but a two-year period was enough to make substantially a clean sweep of these division chiefs as well.

An occasional division chief, such as Alexander F. McMillan in the first auditor's office, escaped these storms, but such cases were rare. Occasionally, too, a division chief would be demoted rather than discharged, and with another turn of the political wheel would reappear in his former office. These cases also were infrequent. Officials at such levels did not then enjoy the protection of the civil service system, and the old tradition of stability in the accounting offices simply disappeared. Republican ascendancy after 1897 and the extension of civil service rules eventually restored the practice that had normally prevailed down to 1885.

TREASURY FUNCTIONS

Most of the central functions of the Treasury were inaugurated in the earliest years of the Republic. They included the collection of the revenue, the audit and settlement of accounts, the management of the debt, and the coinage of money. In 1863 the national bank system was established and, under the immediate direction of the Comptroller of the Currency, the Treasury acquired the new duty of regulating the supply of paper currency and of supervising the national banks.[6]

The Treasury also possessed the important dependent function of supervising shipping and navigation, a duty growing out of the collection of the customs. These related activities included the registration of vessels and their entry and clearance; the maintenance of the Lighthouse Service; the operation of the Revenue Marine Service; the direction of the Steamboat Inspection Service and of the Lifesaving Service. In 1891 it acquired the administration of the immigration laws.[7]

There was thus a recognizable unity in Treasury functions, despite its responsibility for a few marginal activities such as the Marine Hospital Service and the Office of the Supervising Architect. The variety of Treasury activities in 1900 was not far different from those of 1870.

During the 1880's (and indeed earlier) a characteristic controversy developed between the Treasury and the Navy Departments over some of the dependent Treasury activities, notably the old Revenue Cutter Service, known during most of this period as the Revenue Marine Service. The Treasury had possession, the Navy coveted ownership. The story is sufficiently illustrative of a common administrative dilemma to deserve brief rehearsal.[8]

There had been intermittent consideration of the best administrative home for the Revenue Marine Service almost since its establishment. The Treasury acquired it before there was a Navy Department, and in later years the Navy implied that this was the only reason for its original assignment. For about ten years, terminating in 1832, the ships were manned by naval officers while remaining subject to Treasury administration.[9] This dualism worked badly.

The issue was reopened by Secretary of the Navy William E.

---

[6] 12 Stat. 665 (Feb. 25, 1863).

[7] 26 Stat. 1084, sec. 7 (March 3, 1891).

[8] A full account of the course of events, with reprint of the principal documents, is available in a report of the Commission on Economy and Efficiency (April 4, 1912), House Doc. 670, 62d Cong., 2d sess., pp. 269-397. References are to this report.

[9] "Revenue-Cutter Service of the Department of the Treasury," in Report of Commission on Economy and Efficiency, p. 300.

Chandler in 1882.[10] To assess the course of the argument it will be useful to note the salient facts about the organization and functions of the Service. In 1881 it was immediately under the direction of the Revenue Marine Division in the office of the Secretary of the Treasury, a small unit including a chief, assistant chief, and some ten clerks, all subject to appointment by the Secretary. In the Service, there were 198 commissioned officers and about 800 petty officers and seamen. Each of the thirty-six revenue vessels was placed under the superintendence of a collector of customs. The vessels were stationed along the whole stretch of the Atlantic and Pacific coasts and in Alaska. They were small ships, mostly steam propelled and armed with cannon. The crews carried sidearms and cutlasses.[11]

The functions of the Revenue Marine Service were varied. Its prime duty was to ensure the security of the customs revenue. In addition the Service enforced the laws governing merchant vessels, assisted vessels in distress, suppressed mutinies on merchant vessels (which were said to be frequent), reported disarrangements of aids to navigation, and enforced quarantine, the immigration laws, and the neutrality laws. In Alaska it protected the seal fisheries.[12]

The Service was apparently in good condition during the 1880's. Incompetent personnel had been purged early in Grant's administration[13] and recruitment of the officer corps had been put on a competitive basis in 1876.[14] Entrance was confined to young men who earned places in the lowest grade by competitive examination and who were assigned to a year's training duty on a sailing vessel stationed at New Bedford, Massachusetts. The number of cadets was about a dozen.[15]

Secretary Chandler opened the attack designed to transfer the Service to the Navy Department under the impulse of a crisis affecting the Annapolis cadets, more of whom were being graduated than could be absorbed in the Navy. Congress had directed that the excess be

---

[10] *Ibid.*, p. 304.

[11] *Ibid.*, pp. 314-16.

[12] *Ibid.*, p. 316.

[13] Secretary of the Treasury, *Annual Report*, 1870, pp. xi-xii. Nearly one-fourth of the officer personnel was discharged.

[14] 19 Stat. 102 at 107 (July 31, 1876).

[15] Report on "Revenue-Cutter Service" by Commission on Economy and Efficiency, p. 318.

given a year's pay and remanded to private life. The Navy deplored this loss of personnel and sought the Revenue Marine Service as a means for their employment. Secretary Chandler buttressed his case by asserting that the duties of the vessels of the Revenue Marine Service were much the same as those of naval vessels, that the revenue cutters were strictly naval in essence, and that there was an evident absurdity in maintaining a Naval Academy and a small duplicate thereof for training Revenue Marine officers at New Bedford. He proposed to safeguard the rights and privileges of the Revenue Marine Corps.[16]

Chief Ezra W. Clark of the Revenue Marine Division made a stinging reply to Chandler's suggestion.[17] He declared that the functions of the Service were not comparable to those of the Navy, any more than one land service resembled another. He remarked that an annual appointment list in the Revenue Marine Corps of four to six would not afford appreciable relief to the "nearly nine hundred clamorous idlers" among the Annapolis cadets.[18] He argued that the Revenue Marine Service was a national constabulary, not a naval force. He did not hesitate to touch on prejudice against the naval "aristocracy." Popular opinion, Clark declared, was adverse to the interference of the military arm in civil administration in time of peace.[19] "Is it true that we are asked to build up an aristocracy of naval officers in our Country? . . . are the people to be now laid under still further tribute for the benefit of the favored naval officers, and even the civil force displaced in order to afford them continuous tenure?"[20] Finally, the Navy was accused (with some justice) of gross neglect in the management of its own affairs; in a pungent phrase the Navy was called "a floating mass of incompetency."[21]

Although Secretary Chandler renewed his recommendation in 1883, the attempt failed. Secretary Benjamin Tracy tried again in 1889,[22] this time with the assent of Secretary of the Treasury William Windom, the support of the large majority of the Revenue

[16] *Ibid.*, pp. 304-305.
[17] *Ibid.*, pp. 325-36. Letter of Jan. 27, 1883.
[18] *Ibid.*, p. 333.
[19] *Ibid.*, p. 329.
[20] *Ibid.*, p. 330.
[21] *Ibid.*, p. 331.
[22] *Ibid.*, p. 337.

Marine Corps, and a favorable vote in the House. The measure was lost in the Senate. The period closed as it had opened with Treasury in possession.[23]

Among the customs districts that of New York held first place, collecting more revenue than all the other ports of entry combined. The collector of the port of New York was remunerated on a scale exceeding that of the Secretary of the Treasury.[24] The position was, moreover, of high political importance and at times was fought over by contending factions in New York politics. The competence and integrity of the office were criticized freely after the Civil War, and by 1877 complaints reached such a pitch that Hayes appointed a commission, headed by John Jay, to investigate its affairs. At the same time other citizen commissions were instituted to investigate the customhouses at Philadelphia, New Orleans, and San Francisco. Their reports revealed a sorry condition of maladministration, laxness, and corruption, notably in New York.[25]

The Jay Commission disclosed irregularities among the inspectors, weighers and gaugers, samplers, and appraisers, men who dealt with enormous values; and the complaint was rife that the maladministration of the customs service had burdened the merchants, driven trade from New York to other ports, and caused honorable businessmen to abandon some lines of trade because they could not compete with less scrupulous rivals acting in collusion with dishonest officials.[26] Lack of the qualities of intelligence, fairness, experience, exactitude, and promptness, declared the commission, bore heavily upon honest importers.[27] In a remarkably frank passage in his annual report for 1874, Commissioner of Customs Henry C. Johnson confirmed the later findings of the Jay Commission.

[23] *Ibid.*, p. 349.

[24] From 1871 to 1874, Collector Chester A. Arthur had an official income of about $40,000, largely from moieties on collected fines. In 1874 the office was put on a fixed salary basis at $12,000 a year. George F. Howe, *Chester A. Arthur,* p. 49.

[25] For an earlier investigation of the New York customhouse revealing large-scale political favoritism to the firm of Leet and Stocking, see Senate Report 227, 42d Cong., 2d sess. (June 4, 1872).

[26] Reports of Commissions to Examine Certain Custom Houses, House Ex. Doc. 8, 45th Cong., 1st sess. (Oct. 25, 1877), p. 39.

[27] *Ibid.*, p. 50.

. . . . The mercantile community came to regard the customs-service rather as an agency of personal profit to those who obtained admission into it than as a part of the machinery of a popular government for collecting the revenue necessary to its support, and to look upon the customs officer rather as a parasite, unlawfully living upon themselves, than as a public servant in honorable service.

. . . a large, intelligent, and public-spirited class of citizens had, to a lamentable degree, come to look upon their Government as alien in interest and hostile in feeling to themselves.[28]

Jay and his associates found that a part of the force was deficient in proper attention to business as well as in commercial qualifications and integrity of character; that a few were employed more or less in private business to the detriment of the service; and that some were fraudulently accepting money for duties rendered in their official capacity.[29] A large number of complaints bore upon inefficiency, neglect of duty, inebriety, improper conduct, and some were for want of integrity and for accepting bribes. The heads of customhouse departments declared that "men were sent to them without brains enough to do the work, and that some of those appointed to perform the delicate duties of the appraiser's office, requiring the special qualities of an expert, were better fitted to hoe and to plow."[30]

The law against the offer of gratuities to customhouse employees was specific and mandatory.[31] It was habitually disregarded, and apparently some of the subordinate personnel deliberately evaded their duties until a private fee had been paid. The Jay Commission reported:

This law, as it was frankly admitted, has become a dead letter, and the surveyor testified that he had known no prosecutions under it. The disregard by merchants and their clerks and by custom-house brokers of the provisions against outside fees . . . has resulted in the virtual ignoring of the act by custom-house officials, who have enlarged their salaries by the addition of irregular fees, emoluments, gratuities, and perquisites; has demoralized the service, and has given persons employed as agents the opportunity of exacting from merchants fees which they pretend to have paid to officials.

[28] Secretary of the Treasury, *Annual Report*, 1874, p. 222.
[29] House Ex. Doc. 8, 45th Cong., 1st sess., p. 15.
[30] *Ibid.*, p. 38.
[31] Revised Statutes 5452.

The evidence, however, showed that the fees actually paid amounted to large sums in addition to the salaries.[32]

Idleness was endemic. The commission found that the larger number of weighers (salary $2,500 a year) rendered little service to the government; that the weighers' foremen ($1,200 a year) did little but assign their own duties to subordinates; that the work of the weighers' clerks was delegated to men hired as laborers, and that even they had not much to do, so great was their number.[33] Overemployment was common: persons designated as laborers were assigned to useless duty as janitors; as many as ten laborers were assigned to a scale when no more than four could be used; and some were carried on the payrolls who performed no service except to sign their names and receive their pay.[34]

The Jay Commission had no difficulty in identifying the underlying cause of these conditions. It was patronage. "Under the existing system, the incumbents of office in the customs service, however high, responsible, or difficult may be the duties, requiring often the skill and experience of experts, are appointed generally at the request of politicians and political associations in this and other States, with little or no examination into the fitness of the appointees beyond the recommendations of their friends."[35] The commission significantly added: "the recognition of a partisan power outside of the Government, divided among irresponsible leaders claiming the right to dispose of the offices of the customs as the spoils of party, assumes a national magnitude and importance."[36]

Patronage appointments were found also to be the curse of the Philadelphia and New Orleans customhouses. The appraiser at Philadelphia had protected a few of his key assistants; the others were appointed on recommendation of the politically powerful. "In case of a vacancy belonging to a particular Congressman's district, the matter would be referred to him to nominate somebody. This has been the rule, and the member of Congress would feel it an offense if he was not allowed to fill the vacancy."[37]

[32] House Ex. Doc. 8, 45th Cong., 1st sess., pp. 38-39.
[33] *Ibid.*, pp. 50-51.
[34] *Ibid.*, p. 51.
[35] *Ibid.*, p. 15.
[36] *Ibid.*, p. 16.
[37] *Ibid.*, pp. 86-87.

The general course of business at the Philadelphia customhouse under the Grant administration was found to be on a level comparable with that of New York. The evils were recapitulated:

. . . as practices of taking the time of the Government for private business; of receiving presents of wines, &c., from the officers or agents of steamship lines, and permitting such articles to be landed without permit and payment of duty; of drinking in the appraiser's sample-room, and of permitting the appropriation of samples by employes; also the practices of delegating the appointing power and of making appointments, on political grounds, without sufficient assurance of the character and capacity of the appointee; of irregular examination and delivery of packages, not being samples; of granting free permits for dutiable goods; and, finally, the tendency of superior officers to neglect that personal supervision of the work which is their chief duty, and to delegate their personal functions to subordinates, and the tendency of subordinates to abuse such authority.[38]

The New Orleans commissioners of inquiry declared that "in the past a large proportion of the appointments have been made from political considerations only, and such appointments have undoubtedly in many cases been detrimental to the service. . . ."[39]

The San Francisco customhouse had apparently escaped the worst consequences of the general trend toward demoralization,[40] and no evidence was presented relating to the ports of Boston, Portland, Charleston, and lesser offices. We may surmise that customhouse appointments generally were political in nature, but it would be un-

[38] *Ibid.* pp. 98-99. The Philadelphia commission also criticized the practice of a flat pay rate for all employees in a given classification, irrespective of length of experience or ability. "The grocer or mechanic who may have secured the position of examiner of silks, laces, or fancy goods, starts with the same salary which is given to an expert of twenty years' service." "The great fault is, that there is no inducement for an appointee to perfect himself in his duties. In fact, there would seem to be nothing better adapted to encourage mediocrity and repress all zeal for improvement than the present system." *Ibid.*, p. 92.

[39] *Ibid.*, p. 107.

[40] ". . . the testimony of officials, merchants, and others, goes to show that the business is conducted honestly, promptly, and faithfully; nor has the commission . . . been able to obtain any evidence which would justify the belief that any of the officers connected with that department [appraisers] are amenable to the charge of dishonesty, incompetency, or neglect of duty." *Ibid.*, p. 131.

safe to infer that the depth of maladministration and the corruption revealed in New York were characteristic of the customs service in the smaller ports.

The Jay Commission roundly condemned the patronage system and its consequences.

> The commission . . . pronounce this manner of appointment to be unsound in principle, dangerous in practice, demoralizing in its influence on all connected with the customs service, and calculated to encourage and perpetuate the official ignorance, inefficiency, and corruption which, perverting the powers of Government to personal and party ends, have burdened the country with debt and taxes, and assisted to prostrate the trade and industry of the nation. The commission believe that there can be no adequate protection in the customs service for the honor of the Government, the rights of importers, and the interests of the nation, until the service is freed from the control of party, and organized on a strictly business basis, with the same guarantees for efficiency and fidelity in the selection of the chief and subordinate officers that would be required by a prudent merchant.[41]

President Hayes concurred in this view and wrote Secretary Sherman that he wanted the collection of revenues freed from partisan control and organized on a strictly business basis. The vexed practical problem of how to break the patronage system was, however, left unsolved. "Party leaders," declared Hayes, "should have no more influence in appointments than other equally respectable citizens," and he added his opposition to party assessments and party work.[42] Sherman wrote a carefully phrased and guarded letter to the New York collector, recommending "in proper cases" an examination to test the qualifications of applicants, advocating the employment of only one member of a family, and using these words in relation to the crucial problem: "The President properly lays great stress on excluding from a purely business office active participation in party politics. Naturally, in a government like ours, other things being equal, those will be preferred who sympathize with the party in power; but persons in office ought not to be expected to serve their party to the neglect of official duty. . . . If any have been appointed for purely

[41] *Ibid.*, p. 15.
[42] *Ibid.*, p. 17 (May 26, 1877).

political reasons, without regard to their efficiency, now is a good time to get rid of them."[43]

The collector of the port of New York was Chester A. Arthur; the political machine in control of the appointments was that of Senator Roscoe Conkling. Hayes recognized that letterwriting was not the cure for the demoralization of the New York customhouse and, as already recorded, first offered Arthur a chance to resign and then boldly challenged the New York Republican machine by his removal. Control of the customhouse thus passed to the Treasury Department.

Victory was precarious, however, until the patronage system was curtailed by the Civil Service Act of 1883. Its first application included the large customhouses. Suitable standards of qualification for the subordinate positions were quickly established; appointment ceased to be a perquisite of the local machine and its congressional members; tenure was substantially assured. Many years passed, however, before the customs clerks were freed from the practical necessity of making campaign contributions in the form of an assessment of their salaries. The collector of customs remained a major political appointment and a powerful political magnate.

THE MOIETIES PROBLEM

From the inception of the system of customs collection in 1789, Congress had authorized payment of a portion of fines and forfeitures to informers and to the three principal customs officers. One half the amount recovered went to the Treasury, one quarter to the informer, and one quarter was divided among the collector, naval officer, and surveyor.[44] The object of these arrangements was to stimulate zeal in the discovery of concealment or fraud.

The higher the tariff, the greater the incentive to deception on the part of importers and to exertion to expose them on the part of informers. The high tariff acts passed during the Civil War were a case in point, and at the close of the war serious abuses in the moiety system became apparent. An early case involved a Boston importer of wines, who made a compromise settlement of $100,000. The informer

[43] *Ibid.*, p. 19 (May 28, 1877).
[44] 1 Stat. 29, sec. 38 (July 31, 1879).

in this case distributed a part of his share of $25,000 to the collector and to the naval officer.[45] The majority of the House Committee on Public Expenditures condemned the transaction: "Even if these gratuities were not made in satisfaction of, or expectation of, a special *quid pro quo* rendered, or to be rendered by these officers, still the principle involved in making presents to, or receiving the same by, men in office must be demoralizing."[46] The minority of the committee, however, thought the gift not wrong in private morals nor prohibited by law.[47]

In his able summary of this affair, R. Elberton Smith stated the inherent abuses involved in the moiety system. (1) It put a premium on the *detection* of fraud rather than its *prevention*; (2) it authorized indiscriminate seizure of books and "fishing expeditions" to obtain evidence of irregularities; (3) the compromise procedure had developed into a dangerous tool of extortion, with half the proceeds going into the pockets of government officers, some of whom might have had nothing to do with the cases involved; (4) the government failed to receive its proper share of the recoveries.[48]

Secretary of the Treasury George S. Boutwell condemned the whole system in his first annual report, in terms which could leave no doubt concerning the need for reform.

Under existing laws, certain revenue officers and other persons appearing as informers are entitled to shares in fines, penalties, and forfeitures. During the fiscal year 1868-'69 the Treasury Department distributed the sum of $286,073.61 to such officers and to informers in the various cases arising under the customs-revenue laws. A large additional sum was also paid through the Internal Revenue office. The reason on which the laws granting such allowances are based is that officers of the government are stimulated to greater activity in the discovery of frauds and in bringing offenders to punishment. There can be no doubt that such is the effect of the policy; but the experience I have had in the Treasury Department has convinced me that the evils attending the system are greater than the benefits derived from it. It often occurs that revenue officers are led to assert claims in behalf of the government which have no just foundation in law or in the facts of the respective cases; and where real claims exist

---

[45] House Report 15, 39th Cong., 2d sess., pp. 3-4 (Feb. 11, 1867).
[46] *Ibid.*, p. 4.
[47] *Ibid.*, p. 12.
[48] R. Elberton Smith, *Customs Valuation in the United States: a Study in Tariff Administration* (Chicago: University of Chicago Press, 1948), p. 111.

it is often the object of the informers and officers who share in the penalties to misrepresent the case to the department, so as to secure the greatest advantage to themselves. But a more serious evil is found in the practice, quite general, of allowing persons to pursue a fraudulent course until a result is reached which will inure to the benefit of the officers and informers, instead of checking criminal practices at the outset. It is impossible to set forth in exact language the character of the evils that grow out of the present system. I am, however, clearly of the opinion that the government ought to rely upon public officers for the proper performance of their duties without stimulating them by any contingent advantages. . . .[49]

The amounts realized by the lucky customs officers were great. Collector Arthur, as already noted, received about $40,000 a year. Special Treasury agent B. G. Jayne, stationed in New York, took in, over and above his salary, $316,700 as an informer in the four-year period 1870–73 inclusive.[50] Secretary Boutwell, in the passage reproduced in the preceding paragraph, reported an aggregate of nearly $300,000 moiety payments in a single year.

The issue came to a head in 1873 in the so-called Phelps–Dodge case, a firm that was one of the most reputable importers of iron and steel. A technical violation of the customs law involved forfeiture of imports whose total value was about $1,750,000. A compromise settlement for $271,017.23 was agreed upon, despite the fact that the actual undervaluation itself amounted to only $6,658.78 and the duties lost to the government reached only the negligible figure of $1,664.68. As Smith concluded, this was an enormous exaction for a minor violation resulting in an actual loss of duties of less than 1 per cent of the penalty.[51]

In the light of the Phelps–Dodge and other cases, public opinion crystallized in favor of the repeal of the moiety system.[52] The Anti-

---

[49] Secretary of the Treasury, *Annual Report*, 1869, p. vi; cf. the annual report of Commissioner of Customs Henry C. Johnson to the same effect in Secretary of the Treasury, *Annual Report*, 1874, p. 222.

[50] R. Elberton Smith, *Customs Valuation in the United States*, p. 112. Data compiled from report by Secretary of the Treasury on Fines, Penalties, and Forfeitures, House Ex. Doc. 124, 43d Cong., 1st sess. (1874). During the fiscal year 1870-71 the collector and surveyor of the port of New York each received from moieties $49,215.69 and the naval officer $48,195.59. Secretary of the Treasury, *Annual Report*, 1871, p. x.

[51] R. Elberton Smith, *op. cit.* p. 115.

[52] Evidence before the Committee on Ways and Means relative to Moieties and Customs-Revenue Laws, House Misc. Doc. 264, 43d Cong., 1st sess. (1874).

Moiety Act was passed June 22, 1874.[53] It repealed all laws giving any share of fines, penalties, or forfeitures to informers or customs officials, but provided a special fund of $100,000 from which the Secretary of the Treasury could make compensation to informers. Customs officers, however, retained the right to compensation for discovery of smuggling cases. Laws subjecting an entire invoice to confiscation for containing fraudulent items were repealed. Intent to defraud had to be found by a court or jury as a separate finding of fact prerequisite to forfeiture. "Fishing expeditions" were curtailed by requiring court order for the production of books and papers, and a three-year statute of limitation was placed on the commencement of suits.

The number of forfeitures declined rapidly after the passage of this act and some thought that it had gone too far. But the new system was not reversed. It was no longer public policy to depend upon the cupidity of customs officials to enforce the collection of customs.

THE PROBLEM OF UNIFORMITY OF CUSTOMS VALUATION

From time immemorial the collection of the customs has been burdened with a variety of technical considerations, the nature of which is beyond the scope of this work.[54] One, however, raised a universal problem of public administration, that of ensuring uniformity and consistency of action in a number of scattered field offices. For years the weakest point in the administration of the customs laws, apart from laxness and corruption in a few of the largest ports, had been the lack of uniformity in the appraisal of imports. There was an inherent tendency for one port to bid for the import trade against its competitors by valuations tender to the interests of importers. Beyond this, there was inadequate guarantee of uniformity even in a single port, especially in those handling a mass of business such as New York or Philadelphia.

The need of importers for some review of the valuation set by the original appraiser, both in the interest of correctness and uniformity, had long been recognized.[55] The first solution was to call in two

[53] 18 Stat. 186 (June 22, 1874).
[54] See John Dean Goss, *The History of the Tariff Administration in the United States* (New York: Columbia University, 1897), and R. Elberton Smith, *Customs Valuation in the United States.*
[55] Leonard D. White, *The Jacksonians*, pp. 178-81.

discreet and experienced merchants to make a judgment, and in case of their disagreement to require the collector to decide. It was a purely local procedure, useful in settling disputes between the importer and the customs officials, but bearing not at all on the problem of uniformity between ports. To solve this problem Congress authorized four general appraisers in 1851 to travel from port to port and in conjunction with one discreet and experienced merchant to report the true valuation in contested cases.[56] In case of disagreement the collector again had to decide, but this time with the benefit of counsel from a general appraiser familiar with rulings and practice elsewhere. The revised system produced good results but gradually became inadequate with the increasing volume of imports and complexities of tariff schedules.

Two major evils had arisen in the post-Civil War period: loss of revenue to the government by undervaluation, and unfair competition among merchants, the more disreputable of whom resorted to expedients that honorable importers repudiated. Secretary Daniel Manning commented on these matters in 1885. "A very little evasion in the payment of money which ought to go to the Government as duties may, in the strife of buying and selling imported staple articles, make the difference between a profit on one hand or a loss on the other, and may enable a successful evader of duties to outstrip and outsell all rivals in the same line of merchandise. It will be to the discredit of the Government if importers . . . shall be injured, or driven out of their business . . . because of the failure of Congress, or of the Executive, to make dutiable values, and to levy and collect duties, uniform at all places and for all persons throughout the United States."[57]

The system of partial dependence on discreet and experienced merchants was recognized during the 1880's to have outlived its usefulness. In his annual report for 1889 Secretary Windom wrote: "The system of appointing merchants to act as members of reappraising boards, although it may have worked satisfactorily in former years when the volume of importations was comparatively small, and importers owned the goods imported, and when disputes as to value

[56] 9 Stat. 629 (March 3, 1851).
[57] Report on Collection of Duties, Secretary of the Treasury, *Annual Report,* 1885, II, xxv.

were rare, has become, under present conditions, not only ineffective but productive of serious abuses, scandal, and contention, and is injurious alike to the revenue and legitimate trade."[58]

Congress struck out on new lines in the Customs Administrative Act of 1890.[59] The experienced and discreet merchant disappeared, and a Board of General Appraisers was established, consisting of nine men, three of whom were permanently stationed at New York. They were appointed by the President with Senate confirmation and were subject to removal by the President for inefficiency, neglect of duty, or malfeasance. They had original jurisdiction of all controversies over the proper classification of imports, and appeals for reappraisement. The latter cases were first heard by a single general appraiser, with an appeal to a board of three. Their decision was final so far as the administrative branch was concerned. Classification cases and questions of law were heard by a three-man board whose decisions were appealable to the federal courts.[60]

The new system was a success. The Secretary of the Treasury reported in 1891 that up to November first of that year the Board had received 2,107 appeals for reappraisement and had decided 2,051. A considerable body of classification controversies was cleared by judicial decision. The remainder were expected to be decided by January 1, 1892. "This showing," declared the Secretary, "gives assurance that the Customs Administrative Act has realized the purpose of its enactment and afforded what was imperatively demanded—a speedy, just and efficacious means for the settlement of differences between the Government and importers, both as to classifications and values."[61]

To complete the story of the search for uniformity, it is necessary to consider the matter of appeals to the courts. Such appeals had been traditionally authorized and were confirmed by the Customs Administrative Act of 1890. The result was numerous irreconcilable conflicts of interpretation as scores of federal judges handed down their decisions in different ports and judicial districts. The solution of this problem was found in the Payne-Aldrich Tariff Act of 1909, establishing the United States Court of Customs Appeals with ex-

---

[58] Secretary of the Treasury, *Annual Report*, 1889, pp. xxxvii-xxxviii.
[59] 26 Stat. 131 (June 10, 1890).
[60] *Ibid.*, secs. 12-15.
[61] Secretary of the Treasury, *Annual Report*, 1891, pp. xlii-xliii.

clusive jurisdiction to review decisions of the Board of General Appraisers.[62] Thus, after nearly a century and a quarter, a conclusive solution was reached to the problem of uniformity in customs valuations.

TREASURY PERSONNEL STANDARDS

The evidence already presented concerning the New York and other customhouses can leave no doubt that personnel standards at the beginning of this period were deplorably low in these field institutions. Although data are lacking, there is good reason to believe, however, that the smaller ports of entry were able to maintain higher levels among subordinate employees, and even in the large ports there was always a central corps of old-timers who knew customs law and procedure, and around whom swirled the flowing and ebbing tides of patronage.

Personnel standards in the Treasury departmental service in Washington stood in marked and happy contrast to those prevailing in some parts of the field. The evidence on this point is convincing, notably with respect to the auditing offices. In his annual report for 1869, Third Auditor Reader W. Clarke stated: "In closing this report I feel it to be my duty, and a pleasant one, to bear testimony to the general good character of the employés of this bureau. The ladies are prompt to duty, and attentive and industrious in its performance, and above reproach. The gentlemen are sober, moral, intelligent, and faithful, observant of all the rules prescribed for their government, earnest in their labor, with the closest application and the most perfect order."[63]

---

[62] 36 Stat. 11 at 105 (August 5, 1909).

[63] Secretary of the Treasury, *Annual Report*, 1869, p. 131. Cf. the remarks of the third auditor in 1870: "It is but just to say that the clerks in this Bureau have generally been attentive to their duties, correct in their deportment, and useful and diligent in the work assigned them. During the fiscal year ending June 30, 1870, the female copyists have copied and compared 28,986 pages of manuscript; copied 7,445 and compared 7,500 letters; indexed 34,712 names; registered 672 money differences and 4,154 property differences." *Ibid.*, 1870, p. 118. The fourth auditor corroborated these views: "It gives me pleasure to speak in terms of just and cordial commendation of the competent and gentlemanly clerks who compose this office. Their attention to their work, their accord with each other, their courtesy of deportment, and their dispatch of their duties, are worthy of high praise." *Ibid.*, 1870, p. 127.

As Hayes followed Grant, there were few replacements according to the testimony of Secretary John Sherman. "Most of the principal officers had been long in the service. But few changes were made by President Hayes or by myself, and only as vacancies occurred or as an incompetency was demonstrated."[64] In 1880 Sherman praised highly the quality of the departmental organization.

In closing his annual report the Secretary takes pleasure in bearing testimony to the general fidelity and ability of the officers and employés of this Department. As a rule they have by experience and attention to duty become almost indispensable to the public service. The larger portion of them have been in the Department more than ten years, and several have risen by their efficiency from the lowest-grade clerks to high positions. In some cases their duties are technical and difficult, requiring the utmost accuracy; in others, they must be trusted with great sums, where the slightest ground for suspicion would involve their ruin; in others, they must act judicially upon legal questions affecting large private and public interests, as to which their decisions are practically final. It is a just subject of congratulation that, during the last year, there has been among these officers no instance of fraud, defalcation, or gross neglect of duty. The Department is a well-organized and well-conducted business office, depending mainly for its success upon the integrity and fidelity of the heads of bureaus and chiefs of divisions. The Secretary has therefore deemed it both wise and just to retain and reward the services of tried and faithful officers and clerks.

During the last twenty years the business of this Department has been greatly increased, and its efficiency and stability greatly improved. This improvement is due to the continuance during that period of the same general policy, and the consequent absence of sweeping changes in the public service; to the fostering of merit by the retention and promotion of trained and capable men; and to the growth of the wholesome conviction in all quarters that training, no less than intelligence, is indispensable to good service. Great harm would come to the public interests should the fruits of this experience be lost, by whatever means the loss occurred. To protect not only the public service, but the people from such a disaster, the Secretary renews the recommendation made in a former report, that provisions be made for a tenure of office for a fixed period, for removal only for cause, and for some increase of pay for long and faithful service.[65]

[64] John Sherman, *Recollections of Forty Years*, I, 566.
[65] Secretary of the Treasury, *Annual Report*, 1880, p. xlviii.

This fortunate condition was consolidated by the Civil Service Act of 1883, which gave the departmental clerks the tenure that Sherman had recommended. The act came at a timely moment, since the Democratic party, excluded from control of the executive branch for over twenty years, was successful in the 1884 election and took office on March 4, 1885. The initial coverage of the act was small, but it did protect the central clerical forces.

The good effects of the Civil Service Act upon the subordinate personnel were certified by Secretary William Windom, who had served briefly under Garfield as head of the Treasury and who returned under Harrison to his old post. In his annual report for 1889. Windom wrote in these terms:

. . . . The beneficial influences of the civil-service law in its practical workings are clearly apparent. Having been at the head of the Department both before and after its adoption, I am able to judge by comparison of the two systems, and have no hesitation in pronouncing the present condition of affairs as preferable in all respects. Under the old plan appointments were usually made to please some one under political or other obligations to the appointee, and the question of fitness was not always the controlling one. The temptation to make removals, only to provide places for others, was always present and constantly being urged by strong influences, and this restless and feverish condition of departmental life did much to distract and disturb the even current of routine work. . . .[66]

The perennial problem of the Treasury and other departments was the inadequate pay scales allowed by Congress to officials and employees alike.[67] The situation was acute at the close of the Civil War, and remained unsatisfactory for years. In his annual report for 1869, the Comptroller of the Currency, Hiland R. Hulburd, echoed the opinions of his Treasury colleagues when he declared, referring to bank examiners: "The compensation allowed by law is totally insufficient to pay the right kind of men to undertake this duty. The labors of examiners are very severe, involving work by day and travel by night; while the rigid and careful scrutiny required to investigate

[66] *Ibid.*, 1889, p. cvi.
[67] On the general subject of conditions of government employment, see a caustic and telling communication by James Parton, "A Letter to the People of the United States upon their Conduct as an Employer," *North American Review*, CXLI (1885), 480-90.

fully the condition and accounts of the banks is wearying and exhausting."[68] The Commissioner of Customs confirmed this view. "Much inconvenience has been felt, and delay in business occasioned in this bureau by the frequent changing of its working force. The salaries paid to clerks of the first, second, and third classes are not such as men competent to perform the duties required of them here feel that they are entitled to, considering the great cost of living in this city. . . ."[69] The mere fact that hundreds of thousands were demanding such employment was not a controlling consideration, a matter that was cogently explained by the fifth auditor, Henry D. Barron.

. . . . In this view it is manifestly unwise to regulate the pay of clerks by the supply and demand. Persons press for places who are utterly unqualified to fill them, and this keeps up a seeming supply far beyond the demand. The young and middle-aged flock to Washington to obtain clerkships, intending to remain only temporarily, without knowledge of the disabilities attaching to Washington residence, or without much reference to the salaries, and with an over-estimate of the advantages to be enjoyed or the perquisites secured from a connection with the government. This state of things creates a constant tendency and in a measure tempts the employés of the departments to engage in other business, in connection with their public duties—in speculative schemes that unsettle their minds, in boarding-house keeping and other occupations that are annoying and troublesome, to a degree that impairs their usefulness to the government, and which is often the direct cause of scandal attaching to the service, and an efficient promoter of demoralization, bribery, gambling, and kindred evils. This ought not to be, and it is not for the interest or credit of the government that such a state of things should continue.[70]

The Treasury was suffering from the same handicap that later was to afflict the Department of Agriculture and other agencies requiring the services of professional and scientific personnel. It was losing too many of its most promising men. Salty Francis E. Spinner, Treasurer of the United States from 1861 to 1875, put the matter in forthright terms in his annual report for 1869. "Were it not for the fact," he wrote, "that this office is considered a sort of stepping stone, and a

[68] Secretary of the Treasury, *Annual Report*, 1869, p. 30.
[69] *Ibid.*, 1869, p. 73.
[70] *Ibid.*, 1869, pp. 149-50.

school from which young men may graduate, and become tellers, cashiers, and bankers, it would be next to impossible to procure the services of persons of the requisite honesty, competency, and industry to execute the responsible duties pertaining to it. It now turns out that when a young man becomes sufficiently educated to be really useful to the government, he seeks and obtains a more lucrative situation elsewhere. . . . The rule should be reversed. When men have become prominent in private life, for integrity, talents, competency, and industry, in counting-houses and banks, the government should be able, by the salaries that it would offer to persons with such qualifications, to draw them into the public service."[71] Generations were to pass before such an ideal was to approach the realm of the practical.

Treasury made substantial progress in the years from Grant through McKinley. The magnitude and complexity of its task alone compelled improvement, but its greatest boon was the extension of the merit system and tenure to the employees of the larger customhouses. The dramatic conquest of the New York customhouse by Hayes and Garfield had widespread repercussions; the Civil Service Act confirmed and strengthened Treasury control of its field offices.

The significant role played by Treasury during these years was fiscal and political rather than administrative. Its strictly administrative history was of interest, nevertheless, partly because Treasury was deeply involved in general issues such as the appointment and tenure of subordinate employees, partly because it had to solve in its special area other problems that in principle were recurrent, such as the payment of moieties or the means of securing uniformity of action. Treasury was not significant, however, by reason of any administrative supervision that it brought to bear on its sister departments.

[71] *Ibid.*, 1869, pp. 284-85.

CHAPTER SEVEN

The War Department

Both the War and Navy Departments suffered from a common problem: how to coordinate and control the professional bureaus, permanently manned by the officer corps, possessed of the tradition and art of their calling, each jealous of its sister bureaus and all skeptical of the practical value of a civilian Secretary. Complicating this central issue was confusion concerning both military and naval policy, neglect and distrust in Congress, scanty appropriations, and the deterioration that inevitably followed thirty years of peace and the absence of any visible enemy. The country was content in isolation and unwilling to spend money for an army and a navy without an urgent mission.

MILITARY POLICY

The military policy of Congress from 1865 to 1898 was to support an army at the minimum strength to fulfill its minimum missions. These were primarily to man the coast fortifications, maintain West Point, and fight the Indians.

The vast Civil War Army of over 1,000,000 was accordingly rapidly demobilized and the permanent peace establishment organized in 1866.[1] In 1869 all officer appointments and promotions in the line and staff were stopped pending further legislation, and enlistments were abandoned in order to reduce the number of regiments.[2] The peace establishment was fixed in 1874 at 2,161 commissioned officers and 25,000 enlisted men.[3] Agitation continued in favor of further re-

[1] 14 Stat. 332 (July 28, 1866).
[2] 15 Stat. 315, sec. 2 (March 3, 1869).
[3] 18 Stat. 72 (June 16, 1874).

duction, according to Garfield with serious impairment to the efficiency and morale of the army.[4] This figure, however, represented the authorized military force during most of the period under review;[5] actual strength was consistently less.

The duties of the army were uninspiring at best. Garrison life in the seacoast forts was monotonous but comfortable, and the city was near at hand. The forts were, however, neglected by Congress, and gradually became worthless for defense as heavier guns were mounted by foreign navies. Congress did not even implement its own policy. It had approved recommendations of an army board to mount 2,362 guns for seacoast defense, but barely 6 per cent were in position.[6] It was asserted in 1883 that not a single seaboard city could defend itself against a lone hostile ironclad ship.[7]

On the frontier the army was beset with hardships, privation, and danger. Life was often nasty, brutish, and short. The soldier plodded in small detachments across the seemingly endless western plains, sat in lonely and dangerous outposts through parching heat and arctic cold, surrounded in a vast prairie by thousands of Indians against whom he had to wage savage warfare. "And yet the awful marches and these heroic fights were the soldier's main dependence. He got away from the most provincial garrison life into which any government ever forced an army. Living in flimsy shacks, without the commonest conveniences found in the east, he froze in winter and stifled in summer."[8]

During the years from 1865 to 1901 there was a strong undercurrent of hostility to all things military, reminiscent of the old Republicans. It was Albert Gallatin who declared he wished never to see the face of a regular in an American city. Garfield noted this sentiment in

[4] James A. Garfield, "The Army of the United States," *North American Review*, CXXVI (1878), 197.

[5] For an able account of the War Department at the outbreak of the Civil War, see A. Howard Meneely, *The War Department, 1861* (New York: Columbia University Press, 1928).

[6] William Addleman Ganoe, *The History of the United States Army* (New York: D. Appleton and Co., 1924), p. 370.

[7] W. B. Franklin, "National Defense," *North American Review*, CXXXVII (1883), 599. Cf. Brigadier-General H. A. Smalley, "A Defenseless Sea-Board," *ibid.*, CXXXVIII (1884), 233-45.

[8] William A. Ganoe, *History of the United States Army*, p. 352. See also General Nelson A. Miles, *Serving the Republic* (New York: Harper and Brothers, 1911), chs. 6-12.

1878. "It is evident," he wrote, "that during the last three years there has been manifested in Congress a growing spirit of unfriendliness, if not of positive hostility, toward the army."[9] In the debate over the Civil Service Act, a contributor to the *North American Review* declared, "The regular army and the republic are traditional enemies. They antagonize each other at every point. The army, in its separation from the rest of the community, in its organic unity, in its power in arms and discipline, and in its subordination to the will of one man, has, when large, in every age, been a power greater than the state itself."[10]

A new force in American life, organized labor, also was hostile to the army, an attitude in part stemming from the use of federal troops in strike disorders. Samuel Gompers, president of the American Federation of Labor, declared in 1899: "Standing armies are always used to exercise tyranny over people, and are one of the prime causes of a rupture in a country."[11]

This attitude had not disappeared even after the close of the Spanish-American War. The Democratic party in 1900 thought it strong enough to warrant a resounding plank in the platform on which Bryan sought the presidency for the second time.

We oppose militarism. It means conquest abroad and intimidation and oppression at home. It means the strong arm which has ever been fatal to free institutions. It is what millions of our citizens have fled from in Europe. It will impose upon our peace loving people a large standing army and unnecessary burden of taxation, and will be a constant menace to their liberties. A small standing army and a well-disciplined state militia are amply sufficient in time of peace. This republic has no place for a vast military establishment, a sure forerunner of compulsory military service and conscription. When the nation is in danger the volunteer soldier is his country's best defender. The National Guard of the United States should ever be cherished in the patriotic hearts of a free people. Such organizations are ever an element of strength and safety. For the first time in our history, and coeval with the Philippine conquest, has there been a wholesale departure from our time honored and approved system of

[9] James A. Garfield, "The Army of the United States," *North American Review*, CXXVI (1878), 463.
[10] William Martin Dickson, "The New Political Machine," *ibid.*, CXXXIV (1882), 41.
[11] *American Federationist*, VI (1899), 40.

volunteer organization. We denounce it as un-American, un-Democratic, and un-Republican, and as a subversion of the ancient and fixed principles of a free people.[12]

An unpopular department, lacking a compelling purpose, facing an indifferent Congress, deprived of funds, and without an affirmative policy that could command public interest, was almost certain to deteriorate. The record of its *administrative* performance during the Spanish-American War showed clearly enough that it had deteriorated. Ganoe declared its machinery was clogged with the mold of thirty years.[13] Philip C. Jessup described the Department at the close of the war in equally pungent terms.

The Department which Root was asked to take over was a mess. The war had demonstrated its inefficiency and corruption. Its red tape was proverbial. Personal jealousies and spite crippled the efficiency of the personnel. Officers long entrenched in sinecures in Washington had been successful only in firmly establishing their political position with congressional and senatorial backers. Root's predecessor, General Russell A. Alger, was an honest but hopelessly incompetent person who did not even realize that he was officially and personally responsible for the many glaring errors and stupidities which in the Spanish War had characterized every aspect of the American army except the courage of individual soldiers and the intelligence of some officers when they were free to act unhampered by fatuous orders from Washington. . . .[14]

In short, American military policy was that of a country which seemed to have scanty need for an army, which in important sections feared an army, and which for three decades had done almost nothing to develop either the professional or the administrative foundations on which a powerful army could stand.

WAR DEPARTMENT LEADERSHIP

During the eight years of Grant's administration the War Department was directed and controlled by three generals, close personal friends of the President: John A. Rawlins, who had been his aide-de-

[12] Kirk H. Porter, compiler, *National Party Platforms* (New York: Macmillan Company, 1924), p. 213.
[13] William A. Ganoe, *History of the United States Army*, p. 371.
[14] Philip C. Jessup, *Elihu Root* (2 vols., New York: Dodd, Mead and Co., 1938), I, 220-21. Quotations reprinted by permission of the publisher, Dodd, Mead and Co.

camp, his principal staff officer, and his most intimate adviser; William T. Sherman, and William W. Belknap. Rawlins died after a few months and Sherman held this office for only a few weeks. It would have been well if Belknap's term had been equally brief, for he was eventually found to have sold appointments as post trader for his personal profit, was impeached after a last-minute resignation, and barely escaped conviction.

Belknap was the last of the generals to be Secretary of War. He was followed by an unbroken succession of lawyers and businessmen, most of whom were also active in politics. All were men of character and often outstanding ability. None had special qualifications, and none, until Elihu Root took office, left much of a mark on the Department. For them all, Woodrow Wilson's comment on Daniel S. Lamont would be relevant: "There can be no reasonable doubt about his ability to administer the War Department with success, as there would have been little doubt about his ability to occupy almost any other high administrative post with credit and efficiency. The only criticism which his appointment prompts is, that he was, so far as we are able to ascertain, no more fitted for the War Department than for any other. He is, in short, simply a very capable man of unusual executive talents. He has had no special training to be war minister."[15]

After Belknap's disgraceful exit, Judge Alphonso Taft (father of William Howard Taft) was a brief fill-in—three months in 1876 before he went to the office of Attorney General. Grant then turned to the powerful Pennsylvania Cameron family, appointing James D. Cameron, banker and railroad man, son of Senator Simon Cameron. Hayes declined to continue James; his father then resigned his seat in the Senate and the son was promptly elected to fill the vacancy. He became the head of the Pennsylvania Republican machine.

Hayes selected an able Iowa lawyer, active in Republican politics, George Washington McCrary; he served for two years and was succeeded by a Pennsylvania lawyer, Alexander Ramsey. He had moved to Minnesota, had been governor of both the territory and the state, and had served in the U.S. Senate from 1863 to 1875. Ramsey's biographer called him above all a man of practical sense and a shrewd

[15] Woodrow Wilson, "Mr. Cleveland's Cabinet," *Review of Reviews,* VII (1893), 291.

politician.[16] Garfield and Arthur turned to the son of President Lincoln, Robert Todd Lincoln, who was deeply engaged in law and business in Chicago. He became Secretary of War without enthusiasm and left little impress upon the Department.

President Cleveland found a new type, a wealthy New England patrician, William Crowninshield Endicott, a direct descendant of Governor John Endecott and a grandson of a famous Salem merchant, Jacob Crowninshield. Endicott succeeded in laying out a program of construction for coast defense, but Congress was laggard in voting the funds.

Big business interests furnished Harrison's two War Secretaries as well. Redfield Proctor, a graduate of Dartmouth College, was the center of the Vermont marble industry. He succeeded in making small improvements in departmental administration, but the great issue escaped him, as it had eluded his predecessors. His successor, Stephen B. Elkins, operated on a continental scale—banking in New Mexico, coal and railroads in West Virginia, finance in New York City. After leaving the War Department he went into the Senate from West Virginia and made his reputation in the field of railroad regulation. Cleveland's Secretary of War in his second term was the private secretary of his first term, Daniel S. Lamont. Lamont's start in life revolved around political clerkships in Albany where he acquired the wisdom that made him an invaluable political prompter to Cleveland in the campaign of 1884. He returned to public life reluctantly, having established a business connection with the former Secretary of the Navy, William C. Whitney. After four years Lamont returned to business and finance and to the accumulation of a huge fortune.

McKinley made an unhappy error in picking his first Secretary of War, Russell A. Alger, and a magnificent success in his second, Elihu Root. Alger had made a fortune in Michigan lumber, was active in Michigan politics, had been governor of his state and national commander of the Grand Army of the Republic. He had the misfortune to head the War Department during the Spanish-American War. The incompetence of the supply services of the Department and his own inadequacy for the crisis compelled McKinley to ask for his resignation at the close of hostilities. Belknap was the only Secretary who lacked personal integrity; Alger, the only Secretary who

[16] *Dictionary of American Biography*, XV, 342.

lacked personal competence. His successor, Elihu Root, was the greatest War Secretary since Calhoun. He divined the great administrative problem of the War Department and by insight, patient negotiation, and persistence succeeded in solving it.

THE GENERAL STAFF

The central administrative needs of the War Department were to end the friction between the Secretary of War and the Commanding General of the Army, to consolidate army leadership and eliminate the gulf between line and staff, and to provide a central planning agency responsible for defense and war plans and for professional advice to the Secretary of War. There was no dispute that the President was Commander in Chief of the army and the navy, and no confusion about the status of the Secretary of War as the civilian head of the War Department. There were differences of opinion from this point on.

The acknowledged functions of the Department toward the army were in the field of law and finance. What duties, if any, did the Department have with respect to military command? The Commanding General was clearly the source of military orders; but did he also control the special staff agencies, such as the Quartermaster General and the Ordnance department? The matter was in dispute, and the staff agencies actually fell into the orbit of the War Department.[17] These relations had been unsettled before the Civil War[18] and remained in the field of sometimes bitter controversy until Congress finally authorized the General Staff in 1903.

The line of demarcation between the Secretary of War and the Commanding General fluctuated from time to time, particularly with reference to their mutual relations to the so-called staff agencies. The Commanding General insisted that they were part of the army and should receive their orders exclusively from him. The Secretary of War often, and the staff officers generally, considered that these agencies were part of the War Department and could appropriately receive orders directly from the Secretary of War. The Commanding

---

[17] For the documentary record of these agenices, see Raphael P. Thian, compiler, *Legislative History of the General Staff of the Army of the United States . . . from 1775 to 1901* (Washington: Government Printing Office, 1901). These army units did not form a "general staff" in the present sense of the term.

[18] Leonard D. White, *The Jeffersonians*, pp. 240-45; *The Jacksonians*, pp. 190-96.

General asserted that such a line of authority usurped his own powers, but he was frequently overruled. In the 1850's personal hostility between General Winfield Scott and Secretary Jefferson Davis had added new complications to an already difficult problem.

Scott complained, by way of illustration, that upon order of the Secretary of War leaves of absence were granted, details for special service made, orders sent to the geographical departments for the establishment of posts and the movement of troops without his knowledge. He became so irritated that he moved his office out of Washington to Governor's Island in New York City.

For short periods after the Civil War both Grant and Sherman actually occupied simultaneously the offices of Secretary of War and General of the Army. This personal union temporarily resolved conflict but led to curious consequences. Referring to Grant's experience, his biographer wrote, "To preserve the line between his two offices, he followed the practice of issuing orders as Secretary of War from the War Department. Then, having sent the orders across the street to army headquarters by messenger, he trudged after them to obey the orders as General of the Army."[19]

This issue was brought to a head early in Grant's administration by a controversy between Belknap and Sherman. General Orders of March 8, 1869, designated William T. Sherman as General of the Army with a clear statement of relationships that fully safeguarded his position vis-à-vis the bureaus.

The chiefs of staff corps, departments, and bureaus will report to and act under the immediate orders of the general commanding the army.

Any official business which by law or regulation requires the action of the President or Secretary of War will be submitted by the General of the Army to the Secretary of War, and in general all orders from the President or Secretary of War to any portion of the army, line or staff, will be transmitted through the General of the Army.[20]

Sherman soon discovered "that the heads of several of the staff corps were restive under this new order of things, for by long usage they had grown to believe themselves not officers of the army in a technical sense, but a part of the War Department, the civil branch of the Government which connects the army with the President and

---

[19] William B. Hesseltine, *Ulysses S. Grant*, p. 97.
[20] *Memoirs of General William T. Sherman* (4th ed., 2 vols., New York: Charles L. Webster and Co., 1891), II, 441.

Congress."[21] Within less than a month, indeed, the power of the staff officers was reasserted. Secretary Rawlins rescinded the offending paragraphs and directed that all official business requiring the attention of the President or Secretary should be submitted by the chiefs of the staff corps, departments, and bureaus *to the Secretary of War*. Only orders and instructions relative to military operations were to be issued through the General of the Army.[22]

Sherman appealed to Grant, knowing that Grant had favored Sherman's attitude while he (Grant) was General in Chief. Grant avoided the issue, declaring members of Congress had advised him that his first orders were contrary to law and that Sherman and Rawlins should work out a *modus vivendi*. Before this transpired Rawlins died and Belknap succeeded him. In Sherman's language: "He took up the business where it was left off, and gradually fell into the current which led to the command of the army itself as [well as] of the legal and financial matters which properly pertain to the War Department. Orders granting leaves of absence to officers, transfers, discharges of soldiers for favor, and all the old abuses, which had embittered the life of General Scott in the days of Secretaries of War Marcy and Davis, were renewed."[23] Finally Belknap exceeded his authority by removing a post trader who was under Sherman's jurisdiction; Sherman revoked Belknap's order; Belknap induced Congress to transfer authority over post traders to his office, and then removed the controversial individual. Shortly thereafter Sherman took a trip to Europe and on his return, as Commanding General, he moved his headquarters to St. Louis.[24]

Belknap's precipitous resignation in 1876 reversed the situation. Secretary Taft and his two successors, Secretaries Cameron and McCrary, accepted the view that the duties of their office were primarily to advise the President on broad policy issues and, within the Department, to attend to matters of law and finance. Sherman returned to Washington, but the statutory foundations of high-level administrative relationships were not altered.

To understand the organizational faults which practically forced

---

[21] *Ibid.*, II, 441.
[22] *Ibid.*, II, 442 (March 27, 1869).
[23] *Ibid.*, II, 444.
[24] *Ibid.*, II, 454 (Sept. 3, 1874).

friction at the top level of the War Department, three factors must be borne in mind. (1) The rank of Commanding General was understood by many primarily as conferring a status for recognition, not of function. (2) The bureaus had been given much direct statutory authority by Congress which they assumed relieved them from supervision, entitled them to independence of the Commanding General, and suggested that they were attached to the War Department, not the army. (3) The bureaus played the political game to earn and maintain power in Congress. On this point Jessup remarks: "they . . . had acquired enormous political influence by the judicious advancement of cases in which Congressmen's constituents invoked the American panacea for all weak causes—'infloo-ence,' as Mr. Dooley called it."[25]

A Secretary of War was in a relatively weak position vis-à-vis the armed forces. During the period 1869–1901, the term of a Secretary usually did not exceed four years and was frequently less; after the Civil War, except for the two years 1882–84, there was no Assistant Secretary until 1890; and the Secretary had no personal civilian staff except clerks. To impose his will on an elaborate and custom-bound military organization in four years or less was consequently almost an impossible task.[26] He could resign himself to the conduct of the legal and financial business of the Department, leaving the army more or less to itself. He could seek to influence the course of military affairs either through the Commanding General or directly through the staff arms. If he turned to the Commanding General, whose position was determined by rank, he practically committed himself to an officer whom he had not selected and whom he could not remove or transfer.[27] More than one Secretary struggled with General Nelson

[25] Philip C. Jessup, *Elihu Root*, I, 227.

[26] According to President Hayes, the Chief Executive was in no better position than the Secretary of War. Writing to his friend William Henry Smith, he said: "One word more. The Army and the Navy are both sealed books to the President. In a few important matters I have turned over a leaf or two lately, and you see the rumpus it makes!" Rutherford B. Hayes, *Diary and Letters*, III, 634 (Jan. 3, 1881).

[27] General Alexander Macomb was at the head of the army for thirteen years, General Scott for twenty years, and General Miles for eight. ". . . it may be understood," said a contributor to the *Army and Navy Journal*, "why a civilian Secretary objects to turning over the entire affairs to the general of the Army who may not be in harmony or sympathy with the existing administration." *Ibid.*, XXIX, 806 (April 12, 1902).

A. Miles during the 1890's.[28] If he relied upon the staff, a Secretary had to try to master eight or ten entrenched bureaus whose collective mass of business was beyond the capacity of any one man to handle, particularly when deprived of personal aides of standing and competence.

The *de facto* ascendancy of the staff bureaus led to maladministration of army affairs despite the competence and zeal of the responsible officers. Lacking effective civilian or military coordination, they tended to go their respective ways without regard to the needs of the service as a whole. Jealousy and feuds developed as each staff bureau stoutly defended its own prerogatives.

Equally unfortunate was the gulf between staff and line. Assignment to the staff was highly prized since for many officers life in Washington was far pleasanter than in a remote post on the bleak and barren plains across the Mississippi. Moreover, a staff assignment was permanent. There is much testimony to the fact that the needs of the line were not adequately consulted by the staff or perhaps highly considered. Thus General Emory Upton in 1880 wrote: "The Ordnance, for example, manufactures our guns and carriages; the Engineers build the fortifications on which the guns are mounted, and both are turned over to the Army to be tested in war, without an opportunity having been given for the general in chief, or the officers who may die in their defense, to make the slightest suggestion."[29]

A bundle of problems was thus wrapped up in the overhead organization of the War Department and the army. One concerned the status and authority of the Commanding General vis-à-vis both the Secretary of War and the staff bureaus; another involved the need of the Secretary for unified professional advice on military problems and for means of effective control of the army hierachy; still another involved the coordination of the bureaus and a more helpful relation between them and the line.

The Spanish-American War documented these problems, and some army officers foresaw the pattern of their solution. Leadership in the reconstruction of War Department and army relationships,

[28] For an account of Alger's lack of confidence in General Miles, see Russell A. Alger, *The Spanish-American War*, pp. 48-61.

[29] Emory Upton, *The Military Policy of the United States* (1880, 2d impression, Washington: Government Printing Office, 1907), p. 159. For a biography of General Upton, see Peter S. Michie, *The Life and Letters of Emory Upton* (New York: D. Appleton and Co., 1885).

however, could only be taken at the highest level. It was assumed by Elihu Root, who, as he said to McKinley, knew nothing about the army and consented to become Secretary of War only because the President wanted an able lawyer to control affairs in the Philippines. Beginning in 1899, Root cautiously advanced the concept of a new kind of general staff, primarily concerned with war plans and strategy, and a new relationship between the Department, the army command, and the technical staff agencies.

Progress was slow. Stubbornly opposing change were General Nelson A. Miles, Commanding General of the Army, the technical staff bureaus, and many members of Congress who preferred to operate within the existing system. General Miles' performance was indeed extraordinary. Before the Senate Military Committee he praised the existing army system "organized by the genius of Washington, Steuben, Hamilton, and others," victorious in every war in which the army had been engaged. He condemned Root's plan as unsuited to a Republic and more fit for "the monarchies of the Old World." He declared: "The scheme is revolutionary, casts to the winds the lessons of experience, and abandons methods which successfully carried us through the most memorable epochs of our history."[30] By such an array of ignorance and cunning appeal to prejudice, Miles delayed reform.

The solution of the problems of the War Department centered on the establishment of the General Staff Corps, the office of Chief of Staff, and the subordination of the old so-called general staff bureaus to the Chief of Staff. The General Staff also filled a serious gap in military organization revealed in the Spanish-American War, viz., the absence of an effective planning and coordinating mechanism. Although the central idea was borrowed from German and French practices, it was adapted to American preferences and finally accepted by Congress, responding to the gifted leadership of Secretary Elihu Root.[31] The importance of the general staff concept in War Department and army administration can hardly be overestimated.

[30] March 2, 1902, in Senate Doc. 119, 68th Cong., 1st sess., p. 31.
[31] For a documented account of the debate over the establishment of the General Staff, see Major General William Harding Carter, *Creation of the American General Staff*, Senate Doc. 119, 68th Cong., 1st sess. (Jan. 22, 1924). Carter was one of Root's principal advisers. Secretary Root's most extended exposition of the general staff proposal is in *Annual Report of the War Department*, 1902, I, 42-49.

By the terms of the legislation enacted in 1903, a General Staff Corps was established to prepare plans for the national defense and for mobilization in time of war; to investigate and report upon all questions affecting the efficiency of the army; to render professional aid to the Secretary of War and to general officers; and to coordinate the various branches of the military service. The corps comprised the Chief of Staff and forty-four officers detailed from various ranks for a four-year tour of duty, at the close of which they returned to the line.[32]

The Chief of Staff was given supervision over all the troops of the line, and also (of primary importance) over the Adjutant General, the Inspector General, the Judge Advocate, the Quartermaster General, the Subsistence, Medical, Pay, and Ordnance departments, the Corps of Engineers, and the Signal Corps. Congress thus decisively terminated the pretensions of the bureaus, unified command of the army (staff and line), and provided a single responsible channel of communication between the Secretary of War and the army.[33] Congress sought to prevent isolation of the new General Staff Corps by requiring a four-year rotation of officers assigned to it, and by sending them back to their line assignments. The Secretary of War now acquired a responsible body of professional advisers in a position to consider the broad problems of power and strategy which had previously almost wholly escaped attention.

These changes were major innovations, and years of experience were needed to make them fully effective. They modernized the War Department and made unlikely a repetition of the confusion and incompetence that attended the brief war with Spain.

THE WAR WITH SPAIN

Amidst popular and newspaper clamor war had been declared with Spain as of April 21, 1898. The army had been able to make practically no preparations beyond strengthening the coast defense in view of President McKinley's policy of avoiding warlike provocation. It then

[32] 32 Stat. 830 (Feb. 14, 1903).
[33] The principal secondary work on the General Staff is by Major General Otto L. Nelson, Jr., *National Security and the General Staff* (Washington: Infantry Journal Press, 1946).

had an authorized strength of 2,143 officers and 26,040 men, most of whom were stationed on the western frontier. On April 23 the President called for 125,000 volunteers, and on May 25 for 75,000 more. Over a million men came forward.

Regulars and volunteers were concentrated in eastern camps and eventually transported from Tampa and other ports to Cuba. The city of Santiago capitulated on July 15, 1898, after the Spanish fleet had been annihilated; Dewey had already destroyed the Spanish fleet in the Pacific at Manila Bay on May 1; a detachment of the army proceeded to overrun Puerto Rico, and on August 12, 1898, the war came to an end after a brief course of little more than one hundred days. These were enough to exhibit appalling inadequacy in War Department administration despite the excellent record of the Corps of Engineers and the Ordnance department.

The President as Commander in Chief. President McKinley, like Polk and Lincoln, assumed active command. General strategy was settled at White House conferences. Daily sessions were held in the President's office at which the Secretaries of War and Navy, the Adjutant General, and others were present. "McKinley," wrote his biographer, "kept his finger upon every detail."[34] No orders of importance were issued from either the War or Navy Departments without his full knowledge and approval, and they were often revised by him. On great issues he did not hesitate to reverse the judgment of commanders in the field. Thus when General Shafter recommended acceptance of General Toral's first offer of conditional surrender at Santiago, McKinley telegraphed to him: "What you went to Santiago for was the Spanish army. If you allow it to evacuate with its arms you must meet it somewhere else. This is not war. If the Spanish commander desires to leave the city and its people, let him surrender and we will then discuss the question as to what shall be done with them."[35]

In the absence of any means to coordinate army and naval operations, the President had to act as the only authority who could harness the rival ambitions of the two branches of the armed forces. After the spectacular victories at Manila and off the harbor of Santiago the

[34] Charles S. Olcott, *Life of William McKinley*, II, 51.
[35] *Ibid.*, II, 50.

prestige of the navy was high; the army was still without the honors of success.[36]

The navy was in a relatively superior state of readiness, due in part to Assistant Secretary Roosevelt's energy, and it looked with some sense of superiority upon the struggles of the army. Secretary of the Navy John D. Long confided to his diary that there had been "an infinite amount of unpreparation in important details" of army readiness.[37] On May 6 Long put on record the willingness of the navy to convey a force to Cuba, and urged the War Department to move. Alger took offense and intimated that the War Department could take care of itself.[38] Alger was overoptimistic and later had to appeal for naval help. Long's diary suggests some complaisance on his part. The feeling between the two arms was less than cordial and at times uncooperative. A few examples will illustrate the point.

After Cervera's fleet had been destroyed, General Shafter urged that Admiral Sampson be ordered to enter Santiago harbor and bombard the city in order to minimize the loss of life incident to a land attack. Sampson was unwilling to risk his ships. The President was asked to make a decision, but he avoided outright orders. ". . . the President directs that you [Shafter] confer with Admiral Sampson at once for co-operation in taking Santiago. After the fullest exchange of views you will agree upon the time and manner of attack."[39] This telegram settled nothing. More than a week later the Secretary of War formally asked the Secretary of the Navy to order Sampson into Santiago Bay. In response Long cabled Sampson to confer with Shafter, "wishing to do all that is reasonably possible to insure the surrender of the enemy. I leave the matter to your discretion, except that the United States armored vessels must not be risked."[40] Santiago surrendered with the fleet off shore.

[36] There was also the lesser problem of mere communication between the two branches. On May 10, 1898, Secretary Long discovered to his utter amazement that the army planned to sail for Cuba the next morning, "and not a word has been said to me about furnishing a convoy." The President had to intervene to postpone the date of departure. John D. Long, *Journal* (Lawrence S. Mayo, ed.), p. 192.

[37] *Ibid.*, p. 201 (June 27, 1898).

[38] *Ibid.*, p. 188.

[39] Telegram of July 5, 1898, reprinted in R. A. Alger, *The Spanish-American War*, p. 234.

[40] *Ibid.*, p. 238.

To settle the controversy between the army and navy over possession of captured Spanish vessels in Santiago harbor required an opinion of the Attorney General and an order from the President. Secretary Alger directed General Shafter to hold the vessels, and an army guard was put on board. Admiral Sampson claimed possession, refused to recognize the authority of the Secretary of War, and asked for instructions from the Secretary of the Navy. The Attorney General ruled that the vessels were not subject to the laws regarding prizes, and Shafter was required to turn over the vessels to the navy. Later McKinley ordered Sampson to return five ships to the army for transport service.[41]

Another occasion requiring presidential orders involved the naval convoy of army transports from Cuba to Puerto Rico. McKinley ordered Sampson to give General Miles such assistance as they might jointly regard as necessary. Sampson was niggardly and procrastinating. Miles protested to Alger and McKinley handed a sharp note to Secretary Long. "It is evident . . . that Admiral Sampson is not proposing to furnish such assistance as I have heretofore directed. . . . It seems to me a cruiser or battleship, or both, should be detailed for this duty. Please see that the necessary orders are issued at once."[42] Sampson was preparing an expedition against the Spanish coast, and was reluctant to share his ships.

Rivalry between the army and navy was nothing new, but it revealed in wartime a major deficiency in the organization of the government for the effective employment of its armed forces. Each branch lived in isolation. There were no established, continuing, normal means for their mutual consultation and coordination. Officers in each service acknowledged an undivided allegiance to it, and in both they sought jealously to safeguard their respective positions and responsibilities. Secretaries might be personally friendly but they could not escape the influence of their own agencies. There was no organization such as a joint staff. Over-all planning and coordination had to be done in conference at the White House under the ultimate control of the President. He was thus compelled by circumstances, as well as by the Constitution, to be Commander in Chief of the army and the navy.

[41] *Ibid.*, pp. 246-47, 249.
[42] *Ibid.*, pp. 250-53.

War Department administration. The success of the expedition to Cuba depended not only on the professional capacity of the regular army and the energy and preparedness of the volunteers, but also upon the auxiliary services that fed, clothed, housed, and transported troops, cared for their health, and saw to their supplies and equipment. The record of most of these services was far from satisfactory.

In his account of the Spanish-American War, Secretary Russell A. Alger did not hesitate to record some appalling deficiencies.

It is doubtful if any nation rated as a first power ever entered upon a war of offence in a condition of less military preparation than was the United States in 1898. At that time there were not sufficient reserve supplies in the possession of the War Department to fully equip 10,000 men in addition to the regular army as it then stood. . . .

We saw also that the government of the United States did not provide smokeless powder for the Springfield rifles, nor for the field artillery in the early part of the war, simply for the reason that it had none to provide. No type of smokeless powder, indeed, had been adopted even for either of these important adjuncts of war. The issue of smokeless powder subsequently was dependent upon the output of the few plants in the United States capable of manufacturing it. We have also seen that the War Department did not even own or control a single transport, and there was no troop-ship on the Atlantic or Pacific Oceans available to the United States; that many elements of field, siege, and sea-coast artillery were in a transitional state; that the military establishment was palpably deficient in trained artillerists; that the regular army had not been mobilized since the Civil War; one-third of a century had elapsed since the army, as a whole, or any great part of it had been brought together; that there was no strategic staff, and no large number of officers who were experienced in the concentration of troops, or in battalion, division, or corps manœuvres; that there was no place in the United States especially adapted or prepared for army mobilization, and that neither the army nor any officer in it had any experience in meeting, or operating under, the new conditions incident to a campaign in the tropics.

To these causes, most of which may be directly ascribed to the failure of Congress to provide for the emergency of war, must be added another: the statutes under which the military establishment operated were not elastic enough to permit of large purchases of supplies necessitated by the sudden expansion of the army to a war footing.

When the crisis, so often predicted by military experts, at last came it found us totally unprepared for war and with problems to be met at home and abroad which were both unusual and difficult.[43]

The subsequent inquiry of the Dodge Commission, appointed by the President to investigate the conduct of the war, disclosed to the American people a civilian department and a system of army administration wholly unprepared to operate as the military arm of a country with status as a great power. Its revelations furnished the groundwork for the General Staff proposed by Secretary Root and for reconsideration of military policy in subsequent years.

In restrained terms the commission condemned both the War Department and most of the special staff services. So far as the Department was concerned, the commission reported, "In the judgment of the commission there was lacking in the general administration of the War Department during the continuance of the war with Spain that complete grasp of the situation which was essential to the highest efficiency and discipline of the Army."[44] This language was a model of understatement.

The Quartermaster's department was overwhelmed by its task. Tampa, Florida, was selected as a port of embarkation for men and supplies with no awareness of the inadequacy of rail transportation and siding capacity. The resulting confusion was nearly beyond belief. The Dodge Commission reported: "Great complaint was made of railroad congestion at Tampa and the absolute lack of ability to bring order out of chaos at that place . . . 1,000 cars being sidetracked, some of them as far back as Columbia, S. C. . . . The condition of railroad congestion . . . seems unparalleled, showing an almost inexcusable lack of executive ability on the part of those charged with the loading, unloading, and handling of the trains."[45] Confusion was confounded because the contents of cars were not marked, bills of lading were missing, and officers opening cars in the search for beans were said to have found patent leather shoes.

The Quartermaster was also charged with incompetence in transporting men and supplies on the high seas. The number of transports

[43] R. A. Alger, *The Spanish-American War*, pp. 455-57.
[44] *Report of the Commission Appointed by the President to Investigate the Conduct of the War Department in the War with Spain*, Senate Doc. 221, 56th Cong., 1st sess., I, 116 (Feb. 9, 1899).
[45] *Ibid.*, I, 132, 133.

was inadequate; they were poorly equipped for service; and there were not enough lighters to disembark the troops. The vessels were not loaded systematically. A battery with its guns and horses would be placed on one vessel, its ammunition on another. Medical supplies desperately needed at Santiago had carelessly been loaded on a vessel destined for Ponce, Puerto Rico, where they were eventually discovered.[46] The Dodge Commission found the Quartermaster's department neither physically nor financially prepared for war a month before hostilities began.[47]

The Medical department was also subject to criticism, although part of its trouble came from the poor performance of the Quartermaster. The Dodge Commission found only a few medical supplies in store when war broke out, an inadequate list of authorized purchases, lack of training of medical personnel, requisition red tape, and available supplies draining from one place to another. "But no small part of the troubles consequent upon lack of supplies was due to the slowness with which such supplies were transported and the failure to properly deliver them, the responsibility for which rests upon the Quartermaster's Department."[48] This department objected to shipping medical supplies by express on account of the expense! "Fast freight" at times took weeks, in view of traffic congestion. A complete outfit for a 200-bed hospital was actually lost for weeks. Medical stores were loaded in transports under all sorts of freight.[49]

The receiving camp at Montauk, New York, established in the first week of August for returning soldiers, was no credit to its management. The number of sick was vastly in excess of that anticipated. Hospital tents were not ready for them. No laundry was in operation for a month. Sanitation, "with all its defects, was not bad." Discipline was lax and work was hampered by crowds of visitors. Record keeping was imperfect, and it was difficult to locate soldiers in the hospital. "The history of these Montauk hospitals is the history not of careful, thorough preparation and smooth administration, but of hurried adaptation to extraordinary demands."[50]

---

[46] *Ibid.*, I, 134, 135, 142.
[47] *Ibid.*, I, 147.
[48] *Ibid.*, I, 173-74.
[49] *Ibid.*, I, 174.
[50] *Ibid.*, I, 182-83.

The Dodge Commission nevertheless recognized that "a vast deal of good work" was done by medical officers, but found in general that the Medical department was wholly unprepared at the outbreak of war; that after a generation of "contracted and contracting methods of administration" it could not operate freely and without undue regard to cost; that there was inadequate investigation of sanitary conditions; and that the demands made upon the department had not been properly foreseen.[51]

The Engineer Corps, by way of contrast, received a handsome compliment from the Dodge Commission. "Wherever officers of this corps have been assigned to duty the testimony shows that they have acted with great promptness and to the great benefit of the service. The testimony of commanding officers . . . has been in high praise of the services of the Corps of Engineers. This commendation has been because of the efficient preparations made before the beginning of the war with Spain for any emergency, the energy displayed by the officers of the Department and the esprit de corps that permeates the entire force."[52] The Ordnance department also earned praise from the Dodge Commission.[53]

The Spanish-American War, brief and successful though it was, revealed a War Department and an army in urgent need of administrative renovation. The need was the greater because the mission of the army suddenly took on new and strange potentialities. The United States became an imperial power with colonial possessions in the remote Far East and with a dominant national interest in the Caribbean. It rose overnight to the rank of a world power with all the unknown commitments that might be involved. The constructive recommendations of the Dodge Commission for an army readied with reserve supplies for a year, the proposals of Secretary Root for a general staff, the emergence of professional army training institutes, all marked a revolution in War Department administration and organization. The gulf between the Indian-fighter regular army of 1898 and the overseas expeditionary force of 1914 was truly enormous.

[51] *Ibid.*, I, 188-89.
[52] *Ibid.*, I, 195.
[53] *Ibid.*, I, 199.

The Navy Department

The years from 1865 to 1901 include two contrasting periods in naval history. The first, extending from 1865 to 1881, were years of stagnation, political domination, confusion in naval policy, and indifference on the part of Congress. The second, opening in 1882, marked a great revival of interest in a new armored, steam-propelled capital ship navy, a better understanding of naval policy as taught by Admiral Mahan, and vigorous leadership by a succession of able Secretaries of the Navy.

These events comprise the substance of this chapter. The tale of administrative inadequacy that follows should not, however, obscure the fact that during the 1880's and 1890's great progress was made in naval affairs, or conceal the fact that the record of the fighting ships in the Spanish-American War was outstanding. In 1880 the United States hardly possessed a naval force; in 1900 it stood among the leading naval powers. The essential nature of the change can be grasped by a review of departmental leadership, changes in naval policy, and the problems of civilian administration. The principal difficulties arose in the departmental operations, not in the professional naval service. Said Secretary William C. Whitney in 1885, "whatever dissatisfaction the country has ever experienced with the naval arm of our Government will be found to have had its origin, not in the naval service, but in the naval administration. . . ."[1]

THE SECRETARIES OF THE NAVY, 1869–1901

The vigor of naval administration varied during the post-Civil War years under the influence of many circumstances, among which were the character and personality of the civilian Secretaries. Broadly

[1] Secretary of the Navy, *Annual Report*, 1885, I, xxvii.

speaking, these men were relatively incompetent for the first fourteen years but subsequently reached a much higher level of leadership capacity. The major turning point came, both as to naval policy and civilian direction, during the administration of Chester A. Arthur.

The Navy Department, like War, is one of the most difficult for the lawyer or politician to administer. A civilian is usually ignorant of the standards of value, traditions, prejudices, and eccentricities of the professional navy corps. A Secretary, moreover, heads a complex business relating to manufacture, naval architecture, steam engineering, scientific enterprise, naval education, international law, medicine and surgery, astronomy and hydrography. Short-term Secretaries hardly learn the routine of their office, follow the lead of their subordinates, and, according to Charles O. Paullin, "vex . . . the already troubled waters of the navy."[2]

Grant's first Secretary of the Navy, Adolph E. Borie, was a Philadelphia gentleman with short white whiskers—a merchant of substance who was not an applicant for office and who was as surprised as the whole nation at his appointment. He knew nothing about the navy, immediately fell under the influence of Admiral David D. Porter, and resigned after a few months.[3] George M. Robeson of New Jersey, his successor, remained under the influence of the naval officer corps, and in addition was complaisant to Republican politicians on patronage matters.[4] The Navy Department appeared to be run by the naval officers and the politicians, and Robeson's administration was so lax as to require an investigation by Congress.[5]

Hayes' Secretary of the Navy, Richard W. Thompson, a long-time active politician in Indiana, "was somewhat old, slow-moving, conservative and obedient to the strict and narrow interpretation of the law. He shared with his section of the Union its prejudices against the upbuilding of the navy and in favor of economy in naval expendi-

[2] U.S. Naval Institute, *Proceedings*, XXXIX (1913), 1247. This quotation is from an outstanding series of articles by Charles Oscar Paullin, "A Half Century of Naval Administration in America, 1861-1911," in the *Proceedings of the United States Naval Institute*, XXXVIII (1912)-XL (1914), *passim*.
[3] Richard S. West, Jr., *The Second Admiral: a Life of David Dixon Porter, 1813-1891* (New York: Coward-McCann, 1937), pp. 316-17.
[4] *Dictionary of American Biography*, XVI, 31.
[5] House Misc. Doc. 170, 44th Cong., 1st sess. (April 27, 1876); House Reports 788 and 789, 44th Cong., 1st sess. (August 1, 1876).

tures."[6] Hayes had said he wanted in the Cabinet a Republican of the old Whig element. He found a well-respected gentleman who knew nothing of the navy and who was humorously dubbed "The Ancient Mariner of the Wabash."[7] Thompson resigned under pressure, having accepted the chairmanship of the American Committee of the Panama Canal Company, an appointment which he alone thought compatible with his official post.[8]

Secretary William H. Hunt of Louisiana, Garfield's Secretary of the Navy, was an energetic person who began the drive for a new navy, but who retired after Garfield's death.[9] His successor, William E. Chandler of New Hampshire, was an equally energetic and more controversial figure who gave strong support to the emerging revolution in naval construction.[10] Chandler was a politician by vocation; his successor, William C. Whitney, was a businessman who had actively supported Cleveland in the campaign of 1884. Paullin wrote: "Of the five Secretaries, Chandler and Whitney were the most aggressive and positive, and the most ardent for naval reform; they were men of courage, and were willing, if necessary, to stem the tide of naval or political influence. Both were real heads of the department, and exercised more power than any of their predecessors since Gideon Welles."[11] Both had the capacity of making blunt and plain statements. Whitney was popular among naval officers—a rare distinction for Secretaries.

Harrison found a New Yorker to head the Navy Department, Benjamin F. Tracy, a man of marked ability and initiative who quickly accepted both the friendship and the doctrine of Admiral Mahan. Under his direction, and at last with congressional support, the navy expanded its fleet of modern warships and its concept of naval function. Tracy, like his predecessor, Whitney, and his successors, Herbert and Long, served a full four-year term.[12]

[6] Charles O. Paullin, "A Half Century of Naval Administration," *op. cit.,* XXXIX (1913), 752.
[7] Charles Roll, *Colonel Dick Thompson*, p. 213.
[8] *Ibid.*, pp. 255 ff.
[9] *Dictionary of American Biography*, IX, 397.
[10] Leon Burr Richardson, *William E. Chandler: Republican* (New York: Dodd, Mead and Co., 1940).
[11] Charles O. Paullin, "A Half Century of Naval Administration," *op. cit.,* XXXIX (1913), 1248.
[12] *Dictionary of American Biography*, XVIII, 623.

Cleveland's second term Secretary of the Navy, Hilary A. Herbert, was a one-time Confederate army officer, disabled in combat, who served as an Alabama Congressman from 1877 to 1893. He had acquired an unsurpassed working knowledge of the navy, having been three times chairman of the House Committee on Naval Affairs. Like many Secretaries he was professionally a lawyer, and after his tour of duty he practised law in Washington until his death.[13]

McKinley's Secretary, John D. Long, formerly governor of Massachusetts and a member of the House of Representatives, was a man of sterling qualities but of cautious temperament. He was the first "scholar in politics" to sit at the head of the Department, having published a translation of the *Aeneid* and a volume of after-dinner speeches before his official service. After his resignation he wrote a two-volume work, *The New American Navy*.[14] His native caution was balanced, if indeed not overbalanced, by the impetuous energy of his Assistant Secretary, Theodore Roosevelt.

These were the men who for thirty years helped make naval policy and who bore the responsibility for naval administration. To the course of policy and the problems of administration we now turn.

NAVAL POLICY, 1865–1901

With the close of the Civil War the navy underwent an abrupt transition to prewar tradition and standards. A great assemblage of ships and manpower was largely dismantled, and the country returned to a thoroughly outmoded naval policy. There followed sixteen years of drift and inattention, stagnation in shipbuilding, and confusion in thinking about naval policy. For years midwest Congressmen fought a large navy, and its nature was disputed even by the seacoast representatives. Congress finally bestirred itself in the Naval Appropriation Act of 1882, and in the following decade a new navy gradually emerged. Equally important was a clearer awareness of the function of a navy in the imperialist world that was already taking shape and into which the United States was plunged by the War with Spain.[15]

[13] *Ibid.*, VIII, 572.
[14] *Ibid.*, XI, 377.
[15] On the subject matter of this section, see especially the basic work by Harold and Margaret Sprout, *The Rise of American Naval Power, 1776-1918.*

The demobilization of the Civil War navy was pursued rapidly. Ships were sold or dismantled, guns were dismounted, stores were reduced, and sailors released. Prewar naval policy was reestablished by tacit agreement. It consisted of maintaining cruising squadrons (suited to sailing ships) in the Mediterranean, off the coast of Africa, in the Caribbean Sea, and in the Pacific Ocean. Their objectives were protection against pirates, suppression of the dwindling slave trade, and in a vague manner the safeguarding of American commerce in foreign ports. Only the last purpose had meaning after the Civil War, and the specific or unique tasks of the navy in this field were not clear. However this may be, ships were stationed again around the world in accordance with policy fixed at the close of the War of 1812.

Long years of neglect and indifference followed demobilization. There was a strong reaction against military and naval forces after the great exertions of the Civil War, and an insoluble series of disagreements over the types of naval vessels most suitable for an isolated and peaceful country. The dominant school of thought held that the primary wartime tasks of the American navy were (1) to protect the coast against hostile ships off shore, (2) to harry the shipping of a hostile power. A navy for aggression was practically unthought of, and a navy able to take to the high seas with capital ships operating as a fleet was beyond the plans of any responsible civilian or naval leaders of these years. Based on these primary assumptions, controversy raged over the issue of sails versus steam. Sails won a temporary victory. A general order issued in 1869 directed that all naval vessels should have "full sail power." Naval regulations of 1870 expressly forbade using steam at all, except when absolutely necessary.[16]

The case for a strong navy was indeed unimpressive in the late 1860's and the 1870's. No war of conquest was dreamed of—the pressure for southward expansion had evaporated with the abolition of slavery; there was no danger of European aggression; the merchant marine was declining; there were no overseas colonies to defend; the new economy was firmly based on domestic resources of coal and iron and on the productive capacity of American farms. Congressmen, indeed, often were interested in the navy but primarily on account of

(Princeton: Princeton University Press, 1939), and Charles O. Paullin, "A Half Century of Naval Administration in America, 1861-1911," U.S. Naval Institute, *Proceedings*, XXXVIII (1912)-XL (1914), *passim*.

[16] Harold and Margaret Sprout, *Rise of American Naval Power*, p. 167.

the substantial patronage of the navy yards. Executive leadership of the navy under both Grant and Hayes was weak; professional leadership was marred by faction.

The most the navy could do under these two Republican administrations by way of shipbuilding was to repair and recondition vessels in active service or in ordinary. Expenditures for ship repairs suited political needs perfectly, for they provided large payrolls without the necessity of convincing a skeptical country of the usefulness of a bigger navy. Under Robeson over $6,000,000 a year was spent by the construction bureaus, but in 1877 at the end of his administration he "had nothing to show for his work but an obsolete fleet in poor condition."[17]

Naval progress was hampered, if not indeed paralyzed, by differences of opinion among experts and laymen alike. "The contests between wood and iron, and between iron and steel, as materials for the construction of ships; between steam and wind as motive powers; between armored and unarmored ships; between ordnance and armor; and between ships and torpedoes, were all still undecided."[18] These matters were debated endlessly and at times acrimoniously but without resolution. Paullin declared that less was done for the navy under Hayes than during any administration since that of Jefferson.[19]

It was to this state of affairs that Secretary of the Navy William C. Whitney alluded in his annual report for 1885: "At the present moment it must be conceded that we have nothing which deserves to be called a navy. . . . it is questionable whether we have a single naval vessel finished and afloat at the present time that could be trusted to encounter the ships of any important power. . . . This is no secret; the fact has been repeatedly commented upon in Congress by the leading members of both parties, confessed by our highest naval authorities, and deprecated by all. . . ."[20]

The turning point in naval policy came in the Navy Appropriation Act of 1882 during Arthur's administration. This legislation authorized two steam-propelled cruisers of the highest attainable speed (but equipped with full sail power as well), one with a displacement

[17] Charles O. Paullin, "A Half Century of Naval Administration," *op. cit.*, XXXIX (1913), 1224.
[18] *Ibid.*, XXXIX (1913), 1222.
[19] *Ibid.*, XXXIX, 1219.
[20] Secretary of the Navy, *Annual Report, 1885*, I, xxxii-xxxiii.

of from 5,000 to 6,000 tons; the other slightly smaller. Quite as important, the act slowed down the useless expense of repairing old ships and authorized naval boards to condemn ships unfit for service.[21] In 1882 two inspection boards condemned forty-four ships, almost one-third of the total number on the Navy List. By 1893 only nine of the old wooden ships remained in active service.[22]

Both political parties now aligned themselves in favor of new naval construction. In 1883 Congress authorized four steel vessels, including the *Chicago*, *Boston*, and *Atlanta*—protected cruisers that were popularly known as the White Squadron. Under Cleveland's first administration Congress authorized two second-class battleships, one armored cruiser, six protected cruisers, and other small vessels. The battleships were the *Texas* and the *Maine*. President Harrison was a big-navy man and his party was in control of both Houses of Congress. The annual report of the Secretary of the Navy, Benjamin F. Tracy, for 1889 was "one of the most forceful documents in the entire history of American naval policy," calling for a two-ocean navy, twenty battleships, sixty cruisers, and twenty coast defense monitors.[23] A naval board quickly followed with an even more ambitious program. Congress was more cautious, but in the Navy Appropriation Act of 1890 it authorized naval construction intended to secure American naval supremacy for approximately one thousand miles beyond the continental seaboard. Among the new battleships were the *Indiana*, *Massachusetts*, and the famous *Oregon*. By 1897 the North Atlantic Squadron could realistically be called a fighting fleet.

Behind these physical marks of a revived navy was a new understanding of the role of the navy in relation both to naval strategy and to public policy. Its author was Admiral Alfred Thayer Mahan, a member of the staff of the Naval War College.[24] Mahan was a strong nationalist with a definite attachment to imperialism. He argued that

[21] 22 Stat. 284 at 291, 297 (August 5, 1882).

[22] Charles O. Paullin, "A Half Century of Naval Administration," *op. cit.*, XXXIX, 1485.

[23] Secretary of the Navy, *Annual Report*, 1889, pp. 10-12. This report is summarized in Harold and Margaret Sprout, *Rise of American Naval Power*, pp. 207-208.

[24] Charles Carlisle Taylor, *The Life of Admiral Mahan* (New York: George H. Doran Co., 1920); Captain William D. Puleston, *Mahan: The Life and Work of Captain Alfred Thayer Mahan, U.S.N.* (New Haven: Yale University Press, 1939).

an expanding foreign commerce was essential to national prosperity, that such commerce required a strong merchant marine, overseas ports, and an effective navy for the protection of commerce and overseas possessions. Since the United States had no such possessions when Mahan published his major work in 1890, *The Influence of Sea Power upon History, 1660–1783*, he argued that this country needed a powerful fleet sufficient to keep open American ports to neutral shipping in time of war. Coast defense ships and commerce raiders were useless for such a mission, and, confronted with Mahan's analysis, the historic theory of the function of an American navy vanished. Only a fleet of capital ships, able to command the high seas, could guarantee access to our ports—a proposition that had been amply demonstrated during the War of 1812 but had never been acknowledged.

Although Mahan's theory was not wholly original with him, he succeeded in organizing its doctrine systematically and in providing convincing historical demonstration of its soundness. He wrote also at a propitious moment. The country was moving in the direction of naval power, even if without a clear understanding of naval strategy. President Benjamin Harrison favored a large navy; Secretary Tracy was on terms of intimacy with Mahan. He became the intellectual architect of the new navy. The Spanish-American War confirmed the doctrines that he had launched nearly a decade before, provided the overseas possessions that he thought necessary for an expanding commerce, and laid ever more compelling foundations for a capital-ship navy.

Naval policy from the Civil War to the Spanish-American War therefore fell into two periods. From 1865 to 1882 it was dominated by the conviction that the only peacetime task of a navy was to cruise on foreign stations "to protect American commerce"; its wartime mission was merely to prevent hostile forces from entering American harbors, and to harry commerce. After 1882 Congress recognized that the old navy was obsolete and that the day of the wooden sailing ship had finally passed. A new navy, steam propelled and based on capital ships operating as a fleet, had come into existence by 1898. Its mission had been clarified by the teaching of Admiral Mahan and popularized by Assistant Secretary of the Navy Theodore Roosevelt.

NAVAL ADMINISTRATION

"It must be evident," declared Secretary William C. Whitney in his annual report for 1885, "that there is something radically wrong with the Department."[25] Three years before, the same opinion had been expressed in almost the same language by Lieutenant Commander Henry H. Gorringe: "There must be something radically wrong in our system of naval administration that it cannot, with four times the expenditure, maintain a navy as efficient as that of Austria."[26] Inside and outside the Navy Department this opinion was widely held, but there were powerful forces opposing reform.

The basic difficulties revolved around a universal problem of administrative organization: how to delegate adequate authority to bureaus to enable them to act with initiative and energy, and at the same time reserve enough authority in the responsible agency head to ensure coordination, subordination, and responsibility.[27] The navy suffered on the one hand from overpowerful bureaus, each jealously guarding its respective prerogatives, unwilling to yield authority to secure coordination, professionally arrogant, and unmindful of the needs of the Department as such; and on the other hand from the correlative vice of Secretaries whose talents were at times deficient and whose office was inadequately staffed to enable them to exercise the powers of control that were nominally those of the Secretary of the Navy.

The number and duties of the navy bureaus varied from time to time, but their status was firmly fixed in the Department tradition. The five bureaus established in 1842 were reorganized and expanded to eight in 1862.[28] Irrespective of number, the basic functions that were vested in them included the movement of ships, the recruitment and assignment of personnel, the construction and repair of ships, and the procurement of supplies and equipment. The first two operations were naval in character; the latter two, civil—i.e., manufactur-

[25] Secretary of the Navy, *Annual Report, 1885*, I, xxvii.
[26] Henry H. Gorringe, "The Navy," *North American Review*, CXXXIV (1882), 486.
[27] See Alfred Thayer Mahan, "The Principles of Naval Administration," in his *Naval Administration and Warfare* (Boston: Little, Brown, and Co., 1908), pp. 1-48; and "The United States Navy Department," *ibid.*, pp. 49-85.
[28] 12 Stat. 510 (July 5, 1862).

ing, engineering, and purchasing—but all were under the control and direction of naval officers. The chief of the Bureau of Navigation held the greatest power. In Paullin's words: "He, with the consent of the Secretary of the Navy, moves and removes the officers and controls the naval ships. In the naval firmament he is a star of the first magnitude and rivals the Secretary in brilliancy. Until after the Spanish-American War, no other officer of the navy compared with him in power, authority and consequence. . . . He is therefore both feared and hated. . . ."[29]

The status of a bureau chief in the Navy Department had been established in the statutory reorganization of 1842 by providing that the orders of a chief of bureau should be considered as emanating from the Secretary of the Navy, and should have full force and effect as such.[30] Thus over the years developed what Robert W. Neeser called "no less than half a dozen secretaries of the navy, each one, in his own bureau, clothed with executive authority equal to that of the constitutional commander-in-chief. This was a flagrant violation of a fundamental military principle, and it is this that caused such dire confusion, extravagance, duplication of work and irresponsibility, which, according to several secretaries of the navy, have characterized the business methods of the navy department for the last sixty years."[31] The violation of principle may be argued, but in the absence of strong department-wide agencies of coordination and control, the consequences were no less pernicious.

That bureau chiefs did not consider themselves necessarily bound to observe the policy views of the Secretary of the Navy is revealed in the following passage from the testimony of Secretary Tracy in 1892 before the House Committee on Naval Affairs. " . . . I have felt constrained to appear before you to-day in support of the bill now under consideration lest it should come to be understood that the chief of a bureau in the Navy Department, who recently appeared in opposition, did so with my assent and approval."[32]

[29] Charles O. Paullin, "A Half Century of Naval Administration," U.S. Naval Institute, *Proceedings*, XXXIX (1913), 753-54.

[30] 5 Stat. 579, sec. 5 (August 31, 1842).

[31] Robert W. Neeser, "The Department of the Navy," *American Political Science Review*, XI (1917), 60-61. Neeser, who was secretary of the Naval History Society, was a well-qualified commentator.

[32] House Report 1677, 52d Cong., 1st sess., p. 9 (May 20, 1892).

The bureau chiefs with covert support from well-placed members of Congress obviously possessed political power. Paullin, commenting on Secretary Chandler's reforms, observed that he would have gone farther than he did, if he had possessed the support of his bureau heads.[33] Consolidation of bureaus was fought by bureau personnel: the engineers feared loss of status (for which they had waged heavy battles), employees feared a reduction in force and loss of employment, others resisted further concentration of power in the hands of any bureau chief. Admiral Porter called the bureaus "a balky team."[34] Secretary John D. Long sought to consolidate the Bureaus of Construction and Repair, Steam Engineering, and Equipment, but was defeated by a combination of high-ranking officers and members of the naval committees. He declared that the relations among bureau chiefs were sometimes so strained that ordinary courtesy was impaired.[35]

The consequent enfeeblement of departmental administration was reflected in most aspects of agency affairs, two of which may be cited as examples: the design of warships and the duplication of facilities in the navy yards. Commander Gorringe noted in 1882 that under the then prevailing system the hull, the engines, the guns, and the sail power were designed independently of one another in the different bureaus, "the officers of which generally entertain antagonistic views on every question that arises."[36]

Secretary Whitney reported a startling instance of the fatal results of this lack of coordination. After the ship *Omaha* had been commissioned and was ready for sea it was discovered that the several bureaus, working independently, had so completely appropriated the available space as to leave coal room for only four days' steaming at full capacity. Apart from this paralyzing defect, the whole operation was, according to Whitney, "an act of the greatest folly"; the *Omaha* was at best merely an old repaired wooden vessel, whose rebuilding cost the full price of an up-to-date steel ship, and which could neither

[33] Charles O. Paullin, "A Half Century of Naval Administration," *op. cit.*, XXXIX (1913), 1488.

[34] Secretary of the Navy, *Annual Report*, 1881, p. 96.

[35] Charles O. Paullin, "A Half Century of Naval Administration," *op. cit.*, XL (1914), 126.

[36] Henry H. Gorringe, "The Navy," *North American Review*, CXXXIV (1882), 491.

fight nor run away from any contemporary ship of a foreign nation.[37]

The situation within the navy yards was equally indefensible. Every construction bureau maintained its own shops in the several yards, each one with a separate organization of foremen and subordinate personnel. Shops doing the same kind of work, such as carpenter or machine shops, were commonly duplicated or triplicated in the same yard. According to Gorringe, the system required eight distinct and independent organizations in each navy yard, nominally under one commandant but really responsible to the appropriate bureau chief in Washington. "If," he declared, "the object in establishing a bureau system for naval administration had been the multiplication of offices, the division of responsibility, and the obstruction of work, it may be regarded as a success without parallel."[38] Secretary Long discovered that instead of a single power plant in each yard, power was supplied by boilers and engines scattered about the yard and operated by the different bureaus.[39]

Paullin declared that the extension of the bureau system to the yards increased the political and decreased the naval element in their management. The authority of the yard commandant was seriously lessened—as Vice Admiral Rowan put it, the bureau system "pulled out all the teeth of the commandant" and made him a sort of head postmaster whose duty was to pass orders from the bureaus in Washington to their yard representatives.[40]

None of the administrative means appropriate to alleviate such conditions was effectively brought to bear, although the Spanish-American War began the process of reform. Survey of the many efforts to introduce much-needed change throws light, however, on the conditions and limitations of Navy Department administration. What obviously was required was greater strength in the overhead department-wide means of coordination and control. Several ways of attaining this end were open.

In principle, departmental control was properly to be achieved by strengthening the hands of the Secretary. His authority was ample,

[37] Secretary of the Navy, *Annual Report,* 1885, I, xxxix, xli.

[38] Henry H. Gorringe, "The Navy," *American Political Science Review,* CXXXIV (1882), 491.

[39] John D. Long, *The New American Navy,* I, 118.

[40] Charles O. Paullin, "A Half Century of Naval Administration," U.S. Naval Institute, *Proceedings,* XXXIX (1913), 1234.

but his means of action were relatively feeble, and some Secretaries were not inclined even to use those available. Secretaries Borie, Robeson, Thompson, and Goff (1869–1881) fell into this group. However, Hunt and Chandler, Whitney, Tracy, and Herbert (1881–1897) were energetic and intended to be masters in their own house. Long (1897–1902) was more inclined to yield to professional knowledge and guidance. Any civilian Secretary, indeed, is at a marked disadvantage in dealing with a professional military organization. As for Long, he summarized the weakness of his position in the following passage in his journal.

Went with Captain O'Neil, Chief of the Bureau of Ordnance, this morning before the Senate Committee on Naval Affairs, with regard to armor-plate. Of course I know nothing about it, and go through the perfunctory business of saying so, and referring the Committee to Captain O'Neil. When I say I know nothing about it, I mean nothing about the details—which only an expert can know—of the process of manufacturing armor. I make [it] a point not to trouble myself overmuch to acquire a thorough knowledge of the details pertaining to any branch of the service. Such knowledge would undoubtedly be a very valuable equipment, but the range is so enormous I could make little progress, and that at great expense of health and time, in mastering it. My plan is to leave all such matters to the Bureau chiefs, or other officers at naval stations or on board ship, limiting myself to the general direction of affairs. What is the need of my making a dropsical tub of any lobe of my brain, when I have right at hand a man possessed with more knowledge than I could acquire, and have him constantly on tap? At best there is enough for me to do, and to occupy my attention. Some of it is spent on important things, and a very large part on small things, especially personal matters—personal frictions, personal delinquencies, personal appeals, and personal claims.[41]

Even an energetic person like Whitney discounted the role of the head of the Navy Department. "The Secretary," he declared, "may at once be eliminated from the problem. A civilian ordinarily, not skilled in the art of war, nor having the technical knowledge with reference to its implements; having no personal staff, his separate office force consisting, as estimated for and appropriated by Congress, of but one stenographer, one clerk, and three messengers—all the

[41] John D. Long, *Journal* (Lawrence S. Mayo, ed.), pp. 156-57 (Feb. 2, 1898).

other force having general clerical work."[42] Whitney's driving power and business background made a strong impress despite these handicaps, but few Secretaries surmounted them.

Every Secretary, moreover, was mired in a mass of office routine as well as the personal matters to which Long referred. Whitney's biographer records that he had to deal with leaves of absence, assignments, transfers, pay requisitions, trials of boats, inventions and machinery, requests for information and reports on personnel, authority for purchases, general correspondence, memoranda in regard to wrecks and construction, appointments to Annapolis, general navy communications, inquiries, bulletins and notices, and the navy yards.[43] He also had to deal with members of Congress on matters of finance and of patronage, both tasks requiring constant attention. Only an exceptional man could surmount these duties and challenge an entrenched system of bureau autonomy. In any case personal aides for the Secretary would have been essential, and these were the days before the regime of administrative assistants.

Another solution would have been one or more assistant secretaries. The exigencies of war had moved Congress to establish the office of Assistant Secretary in 1861.[44] It was occupied throughout the Civil War by a notable executive, Gustavus V. Fox, but was terminated in 1869.[45] It was finally authorized anew in 1890 and despite some congressional hostility was never again discontinued.[46] The proposal to appoint an Assistant Secretary was not favorably regarded by the naval officer corps. On the other hand Secretary Chandler and Senator Eugene Hale of Maine (who for many years was the Senate authority on naval affairs) both argued for such an office. Paullin commented that this conflict of opinion reflected the rivalry "that has always existed" between the civilian and naval elements in navy management.[47]

Theodore Roosevelt became Assistant Secretary of the Navy De-

---

[42] Secretary of the Navy, *Annual Report*, 1885, I, xxxviii.

[43] Mark D. Hirsch, *William C. Whitney: Modern Warwick* (New York: Dodd, Mead and Co., 1948), p. 264.

[44] 12 Stat. 282 (July 31, 1861).

[45] 15 Stat. 296 (March 3, 1869).

[46] 26 Stat. 254 (July 11, 1890).

[47] Charles O. Paullin, "A Half Century of Naval Administration," U.S. Naval Institute, *Proceedings*, XXXIX (1913), 1250.

partment on the eve of the Spanish-American War, a post ideally suited to his interests and capacities. In his work on the navy, Long characterized his one-time subordinate, then President of the United States. "Mr. Roosevelt," he wrote, "was an interesting personality as assistant secretary of the navy, as, indeed, he is in any capacity." Long continued:

. . . . His activity was characteristic. He was zealous in the work of putting the navy in condition for the apprehended struggle. His ardor sometimes went faster than the President or the department approved. Just before the war, when the Spanish battlefleet was on its way here, he as well as some naval officers, regarding that as a cause of war, approved of sending a squadron to meet it without waiting for a more formal declaration of war. He worked indefatigably, frequently incorporating his views in memoranda which he would place every morning on my desk. Most of his suggestions had, however, so far as applicable, been already adopted by the various bureaus, the chiefs of which were straining every nerve and leaving nothing not done. When I suggested to him that some future historian reading his memoranda, if they were put on record, would get the impression that the bureaus were inefficient, he accepted the suggestion with the generous good nature which is so marked in him. Indeed, nothing could be pleasanter than our relations. He was heart and soul in his work. His typewriters had no rest. He, like most of us, lacks the rare knack of brevity. He was especially stimulating to the younger officers who gathered about him and made his office as busy as a hive. . . .[48]

As soon as war was declared, Roosevelt left the Department against the advice of Long. Later Long recognized his error: "He took the straight course to fame, to the governorship of New York and to the presidency of the United States."[49]

In his private diary, however, Long did not conceal his reservations about Roosevelt: "I lack confidence in his good judgment and discretion. He goes off very impulsively. . . ."[50] Roosevelt had been left as Acting Secretary for one afternoon while Long took a needed rest. The next day Long entered the following passage in his diary. "He seems to be thoroughly loyal, but the very devil seemed to possess him yesterday afternoon. . . . he immediately began to launch peremptory

[48] John D. Long, *The New American Navy*, II, 173-74.
[49] *Ibid.*, II, 175.
[50] John D. Long, *Journal*, pp. 168-69 (Feb. 25, 1898).

orders: distributing ships; ordering ammunition . . . sending messages to Congress . . . authorizing the enlistment of an unlimited number of seamen. . . . He has gone at things like a bull in a china shop. . . . It shows how the best fellow in the world—and with splendid capacities—is worse than of no use if he lack a cool head and careful discretion."[51]

The office of Assistant Secretary was one of the two innovations designed to counteract the force of the navy bureaus. The other was a professional advisory board attached to the Secretary which, it was hoped, could coordinate and where necessary check bureau activities. At the close of the Spanish-American War it was organized under the title, "The General Board."

The issue had been under discussion for at least two decades before the Spanish-American War precipitated action. In 1877 Secretary Thompson organized a board comprising the bureau chiefs and meeting twice a week under Thompson's chairmanship. The board soon terminated. Paullin observed that the centrifugal forces of the Department were too much for it to withstand.[52] *Ad hoc* boards for special purposes were frequent; they were usually set up to look into particular problems and were discontinued after reporting. Thus Secretary Tracy sought to coordinate responsibility for construction of the ships of the new navy by constituting in 1889 the Board of Construction, consisting of five bureau chiefs.

The case for a professional board standing between the Secretary and the bureaus was pushed principally by the line officers, who recalled nostalgically the Board of Navy Commissioners that had served from 1815 to 1842. They looked upon such a board not primarily as a means of curbing the bureaus but as an effective way of "informing" civilian Secretaries of naval needs and policy. Admiral David D. Porter was one of their principal spokesmen.[53] Civilian Secretaries, on the other hand, were suspicious of the enlargement of the naval as against the civilian influence which seemed implicit in the concept, and resisted efforts to give a naval board duties of administration and control. Thus Secretary Whitney favored an

[51] *Ibid.*, pp. 169-70 (Feb. 26, 1898).
[52] Charles O. Paullin, "A Half Century of Naval Administration," U.S. Naval Institute, *Proceedings*, XXXIX (1913), 756.
[53] See his report to Secretary Whitney, Nov. 30, 1885, in the Secretary of the Navy's annual report for this year, I, 272-90.

advisory board comprising not only five bureau chiefs but three additional naval officers. Paullin commented that Secretaries from 1881 to 1897 were jealous of their powers, and naturally opposed any measure calculated to increase the influence of naval officers within the Department.[54] Members of Congress also found proposals for a naval board distasteful. Staff officers, such as the engineers, were opposed to any plan to enlarge the authority of the line. A varied complex of interests and forces thus delayed for many years this solution of the problem of naval administration.

War induced innovation. A Naval War Board, also known as the Naval Strategy Board, was created in the spring of 1898, comprising Rear Admiral Montgomery Sicard, Commodore A. S. Crowninshield, then chief of the Bureau of Navigation, and Assistant Secretary Theodore Roosevelt as chairman. Captain Mahan was put on the Board when Roosevelt went off to active service. It was dissolved in the fall of 1898, but service agitation led in 1900 to the establishment of the General Board.[55]

This Board marked the beginning of the general staff idea in the Navy Department, a concept also under active consideration in the War Department. Its duties were to ascertain the demands that national policy were likely to make on the navy, to prepare war plans, and in this connection to coordinate the work of the Naval War College and the Office of Naval Intelligence, and to advise the Secretary of the Navy. Its functions were advisory only. The line of command led down from the Secretary to the bureaus and their subdivisions. The members of the General Board were the Admiral of the Navy, the chief of the Bureau of Navigation, the chief intelligence officer, and the president of the Naval War College.

Although the establishment of an Assistant Secretary and the creation of the General Board were steps in the right direction, they were insufficient to overcome bureau intransigence. Secretary Long wrote after his retirement: "The several bureaus . . . are tenacious of their prerogatives and guard them jealously, fearing, perhaps, that any innovation will be followed by diminution of their jurisdiction. The temptation to step beyond the limits of a bureau's authority as fixed by the naval regulations sometimes proves almost irresistible.

[54] Charles O. Paullin, "A Half Century of Naval Administration," *op. cit.*, XXXIX (1913), 1262.

[55] General Order 544, March 13, 1900.

The bureau affected sharply resents the encroachment, and there immediately follows an exchange of communications, sometimes highly seasoned. The controversy is ultimately loaded upon the Secretary, who is expected to untangle the snarl in which his subordinates have wound themselves."[56]

The persistence of bureau autonomy and rivalry was documented in the annual report of Secretary of the Navy William H. Moody in 1903.

. . . . The distribution of business among bureaus independent of and unrelated to each other, except through the action of the Secretary, unquestionably creates a condition out of which grow conflicts of jurisdiction between the bureaus, sometimes injurious, and a tendency to consider the interests of the bureaus rather than the interests of the Navy. The division of business in the bureaus exists not only in the Department, but extends to the navy-yards, and even to some extent to the ships in commission. This leads sometimes to excessive and cumbersome organization and lack of harmony of effort, resulting from the fact that there is no coordination of work, except by the voluntary action of bureau chiefs, short of the Secretary's office itself.[57]

It was thus evident to Secretary Moody that the General Board, useful though it was, was not endowed with strength enough to harness the bureaus into a proper team. Following the lead of the War Department, Moody recommended the creation of a general staff established by law, and "responsible for the efficiency of the vessels afloat and the personnel of the Navy," for the collection of information underlying plans of operation, and for advice to the Secretary.[58] Congress did not respond. Secretary George von L. Meyer, however, substantially achieved the same end by executive action in 1909.[59] Congress finally granted legislative recognition in 1916.[60]

PATRONAGE IN THE NAVY YARDS

Until 1883 patronage was the special curse of the navy yards, a burden perhaps greater than the handicaps resulting from jealous bureaus. The passage of the Pendleton Act and its vigorous application

[56] John D. Long, *The New American Navy*, I, 116-17.
[57] Secretary of the Navy, *Annual Report*, 1903, p. 4.
[58] *Ibid.*, 1903, p. 5.
[59] *Ibid.*, 1909, pp. 8-9.
[60] 39 Stat. 556 at 558 (August 29, 1916).

by Secretary Whitney and his successors induced reform on a broad scale.

Secretary Robeson had been exceedingly responsive to the politicians, in conformity with the general policy of the Grant administration. "It is known," wrote the biographer of his successor, Secretary Thompson, "that Secretary Robeson managed the department as if its chief purpose was to carry elections, and all classes and shades of political bummers, no matter to what party they professed to belong, were provided for as far as possible under fraudulent contractors."[61] In retrospect Secretary Long observed that before civil service reform the navy yards employed about 5,000 men, nearly every one of whom had gained place by means of political influence and was dependent on influence for continuance on the government payroll.[62] Paullin quoted the testimony of a supposed timber agent before a House congressional committee that revealed the political demoralization of the civilian navy.

Question. "Are you a timber agent in Florida?"
Answer. "Yes, sir."
Question. "How far do you live from the timber you are expected to guard?"
Answer. "I do not know anything about the public domains, and did not try to find out."
Question. "Did you ever see or visit the timber?"
Answer. "No, sir."
Question. "Did you perform any service under that appointment?"
Answer. "No, sir; nothing but draw my pay."
Question. "What was your salary?"
Answer. "Forty-one dollars a month."
Question. "What is the politics of these agents?"
Answer. "They are Republicans."[63]

So important was the influence of local politicians that several navy yards were familiarly named for their controlling Congressman: the yard at Norfolk was known as Mr. Platt's yard, and that at Mare Island as Mr. Sargent's yard.[64] Chandler's biographer, Leon B. Rich-

[61] Charles Roll, *Colonel Dick Thompson*, p. 235.
[62] John D. Long, *The New American Navy*, I, 55.
[63] *Congressional Record*, 44th Cong., 1st sess., p. 3259 (May 22, 1876), reprinted in Charles O. Paullin, "A Half Century of Naval Administration," U.S. Naval Institute, *Proceedings*, XXXIX (1913), 1233.
[64] *Ibid.*, XXXIX (1913), 1233-34.

ardson, produced evidence that fully justified this designation of
ownership. Thomas B. Reed of Maine was criticized during election
time for failing to provide work at the small Kittery yard. To protect
his political interests he demanded that the demolition of an old
wooden ship begin *at once*.[65] In Massachusetts the young Henry
Cabot Lodge "wanted jobs for his supporters, he wanted their restoration when they lost their jobs, he wanted new jobs created, he wanted
ships sent to Charlestown to be repaired, he wanted old ships sent
to be broken up; and the failure to grant these demands, he insisted,
would have a most calamitous effect upon Republican prospects in
the state."[66] The chairman of the Philadelphia City Committee wrote
Chandler, "Do not take away a large part of our party machinery by
closing the Philadelphia Navy Yard. Nearly 400 of our most active
and useful committee men are employed in the yard and no one
knows as well as you the power of patronage."[67]

Party needs not only had forced patronage into navy yard personnel; they compelled maintenance of unnecessary yards and much
"made work" in repairing old wooden ships; they also induced indefensible purchase of surplus stores. The chairman of the House Committee on Naval Affairs revealed that in 1886 the Department had
on hand $1,242,000 in clothing or in earmarked sums, over four times
that needed in any single year. Commodore Schley estimated that the
Bureau of Equipment and Recruiting had enough canvas to fit out
the entire British navy, and to supply our own for thirteen years although canvas was soon to become obsolete.[68]

Secretary William E. Chandler was the first Department head to
condemn vigorously this degradation of the naval service. In his last
annual report for 1884 he asserted that "we cannot afford to destroy
the speed of our naval engines to make votes for a political party,"
and assailed the waste in maintaining unnecessary yards.[69] His successor, William C. Whitney, found the yards still under political
domination, although the civil service system had covered the departmental clerks. He fought against political influence as best he could
but, according to the testimony of U.S. Civil Service Commissioner

[65] Leon B. Richardson, *William E. Chandler*, p. 310.
[66] *Ibid.*, p. 310.
[67] *Ibid.*, p. 312.
[68] Mark D. Hirsch, *William C. Whitney*, p. 264.
[69] Secretary of the Navy, *Annual Report*, 1884, p. 17.

Roosevelt, over 1,000 men were temporarily employed at the New York navy yard during the presidential campaign of 1888.[70] Secretary Tracy dismissed all the yard foremen, instituted employment boards in each yard, and put men to work (on probation) in the order of their application—a plan that aroused much political opposition. Secretary Herbert continued this system, modified to secure a rough equalization between the two parties. In 1896 Cleveland placed the yard clerks, messengers, and watchmen under the civil service system.[71]

Secretary Long was an ardent friend of civil service reform, and by the turn of the century the influence of patronage in the navy yards had been substantially destroyed. The passage of the Civil Service Act of 1883, a succession of reforming Secretaries, and support from the Presidents gradually blunted the sharp edges of the politicians' battle-axes, for many elections swung over the heads of one of the largest blocks of federal employees. That the efficiency of the yards was greatly improved was the universal testimony of the navy men.

By 1900 obvious progress had thus been made in the capacity of the Navy Department for planning and for action. The Office of Naval Intelligence had been set up in 1882, a departmental library was instituted in the same year, the Naval War College was established in 1884, the office of Assistant Secretary reconstituted in 1890, and the General Board authorized in 1900. These were substantial administrative advances, paralleled by a progressive reduction of patronage in the navy yards.

The standing of the Navy Department at the close of the Spanish-American War was extraordinarily high, in startling contrast to its prestige for nearly two decades after the Civil War. The country was in an imperialistic mood, ready to take its place as a great power. The navy was an essential agency of great-power politics. The dramatic voyage of the *Oregon*, the destruction of the Spanish fleets in Manila Bay and off the Cuban coast, the undisputed control of American waters in the Atlantic and the Pacific were causes for national pride.

[70] U.S. Civil Service Commission, *Annual Report*, 1896-97, p. 180.
[71] Charles O. Paullin, "A Half Century of Naval Administration," U.S. Naval Institute, *Proceedings*, XXXIX (1913), 1490-91.

CHAPTER NINE

The Department
of the Interior

The Department of the Interior might well have been designated the Department of the Great Miscellany. Every government has such an agency, and at one point the Department even had a miscellaneous division, a sort of compounded Miscellany. Interior was organized in 1849 to relieve the existing departments of some of their unwanted baggage: Lands from Treasury, Patents from State, Pensions and Indian Affairs from War. These were the Big Four. There was no semblance of unity then among the major historic components of the Interior Department, and they continued in the substantially independent conduct each of its own business.

THE DEPARTMENT

Functions. When Jacob D. Cox became Secretary of the Interior in 1869, the Department had already acquired a considerable additional number of unrelated dependents. The passage of time merely added to the Great Miscellany. Secretary William F. Vilas declared in 1888, "The scope of the Department's jurisdiction is wide, and the affairs in its keeping are various and disconnected in nature. This rendered symmetrical organization difficult in the beginning; while the addition by Congress, from time to time, of further duties, and the accumulation of business by the rapid development of the country . . . have increased the inconvenience arising from lack of satisfactory arrangement and definition of the functions of the officers of the Department and the methods of work."[1] There was not and,

[1] Secretary of the Interior, *Annual Report*, 1888, p. iii.

indeed, could hardly be a satisfactory arrangement of such a multitude of dissimilar agencies.

However difficult the task of administering the Department of the Interior in 1869, it was even more bothersome in 1900, despite whatever development of the administrative art there had been in the intervening years. The substantive agencies of the Department then numbered over twenty. Besides the central constellation (Land, Patents, Pensions, and Indian Affairs), there were the Bureau of Education, the Commissioner of Railroads, the U.S. Geological Survey, the Census Office, the Architect of the Capitol Extension, two hospitals (Government Hospital for the Insane, and the Freedmen's Hospital), Howard University, the Columbia Institution for the Deaf and Dumb, six territorial governments, including two overseas (Hawaii and Puerto Rico), four local District of Columbia offices, and four national parks, including Yellowstone and Yosemite. To discover unity in such diversity was beyond the power of man, and to weld such an aggregation into a department worthy of the name was beyond the capacity of any Secretary.

The administrative problem was rendered more acute because the Department lacked accommodations which permitted its various agencies to be brought into easy contact with its head. The Secretary's office was in the so-called Patent Office Building (subsequently housing the U.S. Civil Service Commission), where in 1880 were also located, with a desperate lack of room, Lands, Patents, Indian Affairs, and the Bureau of Railroad Accounts. Four other bureaus were located in different parts of the city in rented quarters. "The scattering of the different bureaus constituting this department in widely separated locations," Carl Schurz wrote in 1880, "causes much delay and circumstance in the correspondence between the bureau chiefs and the head of the department, which should always be easy and rapid."[2] The space problem was chronic, and constantly handicapped both the Secretary in overhead control and the subordinate agencies in their daily routine.

Interior, in short, lacked both the organic unity and the housing facilities to enable it to rise above a vast collection of units, large and small, important and unimportant. Compared with Treasury,

[2] *Ibid.*, *1880*, p. 68.

State, War, Navy, and the Post Office, each of which had a substantially homogeneous function, Interior was indeed the Great Miscellany. The absence of organic unity is nowhere more apparent than in the annual reports of the Secretaries during this period, which were scarcely more than an epitome of the separate reports of the subordinate agencies. The Secretaries had nothing to say as the administrative heads of the Department. They usually seemed to be unaware, indeed, of a function of their own.

Overhead organization. The major administrative problem of the Secretary of the Interior was that which in later years was familiarly designated as the span of control. A large number of agencies reported directly to the Secretary, and in law they performed their duties under his supervision and direction. Moreover, in the case of Patents, Lands, and Pensions, his was an appellate office to review decisions unfavorable to applicants. Furthermore, most of the appeals involved a complex mass of law, administrative precedent, and judicial decision—notably Lands and Patents. "The labor involved in the supervising and directing the great diversity of national affairs . . . [in] this Department," declared Secretary Ethan A. Hitchcock in 1900, "is enormous. . . ."[3] It had always been excessive.

What assistance could Secretaries command? Carl Schurz had little: an Assistant Secretary and a chief clerk. The latter relieved the Secretary of housekeeping and supervisory functions, the former dealt primarily with substantive questions of policy or administration. That such help was not enough was the testimony of Secretary Vilas in 1888: "most of the machinery is more or less needlessly cumbered, but especially the head of the Department, whose good service requires above all his freedom from such embarrassments, is laden with the performance of exhausting details of duty that could as well or better be discharged by the assistants or others, and that waste time sorely needed to suitably answer the higher and more important exigencies of supervision of the public concerns under his management."[4] His remedy was a modest one: to secure authority for the Assistant Secretary to sign accounts, warrants, and financial papers.[5]

By 1900 Secretaries had a much more highly developed overhead

[3] *Ibid.*, 1900, p. 3.
[4] *Ibid.*, 1888, p. iii.
[5] *Ibid.*, 1888, p. iv.

organization to relieve them of work. There were now two Assistant Secretaries. There were a whole series of housekeeping offices: the division of appointments and the division of finance; the divisions of stationery and printing and of public documents; the custodian's division and the superintendent's branch in charge of the watch. More significantly, four substantive divisions were interposed between the Big Four bureaus and the Secretary or Assistant Secretaries. These were the division of lands and railroads, the division of Indian affairs, the division of patents and miscellaneous, and the division of Indian territory.[6] Each of these units comprised a chief and eight or ten clerks. Their central task was to prepare material from their respective bureaus for the Secretary.

The position and function of these four divisions were anomalous. They stood between the Commissioners and the Secretary. They presumably sought to protect the Secretary so far as possible from detail, but they ran the risk of making his decisions rather than facilitating his actions. They could easily become bottlenecks. Secretary James R. Garfield abolished them in 1907 in order to throw full responsibility upon the heads of the great bureaus. To quote his words:

. . . four divisions of the Secretary's Office, namely, Indian Territory, Indian Affairs, Patents and Miscellaneous, and Lands and Railroads, were abolished and the work of those divisions distributed to the bureaus and offices dealing with the particular subjects. These divisions had outlived their usefulness, and had become stumbling blocks in the way of good administration, as they brought between the Secretary and the bureau chiefs an unnecessary examination of and action upon the work of the bureau or office. They furthermore had a tendency to lessen the responsibility and authority of the head of the bureau or office and interfere with the cordial and confidential relation that must exist between the Secretary and the head of an office if best results are to be obtained.[7]

The problem was characteristic and in large agencies universal: how a Secretary could control a department effectively without assuming direct responsibility for an impossible mass of detail. It was acute in Interior, both on account of its size and its heterogeneity, and there was little evidence that any Secretary during this period found a workable solution.

[6] *Official Register*, 1901, I, 917 ff.
[7] Secretary of the Interior, *Annual Report*, 1907, pp. 1-2.

Another organizational problem was inherent in the top structure of the Department. The four Commissioners, Land, Patent, Pensions, and Indian Affairs, were presidential appointees by and with the advice and consent of the Senate. In other words, their tenure was the same as that of the Secretary, and presumably political considerations were important in their selection. All were subject to heavy political pressures. It is now impossible to reconstruct the intimate consequences of these considerations, but in principle they were conducive to an independent role for the four Commissioners. A former member of Congress, such as Commissioner of Patents Benjamin Butterworth, might carry as much political prestige as a Secretary of the Interior.

The issue actually came to a head in a controversy between Secretary John W. Noble and the Commissioner of Pensions, "Corporal" Tanner.[8] A former Union soldier, James Tanner, had acquired considerable political standing as a representative of the Grand Army of the Republic and boldly proclaimed a superliberal policy toward his old comrades when President Harrison appointed him Commissioner of Pensions in 1889. He soon came into conflict with Secretary Noble, who sought to control a course of action marked by favoritism if not illegality. Tanner took the ground that the Secretary could not interfere with such of his decisions as were alleged to grant "too much pension"; the Secretary's power of review, he held, extended only to cases in which a claim had not been approved. This high notion of the Commissioner was overruled in an able opinion by the Secretary.[9] Tanner then sought to circumvent an investigation by the Secretary, whereupon Noble told the Commissioner that he was both disrespectful and insubordinate to the last degree.[10] Tanner was shortly thereafter induced to resign.

The legal authority of the Secretary of the Interior was thus fully vindicated, and indeed only an adventurer like Tanner would have presumed to question it. A Secretary's effective influence depended on other than legal considerations. The dispersion of function was so great that perhaps no man could have dominated the whole of this sprawling organism. One remedy would have been to split off some

[8] *Ibid.*, 1889, pp. clii-clxvii.
[9] *Ibid.*, especially pp. clii-cliv.
[10] *Ibid.*, p. clxvii.

of the major bureaus into departments, and this indeed was proposed from time to time. Apart from congressional reluctance to increase the number of departments (with high salaries and greater executive prestige), it would not have been unreasonable to establish separate agencies for Indian Affairs, Public Lands, and Pensions.

To understand fully the Department of the Interior, one further remark is needed concerning the immense pressures that were brought to bear upon it by outside parties. Interior was the focus of a whole series of special interest groups, many of whose members were prepared to use any means to obtain their ends. They included particularly the big contractors for Indian supplies; the big land operators, land corporations, and timber dealers; the mining operators; and the old soldiers, effectively organized in the Grand Army of the Republic. The matter was eloquently stated by Carl Schurz, while still head of the Department. In a letter to President-elect Garfield, he wrote:

The Interior Department is the most dangerous branch of the public service. It is more exposed to corrupt influences and more subject to untoward accidents than any other. To keep it in good repute and to manage its business successfully requires on the part of its head a thorough knowledge of its machinery, untiring work and sleepless vigilance. I shall never forget the trials I had to go through during the first period of my Administration, and the mistakes that were made before I had things well in hand. It is a constant fight with the sharks that surround the Indian bureau, the General Land Office, the Pension Office and the Patent Office, and a ceaseless struggle with perplexing questions and situations, especially in the Indian service. Unless the head of the Interior Department well understands and performs his full duty, your Administration will be in constant danger of disgrace. . . .[11]

The portent of these remarks will become fully apparent in the pages that follow.

The Secretaries. Who were the hard-pressed Secretaries of the Interior? With the exception of Columbus Delano (1870–75), they were men of character and high integrity, although not particularly successful executives. All were caught in the machine and none seemed to surmount it. The post normally went to a westerner, apart from two southern appointments—Lucius Quintus Cincinnatus Lamar from Mississippi, one of the few Confederate officers to attain Cabinet

---

[11] Carl Schurz, *Speeches, Correspondence and Political Papers,* IV, 81-82 (Jan. 2, 1881).

rank after the Civil War,[12] and Hoke Smith of Georgia. Most of the Secretaries had studied and practiced law, and Lamar went from Interior to the Supreme Court. Several were bankers or interested in railroads and investment. Almost all were active in politics and public life, attending national nominating conventions (a mark of the professional), sitting in state legislatures and Congress, serving as governors.

One of the most spectacular political appointments was made by Grant in 1875 in the selection of Zachariah Chandler, the "boss" of the Republican party in Michigan and subsequently chairman of the Republican National Committee. This appointment caused Carl Schurz to write to Rutherford B. Hayes, soon to become Grant's successor, "one of the worst things done yet is the election of Secretary Chandler to the chairmanship of the National Committee. It is in the highest degree improper on principle that a man who wields the patronage and influence of one of the Departments of the Government, should also be the manager of a party in a campaign. . . ."[13] Chandler's record, nevertheless, was good.[14]

These department heads had one characteristic in common, an incapacity to write in general terms concerning their role as Secretary. None of them gave any indication, in such of their official or private writings as have come to attention, that they faced the baffling administrative problem inherent in their position. Officially, they wrote dutifully in their annual reports a restatement of the views of their bureau chiefs; privately, they complained about the pressure of office seeking and their daily labors, but a sense of the art of administration was absent. The history of the Department of the Interior was the history of its bureaus; and to the Big Four we now turn.

THE OFFICE OF INDIAN AFFAIRS

During the thirty years from Jackson's term to the end of Buchanan's administration the general tenor of Indian policy and administration had undergone no major change. The Indians continued

---

[12] Edward Mayes, *Lucius Q. C. Lamar*; Wirt Armistead Cate, *Lucius Q. C. Lamar: Secession and Reunion* (Chapel Hill: University of North Carolina Press, 1935).
[13] Carl Schurz, *Speeches, Correspondence and Political Papers*, III, 260 (July 14, 1876).
[14] Wilmer C. Harris, *Public Life of Zachariah Chandler, 1851-1875* (Michigan Historical Commission, 1917).

to be recognized as dependent nations; their relations with the government were fixed by treaty; they were induced by treaty to yield their homeland and move west to new reservations and again farther west as the tide of white migration pressed upon them. Missionaries sought to Christianize the heathen; Indian agents distributed supplies and annuities; schoolteachers taught elementary education and the household arts to the Indian boys and girls. Vague ideas of assimilating the Indians into white culture and American citizenship persisted, but the Indians also persisted in preference for a simple and nomadic existence. Sporadic but savage wars occurred from time to time as the Indians resisted encroachment or attacked outlying settlements. The Indian problem thus remained both a military and a civilian affair.[15]

After the close of the Civil War the Commissioner of Indian Affairs reported the number of Indians in these figures: civilized, 97,000; semicivilized, 125,000; wholly barbarous, 78,000. The greater proportion, 180,000, had treaties with the United States and were consequently involved in relatively stable and mutually understood relations with the government; another 40,000 lived on reservations and were more or less under the control of the Indian agents; about 55,000 were totally uncontrolled.[16] These figures were estimates.

Before 1850 there remained enough unoccupied land and game

[15] There is a voluminous official and unofficial literature on Indian affairs. For official reports covering the formative years of post-Civil War policy and administration, see Senate Report 156, 39th Cong., 2d sess. (Jan. 26, 1867); House Ex. Doc. 97, 40th Cong., 2d sess. (Jan. 7, 1868); House Report 39, 41st Cong., 3d sess. (Feb. 25, 1871); House Report 98, 42d Cong., 3d sess. (March 3, 1873); House Report 778, 43d Cong., 1st sess. (June 22, 1874). The annual reports of the Commissioner of Indian Affairs and the Board of Indian Commissioners give much detail.

For secondary accounts see, in addition to biographical data, in order of publication: Francis A. Walker, *The Indian Question* (Boston: James R. Osgood and Co., 1874); Francis E. Leupp, *The Indian and His Problem* (New York: Charles Scribner's Sons, 1910); Elsie Mitchell Rushmore, *The Indian Policy during Grant's Administrations* (Jamaica, New York: Marion Press, 1914); Laurence F. Schmeckebier, *The Office of Indian Affairs* (Baltimore: Johns Hopkins Press, 1927); Lewis Meriam, *The Problem of Indian Administration* (Baltimore: Johns Hopkins Press, 1928); J. P. Kinney, *A Continent Lost—A Civilization Won: Indian Land Tenure in America* (Baltimore: Johns Hopkins Press, 1937); Loring Benson Priest, *Uncle Sam's Stepchildren: the Reformation of United States Indian Policy, 1865-1887* (New Brunswick: Rutgers University Press, 1942).

[16] Secretary of the Interior, *Annual Report, 1872*, p. 403.

across the Mississippi to sustain the Indians, however great the hardships of their enforced removal from the eastern country. After the Mexican acquisitions and the rapid settlement of the west coast, the Indians were caught in a massive vise closing in upon them from the east and the west. The advancing fronts suddenly became even more threatening as the Union Pacific Railroad cut across the middle of the Indian territory in 1869 and as other lines pushed ahead of settlement into the northern plains and the southwest.

This critical change was noted in a telling passage of his 1869 report by Secretary of Interior Jacob D. Cox.

The completion of one of the great lines of railway to the Pacific coast has totally changed the conditions under which the civilized population of the country come in contact with the wild tribes. Instead of a slowly advancing tide of migration, making its gradual inroads upon the circumference of the great interior wilderness, the very center of the desert has been pierced. Every station upon the railway has become a nucleus for a civilized settlement, and a base from which lines of exploration for both mineral and agricultural wealth are pushed in every direction. Daily trains are carrying thousands of our citizens and untold values of merchandise across the continent, and must be protected from the danger of having hostile tribes on either side of the route. The range of the buffalo is being rapidly restricted, and the chase is becoming an uncertain reliance to the Indian for the sustenance of his family. . . .[17]

The situation of the Indian thus became more desperate and the years from 1865 to 1870 were filled with war and threats of war.

Indian policy. At the opening of Grant's administration it was obvious that Indian policy had to be reconsidered. Three possibilities were discussed: (1) extermination; (2) compulsory location of the tribes on reservations, with government aid until they could become self-supporting; (3) eventual civilization, with full absorption into white culture.

The prevailing sentiment on the frontier was in favor of the policy of extermination. The savage tribes were entitled, in this view, to no more consideration than dangerous wild beasts, and like them should be killed off to make way for civilization—and land. Such sentiments were abhorred in the East and among the religious denominations.

[17] *Ibid.*, 1869, p. vii.

Compulsory settlement of the tribes on reservations with government rations, clothing, and certain services was by far the dominant opinion and was incorporated in the so-called peace policy established by Grant in 1869.[18] This policy was officially described by Secretary of the Interior Columbus Delano in his annual report for 1873.

The so-called peace policy sought, first, to place the Indians upon reservations as rapidly as possible, where they could be provided for in such manner as the dictates of humanity and Christian civilization require. Being thus placed upon reservations, they will be removed from such contiguity to our frontier settlements as otherwise will lead, necessarily, to frequent outrages, wrongs, and disturbances of the public peace. On these reservations they can be taught, as fast as possible, the arts of agriculture, and such pursuits as are incident to civilization, through the aid of the Christian organizations of the country now engaged in this work, co-operating with the Federal Government. Their intellectual, moral, and religious culture can be prosecuted, and thus it is hoped that humanity and kindness may take the place of barbarity and cruelty. Second; whenever it is found that any tribe or band of Indians persistently refuse to go upon a reservation and determine to continue their nomadic habits, accompanied with depredations and outrages upon our frontier settlements, then the policy contemplates the treatment of such tribe or band with all needed severity, to punish them for their outrages according to their merits, thereby teaching them that it is better to follow the advice of the Government, live upon reservations and become civilized, than to continue their native habits and practices.[19] Third; it is the determination of this policy to see that all supplies of every kind, whether of food or clothing, purchased for distribution to Indians, upon reservations and remaining at peace with the Government, are procured at fair and reasonable prices, so that the Indian meriting such supplies may

[18] Termination of Indian treaties in 1871 was less a mark of policy change than the resolution of a conflict between House and Senate over certain pending treaties disliked by the House. 16 Stat. 566 (March 3, 1871).

[19] A peculiarly harsh treatment was given the Modoc tribe, located in the northwest. After the assassination of two treaty commissioners the army captured most of the tribe, their leaders were executed, the remnant of the tribe was removed east of the Rocky Mountains, tribal relations were broken up and the Modocs distributed among tribes friendly to the United States. "The Indian," reported Secretary Delano, "is greatly attached to his tribal organization, and it is believed that this example of extinguishing their so-called national existence and merging their members into other tribes . . . will be esteemed by them as the severest penalty that could have been inflicted. . . ." Secretary of the Interior, *Annual Report*, 1873, pp. ix-x.

receive the same without having the funds of the Government squandered in their purchase. Fourth; it is the purpose of the Government, as fast as possible, through the instrumentality and by the advice and assistance of the various religious organizations, and by all other means within its power, to procure competent, upright, faithful, moral, and religious agents to care for the Indians that go upon reservations; to distribute the goods and provisions that are purchased for them by the benevolence of the Government; to aid in their intellectual, moral, and religious culture, and thus to assist in the great work of humanity and benevolence, which the policy aims to accomplish. Fifth; it is the further aim of the policy to establish schools, and, through the instrumentality of the Christian organizations, acting in harmony with the Government, as fast as possible, to build churches and organize Sabbath-schools, whereby these savages may be taught a better way of life than they have heretofore pursued, and be made to understand and appreciate the comforts and benefits of a Christian civilization, and thus be prepared ultimately to assume the duties and privileges of citizenship. . . .[20]

The policy objective of absorption with the consequent end of the reservation system was eloquently stated in 1891 by Indian Commissioner Thomas J. Morgan. "The end at which we aim is that the American Indians shall become as speedily as possible Indian-Americans; that the savage shall become a citizen; that the nomad shall cease to wander, and become a resident in a fixed habitation; that hunting shall cease to be a necessity, and become a pastime; that the smouldering fires of war shall become extinguished; that tribal animosities shall end; that the Indians . . . shall . . . assemble in their places of worship to thank the Great Father above for the blessings of a Christian civilization vouchsafed to them in common with us all."[21]

During the three decades from Grant to McKinley energies were exhausted in making the reservation system work effectively. It was stubbornly, if vainly, resisted by many tribes; it was criticized in principle and in detail; it was the source of extravagance, abuse, and graft; but its faults gradually were mitigated by an unusual series of administrative expedients, by the progressive improvement of Indian service standards, and by the mere passage of time.

[20] *Ibid.,* 1873, pp. iii-iv.
[21] Thomas J. Morgan, *The Present Phase of the Indian Question* (Boston: Frank Wood, 1891), p. 21.

Indian administration. Responsibility for Indian matters, long a duty of the War Department, had been transferred to the new Department of the Interior in 1849. Thenceforward the Secretary of the Interior, under the President, was the final authority in Indian administration. His powers and duties were delegated for routine administration to the Commissioner of Indian Affairs, an official appointed by the President with the advice and consent of the Senate. The actual business of this office had perforce to be conducted at distant points in the field. The key figure here was the agent, of whom there were from fifty to sixty or more at different periods. Agents were appointed for four-year terms by the President with the advice and consent of the Senate. They were thus securely anchored to the party organization.[22] Their duties were heavy and ill-defined. They were required to manage and superintend intercourse with the Indians agreeably to law and regulation, to distribute annuities and goods in accordance with treaties and annual appropriations, to remove trespassers and fugitives from justice, and to seize intoxicating liquors. No force of any kind was placed at their disposal for such duties or for the maintenance of order, and the agent had to conduct himself nominally as an ambassador to an alien people with whom an attempt at compulsion was equivalent to a declaration of war.

The field staff included a variety of husbandmen and teachers. The nature of an Indian agency and its dependence on the government may be illustrated by reference to the annual appropriation by Congress to the Crows in 1871.[23] The items of this section included funds to supply 600 male persons over fourteen years of age with a suit of good substantial woolen cloth; 700 females over twelve years of age with a flannel shirt, a pair of woolen hose, twelve yards of calico, and twelve of domestic cotton; 350 boys and 350 girls with cotton and flannel goods to make each a suit and a pair of woolen hose; ten dollars for "each Indian roaming" to purchase such articles as "necessities may indicate to be proper"; seeds and implements for such Indians as continued to farm "(say fifty souls)"; flour and meat; and pay of the subordinate personnel.

These subordinate assistants included typically a clerk to the

22 Revised Statutes, secs. 2052, 2056.
23 16 Stat. 544 at 551-52 (March 3, 1871).

agent and an issue clerk; a physician; farmers, blacksmiths, and carpenters; a herder and a butcher; laborers and one or more apprentices. There was also the staff of the Indian school and an Indian police with such distinctive names as Captain Little Dog, Sergeant Double Runner, and privates Heavy Gun, Wolf Tail, Old Robe, and the like.[24]

The Department of the Interior had an active competitor for the administration of Indian business in the War Department, never fully reconciled to its loss of the Indian Office in 1849. Army officers argued that they necessarily had to take responsibility for subduing and controlling the savage Indians and for protecting the frontier settlements; that divided responsibility was bad and that it should be ended by returning all Indians to their charge; and that army control would eliminate graft and corruption in Indian transactions. Congressional committees three times recommended transfer of all Indian business to the War Department in 1876, 1878, and 1880 respectively.[25]

The Indian Office, aided by citizens concerned about the welfare of the Indians, fought back vigorously and successfully. Its attitude was adequately stated in the following excerpt from an annual report of the Board of Indian Commissioners. "While we have the highest respect for the ability, courage, and humanity of our military officers, we cannot close our eyes to the fact that the men who enlist in the Army in time of peace are among the most vicious of our population; and there is unquestionable and abundant evidence . . . that wherever the latter are brought into close contact with the Indians, the debauchery of the women and the demoralization of the men inevitably follow. . . . The army is admirable in its place, but its function is not that of civil government in a republic like ours."[26] The issue gradually disappeared after 1880; Interior was left in full control.

Fraud and corruption in the Indian service. No one reading Secretary Delano's statement of President Grant's peace policy would have been enlightened as to the actual condition of the Indian

[24] For examples, see *Official Register*, 1891, p. 698.
[25] House Report 240, 44th Cong., 1st sess. (March 14, 1876); House Report 241, 45th Cong., 2d sess. (Feb. 25, 1878); House Report 1393, 46th Cong., 2d sess. (May 8, 1880).
[26] Board of Indian Commissioners, *Annual Report*, 1875, p. 15.

service. It was then and had long been in a deplorable situation, beyond the apparent capacity of the Department of the Interior to correct. The pervading fraud and mismanagement had been revealed by Congressman James A. Garfield on February 4, 1869: "I am compelled to say," he told the House, "that no branch of the national government is so spotted with fraud, so tainted with corruption, so utterly unworthy of a free and enlightened government, as this Indian Bureau."[27] The House Committee on Indian Affairs corroborated this judgment in 1873, placing at the head of their report in bold capital letters the following words: "By this investigation and report the committee hope to do something to rid the Indians and the Indian service of those heartless scoundrels who infest it, and who do so much damage to the Indian, the settler, and the government."[28] The committee declared:

> Great frauds and wrongs have been committed with impunity in the past by means of exorbitant and fraudulent contracts for nominal services as attorneys. . . . there has continually been, and now is, a class of avaricious and unprincipled claim-agents and middle-men, who, for selfish purposes, defeat the mutual interests of the Government, our people, and the Indians, and plundering both the Government and the Indians, disgrace the nation and our civilization. . . .[29]

According to its secretary, Mr. Thomas K. Cree, the Board of Indian Commissioners (to which attention is given shortly) "found the Indian service honeycombed with fraud, from the Indian Office in Washington to the most remote Indian agency, and, as the Board believed, from the head of it to the most unimportant employé."[30]

To cope with the incompetence and corruption in and around the Indian office, both Congress and the President went to work, although neither branch was persistent in reformation. By an act of 1871 every contract with the Indians for services rendered them required the approval of both the Commissioner of Indian Affairs and the Secretary of the Interior.[31] In 1873 the President was authorized to appoint five inspectors for four-year terms, by and

[27] James A. Garfield, *Works*, I, 370.
[28] House Report 98, 42d Cong., 3d sess., p. 1 (March 3, 1873).
[29] *Ibid.*, pp. 2-3.
[30] Charles Lewis Slattery, *Felix Reville Brunot* (New York: Longmans, Green, and Co., 1901), p. 224.
[31] 16 Stat. 544, sec. 3 (March 3, 1871).

with the advice and consent of the Senate. They were to examine each Indian superintendency and agency at least twice a year, making a full investigation of business transactions, contracts, and generally all matters pertaining to the Indian service. They had power to suspend any superintendent or agent.[32] The object in mind was salutary, but senatorial confirmation was not the most certain means to obtain relief from political influence in Indian affairs.

Congress also authorized a citizen Board of Indian Commissioners to watch over the Indian Office and its transactions, and the President transferred the privilege of nominating agents from the western politicians to the various religious denominations. Thus the moral authority of citizens of standing and of the churches was mobilized to correct conditions that apparently were beyond the power of officialdom to control.

The Board of Indian Commissioners. This unpaid citizen board comprised ten persons appointed by the President from men "eminent for their intelligence and philanthropy." Under the President's direction, it was authorized to exercise joint control with the Secretary of the Interior over the disbursements of the annual Indian appropriations.[33] Obvious difficulties were inherent in this organization, notably the division of control between the Secretary and an unpaid citizen board. In due course of time they were influential in causing the resignation of the majority of the first Board.

Subsequent legislation further defined the duties of the Board and the extent of its actual control. In 1870 the Board was authorized to supervise the expenditure of all Indian funds and to inspect all goods purchased for the Indians; the Commissioner of Indian Affairs was directed to consult with the Board in making such purchases.[34] By legislation in 1871, 50 per cent of all payments due to Indian contractors were withheld pending inspection of the accounts and vouchers by the Board, which was given power to approve or disapprove them. This authority was, however, provisional, since the Secretary of the Interior was empowered to modify the Board's action and to authorize full payment to be made.[35] In 1872 each

[32] 17 Stat. 437, sec. 6 (Feb. 14, 1873).
[33] 16 Stat. 13, sec. 4 (April 10, 1869).
[34] 16 Stat. 335, sec. 3 (July 15, 1870).
[35] 16 Stat. 544 at 568 (March 3, 1871).

member of the Board was individually authorized to investigate contracts, expenditures, and accounts.[36]

The Board, working principally through committees, performed herculean tasks. During its first three years the committees appointed to visit reservations traveled 256,000 miles in the performance of their duties.[37] The executive committee between 1871 and 1877 examined accounts aggregating more than $35,000,000 and recommended nonpayment of nearly $1,000,000.[38] The second chairman of the Board, Felix R. Brunot, gave practically all of his time to its work for five years,[39] and all members were active in consulting with the Indian Office, writing articles on the Indian question, preparing extensive annual reports, and traveling in the field.

The Board and the old Indian system were in fact in mortal conflict, and the Board was powerless to do more than investigate and publicize. These activities were not without good results, but they were inadequate to overthrow the system. Many beneficial changes were introduced and procedures were strengthened against collusive bidding, failure to deliver proper goods, and outright corruption. Publicity was a valuable asset and the eminence of the Board members ensured that they would be heard.

The Board encountered, however, two insurmountable obstacles, of which the first was lack of support from the Secretary of the Interior, Columbus Delano. Brunot's biographer recorded that by the close of 1873 the Board members were nearly at the end of their patience.

. . . They freely gave of their busy lives for the sake of the Indian, but when they found repeatedly during the last year that their recommendations were ignored, that bills, laboriously examined by them and rejected by them, were paid, that gross breaking of the law in giving contracts was winked at, and that many matters were not submitted to them at all, they decided that their task was as useless as it was irritating. . . .[40]

The second obstacle was inherent in the administrative organization and involved an insoluble dilemma that the Board itself recog-

[36] 17 Stat. 165 at 186 (May 29, 1872).

[37] Board of Indian Commissioners, *Annual Report*, 1872, p. 6.

[38] *Ibid.*, *Annual Reports*, 1871–1877, *passim*; Elsie M. Rushmore, *Indian Policy during Grant's Administrations*, pp. 24-25.

[39] Charles L. Slattery, *Felix R. Brunot*, p. 147.

[40] *Ibid.*, p. 219.

nized. Either the Board had authority or it did not. In the first case, "the engagements of the members of the Board would hardly permit them to accept the duty." In the second case, they declared themselves unwilling "to continue a service which seems to them as vexatious and arduous as it is ineffective in the correction of abuses."[41] The Board urged Grant to establish a separate Indian Department, and upon his refusal to recommend this course, six original members of the Board resigned.

New members were appointed and the Board continued for many years to serve as a useful agency of visitation and inspection, to which functions it was specifically restricted in 1882.[42]

The Indian agents. The second main drive to clean up the Indian Office was directed against the agents. While there were always conscientious and upright agents who sought fully to protect the interests of the Indians, as a class their reputation was low. "The records are abundant," declared an Indian Peace Commission in 1868, "to show that agents have pocketed the funds appropriated by the government and driven the Indians to starvation. . . . For a long time these officers have been selected from partisan ranks, not so much on account of honesty and qualification as for devotion to party interests and their willingness to apply the money of the Indian to promote the selfish schemes of local politicians."[43]

Grant determined to break the hold of the party machine on the nomination of Indian agents and decided to give the privilege to the religious denominations that had been engaged in missionary work among the Indians—another recourse to outside civilians to correct a situation that apparently defied control by normal hierarchical means.[44] The Society of Friends was first engaged in the work but shortly thereafter many denominations were involved. A controversy promptly broke out over the assignment of agencies among them, the Catholic Church complaining, with apparent justice, that it was denied its due proportion.[45]

The success of this experiment was only partial. A more con-

[41] Letter of Brunot to President Grant (May 8, 1874), in *ibid.*, p. 223.
[42] 22 Stat. 68 at 70 (May 17, 1882).
[43] House Ex. Doc. 97, 40th Cong., 2d sess., p. 21 (Jan. 7, 1868).
[44] Richardson, *Messages*, VII, 109 (Dec. 5, 1870).
[45] Elsie M. Rushmore, *The Indian Policy during Grant's Administrations*, p. 29.

scientious and reliable set of agents was generally forthcoming, but they did not receive full support from the Indian Office. Conditions deteriorated as Grant gave four agencies to his brother, and as Secretary Delano was found to be implicated in shady Indian transactions. Brunot's biographer concluded: "Unhappily, in spite of fine results here and there, the various mission boards missed their opportunity; often irreligious men were sent, and even here politics found an avenue for spoils. But sorrowful as the outcome was, it gave the Indians better agents than they had yet received."[46]

The policy of nomination by the religious bodies was gradually abandoned and came to an end in the early eighties. In 1892 Congress reversed an earlier decision by directing the President to detail army officers as Indian agents when vacancies thereafter occurred.[47] In the interim the President personally controlled the agents' appointments. Commissioner Thomas J. Morgan declared in 1891 that he had never been consulted about them and had absolutely nothing to do with their selection.[48] Morgan also asserted that the popular view that agents were thieves had become a myth.[49] Their character had certainly improved as a consequence of the work of the religious denominations, and the slow but undoubted rise in the standards of official morality.[50]

Indian Commissioners. With few exceptions the Indian Office had only indifferent leadership during this period. Doubtless the most picturesque character serving as Indian Commissioner was General Ely S. Parker, a full-blooded Seneca Indian reared on a reservation but educated (up to age 18) at a Baptist mission school and two New York academies, and at age 24 a sachem of his tribe. He early suffered the handicaps of his minority race. Having read law, he was refused admission to the bar because he was an Indian; offering to fight in the Union army he was rejected by Secretary Seward who told Parker that this was a white man's war.[51] Law foreclosed, he studied engineering at Rensselaer Polytechnic Institute

[46] Charles L. Slattery, *Felix R. Brunot*, p. 146.
[47] 27 Stat. 120 (July 13, 1892).
[48] Thomas J. Morgan, *The Present Phase of the Indian Question*, p. 14.
[49] *Ibid.*, p. 10.
[50] See ch. 17, "Public Service Ethics."
[51] Arthur C. Parker, *The Life of General Ely S. Parker* (Buffalo: Buffalo Historical Society, 1919), pp. 102-103.

and while superintendent of construction for a customhouse and a marine hospital at Galena, Illinois, he became a friend of Grant. In 1863 Parker was commissioned as captain of engineers, was appointed military secretary to Grant, and in 1869 resigned as brigadier general and took office as Indian Commissioner. His reforms quickly made enemies who instigated groundless charges leading to a House investigation. Although fully cleared, his spirit was broken and he resigned in 1871. Subsequently he made a small fortune in Wall Street, lost it by paying the bond of a defaulter, and ended his career in the New York City police department.

Parker was succeeded by one of the most eminent of American public officials, Francis A. Walker. This famous economist and statistician had lost his appropriation as superintendent of the census; to allow him to complete the 1870 census, Grant put Walker into the Indian Office and for two years he in effect managed both. Walker had strong convictions on Indian matters, insisting that the aborigines yield to civilization but that the government discharge its moral obligations to them. On day-by-day policy he would extemporize. "With wild men, as with wild beasts, the question whether in a given situation one shall fight, coax, or run, is a question merely of what is easiest and safest."[52] Walker looked forward to the day when the last hostile tribe became reduced to beg for charity. "This is, indeed, the only hope of salvation for the aborigines of the continent. If they stand up against the progress of civilization and industry, they must be relentlessly crushed. . . . They must yield or perish. . . ."[53] Yielding, however, the Indians should be indemnified. "We are richer by hundreds of millions; the Indian is poorer by a large part of the little that he has. This growth is bringing imperial greatness to the nation; to the Indian it brings wretchedness, destitution, beggary. Surely there is obligation found in considerations like these, requiring us in some way, and in the best way, to make good to these original owners of the soil the loss by which we so greatly gain."[54]

Walker's brief administration of the Indian Office (1871–73)

[52] Commissioner of Indian Affairs, *Annual Report*, 1872, p. 5.
[53] *Ibid.*, p. 9 .
[54] *Ibid.*, p. 10; see also an article by Walker, "The Indian Question," *North American Review*, CXVI (1873), 329-88.

was the high watermark of the reforming influence of the Board of Indian Commissioners and the churches. He was followed in Grant's second term by Edward P. Smith and John Q. Smith, each of whom was investigated and neither of whom bore the best reputation.[55] Secretary Schurz desperately wanted a reliable Commissioner but made a poor choice in Ezra A. Hayt, who had the advantage of former membership on the Board of Indian Commissioners but also the handicap of not possessing the confidence of his fellow members. Schurz finally removed Hayt for a corrupt deal involving his son and a shady Indian agent.[56]

Harrison's Commissioner of Indian Affairs (1889-93), Thomas Jefferson Morgan, was one of the ablest. Colonel of the 14th U.S. Colored Infantry during the Civil War, Baptist clergyman and educator, he served as Commissioner for four years with zeal, energy, and good judgment. He secured the separation of Indian schools from their denominational affiliations, placing them on the same basis as the public schools.[57]

By slow and almost imperceptible degrees the character of the Indian problem had gradually assumed its final form in the thirty years from Grant to McKinley. In 1870 policy was in dispute; civil and military branches were contending for authority; vast stretches of the treeless plains were still occupied by wild Indians, undisturbed by advancing civilization; Indian wars were common and indeed occupied the principal attention of the United States Army. Indians on reservations were the victims of nefarious schemes to defraud them of their property; their government supplies were often deficient and tardy in arrival; and even their hold on their reservations was precarious.

By 1900 the Indian Wars were finished; the last campaign occurred in 1890. All the Indians were on reservations and, with rare exceptions, occupancy of the reservations was no longer in question. Indian title was finally respected as the pressure for their remaining poor land diminished. The moral and administrative quality of the Indian agents had been improved, and graft was less common, if not wholly

[55] Loring B. Priest, *Uncle Sam's Stepchildren*, p. 67.

[56] *Ibid.*, pp. 70-71. Board of Indian Commissioners, *Annual Report*, 1879, pp. 8, 68-70.

[57] *Dictionary of American Biography*, XIII, 187; Thomas J. Morgan, *The Present Phase of the Indian Question*, p. 12.

eradicated. The government more fully recognized its role as guardian and sought to administer Indian affairs for the benefit of the Indian, not for the advantage of white schemers.

The central theme of Indian policy had become paternalistic in quality: to safeguard Indian property rights, to allot land to individual Indian holders for agricultural development, and above all to educate the Indian children in the ways of the white man's culture. The annual reports of the Commissioner of Indian Affairs at the close of the century opened on the subject of education; the second most prominent topic was the allotment of land to Indians and the protection of interests in tribal lands leased for logging, mines, and rights of way for railroads and telephone lines. In 1907 the Secretary of the Interior wrote: "The Indian question will soon become an agricultural land question."[58] Wars and rumors of wars thus receded before less dramatic and fundamentally different administrative relations between the aborigines and the Great White Father.

[58] Secretary of the Interior, *Annual Report*, 1907, p. 6.

CHAPTER TEN

Land, Pensions, and Patents

It would be difficult to discover a more dismal example of administrative confusion, laxness, and frustration than that of the General Land Office. Cursed throughout these decades by the suspicion of corruption, generally lacking powerful leadership, and always half paralyzed by the weight of vast accumulations of unfinished business, the General Land Office had few friends either in Congress or in the western country. Commissioners repeatedly begged Congress for more manpower, but Congress was indifferent, and powerful interests exploiting western resources were unfriendly to a competent and vigorous land office.

Land policy. Early land policy favored the sale of public land with a primary view to reducing the national debt. It endured only until 1800 when policy shifted to disposition under terms that would encourage settlement. Legislation of 1800 provided a liberal credit system for purchasers, reduction in the minimum amount of land that could be purchased, and the establishment of land offices on the frontier—then just across the Allegheny Mountains.[1] The law and regulations required prior survey, deposit of maps and plats in Washington, central authorization to sell, and public auction with competitive bidding at the site of the local land office on an appointed day.

This orderly system was progressively undercut as eager pioneers pushed on ahead of the surveying parties, squatted on virgin territory, and established homes and settlements. To validate their moral

[1] 2 Stat. 73 (May 10, 1800).

[196]

claims, special preemption acts were passed from time to time, and in 1841 a general preemption statute authorized heads of families or single men over twenty-one to make settlements on public lands to which the Indian title had been extinguished, and to enter 160 acres upon payment of the minimum specified price per acre.[2] For various reasons the East fought preemption, which was "a victory of pioneer America over the more established eastern order of society. It was the capstone in the democratization of the public land system."[3]

Preemption as a means of acquiring title stood on the statute books until 1891.[4] It was paralleled by the Homestead Act of 1862, a major law designed to facilitate even more rapid settlement of unoccupied lands by bona fide settlers.[5] This act granted 160 acres of land to actual settlers (or 80 acres of superior quality land) for occupancy and the payment of relatively small fees upon completion of title. Preemption and homesteading precipitated a long struggle between the government, committed to the interest of bona fide farmers on the one hand, and speculators and large-scale land operators on the other. The latter were often successful.

The major technical task of the government was, in short, (1) to extinguish Indian title to lands on the westward moving frontier, (2) to vest good title in the public domain to actual bona fide settlers, and (3) to protect the public domain from spoliation and from fraud. Supplementary responsibilities were imposed in bewildering number and complexity with reference to soldier bounty lands, timber and mineral lands, desert lands, swamp lands, and land grants to railroads and to states and their subdivisions for various public purposes. Land law became complex. For many years the administrative precedents were not organized or available except to the land office clerks, and claims and contests over land ownership multiplied.

For nearly a full century the general land policy was thus designed to divest the government of title to the public lands and to encourage settlement by small owners. The Mississippi valley, the west coast, and the intermountain dry lands were progressively occupied,

[2] 5 Stat. 453, sec. 10 (Sept. 4, 1841).
[3] Roy M. Robbins, *Our Landed Heritage: The Public Domain, 1776-1936* (Princeton: Princeton University Press, 1942), p. 91.
[4] 26 Stat. 1095, sec. 4 (March 3, 1891).
[5] 12 Stat. 392 (May 20, 1862).

but by the last quarter of the nineteenth century doubt arose among forward-looking men about both policy and its administration. Timber shortages appeared possible; soil conservation seemed necessary as floods swept forest-denuded lands; fraud in the acquisition of rich mineral and forest land was common. The policy of disposition of the land and its rapid settlement was challenged by the forces of conservation, forces that were to win their principal victories only after Theodore Roosevelt succeeded William McKinley in the White House.

The General Land Office. The office manned by a single clerk who handled land business in the Treasury Department during Washington's administration had grown into a large and complex organization long before it was transferred to Interior in 1849. It was compelled to expand (so far as a reluctant Congress would permit) to keep up with the movement of the population. "Imagination can scarcely keep pace with the increase of the western country," declared the Land Commissioner in 1851. "The great and fertile valley of the Mississippi, which a few years since was the out-post of civilization and the hunting ground of the savage, has now become the geographical and commercial centre of our ocean-bound republic. . . . Villages, towns and populous cities have sprung up as by magic. . . .[6]

The essential elements of the Land Office as it stood in 1891 included (1) its political overhead, (2) the headquarters divisions and staffs, (3) the field organization, and (4) the inspectional and investigative service. The political overhead comprised the Commissioner and, after 1884, the assistant commissioner.[7] These men were responsible for policy, especially as it involved decisions in contested cases, for operations, for control of the field service, and for congressional contacts. They were harassed even by their routine duties. Commissioner Noah C. McFarland stated in 1883 that half his time was taken up with official interviews, and that he had to sign about 500 letters and documents daily, thus leaving little or no

[6] Commissioner of the General Land Office, *Annual Report*, 1851, p. 3. Senate Ex. Doc. 1, 32d Cong., 1st sess., Part III.

[7] 23 Stat. 186 (July 7, 1884). The prescribed duties of the assistant commissioner were to sign letters, papers, and documents, and to perform such other duties as directed by the Commissioner.

time for more important matters.[8] For many years the principal, indeed the only, subordinate administrative officer was the chief clerk, the primary intermediary between the Commissioner and his organization for housekeeping matters.

The work of the General Land Office was assigned to divisions, numbering at various times from seven or eight to thirteen or more. Each had its own specialty: public lands, preemption claims, railroad lands, swamp lands, contested cases, and the like. Each had a head and a relatively permanent body of clerks, who gradually became expert in their specialties. As will be noted soon, these "clerks" were the crucial body of land office employees. Besides them there were special examiners of contested claims and three inspectors. The work of all these classes was partly clerical in the usual sense of the term, but it generally also involved a wide knowledge of land law, precedents, and judicial decisions. Curtis W. Holcomb, chief clerk, testified in 1881, "The business transacted here is really a profession in itself. No person can acquire it in a brief period."[9]

The mass of pending cases was always so great that the initial examination by a clerk paid from $1,000 to $1,800 a year was usually the only thorough consideration: "the great body of those cases are in fact decided by the division clerks, many of whom are not educated lawyers," the Committee on Public Lands reported in 1882.[10] The chief of the division accepted the facts "as found by the clerk," and limited himself to a review of the legal principles applied by his subordinate. A board of general supervision, one of several successive review boards, could not perform a thorough job "from sheer lack of time and physical strength. They give a rapid glance at such matters as seem to be most important, and only in rare cases do they stop a case on its hurried progress through the official routine. This scarcely amounts to a pretence of a review. The case then goes to the chief clerk and from him to the Commissioner. Neither of these officers have so much time as those through whose hands the cases have come to review them, and they are passed into decisions, no one objecting."[11]

[8] Commissioner of the General Land Office, *Annual Report*, 1883, pp. 32-33.
[9] Senate Report 362, 47th Cong., 1st sess., p. 9 (Dec. 27, 1881).
[10] *Ibid.*, p. vii (April 3, 1882).
[11] *Ibid.*, p. vii.

The success and stability of the organization of the General Land Office were in continuous hazard owing to the resignation of the best clerks for better paid private employment. Commissioner Willis Drummond reported in 1871, "It is now a difficult task to procure and *retain* clerks that can be profitably employed on the more important branches of the work of the office . . . for the reason that the utterly inadequate salaries now paid by the government too often fail to induce the more competent clerks to remain in the Bureau. . . ."[12] A decade later the chief of the public lands division stated: "Some of the best men employed during an administration of 20 years have left us and connected themselves with big corporations or firms, who wanted shrewd, capable, and experienced men; my division has been weakened and crippled during the last two or three years by the loss of five or six good men. . . ."[13] The best men were the ones to leave; the mediocre tended to remain.

The field service, originally clinging to the western slope of the Alleghenies, gradually moved west as land was occupied and the new frontier worked its way toward the Mississippi and, after the Civil War, with increasing momentum across the plains. The pivot of the field service was the land office with two principal officers: the register, in general charge, and the receiver, responsible for financial transactions.[14] In 1891 there were 123 land offices, each with a small complement of clerks.[15] Separately organized were the seventeen offices of the surveyors general, who were responsible for the continuing duty of surveying unoccupied land and preparing maps and plats.

Connection between headquarters and field had been notoriously weak during the 1870's and early 1880's. Congress was finally persuaded to enlarge an embryonic inspection staff, and in 1891 the General Land Office employed 49 special agents to investigate fraudulent land entries and 33 special agents to look into timber depredations. They were well and fully occupied.[16]

The failure of manpower. The General Land Office was harassed

---

[12] Commissioner of the General Land Office, *Annual Report*, 1871, p. 83.

[13] Senate Report 362, 47th Cong., 1st sess., p. 38 (Dec. 28, 1881).

[14] Secretary of the Interior Hitchcock discussed the duality of functions of these officers in his *Annual Report*, 1905, pp. 28-35.

[15] *Official Register*, 1891, pp. 692-96.

[16] *Ibid.*, pp. 685-86.

by two perennial problems: lack of adequate staff and failure to safeguard official transactions from deception and fraud. The Office suffered heavily on both counts.

The mass of business was enormous, and it was carried on in an era when modern office procedures were unknown and handwork methods were universal. The annual report of the Commissioner for 1883 revealed the following partial account of the year's transactions.[17]

Entries and filings posted at all land offices	251,685
Number of entries approved for patenting	53,847
Number of patents issued	50,482
Number of contested cases examined and acted upon	4,274
Number of claims confirmed by the Board of Equitable Adjudication	1,727
Number of cash sales (totaling over 6,800,000 acres)	11,104
Number of letters received	117,800
Number of letters written	88,955

Business poured in more rapidly than even this record of work done could equal. The Senate Select Committee on Methods of Business and Work (the Cockrell Committee) surveyed the General Land Office in 1887–88 and found a depressing backlog of arrearages. As of August 20, 1887, there were in the files, undisposed of, 139,620 pending entries in the public lands division, 67,000 cases in the preemption division, 52,342 cases in the board of review, 12,708 in the contest division (and 14,000 unanswered letters), and 5,000 cases in the mineral division; a total for these five divisions alone of 276,670 pending cases. In addition there was an unknown volume of private land claims; nearly the entire work of railroad land grant

[17] Commissioner of the General Land Office, *Annual Report, 1883*, pp. 4-5, 26.

adjustment; the adjustment of swamp, school, internal improvement, and other congressional grants; Indian allotments; and work incident to fraudulent entries and timber trespass.[18] The Land Office had long suffered from such overwhelming arrearages.

Two solutions were possible: more clerks and examiners, agents and field men; or streamlined methods. The Commissioners sought the answer in more manpower; Congress in better administration. In his annual report for 1883 Commissioner McFarland declared:

> The General Land Office has been deficient in clerical organization from the beginning. There has at no time been a sufficient number of employés to dispose of current work. The increase provided for from time to time has never been proportionate to the increase of business. The volume of work in arrears at the close of each fiscal year has steadily and rapidly grown larger. At the same time, the amount of work accomplished has been greater in proportion than the increase in clerical force. This has resulted from improved system and continued efforts to improve efficiency. . . .
>
> It is a matter of deep complaint, and is felt to be a public shame, that men upon the frontier, who are developing the country by their enterprise and labor, should suffer delay, and have their rights imperiled through a false or simulated economy in the necessary disbursements for the conduct of public business.[19]

At the time these words were written there were pending 600,000 claims under general laws, exclusive of railroad grants, swamp and mineral lands, and private land claims—a backlog of three years' work.[20]

For years Commissioners had begged Congress for help, but with no substantial results.[21] The report of James A. Williamson for 1880 reprinted the representations for more staff made in the previous

[18] Senate Report 507, 50th Cong., 1st sess., p. 143 (March 8, 1888).

[19] Commissioner of the General Land Office, *Annual Report*, 1883, pp. 31-32.

[20] *Ibid.*, p. 32.

[21] There was evidence that the responsible members of the General Land Office worked without cessation, whatever the habits of the rank-and-file clerks. They were never relieved from the pressure of work: "there is more than they can possibly do, continually pressed for action," declared Chief Clerk Curtis W. Holcomb in 1881. "The best clerks in the office have always been in the habit of working out of hours." Holcomb stated that he had known them to work until eleven or twelve o'clock in the evening, and he had himself frequently worked until one or two o'clock in the night. Senate Report 362, 47th Cong., 1st sess., pp. 14-15 (Dec. 27, 1881).

nine successive years, corroborated by the report of the Land Commission of 1879–80.[22] Williamson remarked that no more proof should be required, but he added his own statement of the case.

> Laws have multiplied. . . . Lands are of greater value than formerly, and as the country is settled and filled up, this increase will continue, and with it contests by conflicting claimants will be more numerous and more vigorously prosecuted. . . . it is *absolutely absurd* to expect that the immense and varied interests adjusted by this office can be properly disposed of by clerks who can be hired at $1,000, $1,200, or $1,400 salaries.[23]

> The *necessity* of this office is able men of legal education and mature judgment, and without them the administration of its affairs must be measurably defective and discreditable.[24]

Pressing on the demand for manpower was the need for better quarters. The General Land Office, the Patent Office, and other agencies jostled each other in the Patent Office Building, with such overcrowding as seriously to hamper the conduct of business. It was said that "the clerks have frequently to walk a fourth of a mile to get a paper that is needed."[25] Let Commissioner Williamson state his housing problem.

> . . . The rooms are crowded with clerks' desks, books, files, &c., and large numbers of tract books, which contain the record of every entry . . . and which have to be consulted continually in the daily work of the office, as well as records of patents, are stored in the corridors of the building to a degree rendering these invaluable records insecure, and involving a vast and unnecessary waste of labor, both by reason of their position remote from the clerks, and the fact that the light is so dim that the books have to be carried to some place where light can be secured and then returned again to their places.[26]

Congress was skeptical about the real needs of the General Land Office, and its skepticism was roundly stated in 1888 by the Cockrell Committee.[27] "The condition of the business in the General Land

---

[22] Commissioner of the General Land Office, *Annual Report*, 1880, pp. 2-7.
[23] This had been the congressional relief policy.
[24] Commissioner of the General Land Office, *Annual Report*, 1880, p. 11.
[25] Senate Report 362, 47th Cong., 1st sess., p. iv (April 3, 1882).
[26] Commissioner of the General Land Office, *Annual Report*, 1880, p. 12.
[27] Senate Report 507, 50th Cong., 1st sess., *passim* (March 8, 1888).

Office," reported the committee, "for many years past has been and now is chaotic, and has resulted and now exists from a want or lack of plain, correct, business methods, and requirements, promptly, rigidly, and uniformly enforced upon the local land officers and the employés in the General Land Office."[28] The committee sarcastically added: "It seems strange that the plan of more and better work by the employés instead of an increase has never suggested itself to the General Land Office."[29] This comment was hardly fair to one of the more energetic Commissioners, William A. J. Sparks (1885–88).

The committee strongly condemned the "gross carelessness and negligence" of the headquarters staff in failing to make entries in the plat and tract books since 1832, with the result that there was no single reference source for land office business.[30] The committee was equally caustic about the dereliction of duty among the receivers and registers, whose "failures, omissions, neglects, and carelessness" caused endless delays. "Instead of being required by the General Land Office to perform their proper duties efficiently and carefully, they seem to have been considered for many years past as mere clerks for the General Land Office, to receive applications . . . and then to dump by cartload masses of papers into the General Land Office. . . . It would be difficult to estimate the actual amount of additional work imposed upon the General Land Office by the negligence and carelessness of local land officers. . . ."[31]

The case of the General Land Office in the 1880's thus provided a classic illustration of the conflict between the legislative and executive branches. The position taken by each was tenable: Congress *had* contributed to the breakdown of the agency by failure to provide enough clerks and a sufficient proportion of men trained in law, paid at a salary adequate to hold them in government service. On the other hand, the operations of the General Land Office *were* antiquated and cumbersome; discipline apparently was lax; and the local land offices were often careless and negligent—a condition that had been tolerated too long. It is relevant to recall at this point that receivers and registers were subject to Senate confirmation; that

[28] *Ibid.*, p. 227.
[29] *Ibid.*, p. 228.
[30] *Ibid.*, p. 222.
[31] *Ibid.*, p. 226.

consequently they had to be acceptable to Senators; and that their discipline by official action was not thereby facilitated.

A long deadlock through the 1870's and 1880's thus ensued, growing out of two different and conflicting analyses of the administrative problem inherent in the General Land Office. Congress declined to do much for increased manpower. Administrative improvement came slowly but gradually. Arrearages diminished primarily when the flood of entries decreased.

Fraudulent land operations. The disposal of the western lands after the Civil War disclosed a continuous record of evasion of the intended requirements of the preemption, homestead, and other land laws, and a volume of outright fraud and corruption that was reminiscent of the Indian service. The intent of the land laws was to encourage the genuine homeowner and cultivator of the soil to establish farm units of 160 acres. Land speculators, large corporations, and timber operators competed, all too successfully, with the individual pioneer for possession of the vast riches of land, timber, and minerals. The laws were inadequate to protect the small settler; administration was lax and at times corrupt; and official policy as to land disposition was uncertain.

The administrative system was not adapted to control the pressures that were generated on the frontier. A land district might cover 20,000 square miles; no register could possibly ascertain by inspection the truth or falsity of claims made to establish title to land. Registers and receivers, moreover, depended on fees for their income; they were naturally disposed to accept claims fair on their face rather than to reject them. To some extent, they were in collusion with their clients, but the existence of fraud in the official corps is easy to exaggerate. The greater harm probably came from an inadequate force, lack of field inspectors until the 1880's, and an immense effort by unscrupulous speculators to defeat the true intent of the land laws.

The presence of misrepresentation, laxness, and outright fraud was documented year after year in the reports from the General Land Office and in special congressional inquiries. Congress established a Public Land Commission in 1879 that made a series of voluminous reports, the most useful one prepared by Thomas

Donaldson, *The Public Domain: Its History with Statistics*.[32] This report classified the types of abuse in land acquisition—usually traceable to land speculation. They included speculative filings to hold land until a bona fide purchaser came along who would buy a relinquishment of the filing; fraudulent entries by "gangs of men, ranging from ten to fifty," hired by land corporations to make entries on behalf of their employers; entries made but followed by complete failure to make improvements or merely by construction of a "hold-down" shanty of sod or boards; entry of valuable timber or agricultural lands as mineral claims; entry of "desert" land as such, valuable instead for its timber stands.[33]

Timber land, indeed, was the principal objective of the land companies. Before 1878 there were no specific provisions governing private acquisition of timber land; the Preemption and Homestead Acts presumably included forest as well as agricultural land. Indeed Commissioner Burdett argued in 1874 that the existing laws were powerless to prevent timber depredations, and that the wisest policy the government could pursue was to sell them at a fair appraised value.[34] The Timber and Stone Act of 1878 sought to prevent depredations, but without success.[35] Commissioner McFarland reported in 1883: "Evidence is cumulative that the act approved June 3, 1878, . . . is made use of by corporations and wealthy individual operators, to secure fraudulently for the purpose of manufacturing into lumber or to hold for speculation the accessible forests yet remaining. . . ."[36] So unsatisfactory was this law that the General Land Office recommended its repeal at least twelve times between 1878 and 1900.[37]

Part of the problem lay in the absence of an effective official inspection system. The chief of the timber division, questioned in 1882 by the Senate Committee on Public Lands, engaged in the following colloquy.

[32] 20 Stat. 394 (March 3, 1879); Donaldson's report is printed as House Misc. Doc. 45, Part IV, 47th Cong., 2d sess. (1884).

[33] *Ibid.*, pp. 1219-20.

[34] Commissioner of the General Land Office, *Annual Report*, 1874, pp. 6-7.

[35] 20 Stat. 89 (June 3, 1878), especially sec. 4 with reference to unlawful timber cutting.

[36] Commissioner of the General Land Office, *Annual Report*, 1883, p. 208.

[37] Benjamin Horace Hibbard, *A History of the Public Land Policies* (New York: Peter Smith, 1924), p. 466.

Q. Have you any system of inspection of the timber agents?
No, sir.

Q. You have to take what each one reports to you as being correct, so far as you can believe it?
Yes, sir; they are changed very frequently from one locality to another, and then they do not remain in the service very long. . . .

Q. Are they [other government officers] required to make reports of such depredations?
No, sir; they are not required to do so, but they very frequently report such cases to the Treasury Department, and the department have sent us down that information.[38]

A gigantic timberland fraud was uncovered in the early 1880's involving some of the choicest tracts of the California redwood lands. A special agent reported the operation as early as 1883, together with the fact that he had been offered a bribe of $5,000 to drop the case. He was subsequently suspended and afterward dismissed, "at the instance," the Land Commissioner officially reported, "of great influence brought against him from the Pacific coast and in Washington." A new agent was appointed; he was spied upon; his witnesses were intimidated or spirited out of the country; two were knocked down and dragged from his office. The evidence was nevertheless gathered: "all classes of people were approached by agents and principals of the company and asked to sign applications [for land]. Sailors were caught while in port and hurried into a saloon or to a certain notary public's office and induced to sign applications and convey the lands to a member of the firm. . . . The company's agent presented the applications to the register and receiver in blocks of as many as twenty-five at one time; paid the fees; had the proper notices published; hired men to make the proofs; paid for the lands and received the duplicate receipts; yet the register and receiver and some of the special agents appear to have been the only persons in the vicinity who were ignorant of the frauds." Title thus passed to 22,000 acres of land valued at $440,000.[39]

Laxity and fraud in land operations were vigorously attacked during Cleveland's first administration by Commissioner William Andrew Jackson Sparks. An Illinois lawyer, he served as receiver of

---

[38] Senate Report 362, 47th Cong., 1st sess., pp. 106-107 (Feb. 15, 1882).
[39] Commissioner of the General Land Office, *Annual Report, 1886*, pp. 94-95.

a land office from 1853–1856, sat in the Illinois legislature from time to time, and was a Democratic member of the House of Representatives from 1875 to 1883. Here he distinguished himself as a Jacksonian Democrat with an aversion to civil service reform and with an excitable temperament. As Commissioner of the General Land Office from 1885 to 1888 he was pugnaciously honest and determined to root out abuses.[40] One of his first acts was to suspend all patents for certain regions where widespread fraud was suspected. He set up standards for land agents and lawyers practising before the General Land Office. He fought unauthorized fencing by large operators in the western cattle country. He was so energetic and vigorous that he became subject to widespread attack, and in 1888 because of a disagreement over a railroad grant, Secretary Lamar demanded his resignation.[41]

Three years later Congress repealed the Preemption Act and tightened up the land laws.[42] Vast damage had been done meanwhile by illegal acquisition of rich agricultural, timber, and mineral land, and more was to ensue. Nevertheless, it is possible to date the beginning of land reform from Cleveland's first administration and the efforts of Commissioner Sparks.

THE PENSION OFFICE

One of the oldest constituent elements of the Department of the Interior and the largest was the Pension Office. Recognized reluctantly by Congress in 1833 by authorizing for two years a Commissioner of Pensions, the Office was made permanent in 1849 and transferred from the War Department to Interior in the same year.[43]

Pension legislation. Early pension legislation, dating back to the Revolutionary War, was supplemented in 1862 in order to care for the interests of the hundreds of thousands of men in

---

[40] Harold Hathaway Dunham, *Government Handout: a Study in the Administration of the Public Lands, 1875-1891* (New York, privately processed, 1941), ch. 10.

[41] Sparks had protested carrying out the Secretary's decisions. Lamar replied that "in no other way can the functions of a great department be successfully executed than for the chief to command and the subordinates to obey." Reprinted from *New York Tribune*, Nov. 12, 1887, in Wirt A. Cate, *Lucius Q. C. Lamar*, p. 492.

[42] 26 Stat. 1095 (March 3, 1891).

[43] 4 Stat. 619 at 622 (March 2, 1833); 9 Stat. 341 (Jan. 19, 1849); 9 Stat. 395 (March 3, 1849).

military service during the Civil War.[44] This general pension law was the controlling legislation from 1862 to 1890, although amended and supplemented in many particulars. It authorized pensions for men who had incurred permanent injury or disability while in the military service and in the line of duty, and for dependent widows and children and other direct relatives of men who died in service or subsequently from service-connected injuries or disease. The basis of the act was disability or invalidism. Pensions were in proportion to the degree of disability, and the standard of qualification was the degree to which capacity to subsist by manual labor was lost. This standard was obviously a meager administrative guide.

The most important amendment to the act of 1862 was the so-called Arrearages Act of 1879. Pension office regulations, in accord with the act of 1862,[45] had settled upon the date of application as the effective date when a pension became payable. A tardy application consequently meant loss of pension payments during the preceding years. In 1879 Congress yielded to popular sentiment and required the effective date for a pension to be the date of honorable discharge from military service.[46] The result of this legislation was to validate undreamed of arrears cumulating over more than a decade, amounting in many cases to several thousand dollars and payable in a lump sum. The rate of applications mounted rapidly in the following years. A contemporary commentator observed that in one year "141,466 men who had not realized that they were disabled until the Government offered a premium of a thousand dollars or more for the discovery of aches and disabilities, made application."[47]

The rule of service-connected disability as the basis for pensions was abandoned in 1890 in the third important general pension act of the period.[48] Pensions were henceforth awarded on the ground of ninety days service or more during the Civil War, plus any permanent disability, "not the result of their own vicious habits," which incapacitated applicants from earning a living by manual

[44] 12 Stat. 566 (July 14, 1862).
[45] *Ibid.*, sec. 5.
[46] 20 Stat. 265 (Jan. 25, 1879).
[47] Eugene V. Smalley, "The United States Pension Office," *Century*, XXVIII (1884), 428.
[48] 26 Stat. 182 (Jan. 27, 1890).

labor. With the passage of years it became essentially a *service* pension plan. Widows and children of men who had ninety days service or more received payments without regard to the cause of death; it need not be for service-connected injuries. The Grand Army of the Republic rejoiced over this victory conferred by a Republican President and Congress: "it is," the GAR Pension Committee declared, "the most liberal pension measure ever passed by any legislative body in the world, and will place upon the rolls all of the survivors of the war whose conditions of health are not practically perfect."[49]

In addition to these three basic pension acts, Congress took care of many cases that were barred by some technicality from qualifying under the law and regulations—often, if not always, cases of merit. Thousands of such special acts were eventually passed, and the pressure upon Congress became so great that much laxness and carelessness ensued. President Grover Cleveland vetoed over two hundred special enactments that seemed to him indefensible—at heavy cost in political popularity. These special acts, indeed, had become a sort of congressional patronage, and Cleveland's popularity in the two Houses suffered as well.[50]

By the turn of the century the mass of pension legislation and adjudication defied mastery except by experts. ". . . the whole system," declared Pension Commissioner H. Clay Evans in 1898, "is a most complex and wonderful network or labyrinth of laws and legal opinions. . . ."[51] Two kinds of experts threaded their way through the maze: the Pension Office clerks and examiners, and the private attorneys and claim agents specializing in pension cases. Their interests often collided.

Organization and procedures of the Pension Office. The official body of experts comprised the hundreds of clerks, examiners, and specialists in the Pension Office, headed by the Commissioner of

[49] Quoted in William H. Glasson, *Federal Military Pensions in the United States*, p. 233.

[50] See *ibid.*, pp. 276-79.

[51] Commissioner of Pensions, *Annual Report*, 1898, pp. 19-20. See, for a scholarly monograph, John William Oliver, *History of the Civil War Military Pensions, 1861-1885* (Bulletin of the University of Wisconsin, No. 844, 1917); for basic data, Gustavus A. Weber, *The Bureau of Pensions* (Baltimore: Johns Hopkins Press, 1923).

Pensions. After the Civil War this office was one of the most important among the group below the Cabinet level; it was charged
with political dynamite and carried an exceptionally heavy administrative load. Every President except Hayes appointed his own Commissioner of Pensions. Hayes continued Grant's fifth Commissioner,
John A. Bentley, who was eventually replaced by Garfield under
pressure from the Grand Army of the Republic. The office was held
by at least five able Commissioners during these thirty years: Bentley,
John C. Black (during Cleveland's first term), William Lochren
(during Cleveland's second term), a career man, Dominic I. Murphy,
(for a year at the end of Cleveland's second term), and Henry Clay
Evans (under McKinley). It was also held by a very active politician,
William W. Dudley (under Garfield and Arthur), by a GAR
stalwart, Corporal James Tanner, and by a Commissioner with a very
dubious administrative record, Green B. Raum (both under Benjamin
Harrison). Appointment of Commissioners required the advice and
consent of the Senate, and both Senators and Representatives were
their constant correspondents.

The central operation of the Pension Office—examination and
approval or rejection of claims entered by veterans—was performed
in a considerable number of divisions, each with its own class of
claimants. The division chiefs were the pivots of the organization
and tended to be drawn from among the most capable clerks; they
were not disturbed as a rule by political upheavals for they were too
valuable to displace. In 1891 Commissioner Raum declared that his
agency was "the largest executive bureau in the world." The total
force then numbered 6,241, of which about one-third was stationed
in Washington, and nearly two-thirds located in every part of the
country. The field force included eighteen pension agents (primarily
pay offices), and the medical examiners.[52] The Boston pension agent
had a staff of one chief clerk and twenty-four clerks; Chicago was
larger with forty-four clerks.[53]

Pension agents also required senatorial confirmation and were often
politically active. The experience of John T. Clements, one-time
pension agent at Macon, Missouri, is illustrative. Originally ap-

[52] Green B. Raum, "Pensions and Patriotism," *North American Review,* CLIII
(1891), 211.
[53] *Official Register,* 1891, pp. 673-75.

pointed in 1865 to a district in northern Missouri set up for him as
a friend of President Lincoln, he was removed by President Johnson
in 1866 for opposing his freedmen's policy; he was subsequently imposed on Johnson by the Radical Republicans in 1867, and again
removed in 1871 for opposing Grant's Negro policy. In 1875
Clements was once more in his old office with another turn of the
political wheel, this time endorsed by all the Republican delegation
from Missouri and, as he put it, by "every prominent republican
in the State."[54]

The hundreds of medical boards, composed of three local
physicians paid by fees for each examination and responsible for
certifying the facts concerning the physical condition of claimants,
proved to be unsatisfactory arms of the Pension Office. Charges
were made of their incompetence through the 1870's and later. Commissioner Evans epitomized the criticism in his annual report for
1901. "The same system of securing medical examiners prevails now
as thirty-five years ago, and has prevailed. They are frequently
changed. They know nothing about the pension laws and are not
expected to. They are subjected to no test examination as to their
medical skill, and never have been."[55] The chief of the medical
division added his testimony to the same effect. "The chances are
always in favor of the least qualified. The physician of high standing
in his profession has, as a rule, neither time nor inclination to solicit
political influence; neither has he the time nor taste to exert the
political activity that would be regarded as sufficient to give him
a claim to a place on a board."[56]

There was much complaint in the Pension Office that medical
certificates were incomplete, misleading, and otherwise faulty. They
had to be corrected at great cost in time by being returned to the
local boards. Equally disturbing was the absence of known and reliable standards as to the degree of disability. A test of prevailing practice was somewhat tardily made in 1898 by requiring a soldier
claimant to appear in succession before four local medical boards.
Each made a careful examination and each reported unanimously.
One board could find no ratable disability; one estimated the dis-

[54] House Misc. Doc. 183, 44th Cong., 1st sess., pp. 4, 6 (April 22, 1876).
[55] Commissioner of Pensions, *Annual Report*, 1901, p. 67.
[56] *Ibid.*, 1901, p. 137.

ability as of the grade permitting a pension of eight dollars a month; one, a pension of seventeen dollars a month; and the fourth, a payment of twenty-four dollars a month. For this and other reasons the Pension Commissioner declared "It is beyond the power of this Bureau . . . to cause uniform ratings for like disabilities. . . ."[57]

Applications for pensions originated in every village, town, and place where resided a veteran of the Union forces. They were initiated in thousands of cases by claim agents and attorneys, of whom more will be said at a later point, men who carried the proper forms, who advised the veterans, helped them prepare their papers, and often followed them to Washington. The first step was wholly ex parte; no government agent had an opportunity to question the applicant, to talk with witnesses, or to scrutinize the validation of the papers by local court officials or notaries. It was recognized very quickly that such proceedings were liable to abuse. After the passage of the Arrearages Act, Eugene V. Smalley, a prominent journalist and active member of the GAR, wrote: "Men asked to do the neighborly act of witnessing a pension paper are always compliant, and seldom particular as to what they certify to. No one appears for the Government to cross-examine them. . . . The surgeons are local physicians. Their natural disposition would be to favor an applicant as a neighbor and acquaintance, and perhaps a patient. There is little reason why they should be called upon to protect the Government treasury."[58]

This fundamental weakness in the administrative chain impaired the whole process of examination and of certifying claims. The *system* in the Pension Office was well safeguarded: the military branches were required to confirm claimed military service, papers had to be in order in every particular, medical examiners certified to the degree of disability, doubtful cases went to a board of review and for some years could be referred to a board of re-review. Smalley confirmed the fact that the work of the Pension Office was "methodical, careful, and vigilant within the limitations which law and precedent prescribe." The trouble was that the evidence was all on paper and was all ex parte. "The false swearing looks just as well as the true.

---

[57] *Ibid.*, 1898, p. 12.
[58] Eugene V. Smalley, "The United States Pension Office," *Century*, XXVIII (1884), 430.

So many papers of certain forms, duly signed, sealed, and certified, establish the case."[59]

This, then, was the organizational pattern: a politically responsible Commissioner, fifteen or more specialized divisions with about a couple of thousand clerks and examiners, eighteen regional pension agents, and nearly 4,000 examining surgeons operating independently and free from central supervision. The agency was harassed by an excessive volume of work, antiquated methods, incessant congressional calls, and the political pressure exerted by the Grand Army of the Republic, peculiarly noticeable during Republican administrations.

The Pension Office operated in terms of hundreds of thousands of cases throughout the whole period from Grant to McKinley, but finally substantially caught up with its work in 1900. Complaints of delay were almost universal. ". . . pensioners complain very bitterly if their cases do not receive immediate consideration," wrote Evans in 1899. "There has never been a time when this Bureau has been free of complaint on the part of claimants and others of unusual delays in the adjudication of claims. . . ."[60]

The pressure was extremely heavy following the Arrearages Act of 1879. Congress recognized the political repercussions of tardy action and in August 1882 appropriated funds to double the number of clerks.[61] Subsequent increases of staff more or less kept pace with the work, and under McKinley work and staff were in substantial equilibrium. The number of cases pending on June 30, 1897, was, in round numbers, 578,000; in 1898, 635,000. Thereafter it diminished: in 1899, the number was 477,000; in 1900, 437,000; and in 1901, 403,000.[62] In 1900 Commissioner Evans stated that, excepting some classes, the claims were practically current.[63]

Throughout its history the Pension Office was encumbered by an enormous mass of congressional mail and personal inquiry. This form of constituent business assumed grave proportions, compelling some Congressmen to hire special clerks to handle it, and causing much annoyance to everyone concerned. Congressional mail was causing

[59] *Ibid.*, XXVIII, 430.
[60] Commissioner of Pensions, *Annual Report*, 1899, pp. 12, 26.
[61] 22 Stat. 219 at 247 (August 5, 1882).
[62] Commissioner of Pensions, *Annual Report*, 1901, p. 17.
[63] *Ibid.*, 1900, p. 39.

serious delay in 1884 when it numbered about 75,000 pieces a year.[64] By 1896 congressional calls and letters numbered 799,000 and rose to 1,234,000 in 1898.[65] These inquiries had to be answered, case files had to be called up, and detailed letters written.

The office methods customarily used by the government belonged to the craftsmanship stage. Everything was written by hand until well toward the 1890's and much thereafter. Control of records was by cumbersome indexes and letterbooks, and was governed by a desire to be careful rather than expeditious. Clerks and copyists were the central symbols of the prevailing order.

The elementary filing system of the 1870's broke down after the increase of business due to the Arrearages Act. Claims were filed in blocks according to the first three letters of the surname. Thus all names of claimants beginning with AND would be filed in a single indiscriminate list. It appeared in 1879 that the combination SMI had 4,500 names in it; to discover the records of Smith, William A., would thus require thumbing through the whole block. The combination WIL had 4,900 names; HAR, 3,900; and so on. Since 1861, moreover, the basic records had been transferred several times by copying from old books to new, with inevitable errors. In 1880 another record system was set up, filing names of applicants by their military organizations, such as Company A, 16th Illinois Volunteers, thus enormously facilitating the location of material and enabling clerks in search of records to keep out of each other's way. The new records, however, also went into books—176 volumes of 250 pages each. Filing cabinets were still unknown.[66]

The problem of fraud. The temptation to misrepresent and to defraud in pension applications was great, and the ex parte system of initiating claims strengthened temptation. That the government was deceived by thousands of soldiers and their dependents was universally admitted. Pensioners and their attorneys seemed to have been engaged in a gigantic conspiracy to defraud their own government. To the credit of the Pension Office, it may be said that it made incessant recommendations to improve the system in order to reduce the mass of fraudulent claims, but Congress was indifferent; and within

[64] *Ibid.*, 1884, p. 10.
[65] *Ibid.*, 1898, p. 8.
[66] *Ibid.*, 1880, pp. 6-7.

the system, faulty as it was, the bureau fought deception vigorously. Only under a single administration (Harrison) were the official standards corrupted.

The annual reports of the Pension Commissioners constantly referred to the problem. Grant's Commissioner Van Aerman soon learned, in his words, "that a great number of fraudulent claims upon the Pension Office had been made. . . ." Frauds upon colored persons in the South were common: "an amount of systematic extortion and fraud upon the ignorant pensioners and applicants . . . unparalleled in the experience of this office."[67] In 1875 Commissioner Atkinson reported: "The development of frauds of every character in pension-claims has assumed such a magnitude as to require the serious attention of Congress."[68]

In 1882, the Senate was persuaded to combat misrepresentation by publicity, ordering the names of all pensioners to be printed.[69] According to contemporary testimony, the volumes not needed for official use fell into the hands of pension attorneys for further fraudulent enterprises.[70] As late as 1901 Commissioner Evans declared that the system then in force for settling pension claims "holds out an inducement to those that may be persuaded to file false claims or fraudulent evidence in support of valid ones. In fact the system aids and encourages fraudulent practices of various sorts. It is not to be wondered at that the Government is constantly being imposed upon. When attention is called to the defects which are responsible for these conditions, a mighty howl goes up in certain quarters."[71] The reference was to the GAR and the pension attorneys.

A notable case of an unwarranted pension occurred in the 1890's. Charles D. Long was pensioned at $72 per month for total and permanent helplessness. However, he was, in official language, "a man of apparent vigor, having the full use of all his bodily members save his left arm." He was also, and had been for a considerable time, one of the judges of the Supreme Court of Michigan, and discharged the duties of this high office. When Commissioner Lochren reduced his

[67] *Ibid.*, 1870, pp. 5, 6.
[68] *Ibid.*, 1875, p. 15.
[69] Senate Resolution of Dec. 8, 1882. The list of pensioners was printed in five volumes as Senate Ex. Doc. 84, 47th Cong., 2d sess. (1883).
[70] Eugene V. Smalley, "The United States Pension Office," *Century*, XXVIII (1884), 431.
[71] Commissioner of Pensions, *Annual Report*, 1901, pp. 50-51.

pension to $50, Judge Long resorted to the courts for writs to defeat
the order. His petition was finally dismissed.[72]

There is evidence that public opinion was not firmly on the side
of either morality or law in the matter of pensions to the old soldiers.
The Pension Office was constantly seeking and often secured convictions for fraud, but at times under conditions that were not conducive to continued efforts. A special examiner sent out to Iowa obtained the conviction of a pension attorney for bribery, but was then
himself indicted on specious evidence for having threatened a witness. The guilty pension attorney meanwhile was elected mayor of
his city by a practically unanimous vote.[73]

These matters did not touch the integrity of the staff of the Pension
Office, which maintained an excellent reputation as a whole for faithfulness to duty. During Harrison's administration there was a lowering
of ethical standards under Commissioners James Tanner and Green
B. Raum. "Corporal Tanner" lost both legs in the Civil War, and
became an active member of the GAR, a pension attorney, and a
prominent figure in Washington. He served as a Pension Commissioner from March to October 1889. His appointment gave great
satisfaction to the GAR and the pension attorneys, since he proposed,
as he said, "a pension for every old soldier who needs one." "God save
the surplus." He promptly began to rerate and increase pensions, open
up dubious cases, and overrule precedents. Secretary of the Interior
John W. Noble sought to intervene, but, as already noted, Tanner
was insubordinate and soon resigned.[74]

More damaging to the reputation of the Pension Office was the
record of Tanner's successor, Green B. Raum. He appointed a worthless son as chief clerk of the Pension Office and acting chief of
the appointment division. The son spent much of his time with other
employees out of the office betting on the races; and he was accused,
apparently justly, of seeking loans from employees for favors, of ab-
stracting conscience money for his private use, and of selling an appointment as laborer.[75] A House investigation disclosed that a promi-

[72] *Ibid.*, *1894*, pp. 11-12; *ibid.*, *1895*, p. 14.
[73] *Ibid.*, *1895*, p. 13.
[74] *Nation*, XLVIII (May 30, 1889); *ibid.*, XLIX, 64 (July 25, 1889); Secretary
of the Interior, *Annual Report*, *1889*, pp. lxviii-lxxi.
[75] House Report 1868, 52d Cong., 1st sess. (July 14, 1892), Part 1, pp. i-vi,
passim.

nent pension attorney, George E. Lemon, had endorsed Commissioner Raum's note for $12,000. The House committee majority declared: "it is a fair inference that this indorsement was made in consideration of official action on the part of the Commissioner to George E. Lemon."[76] There was also convincing evidence that Raum used the services of the Pension Office in an unsuccessful effort to defeat a congressional critic.[77] A Democratic majority of the committee recommended Raum's removal "on account of his hasty temper, strong prejudices, and unreasonable animosity," and use of office for private gain and political purposes.[78] Harrison accepted the exoneration of the Republican minority of the committee,[79] but there was no doubt from the evidence that the integrity of the staff had suffered in some quarters.

The damage was repaired by McKinley's able commissioner, Henry Clay Evans. In 1900, his chief clerk declared, with obvious reference to Raum: "The fact is that good order and attention to duty has prevailed; tardiness has been largely limited to unavoidable causes, and there is no loafing in the corridors during working hours, and it is unquestionably a fact that the discipline of the office has never been better than during the time covered by your administration of the Bureau."[80]

Pensions, politics, and pressure groups. The Pension Office faced a massive and well-organized clientele, able to muster strength in both Houses of Congress, and particularly powerful in the Republican party. The Pension Office was not the first official agency to be influenced by a pressure group or by political controversy, but it was peculiarly subject to such external influences. The even balance between Republican and Democratic parties during the 1880's and the early 1890's made the soldier vote a prize of great worth. Membership in the Grand Army of the Republic grew rapidly during the 1880's; in round numbers, 60,000 in 1880; 269,000 five years later; and 427,000 in 1890. Both parties cultivated the old soldiers with promises of pension benefits and administrative improvement, but the

[76] *Ibid.*, p. xxvii.
[77] *Ibid.*, p. xxxii.
[78] *Ibid.*, p. xxxix.
[79] *Ibid.*, p. lxvii.
[80] Commissioner of Pensions, *Annual Report*, 1900, p. 105.

Republicans—"the party that saved the Union"—were the chief beneficiaries.[81]

The aging veterans were active in bringing their influence to bear
both upon Congress and upon the Pension Office. The earliest and
one of the most aggressive of their lobbies, the Pensioners' Committee, was organized in 1875. It was headed by Captain R. A. Dimmick
and circulated over a hundred thousand petitions, pamphlets, and
resolutions.[82] Dimmick sought to capitalize on his alleged success in
securing passage of the Arrearages Act by requesting voluntary contributions from pensioners to meet his expenses. This led to an inquiry
by the House Committee on Expenditures in the Interior Department, which exposed a scheme "whereby a large sum of money would
doubtless have been filched from the pockets of the poor pensioners."
The committee did not hesitate to call Dimmick "a sharper."[83]

The Grand Army of the Republic entered the pension field in 1881,
appointing a Pension Committee that immediately began to wield
great influence. "These men," wrote Glasson, "became the pleni-
potentiaries of the G.A.R. to Washington."[84] One of their first
achievements was to secure from Congress the doubling of the clerical
force to handle the mass of new business arising under the Arrearages
Act. A second was to exert pressure in favor of a bill authorizing pensions on the ground of dependency instead of service-connected disability—a bill vetoed by Cleveland in 1887.[85] A third was to assist
in the defeat of Cleveland in the election of 1888. A fourth and dubious success was the appointment of Corporal Tanner as Commissioner
of Pensions. A fifth victory was the Pension Act of 1890, of which
Glasson remarked that it "was the high bid for the political support
of the 450,000 G.A.R. men and other ex-soldiers, with both the
Republican and the Democratic parties bidding."[86] A sixth was
the eventual removal of Commissioner Evans, who, declared the

[81] See two papers by Donald L. McMurry, "The Political Significance of the
Pension Question, 1885-1897," *Mississippi Valley Historical Review*, IX (1922-
23), 19-36; and "The Bureau of Pensions during the Administration of President
Harrison," *ibid.*, XIII (1926-27), 343-64. Figures for GAR membership in *ibid.*,
IX, 23.

[82] House Report 189, 45th Cong., 3d sess., pp. 100-101 (March 1, 1879).

[83] *Ibid.*, p. 5.

[84] William H. Glasson, *Federal Military Pensions in the United States*, p. 186.

[85] Richardson, *Messages*, VIII, 549 (Feb. 11, 1887).

[86] William H. Glasson, *op. cit.*, p. 238.

Grand Army of the Republic, "is not disposed to administer the duties of his office in that spirit of equity and justice to applicants for pensions which they have a right to expect . . . we are convinced that justice to the soldier is impossible of attainment under the present administration of the Pension Bureau."[87]

The GAR thus brought its influence to bear on elections, Congress, and the Pension Office. Pensions were a major issue in the election of 1888, but thereafter sank to secondary importance. Administration, however, remained a continuing focus of activity. In this field the interests of the GAR seemed to coalesce with those of the leading pension attorneys and claim agents, who, although unorganized, exerted much practical influence. The union of interests was symbolized in the *National Tribune*, the official organ of the GAR and the private property of George E. Lemon, one of the largest operators in the pension field.[88]

The Commissioner of Pensions reported in 1898 that some 60,000 persons were enrolled on the list of attorneys authorized to practice before the agency.[89] About 1,000 of these did the bulk of the business, and among them George E. Lemon did the most. At one point he had over 125,000 cases in charge, for each of which the normal fee was ten dollars.[90]

Many of the pension attorneys and claim agents were men of integrity, handling a relatively small number of cases originating in their localities. A small proportion were scheming knaves, a menace to the government and the pensioners alike. Evans declared in 1898, "The illiteracy, incapacity, and dishonesty which has characterized the work of some of those who have engaged in this business has been a constant source of trouble to clients and tribunal."[91] The Pension Office prosecuted where it could obtain evidence and thus rid itself of many by disbarment; in 1898, 29 were disbarred, 12 suspended, 5 dropped, and 87 employees punished for acting as agents for claimants.[92]

Taken as a group, the pension attorneys, the ex-Union service men, and the GAR had a community of interest: better pensions, wider

[87] Quoted in *ibid.*, p. 245.
[88] *Ibid.*, p. 183.
[89] Commissioner of Pensions, *Annual Report*, 1898, p. 56.
[90] House Report 2683, 48th Cong., 2d sess., p. 14 (Jan. 15, 1885).
[91] Commissioner of Pensions, *Annual Report*, 1898, p. 57.
[92] *Ibid.*, p. 56.

coverage, liberal administration. The more unscrupulous pension attorneys did not hesitate to deceive the Pension Office, and most of them sought to have their cases taken out of turn—a constant struggle between order and favoritism. The business of the Pension Office, complicated and massive at its best and almost impossible at its worst, was not improved by the pressures brought to bear by Congressmen, the Grand Army of the Republic, and the pension attorneys.

Despite these handicaps and an inadequate system, the Pension Office turned out an impressive amount of work. Except during the years of Raum, the evidence showed diligence, perhaps excessive care, and a high sense of official integrity. The major fault in the system, of which Commissioners had complained for thirty years, still existed: the ex parte character of the evidence on which claims for pensions were awarded.

THE PATENT OFFICE

The fourth major component of the Interior Department was the Patent Office, a highly technical organization which over the years managed to keep its staff relatively free from party patronage and to maintain high standards of semiprofessional work. The patent system was established in 1790 in the State Department. Its modern policy and organization were enacted in 1836; administrative developments from Grant to McKinley introduced no novelty, but some of the handicaps under which the office labored were typical of the whole service. Its record of steady accomplishment stands out in bold relief.

The Patent Office was *sui generis* in more than one particular. It had a single and a homogeneous task, to receive applications for patents and to determine whether a patent should issue. It had a small but highly intelligent clientele, the body of American inventors. Its operations required men well trained and experienced in different branches of science and in law. It had no field service, in sharp contrast to the Office of Indian Affairs, the General Land Office, and the Pension Office. All its work was done in Washington, under the immediate supervision of the Commissioner and his chief assistants.

The patent system. The first patent act of 1790[93] established two fundamental criteria for the issuance of a patent, that the device be

[93] 1 Stat. 109 (April 10, 1790).

novel and that it have utility. Thomas Jefferson and his patent clerk were so selective in granting patents that the law was altered in 1793 to provide in substance a mere system of registration, patterned on British precedent.[94] So much litigation ensued that Congress in 1836 returned to "the American system," requiring novelty and utility as the foundation on which a patent would issue.[95] This legislation remained the basis of the patent system for the period covered by this study. It "provided, for the first time in any country, the means of protecting the rights of inventors in an intelligent, scientific, and adequate way, by giving the patent grant a *prima facie* standing of validity and by inaugurating a proper examination system. . . . The effective protection given by this act to the rights of property in ideas soon became a powerful agent in stimulating inventive genius in the United States."[96] The act of 1836 was supplemented from time to time, codified in 1870, and reenacted in 1874 in the Revised Statutes.[97] Despite minor variations in law and procedure, the system stood intact.

The volume of business of the Patent Office was substantial. In 1870 nearly 20,000 applications were received and over 13,000 patents or reissues were awarded. These figures had only slightly increased in 1880, but shortly thereafter practically doubled. In 1890 over 41,000 applications were received and over 26,000 patents were issued. The figures for 1900 were about the same.[98]

The significance of this tide of invention for the prosperity and competitive position of the United States in international trade was not lost upon the Patent Office. Commissioner William E. Simonds in his annual report for 1892 illustrated how American invention had permitted domestic manufacture to replace foreign imports and to compete in the world market. He declared:

. . . . America has become known the world around as the home of invention. We march in the van of human progress. . . .

Our inventors are the true nation builders, the true promoters of

[94] 1 Stat. 318 (Feb. 21, 1793).
[95] 5 Stat. 117 (July 4, 1836).
[96] Gustavus A. Weber, *The Patent Office* (Baltimore: Johns Hopkins Press, 1924), pp. 1-31; quotation is from p. 11. For a brief official history, see Commissioner of Patents, *Annual Report*, 1900, pp. viii-xii.
[97] 16 Stat. 198 (July 8, 1870); Revised Statutes, secs. 4883-4971.
[98] Commissioner of Patents, *Annual Report*, 1900, p. v.

civilization. They take nothing from the public; they ask nothing from the public; they simply add to the sum of human knowledge, to the sum of human possessions, and to the sum of human happiness. . . . The Greeks reserved their highest honors for inventors, and we shall sometime attain to a civilization of like degree.[99]

Organization of the Patent Office. Despite the technical character of the Patent Office operations, its overhead was politically appointed and politically responsible. The Commissioner, the assistant commissioner, and the three examiners in chief (an appellate tribunal) all required the advice and consent of the Senate for appointment.[100] It is difficult to reconstruct the party activity of the various Commissioners, but the office seems in some instances to have been a convenient lame-duck haven. From 1869 to 1901, five Commissioners had been members of Congress, Duell, Paine, Butterworth, Hall, and Simonds, and the latter three became heads of the Patent Office immediately after electoral defeat. Commissioner Simonds spoke out against using the office for political reward in a telling passage in his annual report for 1892.

. . . . The appointment of the Commissioner of Patents and the Assistant Commissioner ought at once and forever to cease to be political, their salaries should be increased, and they should hold office on the tenure of good behavior. . . . The Patent Office is no more political in its nature than is a well-regulated court of law. . . . The fortunes of a political party cannot be advanced or retarded by what is done in the Patent Office. . . .[101]

Simonds strengthened his case by observing that the two positions were primarily judicial in nature; that, lacking previous training and education, Commissioners were prone toward "a cruel travesty of justice"; and that the mere administrative supervision of the office alone required stability and continuity. His was a solitary voice.

The record of tenure of the office proves that political preference was the usual basis of choice. From 1869 to 1901 there were fourteen Commissioners, one of whom held the office twice. Grant had four Commissioners in eight years, and only in Cleveland's second administration did a Commissioner serve out a presidential term. The lack of continuity meant a recurrent element of uncertainty as to

[99] *Ibid.*, 1892, p. v.
[100] 16 Stat. 198, secs. 2, 10 (July 8, 1870).
[101] Commissioner of Patents, *Annual Report*, 1892, p. vi.

policy and staff that "must necessarily," Commissioner Simonds declared, cause "a degree of demoralization."[102] The same complaint had been made in 1877 with reference to the examiners in chief. Commissioner Ellis Spear noted that from 1861 to 1877 there had been fifteen different members. "Under such conditions it must appear inevitable that there could not have been uniformity or the constant exercise of the wisest discretion in the granting of patents."[103]

The business of the Patent Office in fact moved forward primarily under its own momentum, neither requiring nor apparently receiving much leadership from the Commissioners. Indeed Spear declared: "It is impossible for the Commissioner to supervise personally one in a hundred of the patents issued. His duties are too diverse and numerous, and should rather be abridged."[104] The consideration of patent applications and the decision to issue or refuse a patent went on according to long-established routine and in the hands of a highly trained and generally unusually competent body of examiners.

The Patent Office was organized by divisions corresponding to a classification of the subject matter of patents, such as steam engineering, textiles, harvesters, and the like. Each division was in charge of a principal examiner, men who had grown up in the service and who knew the law, practice, and the appropriate art. Each principal examiner presided over a group of assistant examiners divided into four classes according to seniority and competence. The promotion ladder led from the fourth-class assistant examiner up to the first class and the principal examiner.[105] Since 1869 appointments and promotions in the examining staff were normally made by competitive examination, a program begun before the creation of Grant's Civil Service Commission and continued after its demise until the new Commission took over in 1883. Commissioner Spear reported in 1877 that the results had been highly satisfactory. "Men better fitted for the special work have been selected for appointment; the ablest, most diligent, and faithful men have been promoted; and . . . the effect, generally, upon the Office has been to stimulate industry, attention to business, and studious habits."[106]

[102] *Ibid.*, 1892, p. vi.
[103] *Ibid.*, 1877, p. xiii.
[104] *Ibid.*, 1877, p. xiii.
[105] *Ibid.*, 1896, pp. xv ff.
[106] *Ibid.*, 1877, p. ix.

By virtue of an overriding necessity, therefore, the Patent Office became one of the first civil service establishments and remained resolutely attached to the rule of competition. In 1896 there were thirty-three principal examiners, of whom thirty had won their appointments by competitive examination; thirty-four first assistant examiners, of whom thirty-three earned their positions by competition. A similar proportion prevailed in the lower grades. Entrance to the lowest grade was strictly upon competitive examinations, and all promotions were made by examination in the strict order of standing.[107]

The corps of examiners comprised a body of men of unusual talent. They were drawn from among graduates of the leading technological schools of the country and were expected after appointment to take a law degree. Patent law was peculiarly difficult. Commissioner Simonds quoted with approval the Supreme Court's dictum that this field was "the metaphysics of the law." He continued: "A competent Examiner must possess a wide range of scientific and technical knowledge, a trained capacity for analysis and comparison of mechanism, a fair knowledge of law in general, and a thorough knowledge of . . . patent law. . . . The code of procedure and practice in the Patent Office is more complicated than that of any court of law, and necessarily so. . . . there is no similar number of men in the world, gathered into one body, performing duties as delicate and difficult as those performed by the examining corps of the Patent Office."[108]

Their quality and their special competence made the examiners exceedingly valuable to private business firms as well as to the government. There was frequent complaint throughout this period that their low salaries made easy outside competition for the ablest examiners and a consequent loss to the Patent Office. Thus early began a recurrent problem. In 1912 the assistant commissioner of patents, Frederick A. Tennant, declared: "We have great difficulty in holding them, because the corporations take them out of the office, and they are going out now like sheep through a hole in the fence."[109]

Without doubt many young men took the Patent Office examinations with the clear intention of resigning after a few years' experience

[107] *Ibid.*, 1896, pp. xv-xvi, xviii.
[108] *Ibid.*, 1892, p. iv.
[109] *History of the Patent System*, Hearings before the House Committee on Patents (Jan. 10, 1912), p. 24.

to enter lucrative private practice as patent attorneys. In the annual report of the Secretary of the Interior for 1883, Commissioner of Patents Edgar M. Marble complained that " a very large number of examiners and assistant examiners have resigned their positions in this office during the last year . . . for the purpose of entering into practice before the office. The reason of these resignations is found in the fact that insufficient salaries were paid them by the Government. . . . The office is thus made to suffer the loss of experienced men, skilled in particular arts and acquainted with its business, and feels such loss, perhaps, more than any other Bureau of the Government."[110]

Loss of well-trained personnel was one of three nagging administrative problems that harassed the Patent Office without cessation; another was the lack of adequate staff; a third, the lack of decent quarters. Hardly a Commissioner in his annual reports failed to comment on these matters. The complaints were the more bitter because the "Patent Fund," out of which the whole staff was paid, was contributed and sustained entirely by the inventors in the form of fees.[111] Indeed there was a chronic and handsome surplus in the fund, but Congress was tardy in authorizing needed increases of personnel.

In 1880 Commissioner Marble reported, by way of illustration, "The force employed . . . is entirely inadequate to the amount and character of work required. Some of the examining divisions are several months behind with their work."[112] Commissioner Benjamin Butterworth, a vigorous executive and a former member of Congress, made a strong demand for more help in 1883.

I am daily in receipt of communications severely censuring the honorable Secretary and the Commissioner for not employing such additional force as is necessary to bring and keep the work of the bureau up to date. . . . I am daily appealed to by Senators and Members to make applications special. . . . Although well disposed to oblige my friends, I cannot, without violating a well-considered rule of the bureau, comply with these requests. I know these delays are not only vexatious, but in some instances very disastrous to the interests involved. . . .

[110] Secretary of the Interior, *Annual Report*, 1883, II, 380.
[111] 5 Stat. 117, sec. 9 (July 4, 1836).
[112] Commissioner of Patents, *Annual Report*, 1880, p. iv.

The examining corps is greatly behind with its work simply because it is a physical impossibility with the number employed to keep it up. . . .[113]

Congress was not wholly unmoved and from time to time made small additions to the staff. They were never enough, and they came as a rule too late. In 1889 the work was temporarily nearly up to date, due to the "almost heroic efforts on the part of the examining corps, who take pride in the good name of the Office, and who spare no labor within office hours or out of office hours. . . ." But, as Commissioner Mitchell observed, "the work of examination cannot be conducted under whip and spur. Its very nature implies deliberation."[114]

The shortage of manpower was made more exasperating by the shortage of space. The agency was housed in the impressive edifice then and for many years later known as the Patent Office Building. The construction of the building was authorized in 1836, costs to be financed from the surplus of inventors' fees in the Treasury.[115] The Patent Office never succeeded in getting satisfactory quarters in what it considered "its own building," and when Interior moved into the structure with the Land Office, the Indian Office, and the Pension Office, the position of the Patent Office was highly unsatisfactory. It remained so, despite repeated claims for more and better space and ample demonstration of inefficiency caused by cramped quarters. A single quotation will suffice to illustrate the problem.

. . . . The corridor-walls are lined on both sides with unsightly wooden closets and file-cases filled with record-papers. A great number of the force work in basement and sub-basement rooms, intended simply for storage purposes in the original planning of the building.

There are stored more than a thousand tons of copies of patents on five different floors, tucked into every nook and corner where an eager eye can discover a few feet of available space, so disconnected in order and arrangement that it not infrequently happens that to select two copies standing next each other in number one must travel from the sub-basement to the galleries, four stories above. . . .[116]

Lack of space and lack of personnel are not among the fundamental problems of public administration, perennial though they are. They do

[113] *Ibid.*, 1883, p. vii.
[114] *Ibid.*, 1889, p. vii.
[115] 5 Stat. 112, secs. 7-8 (July 4, 1836).
[116] Commissioner of Patents, *Annual Report*, 1892, p. iii.

illustrate, however, on a broader view, one aspect of the many relationships between Congress and the executive agencies. All departments suffered the same handicaps that afflicted the Patent Office; none had adequate space and all could justify requests for larger staff. Congress was stubbornly unwilling to help the executive branch in these elementary needs, and brought relief reluctantly, tardily, and inadequately.

Patent appeals. An elaborate system of appeals against adverse decisions of the Patent Office developed, designed to protect the interests of inventors. They included both administrative and judicial remedies. A decision favorable to the applicant made in the first instance was likely to be conclusive; the finding was reviewed by a primary examiner[117] but as soon as an assistant was well trained and commanded the confidence of his superior, review was likely to be cursory. The machinery of appeals was designed to control adverse decisions.

An applicant for a patent, twice rejected, had a right of appeal from the primary examiner (that is, the first reviewing authority) to the board of examiners in chief. A similar appeal lay in so-called cases of interference, where the issue was one of priority in invention. If dissatisfied with the decision of the board of examiners in chief, the applicant was entitled to appeal to the Commissioner in person. Until 1893 this was the final recourse in an interference case. In substantive cases, however, a disappointed applicant could pursue a further appeal to the Supreme Court of the District of Columbia.[118] This court decided in summary procedure on the evidence produced before the Commissioner, but without jeopardizing the right of any person to contest the validity of the patent in any court where it might subsequently be called into question. Furthermore, if the patent was refused either by the Commissioner or by the Supreme Court of the District of Columbia, the applicant had a further remedy by bill in equity before any competent court. From its decision appeal lay to the U.S. Supreme Court.[119] These judicial appeals reflected the po-

---

[117] The term "primary" examiner instead of principal examiner was used frequently by the Commissioners in their reports.

[118] In 1893 jurisdiction over patent appeals in both types of cases was given to the new Court of Appeals instead of to the Supreme Court of the District of Columbia. 27 Stat. 434, sec. 9 (Feb. 9, 1893).

[119] 16 Stat. 198, secs. 46-48, 50, 52, 56 (July 8, 1870). These procedures were enacted March 2, 1861, 12 Stat. 246.

tentially large property rights that might be involved in patent applications, as well as the complexity of patent law.

The Patent Office deprecated permitting appeals to the Supreme
Court of the District of Columbia, most of which turned on questions of fact, while concurring in a general right of judicial review in
equity. The Patent Commissioner pointed out in his report for 1869
that no such appeal was allowed from decisions of his fellow Commissioners of Pensions, Land Office, Indian Affairs, or Internal
Revenue, and argued that the administrative appeals were adequate
to settle all questions of fact.[120] Despite a strong case, appeal to the
District of Columbia Supreme Court was incorporated into the 1870
revision of the patent law, and continued thereafter.

The internal administrative appeal raised a general question
concerning the relation of the Patent Office to the Secretary of the
Interior. The consolidating act of 1870 provided, "That it shall be
the duty of the Commissioner, under the direction of the Secretary
of the Interior, to superintend or perform all the duties respecting the
granting and issuing of patents. . . ."[121] Did this language authorize
the Secretary of the Interior to reverse, on appeal, a decision of the
Commissioner on the propriety of issuing a patent?

Secretaries differed in their early opinions on this question. Both
Zachariah Chandler and Carl Schurz took the view that they had no
control over the "judicial" action of the Commissioner of Patents,
who was, nevertheless, administratively responsible to them. Secretary
Samuel J. Kirkwood asked the Attorney General for an official
opinion. In this opinion (August 20, 1881), the Attorney General
held that the final discretion in *all* matters relating to the granting of
patents was lodged in the Secretary of the Interior. Henceforth he
was therefore subject to appeals on the substantive correctness of refusal to issue a patent.[122]

The history of the Patent Office from 1869 to 1901 was not one of
innovation or substantial change. Law and policy were well established before 1869; administrative procedures were habitual; Commissioners came and went, but the corps of examiners carried on
their tasks without much concern over their political leadership. More

---

[120] Commissioner of Patents, *Annual Report*, 1869, pp. 11-13.
[121] 16 Stat. 198, sec. 7.
[122] This matter is summarized in Secretary of the Interior, *Annual Report*, 1881,
pp. xxxii-xxxiv.

applications came in year by year, more patents were granted, the search among the records cumulated month by month, but the essential operation remained the same. Secretary of the Interior Noble noted this characteristic in his annual report for 1892: "There has been no great change in the business methods of the Patent Office. It has been so long established and its field of operations are [sic] so distinct that changes of any great moment are not to be expected."[123]

PERFORMANCE AND DOCTRINE

Space is lacking to deal with other important units in the Department of the Interior: the Census Office, fountain of decennial patronage; the Bureau of Education, with strong professional interests and clientele; the Geological Survey, one of the homes of science in government; the national parks, devoted to conservation and recreational opportunities for the American people.

What can be said in review of the administrative significance of the Department of the Interior from 1869 to 1901? A number of observations are relevant. Secretaries of this, like other departments, were not selected primarily on account of their knowledge of the operations of the department or for reasons of demonstrated administrative skill. The evidence is clear that the task laid upon them was too great to master in the absence of executive assistants above the level of bureau chiefs. By the end of the period some such help had been provided, but inadequate in amount and in ignorance of the type of resource later to be given by administrative assistants and career deputy assistant secretaries, finance officers, and personnel officers.

The heterogeneity of function in the Department was matched by variations in the quality of performance. The Patent Office was a model of excellence in comparison with the Indian service; the Geological Survey possessed an *esprit de corps* that was lacking for the most part in the Land Office or the Pension Office.

The Department was peculiarly subject to the influence of outside interests, of which the most powerful was the Grand Army of the Republic. At its height, the GAR was strong enough to control legislation, to influence appropriations, and to dictate the appointment and removal of Pension Commissioners. Congress itself be-

[123] *Ibid.*, 1892, p. 17.

came a pressure group as its members intervened in pension cases principally, but in other cases as well.

Control of the field service was a complex and baffling problem throughout these decades, as well as earlier and later. Progress was made by the establishment and gradual expansion of inspection services, but as late as McKinley's term gross errors and frauds were being exposed among the land surveyors in the west.

The Indian service, harassed as it was by policy problems and by politics, pioneered in one respect: the use of citizen advisory and "watchdog" boards. The Board of Indian Commissioners was a notable administrative invention, and the religious denominations for some years replaced the politicians as sponsors for field agents of the Indian Office.

Finally we may note the absence of contribution to, or interest in, administrative doctrine. There was substantially no writing in the official reports for thirty years that rose above the enumeration of particulars or complaints about contemporary problems. No frame of reference for an administrative doctrine in fact existed, but it is noteworthy that among the many able career executives in middle management, or among gifted personalities such as Carl Schurz, no one speculated about the general nature of the enterprise on which they were all engaged.

CHAPTER ELEVEN

The Department of Agriculture

This newcomer to the administrative scene was unique in more than one respect. It was the first client–oriented department; it was firmly based on science; it had a strong sense of mission; and it represented a new set of relations between the federal and the state governments. Beyond these outstanding characteristics the Department, after it acquired Cabinet status in 1889, enjoyed superior leadership in the succession of able Secretaries and famous scientists who were in charge of its fortunes.

The Department was organized in 1862, a year of agricultural developments whose significance has hardly been surpassed. In addition to establishing the Department (headed only by a Commissioner as a token of less than Cabinet status), Congress also passed the Morrill Act granting land to the states to found and support agricultural colleges,[1] and the Homestead Act, opening up the public domain to home-owner farmer settlers.[2] These were three major statutory foundations of federal agricultural policy for nearly a century.

The charter of the Department of Agriculture was comprehensive. Its "general designs and duties" were to acquire and to diffuse among the people useful information on subjects connected with agriculture "in the most general and comprehensive sense of that word," and to procure and distribute new and valuable seeds and plants. The Commissioner of Agriculture was authorized to conduct practical and scientific experiments and to appoint persons skilled in the natural

---

[1] 12 Stat. 503 (July 2, 1862); William Belmont Parker, *The Life and Public Services of Justin Smith Morrill* (Boston: Houghton Mifflin Co., 1924), ch. 11.
[2] 12 Stat. 392 (May 20, 1862).

sciences pertaining to agriculture.[3] Congress thus formally committed itself to science on a scale far beyond the slender enterprises of earlier years.[4]

The new Department began its life with less than superior leadership. Isaac Newton, its first Commissioner, was a Pennsylvania Quaker, a friend of President Lincoln, who may perhaps not unfairly be described as an agricultural politician. Dr. Warner W. Stockberger, a later distinguished scientist-executive in the Department, observed that "he acquired a large circle of warm friends and became skilled in the art of practical politics."[5] His appointment was severely criticized by the agricultural press, and the removal of a respected chief clerk to make room for his nephew forfeited confidence. To Newton's credit, it must be acknowledged that he also appointed some outstanding scientists: Charles M. Wetherill, educated in chemistry at the University of Pennsylvania and with a Ph.D. degree from the German University of Giessen; Dr. Thomas Antisell, trained in chemistry and medicine at Trinity College, Dublin, and the Dublin School of Medicine; William Saunders, horticulturist from the University of Edinburgh, and others.[6]

Newton died in office in 1867. General Horace Capron, his successor, brought able executive talent to the new Department. Grant's Commissioner, Frederick Watts, was an elderly lawyer and judge with a passion for economy. He is said on occasion to have personally supervised employees tying up seed packets to guarantee no twine was wasted.[7] He was lax in administration, testy and easily ruffled, but he, too, maintained high standards in his scientific appointments. Hayes' Commissioner, William G. LeDuc, another general, fought off the politicians vigorously and made no congressional friends.

His successor, George B. Loring, a noted Massachusetts physician

[3] 12 Stat. 387 (May 15, 1862).
[4] William L. Wanlass, *The United States Department of Agriculture* (Baltimore: Johns Hopkins Press, 1920); John M. Gaus and Leon O. Wolcott, *Public Administration and the United States Department of Agriculture* (Chicago: Public Administration Service, 1940).
[5] Warner W. Stockberger, *Personnel Administration Development in the United States Department of Agriculture: The First Fifty Years* (processed, U.S. Department of Agriculture, 1947), p. 1.
[6] *Ibid.*, pp. 4-5.
[7] *Ibid.*, p. 8.

and surgeon turned farmer and politician, served on the State Board of Agriculture from 1860 to 1877 and was president of the New England Agricultural Society from 1864 to 1889. He was elected to Congress for two terms (1887–91) and was chairman of the state Republican committee from 1869 to 1877. He thus had good credentials, political, professional, and agricultural.

Despite vicissitudes of leadership and some congressional criticism, the functions of the Department steadily expanded during its early years. Small beginnings were made in the control of plant and animal diseases, in the search for new forage plants and grass suitable for arid regions, in agricultural chemistry, in forestry, and in two areas having a primarily economic significance: the collection of crop statistics as an aid to marketing, and the culture of cotton, silk, and especially sugar. Two functions of notable importance were added in the 1880's: the inspection of meat in interstate and foreign commerce, and guidance and leadership to the state agricultural experiment stations established in 1887 by the Hatch Act.[8] The administrative significance of these activities is discussed at a later point.

In 1889, at the close of Cleveland's first administration, the Department was raised to Cabinet status.[9] "For years," declared Secretary Jeremiah M. Rusk in his first annual report, "there had been a demand on the part of a large majority of the farmers of the country that that Department at the seat of government which was organized to represent their interests should be clothed with the same dignity and power that other Executive Departments had, and that it should have its influence in national affairs and be recognized in the councils of the nation."[10] Thus culminated a movement that in its early days had been resisted as a dangerous piece of class legislation, opening the door to demands of other great economic groups for departments protective of their interests.[11]

[8] 24 Stat. 440 (March 2, 1887).
[9] 25 Stat. 659 (Feb. 9, 1889).
[10] Secretary of Agriculture, *Annual Report*, 1889, p. 7.
[11] See three valuable monographs by a one-time director of the Office of Experiment Stations, Alfred Charles True, *A History of Agricultural Education in the United States, 1785-1925* (Washington: Government Printing Office, 1929); *A History of Agricultural Extension Work in the United States, 1785-1923* (Washington: Government Printing Office, 1928); *A History of Agricultural Experimentation and Research in the United States, 1607-1925* (Department of Agriculture Miscellaneous Publication, No. 251, 1937).

Elevation to Cabinet status sustained the triple foundation on which the Department had come to rest during its early years: scientific research, production, and marketing. Succeeding years were to strengthen and deepen these three basic functions. The first Secretary was the last and ablest Commissioner, Norman J. Colman. He served only a few weeks as Secretary, awaiting the inauguration of Benjamin Harrison.[12]

DEPARTMENTAL LEADERSHIP

Agriculture was exceptionally fortunate in its Secretaries, three of whom occupied this post from 1889 to 1913; Jeremiah M. Rusk of Wisconsin, Julius Sterling Morton of Nebraska, and James Wilson of Iowa. Their views concerning the function of government in agriculture were markedly different: Rusk was an expansionist, Morton held to laissez faire, Wilson, a former professor, was particularly concerned with agricultural education. All were men thoroughly familiar with agricultural problems; all were men of integrity; and all were dedicated to the improvement of the farmers' lot.

Jeremiah M. Rusk, known familiarly as "Uncle Jerry," came from a poor farm family, settled in Wisconsin, and almost immediately became a political success: county sheriff, coroner, and member of the state assembly. A brigadier general in the Civil War, he returned to political life as state bank comptroller and a member of Congress from 1871 to 1877. He was governor of Wisconsin from 1882 to 1889 and evidenced a lively and intelligent interest in farm life and movements. Harrison appointed him Secretary of Agriculture in 1889, desiring, he said, "a man who, primarily, had a good practical knowledge of agriculture—not of fancy farming, but of farming as a business, as a means of getting a livelihood; that he ought to come from one of the great agricultural states; that he ought to be a man in close touch with the class described by Mr. Lincoln as the 'plain people'; and that . . . he ought to be a man experienced in public affairs and public administration."[13]

Rusk was impatient with small plans and determined to build a great department. In his first annual report he remarked that in

[12] George F. Lemmer, *Norman J. Colman and Colman's Rural World: a Study in Agricultural Leadership* (University of Missouri Studies, XXV [1953], No. 3).

[13] Ex-President Benjamin Harrison in Henry Casson, *"Uncle Jerry." Life of General Jeremiah M. Rusk* (Madison, Wisconsin: Junius W. Hill, 1895), pp. 1-2.

establishing Agriculture as an executive department, "The intention of our law-makers was not simply to add the luster of official dignity to an industry already dignified by the labor of its votaries, but to give it added influence and power for good in their behalf."[14] After commenting on the broad scale of European departments he continued, "It is my desire to organize the Department upon even a broader plane than these and other countries have established."[15] Disappointed because Congress had not already increased appropriations before he took office, he told the legislative branch that former resources "must not be regarded as a correct basis for the consideration of its present needs, and I, for my part, must absolutely refuse to recognize any such standard of comparison."[16] To emphasize the point he declared, "I beg you to bear in mind that I speak in the name of the agricultural interests of the United States, and I opine that no member of either House will for a moment depreciate the extent, importance and influence of these interests in this country."[17]

Rusk looked far beyond the present to a distant future when the population of the country would exceed 100,000,000 and the value of agricultural products would be double the three or four billion of his time.[18] "It is rarely given to any single man," he wrote, "to superintend the completion of a great work which it has required a wide and mature experience to successfully plan, but the wise builder knows well that without a well-determined plan the building, when completed, will surely be found deficient in some respects. What this Department must eventually be . . . is the consideration which now deeply concerns me."[19] He returned to this theme in his annual report for 1892: ". . . in the affairs of the nation true prescience is an essential attribute to the wise administrator. I must not, therefore, be deemed extravagant if I present designs for the future development of the Department which I conceive to be necessary to meet the demands not only of the near future but those of a score of years hence."[20]

[14] Secretary of Agriculture, *Annual Report*, 1889, p. 44.
[15] *Ibid.*, 1889, p. 9.
[16] Letter to Chairman of House Committee on Agriculture (Feb. 3, 1890), reprinted in Henry Casson, *"Uncle Jerry,"* p. 247.
[17] *Ibid.*, p. 249.
[18] Secretary of Agriculture, *Annual Report*, 1891, p. 63.
[19] *Ibid.*, 1891, p. 62.
[20] *Ibid.*, 1892, p. 62.

The vision of this man of the people was remarkable. He was equally concerned with pure and applied research, with the education of farmers in improved methods, with aid to marketing at home and abroad, and with the inspection of food products on a large scale.[21] He it was, educated in the common schools alone, who sent experts abroad to establish contacts with agricultural institutions in other countries and who indignantly repelled his critics. "The suggestion of sending a well-qualified representative abroad purely in the interest of agriculture is cavilled at as a means of affording a pleasure trip to some broken-down professor. It is time that we rose superior to such humiliating and unworthy puerility."[22]

Cleveland's Secretary of Agriculture, J. Sterling Morton, the originator of Arbor Day, was a Nebraska farmer and agricultural journalist. He was a man of strong opinions and had no reluctance in expressing them, let the consequences be what they might. Rusk had been an expansionist in government programs for farmers; Morton was his opposite—opposed to paternalism, devoted to laissez faire, insistent upon economy, but nevertheless a defender of the scientific work of the Department. In his first annual report in 1893 he declared that "the Department of Agriculture offers opulent opportunities for the exercise of the most pronounced paternalism."[23] Within a few months he had reduced the departmental payroll by over 500 employees.[24] In 1895 he was reported to have said that "if the department of agriculture is to be conducted in the spirit of paternalism the sooner it is abolished the better for the United States."[25]

Morton's biographer, James C. Olson, recorded that he looked with suspicion upon every bill to appropriate money for special purposes, or that would extend the functions of government. Invited to comment on a proposed appropriation to exterminate the Russian thistle, Morton asked whether it was "the business of the Government of the United States to make appropriations out of which men, women, and boys are to be hired, at wages fixed by law, to exterminate weeds,

[21] He even persuaded Congress to spend money for experiments in the production of rainfall, over a half century in advance of science itself. *Ibid.*, 1890, p. 33.
[22] *Ibid.*, 1890, p. 56.
[23] *Ibid.*, 1893, p. 7.
[24] *Ibid.*, 1893, p. 16.
[25] *Chicago Sunday Chronicle*, Sept. 15, 1895, quoted in James C. Olson, *J. Sterling Morton* (Lincoln: University of Nebraska Press, 1942), p. 363.

called Russian thistles, any more than it is the business of that Government to prescribe the manner of plowing, planting, and cultivating cereals, cotton, and tobacco, and to limit the wages to be paid cultivators?"[26]

Morton thus started with a social philosophy the antithesis of that held by Rusk. It naturally predisposed him to economy. He probed every division in search of opportunities to economize, and personally investigated individual accounts. Olson quoted from Morton's Letterbook a communication to an unfortunate director of an experiment station: "I notice that the feed-bill for your horses during the past ten months has averaged $178.77 per month. That I consider extravagant beyond all reason. . . . I wish it distinctly understood that wherever there is an opportunity to economize, it should be embraced with alacrity, and that if you do not economize some one will be put in your place who will."[27]

Laissez faire doctrine and a passion for economy brought Morton into a head-on collision with Congress over the free distribution of seeds. This ancient function, in high favor with Congressmen, had grown to major proportions. Morton criticized the program in 1893, and in 1894 declared in his second annual report, "it is difficult to see how any practical statesman can advocate an annual disbursement of $160,000 for such a purpose. . . . If, in a sort of paternal way, it is the duty of this Government to distribute anything gratuitously, are not new ideas of more permanent value than old seeds? Is it a function of government to make gratuitous distribution of any material thing?"[28] The special agent for the purchase of seeds, Enos S. Harnden, was equally candid. In the same annual report he wrote:

In the light of my experience as a former seedsman, however, I consider the free distribution of seeds by this Department as an infringement upon and interference with a legitimate business, and I believe it should be abolished.

The seed business, whether wholesale or retail, is to-day as much an established legitimate business as manufacturing or trading in any product or merchandise. I hold that this Department has no moral right to interfere with this or any other legitimate business interest by a free political

[26] James C. Olson, *J. Sterling Morton*, p. 359 (Jan. 4, 1894).
[27] *Ibid.*, pp. 356-57.
[28] Secretary of Agriculture, *Annual Report*, 1894, p. 69.

distribution of garden seeds, spades, shovels, or plows, or of new styles of dress goods, or of any other commodity the subject of legitimate trade.[29]

In 1895 Morton exercised his official discretion by rejecting all bids for the purchase of seeds, in effect impounding the appropriation and terminating the function.[30] Congress loved its seed perquisites, however, and promptly passed a joint resolution directing Morton to proceed.[31] He had no alternative.

Whatever the Secretary's views on such activities, they did not affect his support for those functions he considered appropriate. He was as strong an advocate of the Department (in its more restricted role) as had been Rusk. Morton believed that the central purpose of the Department was scientific investigation, and he was gratified to report in 1894 that his economies had not impaired capacity for research. For the fiscal year 1893, 45.6 per cent of the Department's expenditures went toward science; in 1894, the percentage was 51.8.[32] During his four-year term Morton added three new lines of work— development of agrostology, the study of agricultural soils and crop production, and investigation of methods of road improvement.[33] He was an able, courageous Secretary, but not one to expand the Department's functions to trench on the private economy.

Morton retired with Cleveland to be replaced by a professor of agriculture and director of the experiment station at Iowa State College, James Wilson. He was destined to hold the Secretary's office from 1897 to 1913, under McKinley, Roosevelt, and Taft. Wilson had been active in public affairs as well as in practical farming, teaching, and research. From 1867 to 1871 he was a member of the Iowa State house of representatives and sat in Congress from 1873 to 1877, and again from 1883 to 1885. He served on the House Committee on Agriculture. In the interim between his two terms he was a member of the Iowa Railway Commission, and after his retirement from Congress he engaged in farming and in writing for farm journals until his association with Iowa State College in 1891. Wilson was eminently qualified by experience to head the Department of Agri-

[29] *Ibid.*, 1894, p. 211.
[30] *Ibid.*, 1895, pp. 54-55.
[31] 29 Stat. 467 (March 14, 1896).
[32] Secretary of Agriculture, *Annual Report*, 1894, p. 46.
[33] *Ibid.*, 1894, pp. 20-21, 62.

culture. He had a commanding figure, was a tireless worker, and a Presbyterian of high moral principles. Under his administration the Department expanded in all directions. In his final report he summarized the work over which he had presided.

. . . . Bureaus have been created and expanded. Lines of research, investigation, and demonstration have been multiplied. Congress has piled duty on duty from year to year. The corps of experts needed in the increasing amount and variety of service has grown greatly. The department has become a great agricultural university for postgraduate work. Discoveries for the benefit of farm practices and improvements of old ones have been countless. The department has both promoted and begun a revolution in the art and science of agriculture. Its influences for agricultural betterment have penetrated all regions of the national domain. . . .[34]

Agriculture was thus fortunate in its leadership. Each of three successive Secretaries (like others in later years) were men who knew much about agriculture from personal experience and/or from professional activities. Each, moreover, had been active in public affairs and was quickly at home in the official world of Washington. On some policy matters they differed, but they were united in their devotion to agriculture, and above all to the application of science and research to agricultural practice. These men were more than politicians. They possessed a sense of mission, an attribute that permeated the whole Department.

AGRICULTURE: A CLIENT-ORIENTED DEPARTMENT

The Department of Agriculture was concerned exclusively with the affairs of farmers. Secretary Rusk recognized that he was regarded in a special manner as the representative of the agricultural interest in government. In his first annual report he referred to "the class the Department was primarily designed to serve, *i.e.*, the farmers."[35] In his last annual report he noted "that agriculture is the only industry in this country having an individual representation in the National Government, possessing, as it does, an executive department devoted exclusively to its service. . . ."[36] Throughout subsequent reports by Secretaries and division heads runs this undercurrent of devotion to the betterment of farm life.

[34] *Ibid.*, 1912, p. 114.
[35] *Ibid.*, 1889, p. 10.
[36] *Ibid.*, 1892, p. 7.

The orientation of the Department toward its public was in full evidence in the publication program. In pursuance of farmers' interests, scientists worked out discoveries, but to translate science into terms usable by plain farmers was a separate art to which the Department bent much effort. "The very essence of the duties devolving on this Department of the Government," Rusk declared, "is that its results shall be promptly made available to the public by a comprehensive scheme of publication."[37] Science was of little value to farmers unless and until it had been digested, and its findings stated in language that they could understand. Science had, nevertheless, its own intrinsic value and deserved dissemination in scientific circles. There consequently developed a varied series of departmental publications. The annual report early fell into two parts: one concerned with administrative matters, the other—the *Yearbook*—with the science and art of agriculture.[38] The *Yearbook*, with annual editions of 500,000, was the largest single government publication.

A publications division was established in 1890 to ensure oversight and vigor in the Department's program.[39] Special bulletins emanating from the scientific laboratories were encouraged in language suitable for the average layman; and also, in briefer form and plain terms, the practical conclusions of the scientific investigations "on a scale so extensive as to practically reach all the farmers of this country."[40] Rusk reported in 1889 that in nine months the number of publications circulated by the Department was 469,100. The folding room, as the mailing division was called, was hard put to it to keep abreast of the flood.[41]

Rusk also cultivated the rural press. He always prepared the releases covering important transactions of the Department. As Ex-President Harrison noted: "The favor and aid of the agricultural press he regarded as essential, and sought by every means to make it a channel of communication between the Department and the farmers."[42] In his press relations, Rusk was a pioneer.

The Department knew how to use its clientele for mutual advantage, notably in crop reporting. In 1893 the departmental statis-

[37] *Ibid.*, 1889, p. 10.
[38] Authorized by Congress, January 12, 1895. 28 Stat. 601, sec. 73.
[39] Secretary of Agriculture, *Annual Report*, 1890, p. 437.
[40] *Ibid.*, 1889, p. 11.
[41] *Ibid.*, 1889, p. 32.
[42] In Henry Casson, *"Uncle Jerry,"* p. 6.

tician was supported by two corps of field correspondents, each numbering 10,000. One reported crop and other statistics directly to the Department, the other reported similar data to state agents of the Department. Beyond these correspondents the Department maintained a list of over 150,000 selected farmers who from time to time assisted in checking the accuracy of crop reports.[43] Such a complex of client-relations was unknown in other governmental agencies.

Rusk sent his men directly to the farmers, attending agricultural institutes, state and county fairs, and meetings of specialized rural organizations—an activity that he had pressed with good results while governor of Wisconsin. In his first report Rusk included a special section on farmers' institutes. "I regard this institute work as one of the most beneficent movements the agricultural history of this country ever has witnessed."[44] In his second report he was emphatic in his recommendations: "Not only do I deem it to be the utmost importance, indeed a solemn duty devolving upon this Department, that these meetings and gatherings should be encouraged in every possible way by this representative Department in the National Government, but I conceive it to be absolutely necessary for the intelligent conduct of the work of this Department that it should be frequently represented at such meetings. . . ."[45] "Everything," he declared, "that leads to a more intimate acquaintance between the Department and the farmers throughout the country must be mutually advantageous."[46]

None of the older Departments had an opportunity such as fell naturally to the lot of Agriculture. The interests of the Treasury and the taxpayer did not always seem identical, particularly to the latter; the Post Office served the whole people, not one group; the Pension Office was, by bitter experience, suspicious of its "customers" and had to renounce service for policing; neither War nor Navy had a definite clientele whom it served or upon whom it could rely for support in time of need. Agriculture had a special position, and it capitalized on its resources.

[43] Secretary of Agriculture, *Annual Report*, 1893, p. 466.
[44] *Ibid.*, 1889, p. 37.
[45] *Ibid.*, 1890, p. 52.
[46] *Ibid.*, 1889, p. 16.

AGRICULTURE AND SCIENCE

Another of the unique qualities of the Department of Agriculture was its solid foundation in science. The organic act of 1862 directed the Department to conduct practical and scientific experiments and authorized the appointment of chemists, botanists, entomologists, and other natural scientists. Despite the dominant interest of many Congressmen in the free distribution of seeds to their constituents, the departmental personnel was predominantly concerned with science, not seeds; with experimentation, not partisanship; with long-run, not merely immediate gains.

Scientific research and experimentation came into its own during the administration of Commissioner Norman J. Colman. He was one of the principal authors of the Hatch Act of 1887, authorizing funds for the establishment and partial support of the state agricultural experiment stations. A farm journalist professionally, Colman had deep convictions about the value of scientific research in crop production. "The path to success in this experiment-station enterprise," he wrote in 1888, "passes by the fountains of abstract science and by the farms and firesides of the American people." He declared that the Department should bring the best science of the world to the stations and help carry their findings home to the farmer.[47]

Assistant Secretary Edwin Willits, in charge of the scientific bureaus and divisions, declared two years later: "Agriculture to be permanently successful must be founded on, and conducted according to scientific principle. . . . Nature can not be cheated, and her implacable laws will surely find out their transgressors . . . there are arts that promote and arts that prevent injury. Science is at the bottom of each."[48] The halls of the Department, he wrote, "are instinct with science. The chiefs of their divisions and many of their subordinates are eminent in their special lines, and are recognized for their work and their ability the world over as the peers of any like body of investigators, seek where you may."[49]

Willits was not idly boasting in his praise of the scientific corps of the Department. It had always possessed a group of men who stood

[47] Commissioner of Agriculture, *Annual Report*, 1888, p. 14.
[48] Secretary of Agriculture, *Annual Report*, 1890, p. 59.
[49] *Ibid.*, 1890, p. 61.

high in their respective circles. A glimpse at the heads of the scientific divisions in 1891 suggests their eminence. Thirteen were recorded in the *Official Register* for that year; forty years later eight of them had earned a place in the *Dictionary of American Biography*.

The first chief of the Office of Experiment Stations, Wilbur O. Atwater, was a pioneer in agricultural chemistry, holding a Ph.D. from Yale and having two further years of advanced work in Leipzig and Berlin. He had been a professor of chemistry at Connecticut Wesleyan University and director of the first state agricultural experiment station at Middletown, Connecticut. He demonstrated that leguminous plants absorb free atmospheric nitrogen, and with a colleague invented the Atwater-Rosa calorimeter, an instrument that opened new vistas of research. He wrote several hundred scientific papers and translations.[50]

The first chief of the Bureau of Animal Industry, Daniel E. Salmon, held the degree of doctor of veterinary medicine and had studied this specialty in Paris after doing basic work at Cornell University. During his long tenure as bureau chief (1884–1905), he demonstrated both high scientific attainment and great administrative ability. He wrote nearly one hundred papers on veterinary research, and was president of the American Public Health Association and of the American Veterinary Medical Association. After leaving the Bureau he organized the veterinary department of the University of Montevideo, Uruguay.[51]

Bernard E. Fernow, chief of the Division of Forestry (1886–1898), received his professional training at the German University of Königsberg and the Hanover-Münden Forest Academy. He quickly became a leader of the embryonic forestry conservation movement in this country, and after leaving the Department became dean of the Cornell University Forestry School. He also wrote prolifically, having a list of over two hundred articles and addresses on forestry.[52]

The list need not be lengthened to confirm the high quality of the responsible scientists in the new Department. It was indeed instinct with science: astronomer Mark W. Harrington in the Weather Bureau; Dr. Harvey W. Wiley, chief chemist and protagonist of pure

[50] *Dictionary of American Biography*, I, 417.
[51] *Ibid.*, XVI, 311.
[52] *Ibid.*, VI, 336.

food;[53] George Vasey, departmental botanist and distinguished specialist on grasses; Jacob R. Dodge, eminent statistician in charge of crop reporting; Charles V. Riley, noted entomologist; and others. Looking back over the years, Secretary James Wilson wrote: "A choice corps of scholarly experts in their special lines of endeavor has been growing in membership, in breadth of view, and in the practical application of their efforts. They have been and are men both good and true, men with high ideals, often sacrificing greater remuneration in private employment for love of the great results of their public service. No great work can be begun, nor sustained, by this department without such men."[54]

These were years in which scientists had already begun the exchange of ideas and experimental findings through their professional organizations. In many of them departmental scientists participated, and in some of them they played a leading part. Notable among the latter group was the Association of Official Agricultural Chemists, whose annual conventions were held in Washington under departmental auspices, whose secretary was the chief chemist of the Department of Agriculture, and whose proceedings were published as a bulletin of the Chemical Division.[55]

In 1891 Secretary Rusk had occasion to note summer conventions in Washington of ten scientific associations in whose work the Department had a lively interest, including by way of illustration the American Microscopical Society, the Conference of American Chemists, and the Association of Economic Entomologists. Rusk spoke with appreciation of the opportunity for the Department's scientific force to participate in these deliberations.[56]

Rusk did not hesitate, either, to send his scientists abroad to attend professional and scientific meetings, despite the carping criticism against favors to broken-down professors. In 1891 he sent Daniel E. Salmon to the International Congress of Hygiene and Demography in

[53] Harvey W. Wiley, *An Autobiography* (Indianapolis: Bobbs-Merrill Company, 1930).
[54] Secretary of Agriculture, *Annual Report*, 1912, p. 259.
[55] *Ibid.*, 1890, p. 26; Harvey W. Wiley, "Historical Sketch of the Association of Official Agricultural Chemists," in Association of Official Agricultural Chemists, *Proceedings*, 1899, pp. 16-49, U.S. Department of Agriculture, Division of Chemistry, Bulletin 57.
[56] Secretary of Agriculture, *Annual Report*, 1891, pp. 26-27.

London, and the International Congress of Agriculture at The Hague. Salmon was promptly elected first vice president of the International Congress of Agriculture.[57] Rusk also sent Mark W. Harrington and one of his assistants in the Weather Bureau, Professor Cleveland Abbe, to the International Congress of Meteorologists at Munich.[58]

Other departments, notably War and Navy, had pioneered in special areas of science, such as meteorology, oceanography, geology, and exploration. Agriculture was the first department for which science was the central fact of existence. The quality of departmental life in Agriculture was consequently markedly different from that of Treasury, the Post Office, or Interior, where science played almost no part and mass routine required the employment of clerks rather than the service of men trained in science. There were few, if any, doctors of philosophy elsewhere than in Agriculture. Here they dominated the official scene.

THE BUREAU OF ANIMAL INDUSTRY

The quarantine and destruction of diseased animals was the first major regulatory function of the Department of Agriculture, the forerunner of an immense development in later years.[59] The exportation of livestock to Great Britain began in the 1870's. It soon encountered restrictions intended to prevent the introduction of diseased cattle, especially those afflicted with pleuropneumonia. This disease had been prevalent among American herds for many years; state-wide attempts to eliminate it were inept and unsuccessful. Agitation for federal action began by 1880 but Congress was dilatory. A German embargo on American meat imports in 1883 and renewed agitation in the cattle trade finally induced Congress in 1884 to establish the Bureau of Animal Industry.[60] Its duties were primarily to suppress communicable diseases among livestock. The Secretary of the Treasury was empowered to make regulations concerning their export

[57] *Ibid.*, 1891, p. 28.

[58] In 1893, this professional group met in Chicago. Its proceedings were published by the Weather Bureau as a departmental bulletin. Secretary of Agriculture, *Annual Report*, 1893, p. 45.

[59] See Fred Wilbur Powell, *The Bureau of Animal Industry* (Baltimore: Johns Hopkins Press, 1927); and U. G. Houck, *The Bureau of Animal Industry of the United States Department of Agriculture* (Washington: Author, 1924).

[60] 23 Stat. 31 (May 29, 1884).

and transportation, a duty soon transferred to Agriculture. The authority of the Bureau was increased in 1886 by permitting the purchase and destruction of diseased animals.[61] The Bureau now made a determined effort in conjunction with the states. Pleuropneumonia was completely eradicated by 1892.[62]

The European market was not fully restored. Meat inspection so far as it existed was carried on by state and local authorities and was far from adequate. A Senate select committee reported in 1890 that inspection was "in a singularly loose and unsatisfactory condition, without system, and in many localities entirely neglected. . . . we have no hesitation in declaring that the failure of State and municipal authorities, within whose exclusive jurisdiction the matter rests, to provide stringent and efficient inspection of all animals intended for slaughter is in the highest degree criminal."[63] Congress responded to this call for aid to foreign markets by authorizing the inspection of livestock destined for the export trade.[64] Rusk had already made the strongest representations in favor of national inspection of cattle in the interest of both foreign trade and domestic health.[65] Administrative authority over the slaughter and transportation of infected livestock was gradually but steadily enlarged on the basis of this original legislation.

The Bureau of Animal Industry thus became the earliest regulatory arm of the Department of Agriculture. It also engaged in scientific research, formally recognized by Congress in 1896 by appropriations for a pathological division and a biochemic division,[66] but the bulk of its effort went into the eradication of animal disease by inspection and quarantine.

THE EXPERIMENT STATIONS: FEDERAL–STATE RELATIONS

The first agricultural experiment station was established in Connecticut in 1875. By 1886 there were seventeen.[67] They were usually associated with the land grant colleges, and there was some inter-

[61] 24 Stat. 103 (June 30, 1886).
[62] Secretary of Agriculture, *Annual Report,* 1892, p. 28.
[63] Senate Report 829, 51st Cong., 1st sess., pp. 23, 26 (May 1, 1890).
[64] 26 Stat. 414 (August 30, 1890).
[65] Secretary of Agriculture, *Annual Report,* 1889, p. 39.
[66] 29 Stat. 101 (April 25, 1896).
[67] Commissioner of Agriculture, *Annual Report,* 1888, p. 8.

change of faculty and research personnel between them. They were exclusively state institutions, financed by state funds, and had no connection with the Department of Agriculture.

In 1887 Congress passed the Hatch Act setting up cooperative relations between the stations and the Department. By this legislation Congress authorized the establishment of agricultural experiment stations in the land grant colleges and appropriated $15,000 to the support of each one of them subject to the consent of the respective state legislatures. The stations were directed to conduct original research or to verify experiments on the physiology and diseases of plants and animals, on the analysis of soils and water, and to carry on such other research as might be deemed advisable.[68] This was a generous charter of authority. Legislative assent by the states and territories was quickly forthcoming, and the number of stations rapidly increased.

The Hatch Act made no provision for federal control over the state experiment stations or the expenditure of the federal grant. The Commissioner was merely directed "to furnish forms . . . for the tabulation of results of investigation or experiment . . . to indicate, from time to time, such lines of inquiry as to him shall seem most important; and, in general, furnish such advice and assistance as will best promote the purposes of this act." Each station, furthermore, was required to make a full and detailed report of its operations, including receipts and expenditures, to the governor of the state. A copy was sent to the Department of Agriculture and to the Treasury for information. Congress obviously intended no federal control over the research projects, organization, or expenditures of the state experiment stations. It did encourage all the states to establish stations, and it did foresee some vague effort toward coordination of research results, all on a voluntary basis.

At first the Department did not aspire to more. Colman declared that its influence should be exercised mainly in the form of wise and sympathetic help. "It should exercise not dictatorship, but leadership. Its influence should be powerful in bringing the stations together in co-ordinating their work; in making the fruits of other research and reference . . . available to them; in prosecuting lines of pioneer

[68] 24 Stat. 440 (March 2, 1887).

research . . . ; in collating, condensing, distributing their results, and in helping to carry the practical outcome to the farmer. . . ."[69]

The joint program quickly took root. Secretary Rusk reported in 1889: "The development of the experiment-station enterprise in this country is a noteworthy illustration of the readiness of the American people to grasp and to utilize new and valuable ideas. Beginning only fourteen years ago, it has grown out to the farthest limits of the land, enlisted the best colleges and universities and the ablest investigators, and secured both State and national resources for its maintenance. It now employs nearly four hundred workers. . . . It has the favor of a great army of practical farmers, to whom it has brought substantial benefits."[70] An Office of Experiment Stations was set up in the Department and its director, W. O. Atwater, spoke warmly of progress. "Few persons realize the magnitude and the usefulness of the movement represented by the agricultural experiment stations in the United States. This system, established and supported by Congress and aided by the several States, constitutes the most extensive enterprise for agricultural experimenting which any nation has organized."[71]

Commissioner Colman, the architect of the new system, was not, however, unaware of its potential problems. "The prospects," he wrote in 1888, ". . . are full of promise, notwithstanding some manifest dangers which lie in the way of its progress. . . . The greatest danger, that of political interference and manipulation, needs to be carefully guarded against. Whenever it is understood that anything but special fitness constitutes qualification for positions in the management or work of these institutions, deterioration in the workers and the work is sure."[72] In some stations politics intruded nevertheless, and in some, other problems quickly became apparent. They were summarized by the director of the Office of Experiment Stations in 1890.

Atwater reported that the stations were spreading themselves too thin, undertaking more work than they could properly handle.

[69] Commissioner of Agriculture, *Annual Report*, 1888, p. 10.

[70] Secretary of Agriculture, *Annual Report*, 1889, p. 26. In 1890 most of the fiscal support came from Washington—$660,000 out of a total of $785,000 a year. *Ibid.*, 1890, p. 44.

[71] *Ibid.*, 1890, p. 545.

[72] Commissioner of Agriculture, *Annual Report*, 1888, p. 9.

Demands from constituents were numerous and pressing and boards of control wanted answers, not realizing "that to satisfactorily settle questions which seem simple requires a large amount of abstract and long-continued labor."[73] There was need of more "abstract research" as distinguished from the so-called practical. There was failure to secure skilled specialists, due in part to their scarcity. There was too much attention to the farm and too little to the laboratory. "An experiment station is not and should not be a model farm. The man to do good farming is the good farmer; the man to do useful experimenting is the trained specialist."[74] There was too little cooperation in the planning of experimental work. There was too much compliance with the popular complaint that stations were too scientific and not sufficiently practical.[75]

To enumerate these faults was merely to bring them to public notice and to the attention of state boards of control. There was little more that Atwater could do. Rusk in 1891 cautiously recommended that the connection between the experiment stations and the Department should be strengthened, "without in any way limiting the independent action of these several State institutions."[76] He was not specific and did not follow up on his idea.

Raising the standards of scientific work by exhortation was a novel administrative enterprise and it is not surprising that improvement was slow and sporadic. Misuse of funds was a horse of another color, for the prevention of which auditors had sharpened their axes for generations. It was in fact through the fiscal arm that federal authority was put to work vis-à-vis the state experiment stations. The initiative was taken by Secretary Morton in his annual report for 1893.

. . . the law should provide that the Secretary of Agriculture shall have some power to direct and to restrain the disbursements of the Government moneys in each of the experiment stations of the United States, so as to insure only a legitimate expenditure of the same.

Today each State draws from the Federal Treasury its pro rata share for its experiment station, and the only accounting required under the law for that money to the United States Treasury officials is the declaration and vouchers of the State authorities that the money has been

[73] Secretary of Agriculture, *Annual Report*, 1890, p. 540.
[74] *Ibid.*, 1890, p. 541.
[75] *Ibid.*, 1890, p. 543.
[76] *Ibid.*, 1891, p. 27.

expended under their direction. No detailed account as to how the money has been expended, to whom, or for what it has been paid out, is required. Current rumor in some of the States and Territories, so universal, pronounced, accentuated, and vehement as to have secured great credence, indicates that some of the moneys appropriated for experiment stations have been diverted from legitimate public purposes and turned to those of a personal and not patriotic character. . . .[77]

Congress responded, authorizing the Secretary of Agriculture to prescribe the form of the annual financial statement, to ascertain whether expenditures were properly made, and to report to Congress.[78] Thus was imposed the first element of federal control (other than persuasion) upon the state partners in a joint enterprise. Time was to bring new elements of control as experience deepened.

Audit, however, was pervasive. It implied authority to require accounting records adequate for an audit, the formulation of general rules to define the purposes for which federal grants might and might not be used, a federal field force to inspect state financial transactions with power to disallow unauthorized expenditures, and a sanction to enforce the auditors' decisions. Fiscally, therefore, the state experiment stations fell under federal control. The types of inquiry, scientific methods, coordination of research, quality and interest of personnel remained at the disposition of the states subject to the influence but not the authority of Washington.

The Department, however, exercised a steady nonfiscal pressure upon the experiment stations to improve their standards. After the 1894 auditing legislation, the director of the Office of Experiment Stations and his representatives inspected the state projects and by conference with station directors, boards of control, and authorities of the state agricultural colleges were able to do much to clarify the special function of the stations, to raise standards, and to coordinate particular lines of research. Alfred C. True recorded that advice was often given regarding organization, subjects and plans of work, personnel, equipment, and publications.[79] The better stations welcomed this kind of support.

Cooperation was also facilitated by the Association of American

[77] *Ibid.*, 1893, pp. 8-9.
[78] 28 Stat. 271 (August 8, 1894).
[79] Alfred Charles True, A *History of Agricultural Experimentation and Research in the United States*, p. 133.

Agricultural Colleges and Experiment Stations, organized in 1887 with the support of the Department. The Office of Experiment Stations was active in the annual conferences of the Association and published its proceedings as one of the departmental bulletins. The Association in course of time developed strength of its own as a means of influencing the policy and program of the Office of Experiment Stations in Washington.[80]

The community of interests between professional workers in the Department of Agriculture and in the experiment stations was also a powerful bond between federal and state levels of administration. These men were scientists. They had the same type of training, the same dedication to scientific method, the same problems to solve, and the same need for protection against outside influence. In their professional associations they gradually created an *esprit de corps* and common understanding of their mutual interests. Beneath the control relationship evidenced by federal audit of experiment station expenditures there was, therefore, a more subtle but perhaps equally important type of relationship: mutual adjustment by professional persons in the performance of scientific research on common problems for the benefit of a single constituency.

SOME ADMINISTRATIVE PROBLEMS

Like other departments, Agriculture had particular administrative problems and features. To a few of these we turn in the following pages.

Overhead organization. Agriculture was authorized an Assistant Secretary in 1889 when it was raised to Cabinet status. The next subordinate level comprised a considerable number of bureaus, divisions, and offices called into being over the years as new activities were initiated. Secretary Rusk brought order into a somewhat overextended organization by dividing its work into two parts—the scientific, assigned to the Assistant Secretary, the regulatory and developmental, retained by the Secretary.[81]

The number of persons reporting both to the Secretary and to the Assistant Secretary still remained excessive, and in 1892 Rusk recommended the application of what he called the bureau system. To use

[80] *Ibid.*, p. 134.
[81] Secretary of Agriculture, *Annual Report*, 1892, p. 23.

his own words: "The grouping of the several branches of the work into various bureaus, each one having for its chief the right kind of man, would most sensibly facilitate the administration of the work, reducing the number of persons in direct consultation with the head of the Department from 18 to 20 down to about one-third of that number, and placing the chief of each division, as at present organized, under a chief whom he would find readily accessible. . . ."[82] Rusk followed sound principle, interposing a new level of supervision between himself and his division heads, and delegating authority to the bureau chiefs to secure coordination among their subordinates. Over the years this was the course of events.

Rusk recognized also that the bureau system would help solve another problem to which constant reference was made, viz., the difficulty of retaining able men in the departmental service. This system, he declared, "would provide in the Department several offices of sufficient emolument and dignity to attract men of the highest standing . . . men thoroughly qualified to lead in their several specialties, and to command the respect and appreciation of all workers on the same lines not only in this but in foreign countries. Under our present system it is extremely difficult to retain in the departmental service men combining the highest attainments with administrative capacity."[83] Here was the first recognition that has come to notice of the emerging problem of combining science and management in the service of government and retaining in government persons having both skills.

Secretary Morton took a new approach by asking Congress to authorize what was in effect a permanent Undersecretary. He wrote:

. . . . It is not to be supposed that the Secretary of Agriculture, a member of the President's Cabinet, even if a farmer and an experienced executive, will always be a technically trained scientific man. Even if he should be, he occupies the position only four years, and thus scarcely becomes familiar with the difficult and complex work of the Department before he leaves it. The Assistant Secretary of Agriculture is subject to the same conditions. Because he must represent the Secretary in the Administration, he must go with the Administration. These conditions, which are necessary and inherent in our system of Government, it is not proposed to

[82] *Ibid.*, 1892, p. 62.
[83] *Ibid.*, p. 62.

change. A Secretary and an Assistant Secretary are both needed. But another permanent officer is needed to direct the work of the various scientific bureaus of the Department under the general authority of the Secretary.[84]

To this end he asked for a director-in-chief of scientific bureaus and investigations to serve during good behavior with the rank of Assistant Secretary. Congress took no action.

The Department was fortunate in its first two Assistant Secretaries. Edwin Willits was trained in law, had three terms in Congress (1877–1883), and a life-long interest in education. From 1860 to 1873 he was a member of the Michigan State Board of Education, from 1883 to 1885 president of a state normal school, and from 1885 to 1889 president of Michigan State Agricultural College. From this post he went to the office of Assistant Secretary under Rusk. Secretary Morton acknowledged his services to the Department with "a sincere admiration for his rugged honesty, industry, and vigilance."[85]

Willits was succeeded by another university president, Charles W. Dabney, Jr. He was an eminent scientist and educator, trained in chemistry in this country and abroad, state chemist, director of the agricultural experiment station in North Carolina, and president of the University of Tennessee.[86] After leaving the Department, he became president of the University of Cincinnati. It spoke well of the reputation of the Department that two university presidents in succession accepted the office of Assistant Secretary.

Civil service reform. The Department of Agriculture welcomed the protection and the guarantee of open competitive examinations given by the U.S. Civil Service Commission. Moreover, so far as the higher positions of division and bureau chiefs were concerned, it was the regular practice of the Department not to expect resignations with a change of administration and to fill vacancies by promotion from qualified personnel below.

Changes occurring in the higher levels illustrate practice. They were recorded in the following excerpt from the 1893 annual report of the Secretary.

[84] House Doc. 242, 54th Cong., 1st sess., pp. 2-3 (Feb. 11, 1896).
[85] Secretary of Agriculture, *Annual Report*, 1894, p. 19; *National Cyclopaedia of American Biography*, II, 259.
[86] Secretary of Agriculture, *Annual Report*, 1894, p. 19; *National Cyclopaedia of American Biography*, XIII, 310.

Dr. George Vasey, the Chief of the Division of Botany, died early in March, 1893. He was known as a great botanist and a high authority in his specialty throughout the world. His loss is profoundly mourned by his countrymen who were laboring in the same delightful field with himself, and by botanists over the sea, throughout Great Britain, and the Continent. His position was immediately tendered to, and accepted by, Mr. F. V. Coville, his most capable assistant in that division. The other changes occurred because of resignations. Mr. A. W. Harris, Director of the Office of Experiment Stations, resigned to accept the presidency of the Maine State College of Agriculture and the Mechanic Arts, and his place was filled by the promotion of Mr. A. C. True, who was his assistant. Maj. B. F. Fuller resigned his position as Chief of the Division of Accounts and Disbursing Officer, and was succeeded by Mr. F. L. Evans, who had been his faithful first aid for several years.[87]

The extension of the classified civil service went on rapidly during Cleveland's second administration, with the cordial endorsement of Secretary Morton. In 1893 A. C. True, director of the Office of Experiment Stations, noted that he and all of his expert assistants, except the special agents, entered government service through examination under the rules of the Civil Service Commission.[88] In the same year Morton called for a prerequisite diploma from an established veterinary college and an examination in veterinary science for the meat inspectors. "And, furthermore, it is advised that all the inspectors now in the service be required to pass through the same ordeal. . . ."[89] They were placed in the competitive service on July 1, 1894, much to Morton's satisfaction.[90]

In 1894 Secretary Morton also wrote a compelling passage in his annual report with regard to the need for placing the statisticians in the Division of Statistics under the competitive system.

There is no line of investigation which requires more intellectual discipline, more accuracy of judgment, more patience in research, more skill in combining and correlating facts and figures, or more special training for its pursuit, than the line followed by the painstaking and successful statistician. Holding such opinions, the Secretary of Agriculture is convinced that every person employed in gathering statistics under the chief of that division should be admitted to that work only after a thorough,

[87] Secretary of Agriculture, *Annual Report*, 1893, pp. 17-18.
[88] *Ibid.*, 1893, p. 417.
[89] *Ibid.*, 1893, p. 24.
[90] *Ibid.*, 1895, p. 5.

exhaustive, and successful examination at the hands of the U.S. Civil Service Commission. . . ."[91]

Promotional examinations were given by the Weather Bureau itself for its subordinate personnel. "The results of this competitive system have been exceedingly satisfactory. . . . Doubts entertained by many . . . have been dispelled."[92] Finally on May 24, 1895, most departmental employees were put into the classified competitive service, "all the educated and skilled force of specialists and scientists, including all the chiefs of division. . . ."[93] Morton was pleased. In his annual report for 1895 he wrote: "A thoroughly economical and efficient departmental service can only be secured and maintained by extending the provisions of the civil-service law so as eventually to include all the purely nonpolitical ministerial officers, clerks, skilled workmen and laborers. . . . the service of the Government should be put, in all respects, on as good a footing as that of first-class establishments conducting professional or commercial enterprises."[94]

The key to the success of the Department of Agriculture consisted in the quality of its leadership and of its scientific corps. Both science and administration contributed to its vitality, and both were essential ingredients to its success. The Department served the interest of an important segment of the American economy from which it doubtless derived political strength, and in this respect as in others it differed from its sister agencies. It avoided in large measure the handicaps of patronage, partly because its work was highly specialized, partly because Secretaries, bureau chiefs, and division heads had work to do that required competence and stability. In a period when laxness and indifferent standards were common, the record of Agriculture stood out in bold relief as a gratifying symbol of potential achievements in administration and in service to the American people.

[91] *Ibid.*, 1894, p. 64.
[92] *Ibid.*, 1894, p. 24.
[93] *Ibid.*, 1895, p. 58.
[94] *Ibid.*, 1895, p. 59.

CHAPTER TWELVE

The Post Office Department

The romance of the Post Office has often been recorded—the glamor of the pony express and the wandering life of a railway mail clerk, encounters with Indians and desperadoes, devotion to duty in fighting the elements to put the mail through, heroism in train wrecks, and shrewd intelligence in detecting mail "depredators," to use an ancient term.[1]

An intimate, if uncritical, view of the postal establishment at the close of the century is found in Marshall Cushing's *Story of Our Post-Office*, the many illustrations in which convey a remarkable visual sense of staff and equipment. The personnel, from top to bottom, wore fierce mustachios and pompous whiskers, surmounted by a peculiarly vacuous expression that must be ascribed to the photographic art of the 1890's, not to nature. Every portrait was in a mood of deadly earnestness—not a glimmer of humor illuminated the proper official physiognomy. The gaudy but cumbersome mail wagons in use in the larger cities were reminiscent in design and splendor of the mail stagecoaches of an earlier age—the body painted green, carriage and wheels red lead, and on the sides a spread eagle.[2]

Although postmasters were political appointments and often the

---

[1] See by way of example such books as Arthur Chapman, *The Pony Express* (New York: G. P. Putnam's Sons, 1932); LeRoy R. Hafen, *The Overland Mail*, 1849-1869 (Cleveland: Arthur H. Clark Co., 1926); Marshall Cushing, *The Story of Our Post-Office* (Boston: A. M. Thayer and Co., 1893); James E. White, *A Life Span and Reminiscences of Railway Mail Service* (Philadelphia: Deemer and Jaisohn, 1910); Bryant A. Long and William J. Dennis, *Mail by Rail* (New York: Simmons-Boardman, 1951).

[2] A picture of the mail wagon in service in the 1890's (unfortunately only in black and white, but with the spread eagle in full display) is in Marshall Cushing, *The Story of Our Post-Office*, p. 39. The full description of its early forbears is in Leonard D. White, *The Jeffersonians*, pp. 306-307.

cause of factional strife and conflict, there was a group of men who were not disturbed—favorite citizens of small communities. To challenge them would have been cause for universal reprobation. Cushing searched the country in the 1890's to discover the oldest postmaster. He was found in North Lansing, New York, in the person of Roswell Beardsley, who was then eighty-three years old. He had been appointed by President John Quincy Adams on June 28, 1828. Cushing added, "His patrons all love him, and hope his life may be spared for many years. Nobody ever sought to get the office away from Mr. Beardsley. His health is good, and he eats three good meals every day with perfect regularity."[3] Beardsley remained in office until his death in 1902, making a continuous service of nearly seventy-five years under twenty Presidents.[4]

Women had won an established status as postmistresses. Cushing recorded that there were over 6,300, and added: "Sometimes they are popular and successful politicians in their way. Sometimes they are the most important persons in their towns. They know what is going on without reading all the postal cards that pass through their offices."[5] It must be said that the portraits of the postmistresses in Cushing's book are much more human than those of the postmasters, barring a few bleak specimens.

The Post Office was unique in the closeness of its relations to the great mass of people. Congressman Samuel W. McCall (later governor of Massachusetts) wrote an eloquent commentary on this point.

. . . the one Department of the Government that comes in direct contact with all the people, or even a considerable portion of the people, is the Post-Office. They read of the State Department, but never see its agents. They pay the taxes necessary to support the Government . . . but the officers of the Treasury they rarely see. The same thing is true in substance of the other Departments. But the agents of the Post-Office are continually among the people. The 170,000 employees of that Department vastly outnumber all the other civil employees of the Govern-

---

[3] Marshall Cushing, *The Story of Our Post-Office*, p. 461. This author lists 200 postmasters appointed from 1828 through 1865, still in active service. They were in small offices, bearing such picturesque names as Long Swamp, Pigeon Cove, New Bavaria, Broken Sword, and Horse Shoe Bottom.

[4] Joseph L. Bristow, *Fraud and Politics at the Turn of the Century* (New York: Exposition Press, 1952), p. 35.

[5] Marshall Cushing, *The Story of Our Post-Office*, pp. 442, 443.

ment combined. . . . Every crossroads has its post-office. The Department has its special mail trains that rival in speed the fastest expresses. It has its corps of clerks upon every railroad. It has its agents both upon our inland waters and upon almost every sea. It has its carriers upon every city street, and it sends its messengers out into the country on every important highway. There is no hamlet so distant that the emissary of the post-office is not known. . . .[6]

The number of post offices in 1869 in round figures was 27,000; in 1901 nearly 77,000.[7]

POST OFFICE ORGANIZATION

Most administration settles into established routine. The Post Office Department was par excellence the home of routine so far as its central task of collecting, transporting, and delivering the mail was concerned. Collections were made at stated times at specified places on specified routes in the cities; mails were closed at specified hours in the small country offices, were put on the railroad for transportation, sorted and put in the hands of carriers for delivery at regular intervals. Innovation occurred in better equipment, in speeding up deliveries, in extending free delivery, in introducing stamp books, and in other improvements in details.

Functions. The principal additions to the basic functions of collecting, transporting, and delivering the mail occurred before Grant's administration. The postal money order system, the only major new activity, had been authorized in 1864.[8] In 1900–1901 its business exceeded 294 million dollars.[9] Free delivery in the largest cities was inaugurated in 1863[10] and extended to smaller communities from time to time, but this was only an improvement in service. So with rural free delivery, the early experiments in which occurred in the 1890's.[11] Special delivery was inaugurated in 1885.[12] Apart from the banking business of the Post Office, the Department continued in a well-established pattern.

Postmaster General John Wanamaker was not content with these

[6] House Report 2372, 58th Cong., 2d sess., pp. 6-7 (April 12, 1904).
[7] Postmaster General, *Annual Report*, 1900-1901, p. 906.
[8] 13 Stat. 76. (May 17, 1864).
[9] Postmaster General, *Annual Report*, 1900-1901, p. 31.
[10] 12 Stat. 701 at 703 (March 3, 1863).
[11] 26 Stat. 686 (October 1, 1890).
[12] 23 Stat. 385, 387 (March 3, 1885).

ancient functions. He made three major recommendations for the extension of service: Post Office delivery of telegrams in the larger cities by contract with the telegraph companies; postal savings banks; and parcel post.[13] None of these innovations appealed to Congress.

The Postmasters General. The political overhead of the Post Office Department comprised primarily the Postmaster General, the four Assistant Postmasters General, and on the local scene over 75,000 postmasters. No one should suppose, however, that a reasoned line was drawn between this group of officials and the mass of employees. Until 1883 the latter was as vulnerable as the former. At the clearly political level, which had the final authority for management, much time had to be given to relations with Senators and Representatives, to "recognition" of competing factions, and to strengthening the party organization. Since Jackson's time the Department had been a powerful asset in winning elections.

Postmasters General were appointed normally with political considerations in view, but occasionally (as in the case of Cleveland's law partner, Wilson S. Bissell) for personal reasons. The practice of appointing the chairman of the National Committee to the Post Office was not established, however, until the choice of George B. Cortelyou in 1905.[14] A few Postmasters General had sufficient prominence to induce full-length biographies.[15]

For one reason or another incumbency of the office was seldom more than two years. Grant and Arthur each had four Postmasters General, one of whom, John A. J. Creswell, served Grant for five years;

[13] His principal statement on a postal telegraph system was in the *Annual Report of the Postmaster General, 1889-90*, pp. 8-11; on postal savings banks, *ibid.*, pp. 11-14; on parcel post, *ibid.*, pp. 23-24.

[14] Dorothy Ganfield Fowler, *The Cabinet Politician: The Postmasters General, 1829-1909* (New York: Columbia University Press, 1943), p. 287. Miss Fowler amply documented the partisan aspects of the office; unfortunately there is no study of the administrative operations. See also much fascinating political material in Joseph L. Bristow, *Fraud and Politics at the Turn of the Century*. Bristow was Fourth Assistant Postmaster General under McKinley and Roosevelt.

[15] Horace Samuel Merrill, *William Freeman Vilas: Doctrinaire Democrat* (Madison: State Historical Society of Wisconsin, 1954); Herbert Adams Gibbons, *John Wanamaker* (2 vols., New York: Harper and Brothers, 1926); Festus P. Summers, *William L. Wilson and Tariff Reform* (New Brunswick: Rutgers University Press, 1953). One of the ablest Post Office heads, Thomas L. James, for ten years postmaster of New York City and Garfield's selection for Postmaster General, lacks a biography.

otherwise only Harrison retained the same man for four full years, the Philadelphia merchant, John Wanamaker. The administrative impact of Postmasters General was thus necessarily curtailed—for better or for worse—except in the field of appointments.

The organization of the Department in itself was enough to minimize innovation by its head, since endless detail flowed into Washington for decision.[16] Wanamaker quickly recognized this handicap, and in proposing a remedy, wrote an able and unique exposition of the proper function of the Postmaster General.

The Postmaster-General thus relieved of the dead-weight of numberless details, which would be left to the equally safe and prompt action of experienced and less occupied assistants, could intelligently exercise the functions of an administrative officer. He could apply the inventive and creative power of a mind freed from minor things, to the larger work of executive management of greater organization. He would do the planning, originate new ideas and inaugurate new methods, revise and make more practical and effective the regulations, study the systems of other countries, superintend the heads of departments, and give constantly the touch of life to the entire system, making it more representative of the commercial energies and social requirements of the American people. He would ascertain by investigation, study, and experiments, and by encouraging invention, possible improvements that would make the postal organization an agency of larger service and greater convenience. Many of the newer and more useful discoveries in applied science might be utilized and fashioned into a quicker and more satisfactory service than the present agencies, which are now plainly proving themselves too slow. He would secure transit for mail on faster schedules; provide quicker collections and distributions in cities and towns by pneumatic tubes or other improved and more rapid couriers than now exist; push forward American mails as the forerunner of the extension of American commerce; lift the entire service into a larger usefulness for the people and a larger increase for itself.

These and other possible improvements would all be open to the research of a Postmaster-General. His would be the duty and opportunity to study them and the power of the Government, and the interest of the people would aid and stimulate him to lead in enterprise, departures, and experiments. . . . The expanding energies of the human mind, the rapid progress and practical achievements of science, should be seen first rather than last in the conduct of the Government business.

[16] This matter is discussed below.

The venerable clerk who is always with us, faithful to tradition and proudest of all in remembering precedents, should not worry and retard a progressive Department in this progressive age by making a wall of an opinion delivered in 1823 or citing a precedent that governed in 1848. And especially should the postal service utilize in this advanced time of the world everything that can make the mails anticipate the wishes and expectations of the people. The one man who should be expected to ascertain and apply to the postal service all possible better agents, whether they be thus employed in the business world or developed in science, is the Postmaster-General, who under the present methods is allowed no time for studying such great questions or for dealing with anything more than the passing subjects of every day.[17]

Few indeed were the Postmasters General from Grant to McKinley who understood such a function or accepted such a responsibility. All were diligent, signing a never-ending stream of documents and papers that came to their desks; some had considerable business experience, notably Wanamaker; some sought to curtail the influence of politics, such as Marshall Jewell during Grant's brief experiment with examinations and David M. Key, Hayes' first head of the office. One crucial test of the quality of department heads everywhere is the content of their annual reports. Characteristically in the Post Office Department the annual reports comprised brief, unrelated paragraphs obviously emanating from the subordinate offices, mechanically repeating the form and often the content and phraseology of the previous number. The mind of the Postmaster General was conspicuously missing.

To these observations Wanamaker was a notable exception. An eminently successful merchant, a man of deep piety, an apostle of efficient business methods, a far-seeing prophet of what the Post Office could become as a service to the people, he was balked in his major program by an indifferent Congress. He acquired the deep

---

[17] Postmaster General, *Annual Report*, 1888-89, pp. 8-9. See also an equally discerning statement by Don M. Dickinson, one of Cleveland's Postmasters General: "The Postmaster-General should be permitted to devote his entire time and all his ability to shaping policies, improving systems, attending Congress with intelligent aid, exercising a general supervision over division chiefs, providing for the transportation of the great through mails, and in negotiating conventions and regulating our large and increasing postal business with other nations." Don M. Dickinson, "Progress and the Post," *North American Review*, CXLIX (1889), 405-406.

aversion of Civil Service Commissioner Theodore Roosevelt, who believed Wanamaker had yielded to partisanship and tolerated violation of the Civil Service Act.[18] Wanamaker asserted that he was a real civil service reformer, and doubtless his business training would have tended in this direction.

The Assistant Postmasters General. Postmaster General Amos Kendall, building on the experience of earlier years, had fixed the general pattern of organization of the Post Office Department during Jackson's administration. It was based on four major functions: *appointments* (First Assistant Postmaster General); *contracts* for carrying the mail (Second Assistant); *operations* (Third Assistant); *finance*, assigned to the chief clerk under Kendall's immediate supervision. The post-Civil War era opened with the three Assistant Postmasters General; in 1891 a fourth Assistant was authorized, and there were various changes in the assignment of particular functions. The basic organization, however, was stable.[19]

At the close of McKinley's administration the major division of functions stood as follows. The First Assistant Postmaster General had charge of mail delivery, the dead letter office, the money order system, supplies, salaries, and allowances. These last two divisions were vulnerable and, as will be seen, were looted by untrustworthy officials.

The Second Assistant Postmaster General was responsible for foreign mails, contracts, and inspection. The Third Assistant was concerned with postal finance, postmasters' accounts, and related functions. The Fourth Assistant had the delicate responsibility of handling appointments, postmasters' bonds (an incident of appointment), and mail depredations. It could not be maintained that this was an ideal allocation of duties, but to divide the many postal functions into four homogeneous blocks was difficult, if not impossible. Most large organizations need a "miscellaneous division" and the Post Office Department was no exception. The four basic functions of appointment, operations (including inspection), supplies and

[18] For comments on Wanamaker's relations with Roosevelt, see below, ch. 14.
[19] See Lloyd Milton Short, *The Development of National Administrative Organization in the United States* (Baltimore: Johns Hopkins Press, 1923), ch. 16, for a detailed account and reference to statutory enactments. There was a reorganization, mostly a shuffling of the bureaus, about every twenty years—1872, 1891, 1905.

equipment, and finance were, however, segregated into the domains of the four Assistant Postmasters General.[20]

The Fourth Assistant Postmaster General. From both the political and the administrative point of view, the appointment offices were of primary importance. This responsibility was shifted from time to time between the First and the Fourth Assistant Postmasters General; usually one handled the "presidential" appointments (first, second, and third-class offices), the other the multitude of fourth-class posts. Presidents and Postmasters General, indeed, made the decisions in all the larger communities, after consultation.

McKinley's Fourth Assistant Postmaster General (continued by Theodore Roosevelt) was Joseph L. Bristow. "The position of Fourth Assistant Postmaster General," he wrote, "was considered by many as the most desirable bureau office under the Government. It brought the occupant into intimate relations with all sections of the country and put him in the closest touch with the business and political interests of every community. . . . During the early years of an Administration every Congressman and Senator was a frequent visitor to the office of the Fourth Assistant Postmaster General."[21] The chairman of the National Republican Committee, Senator Mark Hanna, opposed Bristow's appointment. He thought Bristow too young and inexperienced and argued that his office ought to be filled by a man connected with the National Committee.[22] One of Bristow's first duties, confirming the astute Hanna's judgment, was to make up a list of "referees" or advisers to recommend postmasters in Democratic districts.[23] Practice had long confirmed the Representative as adviser in Republican districts.

Two old-timers were depended upon for many years to keep the First and Fourth Postmasters General informed concerning impending vacanices and to organize the files of applicants, the names of referees, and other pertinent data. The journalist Frederick Perry Powers reported: "There are two important functionaries known as the appointment clerks. Mr. Edwin C. Fowler has charge of the fourth class appointments, which are under the first assistant post-

---

[20] See *Official Register*, 1901, Vol. II, *passim.*
[21] Joseph L. Bristow, *Fraud and Politics*, p. 41.
[22] *Ibid.*, p. 30.
[23] *Ibid.*, p. 36.

master-general, and Mr. Nathan Smith is in charge of the presidential post-offices, which are under the direct jursidiction of the head of the department. . . . Mr. Smith has been doing this work for a dozen postmasters-general for the past nineteen years and they cannot get along without him. . . . Four years ago when a Democratic postmaster-general came in, Mr. Smith resigned and returned to a Kansas farm, but Mr. Vilas sent for him and he returned."[24]

Indeed, according to Powers, Fowler and Smith were instructed by Vilas to act for First Assistant Postmaster General Malcolm Hay during his absence on account of ill health. There were thousands of vacancies caused by resignation and death. Fowler and Smith knew who were the referees, took their advice, and made out a daily calendar of appointments which Vilas would validate by a single signature.[25] Such was the reliance of the chief political functionary upon the faithfulness and intelligence of the "bureaucracy."

Headquarters and field. The two largest post offices were Washington and New York. In 1894 the latter required 34 superintendents, 100 stamp agents, 1,225 carriers, and 1,614 clerks, a total payroll of 2,973.[26] This is almost precisely the number of federal employees, including postmasters, needed to transact all the business of the government in 1801.[27]

In addition to mail for local delivery, the New York post office handled the great bulk of foreign mail. In a six-month period ending February 10, 1894, it received and forwarded over 11,000,000 trans-Atlantic letters.[28] New York was also the exchange and banking center for the greater part of the postal money order business of the country. For the fiscal year ending June 30, 1893, there were nearly 4,000,000 money order transactions.[29] In more than one respect the office was in effect a bank. Cleveland's Postmaster Dayton had a word of commendation for his staff: "our citizens should not only be highly gratified with the efficiency of those who do such onerous

[24] Fred. Perry Powers, "How Postmasters Are Made," *The Chautauquan*, X (1889-90), 191.

[25] *Ibid.*, X, 191-92.

[26] Charles W. Dayton, "The Postal Service at New York," *North American Review*, CLIX (1894), 30.

[27] Leonard D. White, *The Federalists*, p. 255.

[28] Charles W. Dayton, "The Postal Service at New York," *North American Review*, CLIX, 26.

[29] *Ibid.*, CLIX, 28.

and responsible work, where temptation is aggravated by the smallness of pay received, but should heartily recognize the almost invariable honesty and zeal of those who so thoroughly perform the details of this great and exacting public service."[30]

Between the Washington headquarters and thousands of local post-offices stood the inspection service. It had the dual function of advising postmasters on the efficient and proper conduct of their offices, and of detecting irregularities and fraud. Apparently most of the time of the inspectors was devoted to the latter task. Their number was inadequate.

From its inception the Post Office Department was governed in its intimate detail from Washington. Amos Kendall, Jackson's diligent Postmaster General, wrote personal letters of admonition to distant postmasters who failed to observe the regulations. Washington necessarily became a bottleneck, more and more of an obstacle to prompt decision and action as the Department expanded. Toward the end of the century the congestion at headquarters had become almost intolerable, and a succession of Postmasters General sought relief from Congress through a regional organization. A precedent had already been established in the Railway Mail Service.

At the close of his brief service in Cleveland's first administration, Postmaster General Don M. Dickinson exposed the evil of over-concentration and described the remedy.

> In the postal service alone is there no one save the Postmaster-General in his chief office at Washington, in general authority anywhere throughout the wide territory and the different divisions of the service. We have the local postmaster, but his power ceases when he has performed his function of receiving and distributing the mails. He is responsible to and reports directly to the Postmaster-General in Washington. He cannot remove a letter-carrier without the sanction of that officer. He can remedy no failure of transmission, nor can he expedite it. . . . All complaints of service must go through the department at Washington for remedy. . . . There is no lodgment of original and general power near the people served, and, of course, no responsibility to the people save from the Postmaster-General through the Chief Executive.[31]

[30] *Ibid.*, CLIX, 31.
[31] Don M. Dickinson, "Progress and the Post," *North American Review*, CXLIX (1889), 404-405.

Dickinson's immediate successor, John Wanamaker, proposed a regional organization based on twenty-six districts. In his annual report for 1889, Wanamaker remarked: "The post-offices throughout the country bear little relation to one another. The touch of the Department upon them is very slight. The machinery is set up and then let alone if only certain formal reports are made at stated times."[32] He recommended the appointment of regional supervisors "possessed of enthusiasm for the perfection of the system," to report to the head of the post office at Washington, D.C. He "might readily become the Fifth Assistant Postmaster-General, in charge also of the educational and civil-service work in the entire service and its thousands of post-offices."[33]

Cleveland's law partner, Wilson S. Bissell, who followed Wanamaker, suggested a regional supervisor for each state.[34] Bissell's successor, William L. Wilson, told Congress in 1896 that the then organization of the Department was "as if each private soldier in a great and growing army reported directly to the commanding general, received orders from him and had little other supervision than what was possible from army headquarters."[35] The system could work only because it was a vast repetitive, fixed, and generally routine operation.

Congress was indifferent to repeated recommendations for the delegation of authority to regional directors, and it may be surmised that bureau chiefs in Washington were reluctant to incur a diminution of their authority over the field. Only after nearly a half century had passed was this organizational reform achieved.

[32] Postmaster General, *Annual Report*, 1888-89, p. 7.

[33] *Ibid.*, p. 8.

[34] *Ibid.*, 1892-93, pp. xxxix-xl. Bissell was forthright: "I think that any business man assuming charge of the Post-Office Department feels the weakness of its organization at one point, and that is in the relation of the heads of the Department to its postmasters and other local officers. . . . As a general proposition, it may be said that this great army is organized in companies, without regiments or brigades, so that the company captain makes his report to the general commanding officer; or, in railroad management, it would be like organizing a company with a president and four vice-presidents, but without superintendents, either general or local, the station agents making their reports directly to the one or the other of the general officers. This is a strange anomaly, and is without parallel in any business institution that I have any knowledge of."

[35] Postmaster General, *Annual Report*, 1895-96, p. 12.

THE MERIT SYSTEM IN THE POST OFFICE

Before 1829 the postal service had been nonpolitical in character. Appointment of postmasters was *de facto* for good behavior; removals were not made for partisan reasons; clerks in the larger offices were not disturbed by a change of administration. Custom, not law, prescribed this state of affairs.

During and after Jackson's administration departmental clerks and post office employees were gradually taken over by Democratic and Whig administrations alike. The Department became the great patronage agency of government; the Postmaster General, *the* "cabinet politician." The Civil Service Act of 1883 was aimed in the first instance at the larger post offices and the customs service. Its protection was extended to postal employees in offices having a staff of over fifty and to the departmental clerical force in Washington. Much of the service remained outside the civil service system, but the most vulnerable parts were covered by law and by the inadequate authority of the Civil Service Commission.

The merit system was gradually extended, partly by the increase in number of offices requiring more than fifty employees, partly by covering-in new classes of employees. The principal new categories were the Railway Mail Service, with over 5,000 employees (1889); the free-delivery offices, with over 7,000 employees (1893); the mail-bag and mail-lock repair shops, with about 200 employees (during Cleveland's second administration).[36]

The Post Office Department generally welcomed the merit system and its successive extensions, although it was not energetic in the early years in enforcing civil service requirements in the field. John Wanamaker stated in his second annual report: "I think it would be impossible to find an appointing officer who has not been glad to take advantage of stringent examinations to keep away the mere political place-seekers. They used to be provided; they would surely be provided in all the Departments if they were lacking."[37] In his last annual report he recommended placing all carriers (in small as well as large offices) under civil service.[38] Postmaster General Bissell

[36] U.S. Civil Service Commission, *Annual Report*, 1898-99, pp. 134-36.
[37] Postmaster General, *Annual Report*, 1889-90, p. 39.
[38] *Ibid.*, 1891-92, p. 81.

wrote in his annual report for 1892-93, referring to the Civil Service Act, "Indeed, so great have become the proportions of this Department, and the magnitude of its operations, that, in my judgment, it would be a matter of practical impossibility to conduct its affairs with any near approach to its present degree of efficiency without the benefit and protection of this law."[39]

In its annual report for 1884-85, the Civil Service Commission recorded a large number of enthusiastic comments from postmasters.[40] Two will suffice to indicate their tenor. *New York City:* "It [i.e., the merit system] has relieved me almost entirely from solicitation and altogether from pressure in the matter of appointments. The character and capacity of those appointed under the rules have been good. . . . The general effect of the system upon the moral tone and business efficiency of this office has, as I believe, been excellent. . . . I am convinced its discontinuance or curtailment would be to the last degree injurious to the public interests. . . ."[41] *Cincinnati:* "The relief from solicitation and pressure for office was felt immediately after the law went into effect. . . . Under the old system I had often twenty applications in a day, and during my first year in office more than fifteen hundred. Now I do not average five applications in a month. The character and capacity of the appointees have been of a high average."[42]

Faithful enforcement of the merit system was a constant problem, and no one could assert that the Post Office had been taken out of politics. Congressmen (or referees) continued in substance to name local postmasters, normally for political reasons. It was a great advance when McKinley adopted the policy of not removing fourth-class postmasters until their four-year terms had expired.

Clerks, moreover, continued to rely on congressional aid in time of trouble. In return they did favors for the members from their districts. Bristow noted:

At one time it was discovered that John H. Sumner, a clerk in the appointment division, was keeping the secretary of Congressman Henry D. Clayton of Alabama advised as to the status of post-office cases in his

---

[39] *Ibid.*, 1892-93, p. xxxiv.
[40] U.S. Civil Service Commission, *Annual Report, 1884-85,* pp. 28-37.
[41] *Ibid.*, pp. 34-35.
[42] *Ibid.*, p. 31.

district. Frequently clerks in the department do this in order to court the favor of Democratic Congressmen so as to have a friend at court in the event of a change of Administration. As a rule the department clerk promptly adjusts his politics so as to be in perfect harmony with the opinions of the Administration in power. He is the political weathervane of the capital. . . .[43]

CORRUPTION IN THE POST OFFICE

The system of organization in the postal service was designed in part to prevent fraud and corruption. There were precise rules and regulations, regular fiscal reports, careful audit, a force of inspectors, and an assistant attorney general for the Post Office Department to prosecute cases of delinquency. Despite all safeguards there were a regular but small number of removals and prosecutions for fraud. In the fiscal year 1900-1901 forty-nine presidential postmasters were removed out of a total number of 4,466. Among the fourth-class postmasters, totaling 72,479, there were 687 removals.[44]

A tabulation of offenses by postal employees in violation of the postal laws and rules for the same period included 392 false returns of cancellations, 397 cases of detaining, opening, or destroying letters, and 44 cases of embezzlement of letters. One hundred and forty-one postmasters and assistant postmasters were arrested and something over 125 clerks and carriers.[45] The percentage of removals for cause, including all grades, steadily declined. For the fiscal year 1893–94 it was 4 per cent; it dropped 1 per cent annually for three successive years, and in 1899–1900 it had settled at slightly over 1 per cent, a not discreditable record.[46]

There were two major scandals in the latter years of the Republican era, involving not postal clerks or subordinates, but highly placed officials.[47] The case in the Cuban postal service was that of personal delinquency on the part of the Director of the Posts; the case involving the First Assistant Postmaster General, the assistant attorney general for the Post Office, and their associates was a far-flung

---

[43] Joseph L. Bristow, *Fraud and Politics*, p. 37.
[44] Postmaster General, *Annual Report*, 1900-1901, p. 897.
[45] *Ibid.*, 1900-1901, pp. 918, 920.
[46] *Ibid.*, 1899-1900, p. 111.
[47] The star route frauds are dealt with below. ch. 17.

conspiracy that raised questions not merely of personal integrity but of the whole system of control.

At the close of the Spanish-American War, the government of Cuba was assumed temporarily by the United States and, with the exception of the postal service, was assigned to the War Department. General Leonard Wood was put in charge. The Postmaster General appointed Estes G. Rathbone as Director General of the Department of Posts for Cuba. Rathbone was a protégé of Senator Hanna, and had been a pension examiner, chief post office inspector under Harrison, and at the time of his appointment to Cuba was Fourth Assistant Postmaster General. In the light of subsequent events in Washington, it is important to note that Rathbone was a close personal friend of First Assistant Postmaster General Perry S. Heath.

General Wood quickly observed that Rathbone was living in great extravagance, far beyond his means. An investigation was opened, and Joseph L. Bristow was sent to Cuba to disclose the facts. Rathbone and the head of the Cuban postal finance department, Neely, appointed on Heath's recommendation, were discovered to have made way with about $130,000.[48] The episode grieved President McKinley deeply. Bristow quoted him as saying, "Mr. Bristow, I have been more pained by this scandal than by anything that has occurred during my Administration. These people are our wards. They have had great confidence in our integrity and a reverence for the American name, and to think that the trusted officials whom we have sent there should plunder their revenues and steal their money is a great humiliation to me."[49]

The fraud and corruption that Bristow exposed in 1903 in high levels in the Post Office Department were of long standing, and raised problems of management of a serious nature. The evil-doing began in 1893 and extended unperceived through Cleveland's second term, McKinley's administration, and into Roosevelt's first term. The three principal offenders were James N. Tyner, assistant attorney general,

[48] For the official Post Office comments, see Postmaster General, *Annual Report*, 1899-1900, pp. 17-21.
[49] Joseph L. Bristow, *Fraud and Politics*, p. 100. Bristow was a Kansas journalist, secretary of the Republican State Committee before his appointment in 1897 as Fourth Assistant Postmaster General. He subsequently served one term in the U.S. Senate, 1909-1915. The manuscript of this book was found among his papers after his death in 1944.

A. W. Machen, general superintendent of the free-delivery system, and George W. Beavers, general superintendent of salaries and allowances. Former First Assistant Postmaster General Perry S. Heath was also involved; in all, fourteen responsible Post Office officials were indicted and others were removed. As President Roosevelt observed, "A melancholy feature of the case is that with one exception all the offenders have been for a number of years in the Government service."[50]

Tyner, an Indiana Republican, was in Congress from 1869 to 1875; was Second Assistant Postmaster General, 1875–76; Postmaster General, 1876–77; First Assistant Postmaster General under Hayes, 1877–81; and assistant attorney general for the Post Office under Harrison and McKinley. In deference to his age and bad health he was invited to resign in 1903 in order to avoid removal.

Machen, a smooth scoundrel who had built strong congressional connections, began as a clerk in 1886 in the Toledo, Ohio, office, turned up in Washington in 1893 as assistant superintendent of free delivery and within a few months became superintendent of this division. At that time he was already a bankrupt with a bad reputation for lack of business integrity. On one occasion he was guilty of forgery. Bristow declared, "Financial obligations rested lightly upon him. He never paid a debt except from motives of policy. Moral responsibility seemed to have no weight with him."[51]

George W. Beavers entered the service in 1881 as a clerk in the New York City office, was a postal inspector from 1890 to August 1897, and became chief of the salary and allowance division at that time.[52] "The administration of Beavers was, if possible, more demoralizing upon the integrity of the service than that of Machen. . . . Beavers was reckless in his methods and seemed to care little for the outward appearance. . . ."[53]

These men and others operated principally in the fraudulent purchase of postal supplies, in the illegal appointment of political favorites, and in the sale of promotions. In collusion with contractors

[50] The principal source is House Doc. 383, 58th Cong., 2d sess. (Jan. 11, 1904). The quotation is found on page 6. Heath was subsequently secretary of the Republican National Committee.

[51] *Ibid.*, p. 80

[52] *Ibid.*, p. 129.

[53] *Ibid.*, p. 183. Beavers was endorsed as "reliable, trustworthy, and honest" by the Mayor of Binghamton, New York. *Ibid.*, pp. 166-67.

they purchased quantities of unnecessary, expensive, and faulty equipment, at times wantonly destroying supplies in order to purchase replacements. They blackmailed contractors and took bribes from them. They arbitrarily increased rental of post office quarters, often at the suggestion of Congressmen. They conspired with proprietors of swindling, get-rich-quick schemes for the uninterrupted use of the mails. Unnecessary clerks were loaded upon reluctant postmasters as a favor to prominent politicians.[54] Promotions went by favor and at times for money.

The extent to which these operations extended is illustrated by the record of purchase of time clocks and keys.[55] Berkeley, California, had eleven carriers and seven clerks, but was furnished with three time clocks and 162 keys therefor. South Weymouth, Massachusetts, had two carriers and one clerk; it was supplied with one clock and fifty-eight keys. Bayshore, New York, whose staff comprised the postmaster and his assistant, was nevertheless honored with a time recorder. As Bristow remarked, "Such profligate expenditure is almost incredible." The president of the time-clock company was the one-time mayor of Binghamton, New York, Beavers' political sponsor.[56]

Machen and Beavers went to jail, Tyner died shortly after the investigation, a number of indictments of others were secured, and some summary removals were made. Apart from punishment of the guilty and the purging of the Department, the case raised several general points of interest.

Obviously there was laxity in the scrutiny of qualifications in high post office appointments. The standing of Machen and Beavers could have been disclosed by proper investigation before they were promoted to responsible positions. Political sponsorship prevailed in these and other cases.

Obviously, also, the system of internal control was exceedingly lax. Hundreds of postmasters knew that they were being imposed upon

[54] Violations of civil service regulations in the Washington, D.C., post office are reported in the *Annual Report of the U.S. Civil Service Commission, 1902-1903*, pp. 139-45. The Commission noted that their investigation seemed "to show clearly that most of the irregularities herein set forth were directed by the Department or requested or suggested by high department officials, and in either case came to the postmaster with all the force of a direction." *Ibid.*, p. 142.

[55] House Doc. 383, 58th Cong., 2d sess., pp. 167-68.

[56] *Ibid.*, p. 168.

by someone high in the Washington hierarchy—forced to take useless equipment, to put on the payrolls useless clerks, to agree to excessive rentals. There must have been full cognizance of these matters on the part of the post office inspectors as well as the postal service generally. Yet these frauds went on for a decade undisturbed.

The fault lay with administration, not with the laws. Bristow reported: "What the service most needs, however, is honest, intelligent, and vigorous administration. The corruption disclosed is not due to lax laws but to the dishonesty of those who have been charged with the responsibility of administering them."[57] Vigorous administration was obviously lacking. Tyner worked through his nephew, whose appointment he had arranged. Tyner himself had suffered a stroke in 1902, but had not been replaced. His wife was allowed access to his office early in the investigation, and went off with a batch of papers that were subsequently returned, with incriminating documents missing.[58] No Postmaster General from 1893 to 1903 was apparently aware of the true condition of his Department.

The intimation that members of Congress had been involved in excessive clerk hire and post office rentals induced a House investigation.[59] The result was a vindication of the members, but with the admission that some congressional letters were "carelessly written" and that action in some cases "was not well considered."[60]

THE POST OFFICE INSPECTORS

The inspectors were under the supervision and direction of the Fourth Assistant Postmaster General Joseph L. Bristow at the time of the investigations. He described their duties in his annual report of 1900–1901 as including among others the investigation of complaints against postmasters, the propriety of allowances for clerk hire and other expenses, the collection of balances due from delinquent and retiring postmasters, and violations of postal laws.[61] These duties certainly included the offenses that came to light in 1903. What then can be said regarding the competence of this body of Post Office sleuths, the eyes and ears of the postal administration?

[57] *Ibid.*, p. 185.
[58] *Ibid.*, pp. 65-66.
[59] See House Report 1395, 58th Cong., 2d sess. (March 7, 1904), and House Report 2372, 58th Cong., 2d sess. (April 12, 1904).
[60] *Ibid.*, p. 13.
[61] Postmaster General, *Annual Report*, 1900-1901, p. 913.

There are several possible answers to such a question: that the inspectors were incompetent routineers who failed to grasp the obvious; that they discreetly closed their eyes to conditions which they may have justly concluded were politically inspired or which involved persons in high station; or that they made honest and telling reports that were pigeonholed or reversed by their superiors.

The first assumption was that endorsed by the minority of the House investigating committee.

. . . . Is it not clear that if the inspectors under the control of the Fourth Assistant Postmaster General [Bristow] had been a vigilant body, directed by a vigilant commander, the service would have escaped many of the scandals with which it has recently been tainted?

A small army of inspectors . . . should be able to prevent "wanton destruction of ink"; they should not have allowed to pass unnoticed the fact that there were "many excessive and unnecessary shipments of ink to various post-offices"; . . . they should have learned that the post-office at Columbia, Okla., had enough ink on hand to last for four years. . . . The business of this Department [inspection division] is to watch and guard all other Departments of the postal service. Its chief merit must be found, not in the result of special investigations of demoralizations that have become so great as to challenge general public attention, but rather in the exercise of a vigilance that will prevent wrongdoing.[62]

On the other hand the select staff of inspectors assigned to Bristow's investigation did a superior job. Bristow testified to the excellence of their work: "I can not speak in too high praise of the industry and intelligence of the inspectors and their loyalty to the interests of the service. The success of the investigation is largely due to them. They have sought the truth with eagerness and skill."[63]

The inspectors who made the annual survey of the Washington, D.C., post office had not failed to give timely notice of the dubious practices of Beavers and others. Their reports in 1899 prompted the inspector in charge, William B. Smith, to make a confidential report on July 6, 1899,[64] showing unauthorized expenditures, persons on the payroll performing no service, questionable travel expenses on the part of Beavers,[65] illegal per diem accounts of Machen, and other

---

[62] House Report 2372, 58th Cong., 2d sess., pp. 19-20 (April 12, 1904).
[63] House Doc. 383, 58th Cong., 2d sess., p. 185.
[64] *Ibid.*, pp. 277-94.
[65] *Ibid.*, p. 285.

irregularities.[66] Smith concluded his report by stating: "The responsibility for the many illegal appointments, the payment of two salaries to one and the same person, and the disbursement of thousands of dollars for which practically no service was performed should be placed where it properly belongs and the many abuses corrected." The responsibility was traced directly to the First Assistant Postmaster General, Heath.[67]

No evidence has been discovered with respect to the fidelity and skill of inspectors in the field. That they were overworked is certain. In 1900 they were assigned 169,000 cases; in 1901, 179,000.[68] That some improvement was necessary was clearly indicated.

The administrative record of the Post Office Department from Grant to McKinley was thus a baffling mixture of excellence and imperfection. No one could deny that the postal establishment had kept up with the growth of the country. Its primary function of delivering the mail was performed with astonishing regularity and with constantly increasing expedition. Its banking and financial transactions were safely and expertly performed. The army of postal employees was generally trustworthy and fully competent to do their routine operations, and their quality noticeably improved with the gradual installation of the merit system.

The Department nevertheless operated under grave handicaps. Congress resisted many improvements in organization and operation whose value experience had fully demonstrated, notably authorization for a regional organization. Some Congressmen sponsored questionable applicants for appointment and otherwise insisted upon favors to constituents that could hardly be justified. The influence traditionally due Congressmen in nominating postmasters was always a potential threat to their subsequent discipline and control.

The administrative record of Postmasters General was not impressive. Their tenure of office was usually brief, their interests were primarily the political success of their parties, and while they were generally diligent in transacting the daily business that was referred to them by the Assistant Postmasters General, they do not give the impression that they were masters of their Department. Few, if any,

[66] *Ibid.*, p. 287.
[67] *Ibid.*, pp. 293, 294.
[68] Postmaster General, *Annual Report*, 1900-1901, p. 914.

could claim the rank of statesmen, and few made an obvious contribution other than to keep the wheels turning.

There were some instances of badly misplaced confidence in appointments to high Post Office Department positions, notably Rathbone in the Cuban postal service, Tyner, Machen, and Beavers in headquarters. Their personal delinquencies involved, as President Roosevelt declared, gross corruption. Their success in deceiving the Department for a decade revealed a breakdown in the system of internal control, especially among the force of postal inspectors. Political sponsorship in high levels was in part to blame, and a cautious prudence on the part of many inspectors had its share of responsibility. Despite these aberrations the postal service was generally trustworthy and faithful in the discharge of its duties. No large body of men is without its weak members, and the moral standards of the Department would compare not unfavorably with those of its sister agencies.

From time to time suggestions were made, officially and unofficially, that the Post Office was in effect a huge business operation and ought to be conducted as such. No one in responsible governmental office took such ideas seriously. Few would publicly controvert such views, but generations of contrary practice dictated the inner character of postal administration. The Department was the handmaiden of commercial intercourse and private communication, but it was also the servant of the party in power. Its history compelled it to serve a dual interest, either of which might prevail from time to time.

CHAPTER THIRTEEN

The Battle for Reform

For thirty years after the Civil War the administrative stage was the scene of two major conflicts: one between the legislative and executive branches for governmental power, the other between the professional politicians and the reformers over the merit system and the end of patronage. The two were not unrelated. The recovery of the executive branch and the realization of its higher status and influence depended in part upon wresting control of appointments from Senators, Congressmen, and local machines. This aspect of the struggle has already been dealt with. We turn now to the reform of the civil service, a fundamental issue that in retrospect stands in significance as nearly equal to the renewed authority of the President. Cleveland rightly called the change "radical and far-reaching."[1] No administrative organization of the federal government could have met the needs of the twentieth century without a powerful executive or without a civil service freed from subjection to the demands of party machines concerned primarily with electoral success.

BACKGROUND

It will be remembered that the Federalist and Jeffersonian tradition of permanent tenure, competence, and freedom of federal employees from party obligation had been overthrown by the Jacksonian preference for rotation, for appointment on the basis of party or factional affiliation, and for the subjection of the public service to the demands of party success. The consequence was such a lowering of standards of efficiency and integrity that Congress was induced in 1853 to require a system of pass examinations for the departmental clerks. This

[1] Richardson, *Messages*, VIII, 618 (July 23, 1888).

scheme remained in effect, although with standards varying widely from department to department, from 1853 to the Civil Service Act of 1883. Its influence was good so far as it went, particularly in affording a tenuous basis for the continued employment of a small central corps of clerks whose knowledge of agency business was essential to prevent a complete breakdown of the public service.

The great struggle for civil service reform opened at the close of the Civil War and came to its turning point in the Pendleton Act of 1883 establishing the Civil Service Commission and introducing open competitive examinations. By way of forecast, the principal events of the intervening years were (1) the unsuccessful agitation from 1867 to 1869 of Congressman Thomas Allen Jenckes of Rhode Island for a civil service law; (2) the act of 1871 vesting in the President authority to make rules for entrance to the civil service, leading to the appointment of a Civil Service Commission and its suspension in 1875; (3) a decade of stalemate; (4) the organization of the National Civil Service Reform League in 1881; and (5) the achievement of initial victory in 1883, following the tragic assassination of President Garfield.[2]

THOMAS ALLEN JENCKES

The main figure in the struggle leading up to the enactment of 1871, the terms of which are noted below, was Congressman Thomas Allen Jenckes of Rhode Island, a patent lawyer, a graduate of Brown University, and an active figure in Rhode Island politics before his election to Congress in 1862. Although civil service bills had been introduced in Congress earlier, notably one by Senator Charles Sumner,[3] Jenckes was the first member to give force and leadership to the reform movement. He is entitled to high recognition among

---

[2] The principal secondary works on the subject matter of this chapter are Carl Russell Fish, *The Civil Service and the Patronage* (Cambridge: Harvard University Press, 1904); Frank Mann Stewart, *The National Civil Service Reform League* (Austin: University of Texas, 1929); Dorothy Ganfield Fowler, *The Cabinet Politician: The Postmasters General, 1829-1909* (New York: Columbia University Press, 1943); and Paul P. Van Riper, *History of the United States Civil Service: 1789-1957* (Chicago: Row, Peterson, and Co., 1958).

[3] The bill, which was admirable in its brevity and its foresight, is printed in *The Works of Charles Sumner* (15 vols., Boston: Lee and Shepard, 1874-94), VIII, 452 (April 30, 1864).

a small band of reformers who against great odds finally secured enactment of civil service legislation.

The legislative battle opened in 1867 when Jenckes presented the first report of a Joint Select Committee on Retrenchment. It was a sober document, asserting that a great saving would be made by making "an entire change in the mode of appointment to, and the tenure of office in, the subordinate civil service," proposing examinations on the model of the military and naval services, and setting out at considerable length the appointment systems in effect in Germany, France, and Great Britain.[4] A second brief report, with extensive appendices containing the opinions of scores of highly placed officials in the headquarters and field services, excerpts from Presidents' remarks and the press, and an account of the Chinese civil service (as well as of Prussia, France, and England), was presented in 1868.[5]

Jenckes had offered his first civil service bill on December 20, 1865,[6] but it attracted no attention in the dying reverberations of war. The bill proposed by him in the House report of 1867 came to a vote and at one point mustered substantial strength—66 affirmative to 72 negative votes.[7] Jenckes made two major speeches in the House explaining and defending his bills, as well as others in refutation of the arguments of his opponents.[8] Public interest was considerable. In his correspondence for 1867, 1868, and 1869, there was a stream of letters both from civic-minded citizens and from businessmen and organizations requesting copies of his speech of January 29, 1867. Thus the Collins Iron Company asked for a half-dozen copies, *Lippincott's Magazine* offered compensation for an article, Waldo Higginson and other Bostonians agreed to raise two thousand dollars or more to send a delegation to Washington, and the American Social Science Association mobilized public opinion in New England.[9]

Jenckes also received many letters from officers in the customs

---

[4] House Report 8, 39th Cong., 2d sess. (Jan. 31, 1867). Quote from page 2.
[5] House Report 47, 40th Cong., 2d sess. (May 25, 1868).
[6] *Congressional Globe*, 39th Cong., 1st sess., p. 98.
[7] *Ibid.*, 39th Cong., 2d sess., p. 1036 (Feb. 6, 1867).
[8] *Ibid.*, 39th Cong., 2d sess., p. 837 (Jan. 29, 1867); and *ibid.*, 40th Cong., 2d sess., p. 2466 (May 14, 1868).
[9] The officers of this association in 1868 included Samuel Eliot, president, Henry Villard, and Charles Francis Adams, Jr.

service supporting his bill. The surveyor of customs in Boston wrote, "The opposition you will encounter to your Bill will come I imagine from two important sources. One from the Collectors. Their amount of patronage makes them almost autocrats & though constantly annoyed they naturally would relinquish power reluctantly. The other will be perhaps from M. C.'s. They must inevitably have great control over Collectors and find their power of rewarding constituents by patronage an important feature in elections. . . ."[10] The opposition foreshadowed in this letter outweighed the support that Jenckes was able to muster. He was defeated for reelection in 1870 and retired from public life on March 3, 1871.

THE GRANT CIVIL SERVICE COMMISSION

Jenckes was destined, however, to see the first victory of the reformers. In his second annual message Grant asked for reform of the civil service, governing both the manner of making appointments and tenure. "There is no duty," he declared, "which so much embarrasses the Executive and heads of Departments as that of appointments, nor is there any such arduous and thankless labor imposed on Senators and Representatives as that of finding places for constituents. The present system does not secure the best men, and often not even fit men, for public place."[11] On the last day of the last session of the 41st Congress (March 3, 1871), Senator Lyman Trumbull of Illinois offered a rider to the sundry civil appropriation bill authorizing the President to make rules and regulations for the civil service. Senator George H. Williams promptly moved to lay the amendment on the table—a motion that lost by a single vote. The Senate then concurred (32 to 24), and the rider was rushed at 3 a.m. to the House. With support from Congressmen James A. Garfield, Henry L. Dawes, and William H. Armstrong the provision was carried by a large majority (90 to 20). Its terms follow.

That the President of the United States be, and he is hereby, authorized to prescribe such rules and regulations for the admission of persons into the civil service of the United States as will best promote the efficiency thereof, and ascertain the fitness of each candidate in respect to age,

[10] Jenckes Papers, Box 34, letter of Dec. 12, 1867, in Manuscript Division, Library of Congress.
[11] Richardson, *Messages*, VII, 109 (Dec. 5, 1870).

health, character, knowledge, and ability for the branch of service into which he seeks to enter; and for this purpose the President is authorized to employ suitable persons to conduct said inquiries, to prescribe their duties, and to establish regulations for the conduct of persons who may receive appointments in the civil service.[12]

Congress thus abandoned the effort to enact legislation and authorized the President to reform the civil service by executive rules and regulations, for the operation of which $10,000 was made available. The rider was less a token of Grant's leadership than it was a concession to outside opinion, built up steadily for four years around Jenckes' speeches, committee reports, and bills. Congress was not persuaded to legislate reform, but it did reluctantly permit the executive branch to proceed.

Grant proceeded. He was authorized to appoint suitable persons to advise him concerning the content of rules and regulations, and surprised many by the character and standing of his selections, who soon became known as the Civil Service Commission. The chairman was the leader of the reform movement, George William Curtis; another outstanding member was Joseph Medill, owner of the *Chicago Tribune* and mayor of Chicago after the great fire of 1871; three members were drawn from the civil service; one was a lame-duck Senator, Alexander G. Cattell, and the other an unknown, Dawson A. Walker of Georgia. The Commission was dominated by Curtis and Medill, who promptly disagreed as to whether reform should begin with competitive examinations or with permanent tenure. Curtis, arguing for examinations, eventually prevailed.

The first duty of the Commission was to prepare rules. These were submitted to the President in December 1871, and became effective on January 1, 1872. Grant then asked the Commission to become the agency to put the rules and regulations into effect. The first competitive examination was held on June 5, 1872. The system worked out by the Commission required boards of examiners in each department to conduct agency examinations under the supervision of the Commission. Admission was thus to a department, not to a government-wide service. Applicants were required to be citizens of the United States; to furnish satisfactory evidence in regard to character, health, and age; and to pass a satisfactory examination in speaking,

[12] 16 Stat. 475 at 514 (March 3, 1871); Revised Statutes, sec. 1753.

reading, and writing the English language. They did not require nomination by the head of the department or agency. Appointments were made to the lowest clerical ranks; promotions were made by competitive examinations within the lower ranks. A probationary period of six months was required; aged, incapacitated clerks were allowed to fill subordinate posts; and political assessments were forbidden.[13]

Despite some hopeful signs, the trend of events subsequent to the reelection of Grant in 1872 was against reform and reformers. The Liberal Republicans, who had nominated Greeley in 1872, were anathema to the President, whose support now came wholly from the party wing led by Senator Roscoe Conkling and his group. Both the Democratic party and Republican "Stalwarts" were in opposition. The Commission's rules were assailed as unconstitutional, silly, cumbrous, visionary, and "hostile to the genius of our institutions." Their operation was alleged to produce an aristocracy and to be fatal to the ascendancy of any party. The Commission was called a board of broken-down schoolmasters. A vacancy in the office of surveyor of the port of New York was filled in 1873 by the appointment of a general—an active politician, so offensive that Curtis resigned as chairman of the Civil Service Commission. Grant appointed Dorman B. Eaton to succeed him, but congressional opinion grew ever more adverse. In 1874 the House voted to repeal the enactment of 1871; the Senate refused to concur and voted to appropriate $15,000 for the work of the Commission. The House did not approve the appropriation, and the Commission thus was left in existence but without funds.[14]

The Commission had already foreseen this outcome and its report of April 15, 1874, had recognized that "the decisive issue is fairly raised and ought now to be decided."[15] In his annual message of December 7, 1874, Grant announced that if Congress adjourned without positive legislation for civil service reform, he would abandon the system.[16] Congress adjourned, having taken no action, and on

[13] The rules are printed in Richardson, *Messages,* VII, 157 (Dec. 19, 1871).
[14] In 1873 Congressman Benjamin F. Butler of Massachusetts moved to deny appropriations to the Commission, a motion defeated only by a vote of 85 to 103. *Congressional Globe,* 42d Cong., 3d sess., p. 1635 (Feb. 22, 1873).
[15] Senate Ex. Doc. 53, 43d Cong., 1st sess., p. 7 (April 15, 1874).
[16] Richardson, *Messages,* VII, 301.

March 9, 1875, Grant ordered the abolition of the examining boards throughout the country.[17] Appointments reverted to the pass examination system established by the act of 1853. On the other hand the President's authority to make rules and regulations governing the civil service was neither interrupted nor impaired, although it fell into relative disuse for nearly a decade.

What were the results of this first experiment?[18] In mere numbers, 2,286 persons were examined for original appointment, 1,531 for promotion. Two hundred and eighty-two vacancies were filled in the lowest grade and four hundred and twenty-eight by promotion, a total of seven hundred and ten. The impact on the patronage system had thus not become a substantial threat to old customs.[19]

An important question concerned the success of the competitive system from the point of view of the responsible executive officers. Opinions collected by the Commission in early 1874 showed a wide range on most points but almost unanimity on one: competitive examinations were not suitable for promotions. "A clerk," said second comptroller J. M. Brodhead, "may become master of the business upon which he is engaged by devoting his entire energies to it for a series of years, and by reason of his experience and fidelity [come] to be almost invaluable to an office, and yet when examined on general subjects not be able to pass as good an examination as when he entered the service."[20] The first comptroller agreed: "Promotions should depend upon the qualifications which a candidate has developed through the tests of practical experience . . . and no one outside of the Office . . . can be as well qualified to judge of his merits as the head of the Office in which he has served."[21]

On the other hand, testimony generally favored competitive examinations for original appointment. Brodhead reported that the new men had given entire satisfaction, and added, "I am of opinion that as a class the persons who have entered the service under the civil

---

[17] *Ibid.*, VII, 327.

[18] The story of this experiment is told by Lionel V. Murphy, "The First Federal Civil Service Commission: 1871-75," *Public Personnel Review*, III (1942), 29, 218, 299.

[19] Senate Ex. Doc. 53, 43d Cong., 1st sess., Appendix F, p. 118 (April 15, 1874).

[20] *Ibid.*, Appendix G, p. 147.

[21] *Ibid.*, p. 146.

service rules are superior in point of ability to those obtained under the former mode of examination and appointment."[22] The Post Office auditor was emphatic; he declared that his new clerks had proved, without exception, to be industrious, capable, and efficient, and that the competitive system was "infinitely superior to the former method of *original* appointment."[23] The superintendent of the money order division of the New York Post Office reported, "I cannot but express in terms of the highest praise of the gentlemen so selected, both as to their clerical abilities and gentlemanly conduct, and the moral influence exercised by each and every one of them."[24] The first comptroller (and doubtless others) found another advantage, i.e., relief from importunities for the appointment of unsuitable persons.

Other officials were less than enthusiastic and some were downright hostile to the competitive system. The third auditor reported that the new clerks had given entire satisfaction but were not superior to the clerks appointed in the old manner.[25] The Commissioner of the General Land Office observed, "It is with clerks as with lawyers—an ability to answer questions readily is not a sure test of capacity and fitness for practical duty. . . . He must not only have learning to a certain degree, but he must have natural capacity, industry, application, and executive force sufficient to make that learning available and useful, or he cannot be a valuable clerk."[26] The Commissioner of Customs stood for patronage and republicanism. "I . . . do not believe," he declared, "the interests of the Government are promoted by such competitions. I have always regarded it [sic] as exclusive in its character, giving to the richer portion of the community, who are able to acquire an excellent education, advantages over those who have had only the means to acquire an education sufficient to transact clerical duty faithfully and intelligently. . . ."[27] There were thus some practical as well as political reasons for opposition to the new examination system, especially promotional examinations.

Could Grant have done more to save his program? Why was he

[22] *Ibid.*, p. 147.
[23] *Ibid.*, pp. 149-50.
[24] *Ibid.*, p. 178.
[25] *Ibid.*, p. 148.
[26] *Ibid.*, p. 161.
[27] *Ibid.*, p. 148.

not more aggressive in 1873 and 1874? His own experience might well have led him to reject the patronage system. In 1859, while an unknown figure in public life, he sought appointment as county engineer of St. Louis County, Missouri. The Democratic county commissioners were outvoted by the Free Soil commissioners and he lost the appointment.[28] As an ex-President, he is reported to have said, "There is no man in the country so anxious for civil service reform as the President of the United States for the time being. He is the one person most interested. Patronage is the bane of the Presidential office. . . . He is necessarily a civil service reformer, because he wants peace of mind."[29]

On the other hand, as revealed in an earlier chapter, Grant believed that Congress was the body to determine policy, that his main duty was to execute the law as Congress enacted it, and that his duty was fulfilled when he had made his recommendations. It was in strict accord with this doctrine that he told Congress, unless they took action to indicate approval, he would construe inaction to mean disapproval and would discontinue the system. After retirement he said, "Civil service reform rests entirely with Congress."[30] Moreover, despite his request for reform legislation, his heart was never in the battle if we can believe the remarks ascribed to him after his retirement from the White House. "As to competitive examinations," he said, "they are of questionable utility. One of the most brilliant candidates before the civil service board was in jail very soon after his appointment, for robbery. The way to achieve the best civil service is, first to influence Congressmen, and induce them to refrain from pressure upon the Executive; then pass laws giving each office a special tenure; then keep the Republican party in power until the process of education is complete. As it is now, the only danger I see to civil service reform is in the triumph of the Democratic party."[31] Grant was in favor of peace of mind, but declined to follow the reformers' prescription for its achievement.

Finally, the President was at war with the Liberal Republicans, who

[28] Ulysses S. Grant, *Letters to His Father and His Youngest Sister*, p. 19 (Sept. 23, 1859).
[29] John R. Young, *Around the World with General Grant*, II, 264-65.
[30] *Ibid.*, II, 264.
[31] *Ibid.*, II, 268.

wanted reform, and was forced to find support in the wing of the party that was hostile to reform. Reformers became more and more repugnant to him as a class. They were, he thought, theorists, not practical men. Some of them, he said, were as anxious for patronage as others.[32] In conversation with John R. Young on his trip around the world Grant was reported to have said, "The most troublesome men in public life are those over-righteous people who see no motives in other people's actions but evil motives, who believe all public life is corrupt, and nothing is well done unless they do it themselves. They are narrow-headed men, their two eyes so close together that they can look out of the same gimlet-hole without winking."[33]

STALEMATE

The collapse of the reform set in motion by the act of 1871 left patronage and spoils with no check save the pass examinations instituted in 1853. They possessed some value, but they were wholly inadequate to correct the evils of which the reformers complained. For the remainder of Grant's term, reform stood still.

The election of Rutherford B. Hayes after an unprecedented controversy over the electoral college returns gave the reformers hope. Hayes had made a good record as governor of Ohio and had written a stirring endorsement of civil service reform in his letter accepting the Republican nomination. The appointing power, he declared, had passed into the control of members of Congress in many cases; appointments had become not merely rewards for party services but rewards for services to party leaders; and the system had degenerated into an intolerable burden and an unwarrantable hindrance to the proper discharge of the business of Congress. "It ought to be abolished. The reform should be thorough, radical, and complete."[34]

Congress was not, however, disposed to such a revolution and refused to pay attention to Hayes' repeated requests for legislation. In his third annual message, delivered to the new Congress on December 1, 1879, Hayes made his major plea for civil service reform, again asking for an appropriation to revive the Civil Service Commission. "Every citizen," he declared, "has an equal right to the honor and

[32] *Ibid.*, II, 263.
[33] *Ibid.*, II, 365.
[34] Rutherford B. Hayes, *Letters and Messages*, pp. 5-6 (July 8, 1876).

profit of entering the public service of his country," a proposition that brought ideas of democracy to the support of the merit system rather than rotation and party or factional exclusion. "The authority of appointment and removal is not a perquisite, which may be used to aid a friend or reward a partisan, but is a trust, to be exercised in the public interest," a phrase that was to be repeated later by President Grover Cleveland. The increasing number of public employees had long since made it impossible, Hayes continued, for heads of departments to examine personally the qualifications of office seekers. A different system had become inevitable.[35]

Congress still remained indifferent and Hayes prudently did not press reform as far as he might have done by executive direction. He took the same ground as Grant, that major reform depended on Congress, and that change in any event must be gradual. His personal convictions about the wisdom and necessity of reform were, however, firm, although toward the end of his term he recorded in his diary that he had not done as much to improve the civil service system as he had hoped.[36] He may well have gone as far as he could, faced by a captious, office-loving Congress, and an unconvinced general public. The Republican party in its 1880 convention adopted a reform plank against heavy opposition; the temper of the convention was perhaps better expressed by delegate Flanagan of Texas, who asked, "What are we here for, if not to get the offices?"[37] This slogan would be understood by the professionals in both party camps.

In the departments the nature and quality of such examinations as prevailed varied according to the attitudes of Secretaries and bureau chiefs. Each department head was allowed to fix his own standards within the broad range of the act of 1853; Schurz in Interior used competitive examinations, while Sherman in Treasury did little.

[35] Richardson, Messages, VII, 562. Hayes made another interesting move to advance the cause by encouraging Dorman B. Eaton, whom he continued to recognize as the head of the Civil Service Commission even though in a state of suspense, to visit England and study the progress of civil service reform there. Eaton wrote a substantial volume, first published as a public document, and subsequently as a commercial publication, Dorman B. Eaton, Civil Service in Great Britain: A History of Abuses and Reforms and Their Bearing upon American Politics (New York: Harper and Brothers, 1880).

[36] Rutherford B. Hayes, Diary and Letters, III, 597 (April 11, 1880).

[37] The Reminiscences of Carl Schurz (3 vols., New York: McClure Co., 1907-1908), III, 395.

Nevertheless, he did not disturb the examinations he found in effect in the Lifesaving Service and in the Revenue Marine Service. Sumner I. Kimball, general superintendent of the Lifesaving Service, told the Pendleton Committee in 1882 that he was a strong party man himself, but declared that this agency was different from most other branches of the civil service. "The Life-Saving Service is an expert service; a technical one, in which it is absolutely indispensable to have the very best obtainable men. In organizing it . . . I found it necessary to adopt such means as would exclude politics."[38]

The showpiece of Hayes' administration was Interior. With full support from the President, the reformer-politician at its head revived the examination procedure briefly established in 1871 and put the Department so far as possible on a merit basis. Thus in the Pension Office all original appointments of clerks were made after competitive examination, efficiency records were kept, and promotions given to the most competent while those who fell behind were demoted. "This system," said Carl Schurz, "has proved to be a powerful stimulus, and the result is that almost everyone in the Pension Office does his utmost."[39] In the Patent Office an examination system had been introduced in 1869 and owing to the technical character of the work had survived all the vicissitudes of the 1870's. The system was continued by Schurz and operated by Henry Hobart Bates, examiner in chief of the Patent Office. The test was carefully conducted and included questions on general information, arithmetic, capacity to write effectively, problems in mensuration, and the essential branches of mechanics and natural philosophy. In 1880 the examination attracted about eighty-five applicants for five or six places.[40] Bates testified that the Patent Office got bright young men, "much better than the average of appointments."

Even in the Interior Department under Schurz, however, the "competitive" examination was limited to the candidates approved by the Secretary and the appropriate bureau chief. ". . . these candidates," said Bates with respect to the Patent Office, "were admitted somewhat with reference to political reasons. . . . they had those who recom-

[38] Senate Report 576, 47th Cong., 1st sess., p. 212 (March 18, 1882). For a fascinating account of the examination plan in the Lifesaving Service, see *ibid.*, pp. 212-14.
[39] Carl Schurz, *Speeches, Correspondence and Political Papers*, III, 490-91.
[40] Senate Report 576, 47th Cong., 1st sess., pp. 194-95 (March 18, 1882).

mended them; and it is not everybody who applies by any means that is admitted. The Commissioner and the Secretary admit those people whom they suppose are eligible for any reason, political or otherwise, and they exclude others."[41]

The same practice prevailed in the customhouses, and presumably was not uncommon in other agencies. The result was to facilitate factional and party discrimination. Grant's first collector of customs in Baltimore, John L. Thomas, made this fact quite clear in his testimony before the Pendleton Committee in 1882. The following colloquy took place.

Senator Walker. You spoke of putting out Johnson Democrats; that was in 1869?

Mr. Thomas. Yes, sir.

Senator Walker. Did that get rid of the Democrats in your office pretty much?

Mr. Thomas. I believe it did.

Senator Walker. Since that time have many Democrats been appointed?

Mr. Thomas. None that I know of. I did not appoint any.

Senator Walker. You know of none since?

Mr. Thomas. No, sir.

Senator Walker. There were no Democrats, or few, if any, in the Baltimore custom-house when you left there?

Mr. Thomas. I do not think there is any one in the service there who is not a Republican. . . .

Senator Mitchell. When you had competitive examinations, how did you determine who should be admitted to them? Was there any preliminary evidence as to character or politics . . . ?

Mr. Thomas. Always, whenever we did not know the applicant; but in nine cases out of the ten the applicants were always known. Of course in relation to politics, I do not suppose there was anybody of the opposite political party who ever applied for a position there. I did not know of any. The applicants were all known to be Republicans, and generally in every application they would state what their services were to the party.

Senator Walker. Was it not pretty well understood that no other need apply?

Mr. Thomas. I think so.[42]

The net result of the suspension of Grant's Civil Service Com-

[41] *Ibid.*, pp. 198-99.
[42] *Ibid.*, pp. 186-87 (March 4, 1882).

mission was therefore a stalemate between powerfully entrenched vested interests on the one hand and a small group of able publicists and reformers on the other. Despite good intentions, Hayes made almost no actual progress. Garfield had too little time to disclose what course he might have preferred; Arthur allowed the situation to come to a crisis without initiating action.

THE DEFENSE OF PATRONAGE

The forces that had to be overcome by the civil service reformers were enormous. The whole country was habituated to patronage from the experience of two generations. To a young man becoming aware of public affairs after the Civil War, patronage must have seemed the natural order for a republic. It generally prevailed in the governments of states and cities as well as in Washington and the field services. Patronage seemed essential to support the political parties, and everyone knew that parties were necessary in a democracy. Tradition, habit, and democratic theory joined with the sentiments of practical politicians to support an almost impregnable assumption that patronage was both necessary and proper.

Much of the defense of patronage could therefore rest on the mere coinage of slogans, and the reformers had a great deal of this to endure. In the course of the second debate on the Jenckes bill in 1869, Representative John A. Logan of Illinois declared, "the bill is bad in theory, wrong in principle, opposed to the genius and spirit of our institutions and our people, and probably unconstitutional. . . ."[43] A few years later Congressman William Williams of Indiana declined to embrace "this new revelation of these latter-day saints, which ignores the established customs of the country from its organization," and which delegated to "an examining board of schoolmasters or new-fledged collegiates the power to dictate the officers in the civil department of this Government. . . ."[44] Congressman George C. McKee of Mississippi declared that President Grant's civil service rules had been imported from China at government expense and that reform was a fraud and a snare.[45] When the defenders of patronage came to make their case, rather than resort to slogans, they put it on four

[43] *Congressional Globe*, 40th Cong., 3d sess., p. 262 (Jan. 8, 1869).
[44] *Ibid.*, 42d Cong., 2d sess., pp. 1101, 1102 (Feb. 17, 1872).
[45] *Ibid.*, 42d Cong., 3d sess., p. 1631 (Feb. 22, 1873).

principal grounds: that civil service reform was antirepublican; that
the rule of rotation was correct for a republic; that reform would
destroy the party system; and that examinations were impracticable
and a poor substitute for the judgment of members of Congress and
of heads of departments.

The antirepublican theme was repeated again and again. Logan declared that the whole civil service plan was taken "openly, boldly,
and without disguise from monarchical Governments...."[46] Williams
declared that life tenure was "totally anti-republican, and subversive
of elective Government," and that it was "against the genius of our
republican institutions, and only fit for the iron heel of monarchical
despotism. . . ."[47] A less fervid variation turned on the proposition
that the civil service system would beget caste and aristocracy.

The propriety of rotation was defended as one of the bulwarks of
republican government. Logan told the House in 1869:

> . . . . It is by having their agents constantly before them that their acts
> may be denounced or confirmed that the people maintain their supremacy
> and enforce their will. This, sir, is the theory and practice of our Govern-
> ment. Immediate responsibility we all incur, and speedy settlements we all
> must render. The appointment of subordinates or the nominations for
> appointments are just as much a part of our responsibility as any other
> which we have, and a share in those appointments and the right to become
> for a time a portion of the administrative force of the Government is one
> of the recognized rights of the people of which it is proposed by this
> bill, utterly and forever, to deprive them.[48]

More than a decade later the argument retained vitality, eloquently
put by William Martin Dickson in the *North American Review*.
"With a reasonable rotation," he wrote, "every citizen of political
aspirations and experience who reaches middle life and conducts
himself well may hope to crown his family with the reflected honor
which office confers. This prospect is a motive to good work. This is
the peerage which the republic offers, not to a particular class, but
to every one who serves her."[49]

---

[46] *Ibid.*, 40th Cong., 3d sess., p. 262 (Jan. 8, 1869).
[47] *Ibid.*, 42d Cong., 2d sess., p. 1102 (Feb. 17, 1872).
[48] *Ibid.*, 40th Cong., 3d sess., p. 263 (Jan. 8, 1869).
[49] William Martin Dickson, "The New Political Machine," *North American
Review*, CXXXIV (1882), 50.

Civil service reform was repeatedly assailed as a threat to the party system. Thus Senator Joseph E. Brown of Georgia declared: "In a free republican government like this those who belong to both parties fight for office as well as principle. Do you believe that the Democratic leaders in all the different States would work with the same energy, and zeal, and ability as they would if you held out to them a chance of a change of the offices, with the change of the Executive? It would be contrary to all the history of the past to expect any such work."[50]

That examinations were impractical and unnecessary was another argument against reform. "The duties of civil officers," Senator Matthew H. Carpenter of Wisconsin reminded his colleagues, "are regulated by law; what they may do, and what they may not do, prescribed by law; and any intelligent man may shortly acquaint himself with the duties of any civil office. . . ."[51] The Senator had been reading his Jackson!

Representative James B. Beck of Kentucky declared, "It is folly, often worse than folly, to test competency or efficiency by mere capacity to answer questions in grammar or arithmetic." He documented his case: "Take, for instance, the men who are engaged in the life-saving stations along our coast. They are men who have been trained for years in that service until they have attained the utmost efficiency; they can man their boats, brave the storms, and save the lives of human beings in the midst of tempests. If these men are required to go before the civil-service commission to come into competition with schoolmasters who may not have the courage to go within a hundred feet of a wave nor the slightest qualification for that special service, yet because he knows something about geography and something about spelling the schoolmaster will get the place. . . ."[52] Senator Carpenter had already announced this result to his colleagues in the upper House: "So, sir, it comes to this at last, that . . . the dunce who has been crammed up to a diploma at Yale, and comes fresh from his cramming, will be preferred in all civil appointments to the ablest, most successful, and most upright business man of the country, who either did not enjoy the benefit of early education, or from whose mind, long engrossed in practical

[50] *Congressional Record*, 47th Cong., 2d sess., p. 277 (Dec. 14, 1882).
[51] *Congressional Globe*, 42d Cong., 2d sess., p. 457 (Jan. 18, 1872).
[52] *Congressional Record*, 43d Cong., 1st sess., p. 4895 (June 11, 1874).

pursuits, the details and niceties of academic knowledge have faded away as the headlands disappear when the mariner bids his native land good night."[53]

The alternative was obvious. ". . . I know of no better source of information as to the capacity, honesty, and integrity of applicants for positions to the President, or heads of Departments," declared Congressman Williams, "than can be furnished by the members of Congress. . . ." ". . . who," he asked, "are the best qualified to judge of the merits and qualifications of persons seeking employment in the civil service of the country, the heads of Departments, familiar with all the duties of the office and the talent requisite to fill it, or a board of examiners who know nothing whatever of the particular duties to be performed?"[54]

These were the principal bulwarks erected by the defenders of patronage against the attacks of the reformers. They were reinforced at various other outposts held by those who feared for the right of the Civil War veterans, who foresaw diminished responsibility of Congress, who anticipated the collapse of the apportionment of appointments by states to the exclusion of citizens from distant parts, and who were certain their constituents could not pass the examinations. Representative McKee spoke for this class of citizens: "I had a constituent here," he exclaimed, "who knew more than your whole civil service board. He was brought up here from Mississippi and they found him incompetent for the lowest grade of clerkship; and yet he is now cashier or teller of one of the largest banks on the Pacific slope. And they gave the appointment to a spectacled pedagogue from Maine. . . ."[55]

The argument was anti-intellectual. The prestige of the practical man stood head and shoulders above that of the college graduate. Indeed there was an undercurrent of hostility toward an educated person, assumed to be a son of the well-to-do. Logan of Illinois declared that the Jenckes bill would lead straight to two national schools —one for the military and the other for civil education. These schools, he said, would monopolize all avenues of approach to the government, and the next care of their graduates would be to get their children

---

[53] *Congressional Globe*, 42d Cong., 2d sess., p. 458 (Jan 18, 1872).
[54] *Ibid.*, 42d Cong., 2d sess., pp. 1103, 1104 (Feb. 17, 1872).
[55] *Ibid.*, 42d Cong., 3d sess., p. 1631 (Feb. 22, 1873).

there also.[56] Senator Carpenter sustained a national school for the military services "because their duties require scientific knowledge and long experience for their proper performance,"[57] but a civilian training institution was a horse of another color.

The argument reflected the history of forty years. Party, patronage, the public service, the expectations of office seekers, the aspirations of Congressmen, Senators, and Presidents, the demands of locality, all intertwined to make the doctrine of rotation not only natural, but apparently the essence of popular government itself. These were the major forces that the reformers faced and had to overthrow.

THE CASE FOR REFORM

The advocates of civil service reform sought two major objectives: greater efficiency and economy in the public service, and the moral regeneration of public life, both political and administrative. The great debates of 1867 and the years immediately following emphasized economy and efficiency, a natural consequence arising from the existence of an immense public debt at the close of the Civil War and from the fact that the initiative came from the Joint Select Committee on Retrenchment for which Congressman Jenckes reported. This objective, while never lost from sight, was soon overshadowed by the more powerful drive for moral reform. During the twentieth century the balance swung again to economy and efficiency as the primary end of civil service reform—a shift reflecting the gradual but steady improvement in the ethical standards of public life.

There were many corollaries growing out of these two major drives against patronage and spoils. The political party, it was said, was destroyed as an instrument of rational analysis in forming public policy, and party conflict was reduced to a mere struggle for office between the ins and the outs. Public life was made unattractive to able men and was monopolized by manipulators of caucuses and conventions. The public service was rendered unattractive to young men of promise. The position of Congress, in *de facto* command of the appointing power, was exaggerated and the constitutional balance upset. The rising power of corporations was observed with alarm—a

---

[56] *Ibid.*, 40th Cong., 3d sess., p. 265 (Jan. 8, 1869).
[57] *Ibid.*, 42d Cong., 2d sess., p. 457 (Jan. 18, 1872).

power exerted in part by outright corruption of weak men, in part by combinations with the party machines to secure mutual benefit.

Efficiency and economy. In the major speech on his bill to regulate the civil service Jenckes left no doubt as to his immediate objective. "This measure," he told the House, "proposes to extirpate, eradicate, or, in plain Saxon, dig up, root out, and throw aside any, every, and all kinds of 'patronage' in appointments to the public service. The word, the thing, the act, have no place in a republic."[58] To eradicate patronage, however, was only a means to an end. The end that Jenckes had primarily in mind was economy, efficiency, and plain honesty in the public offices. ". . . the true interests of the Government can be best served, its expenses lessened, the character of its officers improved, and its business more effectually done, by an entire reformation in the mode of making appointments in the civil service. . . . at present nearly every one of these subordinate offices is filled by some person who gained his appointment by the recommendation of personal and political friends, and not by the application of any test to discover his fitness for the place he occupies."[59] The expense of government and inadequacy of its results, he declared, were due to "the quality and character of the *personnel* of that service and their mode of appointment. . . ."[60] "The great point to be gained is in competency, efficiency. . . ."[61] "Let us seek to obtain skill, ability, fidelity, zeal, and integrity in the public service, and we shall not be called upon to increase either salaries or the number of offices. It is safe to assert that the number of offices may be diminished one third, and the efficiency of the whole force of the civil service increased one half, with a corresponding reduction of salaries for discontinued offices, if a healthy system of appointment and discipline be established for its government."[62]

Significant of a new force operating within the public service area and supporting the claim for more competence in government was a resolution of the National Manufacturers' Association at its first annual meeting in Cleveland on May 27, 1868.

[58] *Congressional Globe,* 39th Cong., 2d sess., p. 840 (Jan. 29, 1867).
[59] *Ibid.,* p. 837.
[60] *Ibid.,* p. 838.
[61] *Ibid.,* p. 838.
[62] *Ibid.,* pp. 838-39.

Resolved, That for the integrity and permanence of our Government, it is indispensable that public affairs be conducted on business principles, and that the dangerous custom of giving public posts to political paupers and partisan servants, regardless of their fitness, should be discontinued, as such custom absorbs a large share of the public revenue, and thus imposes useless and grievous burdens on the people, tends to growing demoralization in public and private character, destroying true freedom and bringing ruin at last.

Resolved, That we heartily approve the Civil Service Bill of Hon. Thomas A. Jenckes, now before Congress, as well and wisely adapted to remedy the great evils in our revenue and other civil departments, caused by incapacity and fraud, and to place men more competent and reliable in places of honor and trust. . . .[63]

Moral reform. The demand for moral reform was most effectively urged outside the halls of Congress by a small band of citizens who were dismayed by the corruption of the postwar years, and who eventually came together in the National Civil Service Reform League. The home of the League was in New York, where the greatest evils of patronage and spoils had been manifest. The New York Civil Service Reform Association was organized in 1877; other groups came together in Boston, Philadelphia, Milwaukee, San Francisco, and elsewhere; and in 1881 the National Civil Service Reform League was formed with George William Curtis as president.[64] Its first task was to agitate for a federal civil service law and to secure corresponding legislation in the states; its second was to defend and extend the legislation that was eventually forthcoming. Around the League were now concentrated the reform forces, and seldom have so few men with such meager resources produced such major results. They were, of course, carried forward by a tide of opinion which was progressively shocked by the evils of the spoils system, by a growing irritation on the part of the business community over the waste and abuses inherent in partisan conduct of the public offices, and by the concern of thoughtful men over the prostitution of party and the weakness of the executive power.

The function of the League was to foment opinion and to focus it for action. For this purpose such leaders of the League as Curtis,

[63] Copy seen in Jenckes Papers, Box 37, in Manuscript Division, Library of Congress.

[64] Frank M. Stewart, *The National Civil Service Reform League, passim.*

Schurz, Dorman B. Eaton, Everett P. Wheeler, and Charles J. Bonaparte were supremely qualified. They could speak and write with deadly effectiveness, they had standing in the community, they had courage, and they were in earnest. During the crucial period of agitation their financial resources barely exceeded an annual income of one thousand dollars, and through the years to 1901 averaged less than three thousand dollars. They had, however, a cause suffused with moral fervor and the eloquence of conviction.

Their leader, George William Curtis, was a scholar, artist, orator, and very Christian gentleman. "Without injustice to others," wrote Carl Schurz, "whose part in the work cannot be overlooked, it may well be said that Curtis, by his wide knowledge and experience, his ripe and calm judgment, his gentle temper and his scarcely asserted but easily acknowledged authority, was most perfectly fitted for that essential task of leadership in such a cause. . . . He was . . . to the day of his death, more than any other person, the intellectual head, the guiding force and the constant moral inspiration of the civil service reform movement."[65]

Curtis was one of the most popular after-dinner speakers of his time, and repeatedly condemned the moral degradation of the public service and advocated civil service reform as its cure. "What we affirm is," he asserted, "that the theory which regards places in the public service as prizes to be distributed after an election, like plunder after a battle, the theory which perverts public trusts into party spoils, making public employment dependent upon personal favor and not on proved merit, necessarily ruins the self-respect of public employés, destroys the function of party in a republic, prostitutes elections into a desperate strife for personal profit, and degrades the national character by lowering the moral tone and standard of the country."[66] Five years earlier he had written, "Civil service reform is not merely the observance of certain rules of examination. It is the correction of corruption in politics, and the restoration of political parties to their true function, which is the maintenance and enforcement of national policies. . . . The key-note of reform is struck in the President's

[65] Carl Schurz, "George William Curtis," in *Speeches, Correspondence and Political Papers*, VI, 410 (Dec. 7, 1903).

[66] George William Curtis, "Party and Patronage," in *Orations and Addresses of George William Curtis* (Charles Eliot Norton, ed., 3 vols., New York: Harper and Brothers, 1894), II, 502 (April 28, 1892).

saying that public office is a public trust, not a party perquisite."[67]

Curtis was supported in the campaign for moral reform by Carl Schurz, who became a civil service reformer when he stepped off the ship that brought him to America. In 1871 he told the Senate, "in my opinion, the question whether the Departments at Washington are managed well or badly, is, in proportion to the whole problem, an insignificant question after all. Neither does the question whether our civil service is as efficient as it ought to be, cover the whole ground. The most important point to my mind is, how we can remove that element of demoralization which the now prevailing mode of distributing office has introduced into the body-politic."[68] In 1872 he wrote, "I have long considered the reform of the civil service, the destruction of the corrupting and demoralizing influences of the patronage, the elevation of the moral tone of our political life, as one of the most important problems, second, perhaps, to none among these we have to solve for the success and perpetuation of our republican institutions."[69]

In the eighth report of the Civil Service Commission there is a passage in the same vein that may reasonably be ascribed to Commissioner Theodore Roosevelt.

While one of the main purposes of the law is to improve the public service, yet this can hardly be considered its prime object. Its prime object is to remove from American politics the degrading influences of the patronage system. Certainly, during the last sixty years, no other one cause has been so potent in tending to degrade American politics. The men who are in office only for what they can make out of it are thoroughly unwholesome citizens, and their activity in politics is simply noxious. . . . Decent private citizens must inevitably be driven out of politics if it is suffered to become a mere selfish scramble for plunder, where victory rests with the most greedy, the most cunning, and the most brazen. The whole patronage system is inimical to American institutions; it forms one of the

[67] "The Last Assault upon Reform," editorial in *Harper's Weekly*, XXXI, 358 (May 21, 1887).
[68] Carl Schurz, *Speeches, Correspondence and Political Papers*, II, 123 (Jan. 27, 1871).
[69] *Ibid.*, II, 318 (Jan. 20, 1872). See also, William Dudley Foulke, *Fighting the Spoilsmen*, and his A *Hoosier Autobiography* (New York: Oxford University Press, 1922).

gravest problems with which democratic and republican government has to grapple.[70]

The civil service reformers, notably Curtis, argued that reform would tend to return the political parties to their proper function. "What," asked Curtis, "is the legitimate sphere of party action? Parties divide upon questions of national policy. In a free country they appeal by public speech and in the public press to the judgment of the people. . . . But they can succeed only by legislation. Consequently each party strives to elect to the various legislatures representatives who will put its policy into law, and to commit the chief executive offices . . . to friendly hands. This is the legitimate scope of party action."[71] Later he stated his conception of the proper relationship between party as thus understood and reform. "Civil-Service reform," he wrote, "proposes to restrict the arbitrary power of party. It does not, of course, contemplate the dissolution of parties, or suppose that popular government will be carried on without the organization of citizens who desire to promote public policies upon which they agree. Indeed, the reform will necessarily promote the legitimate power of party by making it a representative of opinion to a degree which, under the spoils system, is impossible."[72]

A variation of this view, repeated over many years, asserted that devotion to appointments and patronage was a handicap to Congress as well as to the majority party. The point was made by Henry Cabot Lodge as late as 1889. ". . . the system of patronage is peculiarly odious. It has converted Congress into a machine for the division of offices, for which it was never intended, and by which its powers are cramped, its action is impeded, and its character injured."[73] Despite these views, Lodge took full advantage of his patronage prerogatives.

Discussion of party, patronage, and the reform of the civil service showed no obvious terminus as a new Republican administration succeeded Hayes on March 4, 1881. The scene abruptly changed with the shocking attack on President Garfield by a disappointed office seeker and with his death after weeks of suffering. The country

[70] U.S. Civil Service Commission, *Annual Report*, 1890-91, p. 13.
[71] George W. Curtis, *Orations and Addresses*, II, 135 (Sept. 20, 1878).
[72] *Ibid.*, II, 505 (April 28, 1892).
[73] Henry Cabot Lodge, "The Coming Congress," *North American Review*, CXLIX (1889), 300.

was aroused. Public opinion finally was convinced that the spoils system at least had to be curtailed, and the civil service reformers, aided by many of the leading journals and newspapers, gave opinion no opportunity to waver.

Apart from the universal indignation caused by Garfield's death, the nature of the public service had become such that patronage was more and more obviously an anachronism. Senator Henry L. Dawes made the point effectively. ". . . the method of appointment to office in this country has got to be changed. It can be administered but little longer in the methods of the past. It has outgrown those methods adapted for an old system of things never sufficient for them; but it was never dreamt by those who created it that it would be applied to the condition of things now existing in this country. It can no longer be that 200,000 office-holders can be appointed in the methods that were fit and proper for the appointment of 1,000. Two hundred thousand in the very near future are to be appointed. . . ." And again, ". . . were it not for the debauchery of this service itself the necessity of a safe administration would be so apparent that the thoughtful and earnest statesman of whatever party . . . would see that this must be changed somehow."[74]

The civil service reform bill passed the Senate (38 to 5); a motion to recommit in the House was defeated (113 to 85); and the House then concurred by a strong majority (155 to 47).[75] President Arthur, once removed as collector of the port of New York for flagrant partisan abuses, had correctly read the handwriting on the wall and signed the bill without hesitation.[76]

The struggle for reform passed into a new stage, the struggle to defend the victory and to ensure survival of the new regime.

THE CIVIL SERVICE ACT OF 1883

It remains to summarize the terms of the Civil Service Act, often referred to as the Pendleton Act. It established by law a bipartisan Civil Service Commission of three members appointed by the President with the advice and consent of the Senate for an indefinite term but subject to removal by the President. It gave statutory

[74] *Congressional Record*, 47th Cong., 2d sess., pp. 467-68 (Dec. 20, 1882).
[75] *Ibid.*, pp. 661, 867.
[76] 22 Stat. 403 (Jan. 16, 1883).

authority to the fundamental rules of operation, including the requirement of open competitive examinations, appointment from among those earning the highest grades, apportionment of the departmental service among residents of the various states according to population, a probationary period, and protection of the classified service against political pressure.

The Civil Service Commission was vested with two crucial powers —control of the examinations and authority to investigate the enforcement of its rules. The departments were directed to classify (that is, to include in the competitive service) their departmental employees; the Treasury was required to classify subordinate custom-house personnel in offices employing more than fifty; the Post Office was under a similar injunction. Of great significance was the authority conferred upon the President to extend the classified service by executive order from time to time.

The remainder of the act was concerned with limiting the solicitation of campaign funds by officials from employees, and in public buildings. The law was so successfully drafted that its basic provisions stood without amendment throughout the Republican era and beyond. Sumner and Jenckes, Trumbull, Curtis, and Schurz were finally vindicated by the acquiescence of Congress in the doctrine that the civil service should be competent, politically neutral, and an integral segment of the executive branch. At the moment these were victories of principle, gradually to be achieved in practice over the succeeding decades.

CHAPTER FOURTEEN

The Struggle for Existence

What would be the fate of the new Civil Service Commission? The destruction of the Grant Commission by the refusal of Congress to appropriate funds was well remembered; the enemies of this Commission were numerous and well placed. The danger of outright repeal of the act of 1883, although repeatedly proposed, was relatively slight, but more subtle ways of reaching the same end were at hand. As late as 1899 an advocate of reform wrote, "Those of us who have fought for the principle of civil service and have got it, feel like a sailor out on the yard-arm in a storm, who holds on to the sheet, which he is striving to reef, with his teeth as well as with his hands and his feet! Every now and then some cloud appears in the sky, that makes us feel that everything we had fought for and won in the great struggle for civil service is in danger of being imperilled; if not of being lost. The conviction of the country in regard to the soundness of the principles of civil service wabbles about, so to speak, in such a way as creates in the hearts of many of us the keenest apprehension."[1]

Formal support for competitive examinations was regularly introduced in both party platforms, but these planks were not convincing. In 1896, indeed, the Democratic platform declared opposition to life tenure in the public service and support for fixed terms of office, appointments to be based on merit nevertheless. This "straddle" looked toward rotation, not to careers.

[1] H. C. Potter, "National Bigness or Greatness—Which?" *North American Review*, CLXVIII (1899), 436. For two articles condemning the civil service system, see General John Pope, "Common-Sense and Civil-Service Reform," *ibid.*, CXLIX (1889), 265; J. S. Clarkson, "The Politician and the Pharisee," *ibid.*, CLII (1891), 613.

COUNTERCURRENTS

So far as the attitude of rank-and-file politicians was concerned, the passage of the Pendleton Act involved no conversion to grace. Carl Schurz might have written in 1885 (or 1895) what he actually wrote in 1882. "A very large majority of the professional politicians of both parties continue to hate civil service reform with a sincere and robust hatred, because it threatens to spoil their business, to throw most of their arts out of the market, and to deprive them of their plunder."[2] After two years' experience Dorman B. Eaton wrote, "The old spoils-system spirit is, however, still alarmingly audacious. I could fill an article with illustrations."[3]

Many members of Congress were thoroughly convinced of the soundness and necessity of the new system; many were skeptical, and some were hostile. The temptation to attack the administration for supposed failure to observe the civil service rules was too much for either party to withstand, and the Commission was repeatedly investigated from 1888 to 1898. The first of these investigations was authorized by a Republican Senate in 1888; it revealed the failure of the Cleveland administration to prevent political assessments in the field service, and was released on October 10, 1888, in time to be influential in the pending presidential election.[4] The second was authorized in 1890 in the midst of the Harrison administration, and was directed against alleged evasion of the law by the Civil Service Commission itself. The Commission was cleared of serious fault, but the House committee recommended its replacement by a single civil service commissioner.[5] The third investigation arose out of a head-on conflict between the Commission and the Post Office Department (in terms of personalities between Theodore Roosevelt and John Wanamaker) over evasion of the civil service law in the Baltimore post office and the respective authority of the Commission and the Department to punish offenders.[6] The fourth involved an attack on Cleveland's executive order of 1896 extending the civil

[2] *Ibid.*, CXXXIV (1882), 451.
[3] Dorman B. Eaton, "Two Years of Civil Service Reform," *ibid.*, CXLI (1885), 23. See also a pessimistic article on the achievements of reform by Frederick Perry Powers, "The Reform of the Federal Service," *Political Science Quarterly*, III (1888), 247.
[4] Senate Report 2373, 50th Cong., 1st sess. (Oct. 10, 1888).
[5] House Report 4038, 51st Cong., 2d sess. (March 2, 1891).
[6] House Report 1669, 52d Cong., 1st sess. (June 22, 1892).

service and laid the groundwork for a McKinley order rolling back the coverage of the act.[7] This inquiry involved a major attack upon the Commission, which had become the object of much adverse (although ill-founded) rumor. Congress, animated in part by a desire of succeeding majorities to expose their party adversaries of previous years and in part by the opposition of patronage-minded members, thus kept the Commission under almost constant, and at times unfriendly, scrutiny for a full decade.

Potential danger in Congress was evidenced not only by this series of investigations but also by the declamation of a few of the more violent advocates of party patronage. Senator Preston B. Plumb of Kansas observed in 1889, "I do not subscribe to that doctrine of civil-service reform which has been developed by a morbid desire to pattern after the British form and detail of government. . . . I believe that it [the civil service system] has been rotten to the core, one-sided, grasping, avaricious in a certain way, which has not tended to benefit the other branches of the civil service. . . ."[8] Senator Arthur P. Gorman of Maryland declared, "The fault comes from the system. It is un-American."[9] Senator William M. Stewart of Nevada, a persistent opponent of reform, asserted in 1888 that the law was "a bad one; that instead of fixing responsibility and securing reliable officers it has a tendency directly the other way."[10] In 1891 he told his senatorial colleagues, "It is impossible to properly discharge the work of the Executive Departments unless the heads of those Departments can select those whom they think proper and competent to do the clerical work, and whom the heads of the Departments can control, and I think it has a tendency to demoralize the service."[11]

In 1890 Congressman Charles H. Grosvenor of Ohio, a prominent officer of the Union Army and an active political figure, learned that the Civil Service Commission was recruiting clerks in Louisiana and Arkansas in order to fill the quotas of these states. In wrath, the Congressman rose to his feet and appealed to the House. "I want," he said, "as an ex-Union soldier and on behalf of the ex-Union

[7] Senate Report 659, 55th Cong., 2d sess. (March 9, 1898); and Senate Doc. 41, 55th Cong., 2d sess. (Jan. 5, 1898).

[8] *Congressional Record*, 50th Cong., 2d sess., p. 1513 (Feb. 5, 1889).

[9] *Ibid.*, 50th Cong., 2d sess., p. 1607 (Feb. 7, 1889).

[10] *Ibid.*, 50th Cong., 1st sess., p. 9155 (Oct. 4, 1888).

[11] *Ibid.*, 51st Cong., 2d sess., p. 3417 (Feb. 27, 1891).

soldiers of this country, to express my unqualified condemnation of that act. That alone will forever damn the Civil Service Commission in the estimation of the people of this country. . . . I want to abolish this board. It is abnormal, and it is a growth that was never contemplated by the Constitution. . . . I would turn out an irresponsible board which defies the common law of the country and the general sentiment of mankind. . . . I went to the last State convention and was assured by more than five out of six Republicans there that if I would introduce a resolution to repeal the civil-service law that they would vote for it."[12] No one could be quite sure for how many of their colleagues Plumb, Gorman, Stewart, and Grosvenor were speaking.

The heads of departments, generally friendly to the civil service system, were quoted *in extenso* by Commissioner John R. Proctor in testimony before the Senate Committee on Civil Service and Retrenchment in 1898. Typical of their attitude was that of former Secretary of the Treasury William Windom, pronouncing the examination plan preferable in all respects to the older method, and that of former Secretary of the Navy Benjamin F. Tracy: "The persons appointed under this system are unquestionably more efficient, as a whole, than those selected under any system of pure patronage."[13]

On the other hand some were disposed to remain officially ignorant of violations in the field services, and some were hostile.[14] Postmaster General John Wanamaker was in frequent conflict with the Civil Service Commission, in contrast to most of President Harrison's department heads. "Wanamaker," wrote Commissioner Roosevelt to Henry Cabot Lodge, "has been as outrageously disagreeable as he could possibly be. . . . We have done our best to get on smoothly with him, but he is an ill-conditioned creature."[15]

[12] Remarks uttered on August 23, 1890. House Report 4038, 51st Cong., 2d sess., pp. 96, 97.

[13] Senate Report 659, 55th Cong., 2d sess., p. 743 (Feb. 3, 1898).

[14] See Leon B. Richardson, *William E. Chandler*, pp. 314-15; Mark D. Hirsch, *William C. Whitney*, pp. 350-54; Horace S. Merrill, *William Freeman Vilas*, pp. 103-105.

[15] Theodore Roosevelt, *Letters* (Morison ed.), I, 171 (July 11, 1889). Roosevelt lacked a balanced view of Wanamaker's policy on the merit system. As noted in Chapter 12, Wanamaker strongly endorsed the Civil Service Act and proposed to extend it. On the other hand, he accepted the patronage system without hesitation where it existed, and resisted the efforts of the Civil Service Commission to police the Post Office Department.

Mr. Wanamaker blandly told the House investigating committee in 1892, "I consider myself the highest type of a civil-service man."[16] His biographer, however, stated that Wanamaker had no profound objection to the theory that to the victor belonged the spoils.[17] He wrote to a Pittsburgh correspondent, "all the traditions are fixed that the Congressman must have the casting vote in making the post-masters within the district that he represents. . . ."[18] Roosevelt told the House committee, "The Postmaster General says once and again that he is not and has not been antagonistic to the Civil Service Commission. I regret to state that I must emphatically dissent from this statement."[19]

Presidents, for their part, were in a difficult position. The civil service reformers drove them hard, and watched for every evidence of backsliding while urging extension of the system to new offices and agencies. In his annual message for 1893 Cleveland denounced "the querulous impracticability of many self-constituted guardians."[20] On the other hand the "insiders" in every administration reminded Presidents that they had been elected by the untiring efforts of thousands of small leaders whose interest could be sustained only by adequate reward. It is not surprising that the National Civil Service Reform League found much to criticize and condemn, or that active politicians were dismayed by the steady growth of the merit system at the expense, they feared, of party solidarity and strength.

The official pronouncements of each successive President were all that the reformers could desire, but performance lagged behind promise. Cleveland was the reformers' choice in the election of 1884 but at the end of his first administration the National Civil Service Reform League condemned "the practically complete partisan reconstruction" of the unclassified service and the failure of the President to resist political pressure.[21] Harrison was in favor of the merit system and appointed Roosevelt as a Civil Service Commissioner, but he refused to control Wanamaker. Roosevelt found Harrison a weak

[16] House Report 1669, 52d Cong., 1st sess., p. 8 (testimony of April 25, 1892).

[17] Herbert Adams Gibbons, *John Wanamaker*, I, 301.

[18] Quoted in Dorothy G. Fowler, *The Cabinet Politician*, p. 215.

[19] House Report 1669, 52d Cong., 1st sess., p. 63 (June 22, 1892).

[20] Richardson, *Messages*, IX, 457 (Dec. 4, 1893).

[21] Frank M. Stewart, *The National Civil Service Reform League*, p. 51. Despite President Arthur's early record as a machine politician in New York, he gave full support to the new Civil Service Commission. U.S. Civil Service Commission, *Annual Report*, 1884-85, p. 55.

support. McKinley was favorable in principle, but in 1899 he issued the first executive order substantially diminishing the coverage of the civil service.

The problem faced by Presidents, particularly acute in the early years of the new civil service system, was understood by thoughtful citizens who were committed neither to spoils nor to reform. Referring to Cleveland, Ballard Smith wrote in 1888: "As a Democrat and representative of the principles of the Democratic party he could, loyally to himself or to Democratic principles, make no compromises whereby those ideas of government could be overthrown by the triumph of the opposing party. . . . A partisan and hostile postmaster in the city of New York in 1884 would have brought about the defeat of the Democratic party. . . . it seems an axiom not worth discussion to those who believe in the principles of the party that a Democratic President should choose lieutenants for the influential public offices entirely and with enthusiasm in accord with the principles he represents."[22] Looking back on Cleveland's lack of party support on the gold standard issue during his second term, the editor of the *New York Evening Post* declared that his trouble began in his first term, when he refused to consider that one of his chief duties as a Democratic President was to satisfy Democratic hunger for office.[23]

Presidents, indeed, were on the horns of an awkward dilemma. They had been elected, so it appeared, by the strenuous efforts of the rank and file in city precincts and country polling places—a professional army of party workers who were for the most part but dimly aware of the virtues of high tariff or low tariff, free coinage of silver, or the possession of the Philippine Islands, but who knew the value of an office or a contract. They worked in part for the mere excitement of the campaign, in part for the savor of success, in part doubtless for high principle. They also cherished anticipations, and without the reward of office or perquisite their energies in succeeding campaigns might easily dwindle. This was the expectation of many decades, and Presidents could not ignore it.

At the same time, Presidents were responsible for the due and

[22] "The Political Effect of the Message," *North American Review*, CXLVI (1888), 212-13.

[23] *New York Evening Post*, July 16, 1896.

effective administration of the laws, the collection of the revenue, and the honest use of public funds. These objects, demanded not only by reformers but by businessmen and merchants, could not be gained by reliance on ward-heelers. The task of Presidents was one of balance and compromise, recognizing both the needs of the public service and of party organizations. No one could foretell from time to time which way the presidential balance would tip under the weight of contradictory impulses.

Old traditions had not yielded under the new regime so far as the *exempt service* was concerned. In the Senate investigation of 1888, the collector of internal revenue of the first Pennsylvania district (Philadelphia), a Cleveland appointee who had been occupied "in railroading," took part in the following questions and answers.

Q. Of the sixty-two employés that you found there [i. e., in the collector's office], how many of them have you now?
A. Four.
Q. All the rest have been changed?
A. Yes, sir; by resignation. They all resigned. Most of them resigned when I first went in there, with the exception of the gaugers, and they resigned as other people became competent to take their places. . . .
Q. I suppose nothing more was needed than an intimation that their places were wanted?
A. That was all.
Q. Nobody objected or made any fight?
A. No, sir. In fact they taught our people; the old gaugers went with them and taught the new gaugers their duties. . . .
Q. What are the politics of the men that you have under you now in the internal-revenue department?
A. They are all Democrats; that is, with the exception of some whom I judge to be Republicans; I never have asked them. Those who remain have been there some time.[24]

An employee of the Baltimore post office, one-time chief of the city division, was asked whether all the clerks in his former division had been removed. He answered, "Yes, sir; I do not think there are hardly any left; there may have been one left." Asked if he knew of any Republicans being appointed, he replied, "I do not."[25] John

---

[24] Senate Report 2373, 50th Cong., 1st sess., Part 2, "Civil Service in Pennsylvania," pp. 137-38 (April 6, 1888).
[25] *Ibid.*, Part 3, "Civil Service in Maryland," pp. 59-60 (June 8, 1888).

W. O'Brien, a Democratic weigher in the port of New York, somewhat reluctantly admitted that the majority of the laborers in the
port of New York had been recommended by Democratic politicians,
or were Grand Army men. "I take care of the soldiers," he testified,
"they come to me for that. I never ask a soldier's politics."[26]

The political organizations were violating no law in such operations in the exempt service, and Republicans were no different from
Democrats. Both parties, moreover, enjoyed the patronage available
in state and city governments. While, therefore, the proportion of
federal patronage was being reduced, the combined federal, state, and
local patronage remained great. Indeed the number of federal
patronage positions actually increased from 1883 to 1901, rising from
about 118,000 in 1884 to about 150,000 in 1901, an increase due to the
over-all expansion of the service. The spoils system, in short, fully
maintained its vitality for many years after the passage of the Pendleton Act, and constituted a covert threat to the life of the merit idea.

ALTERNATIVES TO COMPETITION

The hostile forces noted in the preceding pages were never strong
enough to do more than threaten repeal of the Pendleton Act. They
were consequently forced to consider alternative lines of opposition
which might at least contain the reform movement and confirm party
control of the major sector of the public service. They were defeated
in part by the initial error (from their point of view) of authorizing
the extension of the merit system by executive order. Thus, as we
shall see, the system grew in this way at the expense of partisan
patronage.

Four alternatives to the competitive system presented themselves:
(1) evasion; (2) starvation by crippling the resources of the Civil
Service Commission; (3) substantial abandonment by a return to
the system of agency boards; and (4) a fixed term for all government
employees. Much controversy developed over each possibility.

(1) *Evasion.* In the Washington offices there was relatively little
evasion of the civil service rules, apart from a few resisting bureaus.[27]
In the field, the problem of enforcement, even for the small propor-

---

[26] *Ibid.,* Part 1, "Civil Service in New York," p. 127 (May 23, 1888).
[27] Charles Lyman, "Ten Years of Civil Service Reform," *North American Review,* CLVII (1893), 574.

tion of civil service positions, was serious. In 1890 Commissioner Roosevelt summarized the situation in this passage from a letter to a House investigating committee. "We will submit figures to you concerning the appointments and removals in the Departments, which go to show that in the departmental service at Washington, aside from a small special division of the Pension Bureau, the law is working satisfactorily, and is being, and has been for the last half dozen years, observed with *substantial* integrity. . . . On the other hand, in the local offices there exists the widest variety in its observance, and in only a few is it as well observed as in Washington. We do our best to prevent any evasion or violation of the laws at the local offices, but it is wholly impossible under present circumstances to make matters in these offices as they should be."[28] Even in the subordinate offices in Washington Roosevelt found considerable abuse on the part of unscrupulous supervisors who persecuted clerks of the opposite party affiliation until they resigned, or who preferred trumped-up charges. This type of evasion was hard to reach.

The Senate investigation of 1888 gave ample evidence of evasion of the civil service law and rules in four of the admittedly most difficult jurisdictions: New York City and Philadelphia, Maryland and Indiana. Despite the partisan flavor of the investigation, the majority were fully justified in their findings (1) that partisan changes had been made in a wholesale way; (2) that federal officials throughout the country had freely and openly participated in political conventions and had used their official influence; and (3) that federal officeholders were assessed for political purposes. The minority of the committee were reduced to general denials, to aspersions upon the testimony of the National Civil Service Reform League representatives, and to charges that the Republicans had been equally guilty and that the report was a campaign document. The record of evasion was, however, beyond controversy, bold, widespread, and at times defiant.[29]

[28] Theodore Roosevelt, *Letters* (Morison ed.), I, 226 (June 23, 1890).
[29] Senate Report 2373, 50th Cong., 1st sess. (Oct. 10, 1888); majority report summarized at pp. 46-47; minority report at end of testimony. A form of evasion in the Office of Internal Revenue was to appoint deputy collectors (exempt positions) to do the work of clerks (classified positions) in the field offices. This device baffled the Civil Service Commission for many years. See Official Deputies of Internal Revenue, Senate Doc. 58, 55th Cong., 2d sess. (Jan. 13, 1898).

Theodore Roosevelt plunged into the fight to reduce evasion with energy. Appointed to the Civil Service Commission in May 1889, in June he was already wielding the big stick over errant postmasters. Describing his first field trip to Henry Cabot Lodge, he wrote, "We had only a week's trip but we stirred things up well; the President has made a great mistake in appointing a well-meaning weak old fellow in Indianapolis, but I think we have administered a galvanic shock that will reinforce his virtue for the future. Cleveland's post-master at Milwaukee is about as thorough paced a scoundrel as I ever saw—an oily-Gammon, church-going specimen. We gave him a neat hoist. The Chicago postmaster is a trump. . . ."[30] The Milwaukee postmaster, Paul, was supported by Wanamaker, and a lively battle ensued.

Returning to Washington from his western trip, Roosevelt went to Baltimore to investigate the management of this post office. Cleveland's first appointee (Veazey) had turned out four-fifths of the old employees within a year, a record that Roosevelt declared was scandalous. "Mr. Veazey," wrote Roosevelt, "was one of those products of the patronage system whose antics would be comic were it not for their deeply tragic effect upon the public service and upon honest political life. . . . It seems likely that he habitually and grossly violated the law both as to appointments and removals. . . ."[31] Veazey's successor, Brown, removed four-fifths of those who had survived Veazey. Since at that time cause for removal was not usually stated, the Commission could only infer political reasons, and the indignant Roosevelt recommended that unless a postmaster was able to justify removal of a very large percentage of his employees, he should be deemed to have violated the civil service law and be himself dismissed.[32]

At the end of his service as Commissioner, Roosevelt admitted that there had been violations or evasions of the law which the Commission had been unable to prevent. "In every case, however," he declared, "we made a resolute fight, and gave the widest publicity to the wrongdoing. Often, even when we have been unable to win the actual fight in which we were engaged, the fact of our having

[30] Theodore Roosevelt, *Letters* (Morison ed.), I, 166 (June 24, 1889).
[31] *Ibid.*, I, 178 (August 1, 1889).
[32] *Ibid.*, I, 181.

made it, and the further fact that we were ready to repeat it on provocation, has put a complete stop to the repetition of the offence."[33] Evasion remained a problem for years yet to come, if on a diminishing scale.

(2) *Starvation.* The Civil Service Commission was chronically understaffed and not infrequently in danger of the total loss of its appropriation. The principal attack on the Commission came over its financing. ". . . in every Congress," wrote Roosevelt in 1895, "resolute efforts are made by the champions of foul government and dishonest politics to cut off the Commission's supplies."[34] More than once, indeed, the whole appropriation was stricken by the Committee of the Whole (where no vote was recorded) only to be restored in the open House. The battle was unremitting; requests for three or four additional clerks were made the occasion for an assault upon the Commission. In the short session of the fiftieth Congress, Senator Gorman arose in wrath. "Why," he asked, "should the Civil Service Commission come to this body and ask for an increase of its force? What earthly necessity is there for it except to build up another huge department? . . . I assert . . . that they have now a larger force employed in this office than is necessary. . . ."[35]

The Commission was never left without an appropriation, but it constantly had to complain about inadequate funds. In 1890 it was three months behind in its work and steadily falling into greater arrearages. In 1893 the situation became so serious that a special appeal was made to President Cleveland, the Commission then being 5,000 papers behind schedule.[36] Some relief was forthcoming.

Another aspect of the fiscal problem lay in the fact that Congress declined to appropriate funds for a full staff, but forced the Commission to accept employees on detail from other departments to do the bulk of examination rating. In 1893, twenty-two employees were on detail, ten of whom were incompetent, unfit for their work, and themselves unable to pass a creditable examination. "The departments," said Roosevelt, "very naturally object to detailing their efficient men. The temptation is almost irresistible to detail those

---

[33] Theodore Roosevelt, "Six Years of Civil Service Reform," *Scribner's Magazine*, XVIII (1895), 239.

[34] *Ibid.*, XVIII, 245.

[35] *Congressional Record*, 50th Cong., 2d sess., p. 1607 (Feb. 7, 1889).

[36] Theodore Roosevelt, *Letters* (Morison ed.), I, 323 (June 24, 1893).

who cannot do good work, but whom, from motives of sympathy or because of the influence which is back of them, the departments do not like to discharge."[37]

(3) *Return to the agency board system.* Ever since 1853 agency examining boards had been required by Congress for the noncompetitive examination of clerks. The Grant Commission in effect continued the agency boards, subject now to some supervision, to open competition, and to some standardization of requirements. The suspension of the Commission again left the agency boards in full possession of the field. In 1882 it was strenuously argued that the only change needed in the system was to make these boards more effective bodies, keeping responsibility for selection completely within each respective department. It was true, as the reformers pointed out, that many of these boards were mere tools of the department heads; that they examined only those persons whom the department heads recommended; and that they were ill placed to resist pressure to pass official favorites. These arguments were unconvincing—to the opponents of reform.

It is not surprising, therefore, that the Civil Service Commission was attacked under the guise of a return to agency responsibility and agency examining boards. Critics appealed to business practice. Senator William M. Stewart of Nevada declared in 1889 that the examination system would be repudiated by any businessman in the United States. "If there is to be a civil-service examination," he declared, "it ought to be conducted in the same way that a business examination would be conducted to obtain persons to fill business places. This whole system, it seems to me, is a fraud, a farce, and a delusion, and excludes from the public service as a rule those best qualified to fill the places. I am opposed to it, unless it is reduced to some rational business basis. . . ."[38] Two years later he reiterated this opinion: "Now, if the heads of the divisions had the same opportunity [as the businessman] . . . they could certainly make better selections than can be made by an abstract examination generally having no relation to the business in hand."[39]

The House select committee investigating the Civil Service Com-

[37] *Ibid.*, I, 324.
[38] *Congressional Record*, 50th Cong., 2d sess., p. 1515 (Feb. 5, 1889).
[39] *Ibid.*, 51st Cong., 2d sess., p. 3412 (Feb. 27, 1891).

mission in 1890 had before it bills to abolish the Commission and to establish a series of departmental examining bureaus. Their object, said the chairman, was "not to make any examination less severe, nor to do away with the merit system, but to avoid these examinations over the country, to examine so many and put them on the eligible list. . . ."[40] He had before him a willing witness in the person of the superintendent of the census, Robert P. Porter. The chairman asked him if the efficiency of the clerks would not be improved by independent agency examining boards, to which Porter replied, "I think it unquestionably would be better than the present civil-service method." He was asked if agency examining boards might not facilitate political selection. Porter responded: "I think there is no harm in that if you could get good people. I am in favor of that, if you get efficient clerks. I think the party in power should have something to say about it. I think it is wholesome and a good thing."[41] His attitude was further revealed in another passage of his testimony. "I am myself in favor of examinations . . . though I am not in favor exactly of any system of barnacleism. The greatest danger is the system of permanent civil-service appointments and that danger is becoming greater and is being fitted to certain classes and shutting out the common people from these examinations."[42]

Superintendent Porter, to whom credit was due for requiring even a pass examination for the unprotected Census Office employees,[43] was endorsed by Congressman Grosvenor. "Now," he said, "this bureau demonstrated to the country that the true application of the doctrine of civil-service reform was to have an examination in each Department. . . . The system which I ask involves simply that the heads of these great Departments . . . and the chiefs of the great bureaus shall be permitted to send before a board young men, applicants for positions, and let them make the examination just as strict as the wants and demands of the bureau require."[44]

At a later session of the House committee appeared Commissioner

<hr/>

[40] House Report 4038, 51st Cong., 2d sess., p. 124.

[41] *Ibid.*, p. 124 (Sept. 9, 1890).

[42] *Ibid.*, pp. 112-13.

[43] Indeed Porter claimed that his agency examination for clerks was more thorough than that of the Civil Service Commission. *North American Review*, CLI (1890), 667.

[44] *Congressional Record*, 51st Cong., 2d sess., p. 2635 (Feb. 13, 1891).

Roosevelt, "loaded," as he said, "for Mr. Porter." He accused Porter of advocating the reintroduction of the old patronage system into the departmental service. "His advocacy of a system of non-competitive or pass-examinations does not change his position in the least, for non-competitive examinations serve only as a cloak to hide the nakedness of the spoils system. Pass-examinations or non-competitive examinations are absolutely useless as checks upon patronage appointments."[45] Commissioner Roosevelt accused the Congressmen who stood behind Porter. "The Congressmen who introduce bills to provide for the departmental pass examinations are of course merely trying to reintroduce the spoils system into the departmental service. I want to make that statement with as much emphasis as I am capable of. I have no fear that this law will ever be repealed; but there is always danger that under pretense of friendship it may be done away with, and departmental or pass examinations introduced into the public service at large."[46] The vehemence of Roosevelt's rejoinder cooled the demand for agency boards and, with support elsewhere, warded off this attack.[47]

(4) *Fixed term.* A final alternative to the competitive examination system and its corollary, continuity of employment, was the proposal to limit by law the term of all subordinate employees. Garfield had favored a four-year term, with protection from removal during these years except for cause specified by law. He doubted whether more could be secured from Congress.[48] His Commissioner of Internal Revenue, Green B. Raum (later Commissioner of Pensions), made an elaborate defense of the fixed term proposal in 1881.

> ... it is inconsistent with the genius of our government, and contrary to the public sentiment of the people to have the great body of the officers and employés of the executive branch of the government to hold their positions by a life tenure, or during good behavior. Such a system would create a privileged class removed from the influences of popular sentiment,

[45] House Report 4038, 51st Cong., 2d sess., p. 142 (Jan. 29, 1891).
[46] *Ibid.*, p. 148.
[47] The value of an agency board under proper auspices and in friendly hands was not, however, lost from sight. In 1897 Secretary of the Interior Cornelius N. Bliss suggested an agency board comprising the Secretary and the four Commissioners (Lands, Indian Affairs, Pensions, and Patents) to examine special agents such as land and timber agents, mineral-land commissioners, and Indian agents. Senate Report 659, 55th Cong., 2d sess., p. 98 (May 1, 1897).
[48] *Garfield-Hinsdale Letters,* p. 454 (July 25, 1880).

which in this country is a constantly operating force favorable to honest, efficient administration. It would repress the laudable and honorable ambition of other citizens to serve the government in official positions and would manifestly tend to weaken the hold that our system of popular government has upon the minds of the people.[49]

Raum consequently recommended an initial probationary appointment of one year and, if found worthy, a subsequent appointment for three years; restrictions against arbitrary removal; and retiring pay at the end of four years' service.[50]

This alternative to reform persisted after the passage of the Pendleton Act. A bill for a four-year term was introduced in 1894, concerning which the Civil Service Commission declared: "Practically, this, of course, means to make the spoils system in its worst form obligatory instead of permissive. . . . The bill might properly be entitled, 'A bill to secure hopeless inefficiency in the governmental departments.' "[51] A five-year tenure bill was pending in 1898.[52]

The final appearance of this plan occurred in 1912, now motivated by a desire to find an alternative to a civil pension. Congress tacked a seven-year tenure limitation on the legislative, executive, and judicial appropriation bill of 1912. President Taft nevertheless vetoed the bill.[53] The issue had long lost force as a means of defending patronage, and the enactment of a retirement plan in 1920 robbed it of any strength or standing.

EXTENSION OF THE MERIT SYSTEM

Opponents of competitive examinations were naturally against extension of the coverage of the merit system, but they were handicapped by the clear authority of the President to proceed by executive order. The original coverage was about 14,000 positions in a service of approximately 100,000. Every President made additions and some made exceptions to the classified competitive service. By 1900 the positions under the merit system numbered about 106,000. In the midst of perils and investigations, the cause of reform thus slowly gained strength.

[49] Secretary of the Treasury, *Annual Report*, 1881, p. 71.
[50] *Ibid.*, p. 72.
[51] Senate Report 659, 55th Cong., 2d sess., p. 724.
[52] *Ibid.*, p. 725.
[53] *Congressional Record*, 62d Cong., 2d sess., pp. 11025-26 (August 15, 1912).

The struggle for extension involved three major episodes—the coverage of the Railway Mail Service by Cleveland, of the Indian service by Harrison, and of the service generally by Cleveland at the close of his second term. This act brought about the first thoughtful consideration of the problem, where to draw the line between the permanent and the excepted branches of the civil service. After an elaborate investigation McKinley retreated from the advanced ground taken by Cleveland.

Cleveland ordered classification of the five thousand railway postal clerks toward the close of his first term, but not early enough to enable the Civil Service Commission to execute his directions before the Harrison administration took office. In the interval between March 4 and May 15, 1889, about 2,300 clerks were removed and Republicans put in their places. Roosevelt later wrote, "This was an outrageous act, deserving the severe condemnation it received; but it was perfectly legal."[54] The delay in completing the classification was widely supposed to have been due to Republican intentions to reclaim their share of the jobs, but the Commission declared, with some justice, that they could not have worked more rapidly. The Railway Mail Service had been subject for years, as Commissioner Lyman stated, to "sudden and numerous changes." It now settled down, and the change of administration in 1893 "scarcely produced in it a ripple of excitement."[55]

The mismanagement of Indian affairs for many decades had been a disgrace to the Republic.[56] The appointment of Indian agents and indeed of the whole service was controlled politically; it was important primarily in the western states where ideas of civil service reform were slow in taking root. Harrison made a beginning in the improvement of the Indian service by extending the merit system to cover 626 field employees: physicians, school superintendents, schoolteachers, and matrons.[57]

During his second term, Cleveland gave much encouragement to the reformers by many extensions of the competitive service, in-

[54] Theodore Roosevelt, "Six Years of Civil Service Reform," *Scribner's Magazine*, XVIII (1895), 242.
[55] Charles Lyman, "Ten Years of Civil Service Reform," *North American Review*, CLVII (1893), p. 575.
[56] See ch. 9.
[57] U.S. Civil Service Commission, *Annual Report*, 1890-91, p. 72.

cluding among others lighthouse keepers and the clerical force of the Pension Office. Finally in his last year of office he added nearly 30,000 positions in a single stroke.[58] This sweeping order covered almost the whole of the departmental service, including all heads of divisions and chief clerks. In the Internal Revenue Bureau there was a total force of 3,502, of whom 3,387 were included in the competitive classified service. The remainder comprised the Commissioner, 63 collectors, and 51 deputy collectors receiving $300 or less.[59]

The incoming Republicans declared in 1897 that this was going too far. Objections based on mere desire for the offices were not novel and need not again be recorded. Now, however, appeared a new problem: to what extent does an incoming administration need to control higher and middle level personnel in the interests of effective direction of the great departments and agencies that are to carry out its policy?[60] In a simpler age the problem substantially did not arise since most agencies were small and easily manageable, with the exception of the War and Navy Departments. Later the problem was avoided in large measure by the appointment of masses of subordinate employees, who were subject to political discipline in the highest degree. Now partisan responsibility of clerks was diminished or eliminated; the organizations were large and relatively complex; and incoming Secretaries and bureau chiefs began to complain that they were administratively handicapped in controlling their agencies because they could not appoint their subordinates. Where should the line be drawn between the permanent public service and the political high command?

Woodrow Wilson was one of the first to identify the problem, in his *Congressional Government*. One of the conditions precedent to civil service reform, he wrote, "is the drawing of a sharp line of distinction between those offices which are political and those which are *non*-political." Wilson was baffled in fixing the line, even suggesting that department heads might fall in the nonpolitical category.[61]

---

[58] Amendment to Rule III, Civil Service Rules in Richardson, *Messages*, IX, 702 (May 6, 1896).

[59] Senate Report 659, 55th Cong., 2d sess., pp. 199-200 (May 21, 1897).

[60] An early discussion of the point occurred in an article by Frederick Perry Powers, "The Reform of the Federal Service," *Political Science Quarterly*, III (1888), 278-80.

[61] Woodrow Wilson, *Congressional Government*, pp. 289-91.

Senator Hoar made a preliminary effort to draw the line in 1889, in stating the proper coverage of the Civil Service Act.

> I would apply it, if I had my way, to every official in the country in an executive office whose duties were not of a political or a confidential nature and whom it was not expedient to have in sympathy with the administration when that administration was carrying out its political theories and policies in regard to which its opponents would be expected not to be in sympathy. . . .[62]

The Senator was immediately asked whether the presidential postmasters were "below the line," and had to confess that he could not answer the question.

The discussion revolving about Cleveland's wholesale extension of the merit system in 1896, leading in 1899 to McKinley's "roll back," included a series of reports from departmental officials. Most of them argued that bureau chiefs, division chiefs, and chief clerks were "above the line" and should be politically responsible.[63] One of the most thoughtful statements of this position was submitted by Binger Hermann, Commissioner of the Land Office.

> The chiefs of divisions should be especially exempt from the classified service, because their relations are not only confidential to the Bureau head but they constitute the last line of demarkation between the political relations of the Administration and the justly clerical or civil-service divisions of the Departments. The chief of a division is its presiding officer, and his general deportment should be such as to command the respect and add to the discipline of the corps. He should be selected especially as to his general fitness as such chief.
>
> If it is assumed that the dominant party shall shape the legislation of the country in consonance with the policies which it sustains, it has a right to know that the chiefs of divisions, who first shape recommendations as they are called for through the various divisions, are in perfect sympathy with the party policies. The most important legislation in Congress emanates from the division in the form of reports or measures pending in Congress and which are usually first submitted to the heads of the Departments, and by them to the heads of Bureaus, who in turn submit to the chiefs of divisions.[64]

To this the Civil Service Commission replied: "The great bulk of

---

[62] *Congressional Record*, 50th Cong., 2d sess., Vol. XX, Part 2, p. 1608.
[63] Senate Report 659, 55th Cong., 2d sess. (March 9, 1898).
[64] *Ibid.*, p. 101.

the offices of the Government are purely administrative business offices. . . . There are properly very few of the many offices in the gift of the Government which are really political in character, after we pass below the highest, such as the members of the Cabinet and the ministers to foreign countries."[65]

The dispute never passed beyond generalities. Neither the Commission nor the agencies made a convincing case, but the passage of time gradually confirmed the position of the Commission.

The crucial case at this time was the status of chief clerks and division heads, with respect to whom agency spokesmen insisted that they retain the right of selection. Secretary of Agriculture James Wilson testified that his experience had led him to conclude that "it is difficult to get heads of divisions with sufficient practical experience through civil-service examination. We want men in my Department who not only have a good foundation education, but also a good deal of practical knowledge of the world; and we are quite likely to get bright school boys."[66] Secretary of the Interior Cornelius N. Bliss urged that the chief clerk and the heads of divisions in this Department should be exempt. "These officers occupy confidential relations to the Secretary, and on their briefs or recommendations he is dependent, to a large extent, for the proper conduct of his office."[67] The Commissioner of the General Land Office submitted the same recommendations.[68] In a vigorous and forthright letter Benjamin Butterworth, Commissioner of the Patent Office and a long-time advocate of civil service reform, roundly condemned its extension into the higher levels. ". . . the rules," he declared, "should embrace in the main merely the clerical force, and certainly not those of the executive staff."[69]

While opinion among the executive officers was not unanimous, there was a strong preponderance holding that the classified service had been extended too far, and should be curtailed not for the advantage of party politics but for the necessities of responsible administration. Thus drew together for this occasion two groups whose interests were markedly different, if not contradictory. The result was

[65] U.S. Civil Service Commission, *Annual Report*, 1890-91, p. 15.
[66] Senate Report 659, 55th Cong., 2d sess., p. 40 (April 24, 1897).
[67] *Ibid.*, p. 98.
[68] *Ibid.*, pp. 100-101.
[69] *Ibid.*, p. 181.

an executive order by President McKinley on May 29, 1899, withdrawing from the competitive classified service about 10,000 positions. "The principal purpose of the order," McKinley told Congress, "was to except from competitive examination certain places involving fiduciary responsibilities or duties of a strictly confidential, scientific, or executive character which it was thought might better be filled either by noncompetitive examination, or in the discretion of the appointing officer, than by open competition."[70] The civil service reformers declared that the real object was to restore patronage to the Republican party. Both the President and the reformers could justify their assertions.

THE UNITED STATES CIVIL SERVICE COMMISSION

While he was a Civil Service Commissioner, Theodore Roosevelt stated that there was no office in the country needing higher qualifications, and added, "it is very difficult indeed to find a man possessing the peculiar combination of qualities necessary to fill it well."[71] President Arthur found two outstanding men for the majority members of the first Civil Service Commission, Dorman B. Eaton and John M. Gregory, and a well-known public figure for the Democratic minority member, Leroy D. Thoman. Eaton, a decade earlier, had succeeded George William Curtis as president of Grant's Civil Service Commission and had been a great force in the reform movement. Gregory had been a leader in public education in the midwest, had served as president of Kalamazoo College, and was the first president of the University of Illinois (then known as the Illinois Industrial University). Thoman had been a probate judge and had a wide reputation as a public speaker. His interests were in law and politics. This group broke up in 1885 when Gregory and Thoman resigned, followed by Eaton's resignation in 1886.

Three undistinguished short-term Commissioners followed (Trenholm, Edgerton, and Oberly), one of whom, Edgerton, won the dubious distinction of summary removal by Cleveland on February 10, 1889, for his lack of sympathy with the merit system. Edgerton promptly confirmed the President's judgment in removing him (and his lack of discernment in making the appointment) by accusing

[70] Richardson, *Messages*, X, 180 (Dec. 5, 1899).
[71] House Report 4038, 51st Cong., 2d sess., p. 91 (August 12, 1890).

Cleveland of being "a mugwump of mugwumps" and by announcing defiantly that *he* was not such.[72]

Then appeared in Washington one of the strongest Commissions in the whole history of this body, comprising in order of appointment Charles Lyman (1886–1895), Hugh S. Thompson (1889–1892), and Theodore Roosevelt (1889–1895). Lyman was an example of the career clerk holding office through the years when the spoils system was at its worst. A poverty stricken farmer's boy in Connecticut, he enlisted in the Union army and fought through heavy engagements until 1863, when he returned to Hartford for a business course in the Bryant and Stratton commercial college. He became a clerk in the office of the second auditor in 1864; an assistant division chief in 1869 and a member of the Treasury board of civil service examiners; chief clerk of the Treasury Department in 1878; the first chief examiner of the Civil Service Commission in 1883; a member of the Commission in 1886 and its president from 1889 to his resignation in 1895. In 1897 he was back in the Treasury again as chief of the division of appointments.[73] The impatient Roosevelt found him thorough, reliable, but terribly slow. He wrote to his young friend, Lodge: "Lyman is a good, honest, hard-working man, very familiar with the law; but he is also the most intolerably slow of all the men who ever adored red tape."[74] After another month Roosevelt's patience ran out: "As for Lyman," he wrote, "he is utterly useless; I wish I had one more good Republican on the Commission; Lyman is utterly out of place as a Commissioner; I wish to Heaven he were off."[75] Dorman B. Eaton, however, held that Lyman was invaluable in his understanding of the practical work of the Commission. Cleve-

---

[72] *Dictionary of American Biography*, VI, 19. In 1890 Commissioner Lyman remarked (in relation to the preparation of rules for the Railway Mail Service), "Mr. Edgerton . . . took no part in this work, as he knew little or nothing about it, and took no interest in the subject." House Report 4038, 51st Cong., 2d sess., p. 35 (August 9, 1890). The *Washington Evening Star* commented (Feb. 11, 1889): "He was too positive and enthusiastic a politician, and too outspoken in his declarations of a lack of sympathy with the spirit of the law which he was appointed to enforce. . . . The commission could not expect to accomplish much with the severest public critic of its objects and methods one of its members and participating in its councils."
[73] *National Cyclopaedia of American Biography*, XIII, 373.
[74] Theodore Roosevelt, *Letters* (Morison ed.), I, 192 (Sept. 27, 1889).
[75] *Ibid.*, I, 199 (Oct. 19, 1889).

land asked for his resignation in 1894; it became effective in 1895.[76]

Hugh S. Thompson (the Democratic minority member) was a different type, thoroughly congenial to Roosevelt. Almost immediately after his appointment, Roosevelt wrote Lucius B. Swift: "I think Thompson is a trump,"[77] and in his testimony before a House committee in 1890 he declared, "If you get a man like that you could keep him always, under every administration, and be sure the law was obeyed."[78] Thompson was a native of South Carolina, served briefly in the Confederate army, made a wide reputation in the field of education as principal of the Columbia Male Academy (1865–1880) and as an orator. He was state superintendent of education from 1877 to 1882 and made a brilliantly constructive record in this office. Twice elected governor of South Carolina, he resigned in 1886 to become Assistant Secretary of the Treasury, and in 1889 began three years' service as a member of the Civil Service Commission.[79]

Theodore Roosevelt had hoped to become Assistant Secretary of State under Harrison, but reluctantly accepted appointment as a member of the Civil Service Commission in 1889, convinced that his political career was thus brought to an end. He instantly became the dynamic force within the Commission and at the end of a month wrote Lodge, "I have made this Commission a living force. . . ."[80] He brought to it moral fervor, personal independence, physical energy, and a complete willingness to fight a good battle for the merit system. ". . . if any Department," he declared, "makes an attack upon me or upon the Commission I represent I will . . . answer it in public, if it is made in public. I should hold myself derelict in my duty . . . if I did not make public answer to a public attack upon the Commission."[81]

Roosevelt held his commissionship until 1895, half way through the second Cleveland administration. Leadership then passed to another able Commissioner, John R. Proctor, a Kentuckian and an ex-Confederate, who professionally was a geologist. His removal as director of the Kentucky geological survey because he refused to make

---

[76] Grover Cleveland, *Letters* (Nevins ed.), p. 354 (June 29, 1894).
[77] Theodore Roosevelt, *Letters* (Morison ed.), I, 162 (May 16, 1889).
[78] House Report 4038, 51st Cong., 2d sess., p. 91.
[79] *Dictionary of American Biography*, XVIII, 458.
[80] Theodore Roosevelt, *Letters* (Morison ed.), I, 167 (June 29, 1889).
[81] House Report 4038, 51st Cong., 2d sess., p. 150 (Jan. 29, 1891).

a place for the son of the governor attracted national attention and the notice of Theodore Roosevelt, who wrote Carl Schurz, "By the way, I believe I have discovered a first class southern Democrat for Civil Service Commissioner."[82] Proctor served a full decade on the Commission (1893–1903) and won universal praise from the friends of civil service reform. He had a sense of humor and a knack of good-natured ridicule of the spoils system. He was said to have the best qualities of the traditional southern gentleman.[83] Proctor's immediate predecessor, General George D. Johnston, had so seriously obstructed the work of reform that Cleveland was compelled to remove him after a year's service.[84]

McKinley's appointments to the Commission displayed no interest in the vigorous enforcement of the law. When William Gorham Rice, a sincere friend of the merit system, resigned in 1898, the President nominated Mark S. Brewer, a choice described by Charles J. Bonaparte of the National Civil Service Reform League as one of the most deplorable of McKinley's public acts. After Brewer's death in 1901 McKinley appointed a lame-duck Congressman, William A. Rodenberg, who, on February 17, 1900, had voted to strike out the appropriation for the Commission. He resigned in 1902 to campaign successfully for his former seat in the House.[85]

The high level of energy and devotion that was attained from 1889 to 1895 was lost under McKinley despite the presence of Commissioner Proctor. To use the Commission as a haven for lame-duck Congressmen, or for the reward of persons cool to the merit system, was an alarming symptom of indifference in the highest levels. Fortunately three men of courage and conviction covered most of the years from 1883 to 1901—Dorman B. Eaton, Theodore Roosevelt, and John R. Proctor.

The Civil Service Commission, however, was under fire as an administrative device, as well as for performing its duty in enforcing the law. In the course of the 1890 hearings the House committee

[82] Theodore Roosevelt, *Letters* (Morison ed.), I, 318 (May 27, 1893).

[83] *Dictionary of American Biography*, XV, 241. Name also appears occasionally as Procter.

[84] William D. Foulke, *Fighting the Spoilsmen*, p. 104.

[85] Adelbert Bower Sageser, *The First Two Decades of the Pendleton Act: a Study of Civil Service Reform* (Lincoln: University of Nebraska, 1935), pp. 212-13.

raised the issue whether a single commissioner would not be preferable to a bipartisan body. Commissioner Lyman declared himself
opposed to triumvirates as administrative instruments, asserted that
they were less efficient than single administrative heads, and cited
delays due to the inattention of one member of the Commission.[86]
Commissioner Roosevelt testified, "The ideal constitution of an office
of this kind would be to have one commissioner. . . . But I question
very much if under existing circumstances it would be wise to change
the three-headed commission to a single commissioner, because at
present we have a constant struggle to make the public understand
that we are acting in a strictly non-partisan way."[87]

The House committee was not convinced, however, of the value
of a three-man commission. In the course of the hearings, a member
remarked, "I think the public have come to believe that the Commission, previous to the present one, has never been harmonious, and
that the minority man has always been the controlling factor in
the execution of the law."[88] Roosevelt denied the statement so far
as his Commission was concerned, and the matter was not pursued.
When, however, the committee made its report, it recommended
abolition of the Commission, replacing it with a single commissioner
to be appointed by the President with the consent of the Senate.[89]
The bill also proposed two deputy commissioners, appointed in the
same manner, to serve as chief examiner and as secretary of the
Commission respectively. The chief examiner was required not to
belong to the same political party as the commissioner. The bill did
not secure congressional approval.

The introduction of open competitive examinations and tenure
during good behavior occurred in a period of political instability,
the most difficult for success. It was not surprising, therefore, that
there were skeptics who confidently looked forward to the early
demise of the Civil Service Commission, that bills were successively
introduced in Congress to abolish it, and that attacks on the Commission and on its procedures were unremitting. The merit system
nevertheless survived, due in part to the moral fervor of the re-

[86] House Report 4038, 51st Cong., 2d sess., pp. 52-53 (August 11, 1890).
[87] Ibid., pp. 66-67.
[88] Ibid., p. 91.
[89] Ibid., p. iii.

formers and a friendly press, in part to the sheer necessities of administration. Theodore Roosevelt imparted a dynamic energy and fighting qualities that gave the Commission much needed public recognition and that tended to meet offense with counteroffense. During his six years, as he himself declared, he made the Commission a living force. The danger of repeal or of inertia gradually receded. By the end of the century it had ceased, and when the former Civil Service Commissioner became President the experiment was a settled and accepted element of the federal administrative system.

CHAPTER FIFTEEN

The Search for Political

Neutrality

During the years when the United States Civil Service Commission was gaining its early experience and fighting for its own existence against hostile forces, it was engaged in an unceasing battle to free the classified competitive service from the clutches of the party organizations. Both implicitly and explicitly the Pendleton Act accepted the doctrine that clerks and other employees entering the service by open competitive examination should not be subjected to any party responsibility, should be free from party pressure, and, conversely, should not engage actively in party management. The latter expectation was on the whole not difficult to attain.

It was not easy, however, to reverse the practice of many decades by which both parties seized upon the public service as a source of strength in party warfare. Clerks and government agents owing office to party leaders had been expected to recognize their party obligations by active membership in the organization, by canvassing voters and bringing them to the polls, and by contributing to campaign funds. Dereliction in these duties might lead to loss of office; and party defeat meant wholesale retirement to private life.

The Civil Service Act and related legislation stood squarely against this ancient tradition, in principle for both classified and unclassified employees. Three issues were prominent during these years: the restriction of what later came to be known as pernicious political activity, protection against party assessments, and safeguards against arbitrary removals. Progress was made on all fronts, but full victory was hardly achieved.

POLITICAL ACTIVITY

The character of the public service of the federal government prior to 1829 had been neutral with regard to partisan activity, barring exceptions in the customs service and post offices in a few of the larger ports and cities. After 1829 public employees were steadily forced into allegiance to the party in power and were expected to engage freely in politics and to pay assessments to help finance party work.

The fifth fundamental rule in the Civil Service Act laid the cornerstone for the doctrine of political neutrality in the competitive service and for the restriction of offensive political activity. It provided that "no person in the public service is for that reason under any obligations to contribute to any political fund, or to render any political service, and that he will not be removed or otherwise prejudiced for refusing to do so." The sixth fundamental rule prescribed that "no person in said service has any right to use his official authority or influence to coerce the political action of any person or body."[1] This rule was aimed in part at official control of caucuses, party primaries, and nominating conventions. Although the battle against political activity and party assessments was fought out as a single engagement, it will be convenient to deal with each sector separately, beginning with the former.

The explicit terms of the Civil Service Act were designed to protect clerks and other employees from being forced into political work. Although they did not forbid such activity, there was an implicit understanding that persons in the classified service at least should refrain from active partisanship. The Commission was vested with no authority to enforce penalties against any employee who became an active partisan. The heads of departments could make and enforce their own agency regulations, but this operation was outside the terms of the Pendleton Act.

The Commission moved cautiously. In its second annual report, it laid down one basic proposition: that the right of officials and employees to vote and to express their opinions freely was beyond

[1] 22 Stat. 403, sec. 2 (5) and (6) (Jan. 16, 1883).

question. The Commissioners, however, ventured the opinion that in the degree officials "become proscriptive partisans, they forget the proprieties of their position and are likely to become poor public servants."[2]

Presidents were in a stronger position to take the initiative. Hayes had addressed a circular letter to all departments, stating that no officer should be required or permitted to take part in the management of political organizations, caucuses, conventions, or election campaigns—an order that was not taken seriously by his fellow Republicans.[3] Cleveland, on July 14, 1886, issued an executive order warning all officeholders, classified or unclassified, against active participation in politics.[4] Years later the Commission reported that no rule could be applied equally against the two categories and that "its universal and immediate enforcement was found to be impracticable."[5] Late in his presidential career Theodore Roosevelt wrote: "Cleveland was led into absolutely hypocritical professions and conduct both because he made sweeping promises and issued sweeping orders applying to everybody, classified and unclassified alike, and then did not live up to them even as regards the classified places."[6] Roosevelt, as will be noted below, sought to do less, but to execute what was proposed.

The Civil Service Commission gradually stiffened its attitude as it sought for some means to induce less partisanship. It declared flatly in 1890: "The Commission believes that the public service should be divorced from politics," and proposed a new formula. "There is no intent," declared the Commission, "to interfere with the proper political action of public officers, but the Commission holds that no officeholder belonging to a dominant party should act in any way which would cause a scandal or create friction in any office if the person belonged to the party in opposition instead of to the party in power."[7] This Golden Rule of political propriety made little impress upon settled habits.

In 1893 Commissioner Roosevelt personally drew up a new state-

[2] U.S. Civil Service Commission, *Annual Report*, 1884-85, p. 47.
[3] Richardson, *Messages*, VII, 450-51 (June 22, 1877).
[4] U.S. Civil Service Commission, *Annual Report*, 1886-87, pp. 541-42.
[5] *Ibid.*, 1906-1907, p. 8.
[6] Theodore Roosevelt, *Letters* (Morison ed.), VI, 1229 (Sept. 10, 1908).
[7] U.S. Civil Service Commission, *Annual Report*, 1890-91, p. 12.

ment of principle. He withdrew from any substantial restrictions on the unclassified service, merely stating that such officeholders "must not *use their offices to control political movements,* must not neglect their public duties, must not cause public scandal by their activity."[8] His rule for the classified service declared: "A man in the classified service has an entire right to vote as he pleases, and to express privately his opinions on all political subjects; but he should not take an active part in political management or in political campaigns, for precisely the same reasons that a judge, an army officer, a regular soldier, or a policeman is debarred from taking such an active part."[9]

These standards were repeated by Roosevelt in a letter to the Commission in 1902, and in its twenty-fourth annual report the Commission declared that they were practical guides. Enforcement, however, was primarily the duty of department heads and much lack of uniformity resulted.[10] The Commission investigated; the heads acted if they thought appropriate. The trend, however, was steadily toward the elimination of political activity by members of the classified service. In 1904 the Secretary of State told his employees that they were prohibited from such active participation in campaign work as was incompatible with their official duties, and particularly from serving on committees collecting and disbursing political funds. In 1905 the Commissioner of Internal Revenue notified his classified employees that they must "absolutely refrain from political activity." In 1908 the Navy Department ruled that laborers and mechanics in yards or stations would be discharged for political activity.[11]

The Commission became the enforcing agency on June 15, 1907, when President Roosevelt put into the Commission's rules the standard that gradually had taken shape: that persons in the competitive classified service, while retaining the right to vote as they please and to express privately their opinions, "shall take no active part in political management or in political campaigns."[12] The Commission began to rule on such matters as service on political committees, delegates to conventions, political activity and leadership, publication of a partisan newspaper, membership in political clubs, circulation of

---

[8] Theodore Roosevelt, *Letters* (Morison ed.), III, 273-74.
[9] U.S. Civil Service Commission, *Annual Report,* 1893-94, p. 21.
[10] *Ibid.,* 1906-1907, p. 8.
[11] For these and similar agency rules, see *ibid.,* 1906-1907, pp. 55-57.
[12] *Ibid.,* p. 9.

political petitions, and service as election commissioners.[13] Many years later, these and similar prohibited political activities were enacted into law.[14]

By the end of President Roosevelt's second term, the new standard of partisan neutrality in the competitive service was solidly established. There were lapses, to be sure, but the great bulk of the competitive service welcomed protection, and party managers on the whole respected their exclusion from active political participation.

POLITICAL ASSESSMENTS OF OFFICEHOLDERS

Officeholders, high and low, had been subjected to assessments on their salaries since the early days of Jackson's administration.[15] By 1860 both political parties had come to depend heavily upon this source of income. The ethics of the levy and its evil effects upon the public service were condemned by many leading men, but in vain. Collections were lawful, and clerks were helpless.

The return of peace in 1865 brought no change in the custom of party assessments. The Missouri Republican State Committee sent out a circular in 1870 in the following terms.

[*Confidential and Important*]

ST. LOUIS, October 24, 1870.

DEAR SIR: The State Republican committee have great and imperative need of funds at once, to carry the campaign to successful issue. An assessment of one per cent. on the annual gross receipts of your office is therefore called for, and you will please inclose that amount, without delay, to the treasurer, E. S. Rowse, in the envelope inclosed.

This assessment is made after conference with our friends at Washington, where it is confidently expected that those who receive the benefits of Federal appointments will support the machinery that sustains the party which gives them pecuniary benefit and honor. The exigencies are great, and delay or neglect will rightly be construed into unfriendliness to the Administration. We do not look for such a record from you, and you will at once see the propriety and wisdom of the earliest possible attention to the matter.

ISAAC SHEPPARD,
Chairman of Committee.[16]

E. S. ROWSE, *Treasurer.*

[13] *Ibid.*, p. 10.
[14] 53 Stat. 1147 (August 2, 1939).
[15] Leonard D. White, *The Jacksonians*, pp. 332-36.
[16] Carl Schurz, *Speeches, Correspondence and Political Papers*, II, 48-49.

Zachariah Chandler, Secretary of the Interior under Grant, secured the President's endorsement of a letter, which, said Grant,

it has been intended to distribute among Federal officials with the view of soliciting contributions (voluntary ones; for it does not contemplate that any one should be compelled to respond on pain of losing his position) for the laudable purpose of maintaining the organization of the republican party. Money is necessary for this purpose, to buy and distribute documents, print tickets, send speakers into the field, etc., and I do not see that any parties are more directly interested in this than the office holders whose places yield them a compensation of more than $1,000.00 pr. Annum. I understand it is to be distributed to none others.

You may say if you please to the balance of the Cabinet that my views on this subject are as here expressed.[17]

These illustrations well represent the attitude and intent of the party managers. Daniel Webster's judgment, that "nothing can be a greater abuse of official station, or greater misuse of the money paid for public services," went unheeded both in his day and by later generations.[18]

During the 1876 campaign, Rutherford B. Hayes wrote Carl Schurz, "I need hardly assure you that if I ever have charge of an Administration this whole assessment business will go up, 'hook, line and sinker.' "[19] His admonition against the assessment of custom-house officials and of departmental subordinates in 1877, however, was disregarded.[20] In 1880 a request for contributions went out, apparently with Garfield's endorsement.[21]

Nevertheless, the tide of opposition to partisan assessment of office-holders began to secure results after Grant's retirement. Congress already had been persuaded to enact a very moderate restriction, prohibiting executive officers or employees from requesting anything of value from other officers or employees for political purposes, or giving or receiving such.[22] That even this modest ban had some in-

[17] Quoted in Allan Nevins, *Hamilton Fish: The Inner History of the Grant Administration* (New York: Dodd, Mead and Co., 1936), p. 781 (July 2, 1875).

[18] Leonard D. White, *The Jacksonians*, p. 334.

[19] Carl Schurz, *Speeches, Correspondence and Political Papers*, III, 339 (Sept. 15, 1876).

[20] Richardson, *Messages*, VII, 450 (May 26, 1877); *ibid.*, VII, 451 (June 22, 1877).

[21] Harrison Cook Thomas, *The Return of the Democratic Party to Power in 1884* (New York: Columbia University, 1919), pp. 82-88.

[22] 19 Stat. 143, sec. 6 (August 15, 1876).

fluence became evident in the case of General Newton M. Curtis. In 1880 the General had been appointed a Treasury expert to look into suspected customs frauds. He was also elected treasurer of the New York Republican State Committee for the presidential election of 1880, and while holding both offices he received contributions from the New York customhouse employees. At the instance of the National Civil Service Reform League, he was convicted for violation of the act of 1876. Upon appeal to the Supreme Court his conviction was sustained. Chief Justice Waite set forth the philosophy of the act in terms to which little could be added.

The evident purpose of Congress in all this class of enactments has been to promote efficiency and integrity in the discharge of official duties, and to maintain proper discipline in the public service. . . .

A feeling of independence under the law conduces to faithful public service, and nothing tends more to take away this feeling than a dread of dismissal . . . what begins as a request may end as a demand, and . . . a failure to meet the demand may be treated by those having the power of removal as a breach of some supposed duty, growing out of the political relations of the parties. Contributions secured under such circumstances will quite as likely be made to avoid the consequences of the personal displeasure of a superior, as to promote the political views of the contributor,—to avoid a discharge from service, not to exercise a political privilege. . . .

If there were no other reasons for legislation of this character than such as relate to the protection of those in the public service against unjust exactions, its constitutionality would . . . be clear; but there are others . . . equally good. If persons in public employ may be called on by those in authority to contribute from their personal income to the expenses of political campaigns, and a refusal may lead to putting good men out of the service, liberal payments may be made the ground for keeping poor ones in. So, too, if a part of the compensation received for public services must be contributed for political purposes, it is easy to see that an increase of compensation may be required to provide the means to make the contribution, and that in this way the government itself may be made to furnish indirectly the money to defray the expenses of keeping the political party in power that happens to have for the time being the control of the public patronage. . . .[23]

[23] *Ex parte Curtis,* 106 U.S. 371 at 373-75 (1882). Cf. an article by Dorman B. Eaton, "Political Assessments," *North American Review,* CXXXV (1882), 197-219.

The Pendleton Act amplified the 1876 prohibitions against assessments. Members of Congress, executive, judicial, military and naval officers, clerks, and other employees were forbidden to solicit or to receive any assessment for any political purpose from any other officer, clerk, or employee.[24] Solicitation by any person in any public building was prohibited.[25] No employee was subject to penalty for giving or withholding political contributions.[26] No person in the public service was allowed to give any other such person, directly or indirectly, any political contribution.[27] Congress attached severe penalties for violation: upon conviction a fine up to $5,000 or imprisonment up to three years, or both.[28] The Civil Service Commission immediately made a rule (xxiii) that violation of these sections of the Pendleton Act was also good cause for removal.

The provisions of the Civil Service Act relating to political assessments were directed against *all* federal officers and employees, legislative, executive, and judicial. They were not limited to the small number that were then covered into the classified competitive service. The evil was considered by Congress (both in the 1876 and 1883 enactments) to be so serious as to warrant restriction in some measure in all branches of government. There were, however, plenty of loopholes and the problem of enforcement proved almost insurmountable.

The Commission noted in its first annual report that the "influence of old habits and theories affects conduct long after new standards of duty have been accepted" and admitted that "the utility of such rules must in some degree rest in their power as precepts."[29] Nevertheless the Commission recorded in successive annual reports its opinion that the evil was diminishing. In 1885 the Commission wrote that contributions had been many times less despite persistent attempts "to extort money by unjustifiable appeals to the fears and hopes of the clerks. . . ."[30] Two years later the Commission reported, "At the present time all fear of the political assessor has disappeared from among the officers, clerks, and employés of the three branches of the

---

[24] 22 Stat. 403, sec. 11 (Jan. 16, 1883).
[25] *Ibid.*, sec. 12.
[26] *Ibid.*, sec. 13.
[27] *Ibid.*, sec. 14.
[28] *Ibid.*, sec. 15.
[29] U.S. Civil Service Commission, *Annual Report*, 1883-84, p. 8.
[30] *Ibid.*, 1884-85, p. 27.

executive civil-service. They are not now required to endure his hateful presence."[31] By 1890 the Commission was less certain. The prohibitions on assessments, it reported, "while they have not succeeded in entirely stopping the evil, have undoubtedly much abated it." In language probably written by Commissioner Roosevelt, newly arrived on the Commission, it was said: "Weak clerks . . . often feel that they put in jeopardy their places if they do not placate the people soliciting them. As a matter of fact, the Commission believes that there is now but little reason for this fear, but it also believes that the fear exists in a great number of cases, and that many clerks are practically compelled to contribute when they do not wish to. . . ."[32] There was considerable evidence to support this opinion.

Party financiers promptly began to discover ways and means of securing contributions from officeholders without running foul of the penal provisions of the Pendleton Act. One scheme was to form associations, political in character if not in name, and to collect dues for membership. The Commission noted this move in its second annual report. Commissioner Roosevelt exposed such a club in Indianapolis and in a report to the Commission described another, the Old Dominion Republican Club.[33] Another device was to exact money from the federal clubs to be used in aid of *state* elections. The Commission had to admit that this was no violation of the law.[34]

Another evasion was solicitation by mail. During the mid-term campaign of 1894 an agent of the Democratic State Committee of California addressed the following letter to employees of the San Francisco customhouse and post office.

Feeling that as an office holder you are desirous of seeing the present Administration perpetuated, and to that end are anxious that the DEMOCRATIC ticket be successful at the coming election, you are advised that it has been decided to ask of you a subscription toward defraying the expenses of the coming campaign.

It is suggested that an amount equal to two (2) per cent of your yearly salary would be about the sum you should subscribe; and it is

[31] *Ibid.*, 1886-87, p. 143.
[32] *Ibid.*, 1889-90, pp. 23, 24-25.
[33] *Ibid.*, 1884-85, p. 27; Theodore Roosevelt, *Letters* (Morison ed.), I, 302 (Dec. 15, 1892).
[34] U.S. Civil Service Commission, *Annual Report*, 1885-86, p. 23.

trusted that your patriotic sentiments and sound Democracy will prompt you to respond without delay.[35]

The Commission appealed to the Attorney General; he ruled that solicitation by letter was not solicitation within the meaning of the Pendleton Act. "This seems," Richard Olney stated, "to be one of those instances where the personal liberty of the citizen and the inviolability of his private letters have been deemed of higher importance than the complete success of an enactment."[36] The Commission had construed the words "solicit in any manner whatever" to apply to solicitation by letter, and ruefully had to report that in 1894 there had been more solicitation by letter "than in any recent non-Presidential campaign of which the Commission has knowledge."[37] Olney's ruling was reversed in 1902.[38]

Coercion is an elusive term, and it was often difficult to determine whether a contribution was made with a free will or otherwise. The Pittsburgh internal revenue office in 1894 was not under civil service regulations, although controlled by the provisions against assessments. An investigation of the office by the Commission resulted in the following report. "In this office there has been no coercion and no assessment contrary to law. Unquestionably, however, the office in its present condition, being outside the civil-service law, is used as a cog in the machine of whichever party is in power. . . . The men thus appointed have, of course, always been active ward workers—leaders at the primaries and the polls. They have not been assessed or coerced, save by the feeling of their party associates." They were expected, nevertheless, to contribute sums ranging from $35 to $150, amounting in gross to six or seven thousand dollars. "These payments are taken as a matter of course."[39]

An investigation of the Columbus, Ohio, post office in 1895 revealed the culmination of assessment theory and practice. "It was found that it had been for years the practice of many employees, without regard to their party affiliations, to contribute to the campaign

[35] *Ibid.*, 1893-94, p. 22.
[36] *Ibid.*, pp. 116-17.
[37] *Ibid.*, p. 22.
[38] 24 *Opinions of the Attorneys General* 133 (Oct. 17, 1902).
[39] U.S. Civil Service Commission, *Annual Report*, 1893-94, pp. 23-24.

fund of whatever party was in power."[40] The Commission was obviously fighting against a deeply ingrained custom.

What weapons did it possess? Both the act of 1876 and the Pendleton Act specified the courts as the enforcement agency. By implication the prosecution of alleged violations therefore fell to the United States district attorneys. Although they were under the general direction of the Department of Justice, they had always retained considerable discretion in deciding whether to prosecute or not, on the basis of the evidence at hand. Obviously much depended on the temper of the Attorney General and the scores of district attorneys. Results were mixed, and in the early days not promising. Commissioner Roosevelt wrote in 1892, "Until you have been in this position yourself I don't think you can understand the extreme difficulty of getting these cases prosecuted. The district attorneys are as a rule very lukewarm. . . ." Exceptionally the district attorney in Kentucky had secured six indictments. Roosevelt continued, "I don't believe we will be able to get these six men convicted, but we have done well in getting them indicted at all."[41]

The Commission did have full power to investigate, and it exercised this authority vigorously. The Commissioners individually took to the field, held hearings, made reports, and sought to publicize fully any violation of the prohibition against assessments. Roosevelt's investigation of the Baltimore post office during a local election in 1891 was one of the most spectacular. He recommended removal of twenty-five federal officeholders, but neither President Harrison nor Postmaster General Wanamaker took any action. Roosevelt gave interviews to the press and condemned Wanamaker in a speech before the National Civil Service Reform League. The House made an investigation, in the course of which the enforcement power of the Commission came into question.

Postmaster General John Wanamaker had declined to remove any of the men accused by Roosevelt, the post office inspectors having reported that there had been no violation of the law.[42] The following colloquy ensued between the chairman of the committee, Congressman Charles J. Boatner (a civil service man), and Wanamaker.

[40] *Ibid.*, 1895-96, p. 22.
[41] Theodore Roosevelt, *Letters* (Morison ed.), I, 280 (May 7, 1892).
[42] House Report 1669, 52d Cong., 1st sess., p. 14 (April 25, 1892).

MR. BOATNER. Of what use is the Civil Service Commission if the heads of Departments have authority to go behind its reports and direct investigations on their own account? Of what use is it to the Government to authorize the Commission to make these investigations and reports if they are not to be acted upon?

MR. WANAMAKER. This is the first intimation that has ever come to me that the Civil Service Commission, or any other commission, has such control of any Department that it can step in and order the dismissal of employés at its own sweet will, whether they are employés of the Treasury, the Interior, or the Post-Office Department.

MR. BOATNER. Then, what effect do you give to a recommendation or report of this character? Do you consider it merely advisory, or as simply calling attention to the supposed existence of irregularities?

MR. WANAMAKER. It is not the duty of the Civil Service Commission, as I understand it, to make and [sic] report to the head of a Department. I understand that it is responsible to the power of its appointment, and that whenever a notice reaches me from any source, from the Civil Service or any other Commission, that irregularities exist, it is my duty to properly investigate.[43]

Wanamaker's position was upheld by the Assistant Attorney General, James N. Tyner (Grant's Postmaster General). "I do not see how the . . . Commission can consistently call upon the head of any Executive Department to dismiss an officer or employé for a violation of the law until it shall have taken the necessary steps to judicially determine the guilt or innocence of the accused."[44] The Commission was thus thrown back upon the Department of Justice, unless a department head chose to follow the recommendations of the Commission. Some did, and a few cases of judicial prosecution succeeded from time to time.[45]

The principal weapon of the Commission was publicity. Investigations were held for their deterrent effect as well as for punishment, and were often effective. Beyond this the Commission could and did condemn political assessments in its annual reports, which were presumably read at least by members of the civil service. Finally it took the initiative by having circulars posted in public buildings prior to election time, notifying employees of their rights and warning

---

[43] *Ibid.*, p. 10.
[44] *Ibid.*, p. 91 (Opinion of June 15, 1892).
[45] U.S. Civil Service Commission, *Annual Report*, 1896-97, pp. 20-21.

against violation of the law. In July 1892, well before the presidential campaign had opened, the Commission published a general notice calling attention to the law on political assessments, stating that government employees must be left absolutely free to contribute or not to either party, and declaring its intention to secure prosecution of any violators. "The Commission thoroughly understood that its efforts would be liable to criticism, but deemed its duty to be clear, and did not feel it would be right to hesitate because of any hostility it would arouse or misconstruction of motive to which it might be exposed. . . . It did this believing that publicity itself is one of the best weapons with which to fight this evil. The American people have a very hearty contempt for blackmailing, and especially for black-mailing defenseless people. . . ."[46]

The struggle to protect the federal civil servants from political as-sessments was unremitting and complete victory was not achieved during the Republican era. Progress was steady, if slow. The Commis-sion was over optimistic when it reported in 1898 that "this practice, once general, has almost entirely ceased,"[47] but it could claim sub-stantial improvement. The major parties turned to state, county, and municipal employees whose status was more vulnerable, and to other sources of income.

PROTECTION AGAINST ARBITRARY REMOVAL

The original civil service reformers were not greatly concerned about protecting career employees against the removal authority of department heads. They argued that if politicians could not name their henchmen to vacancies caused by removals, the incentive to re-move would be destroyed. Thus George William Curtis: "The re-movals would not be made except for the pressure of politicians. But those politicians would not press for removals if they could not secure the appointment of their favorites. Make it impossible for them to secure appointment, and the pressure would instantly disappear and arbitrary removal cease."[48] The argument of the reform group was on the whole sustained by early experience in the competitive service. An investigation by the National Civil Service Reform League in 1886

[46] *Ibid.*, 1891-92, pp. 3-4.
[47] *Ibid.*, 1897-98, p. 34.
[48] Curtis, *Orations and Addresses*, II, 192 (Sept. 8, 1881).

showed that the removal rate among some 5,000 classified employees was annually about 6½ per cent; in the unclassified service it ranged from 25 per cent in the foreign service to 71 per cent in the Interior Department.[49] The Civil Service Commission, however, believed the situation of the classified service unsafe without statutory protection against unjustifiable removals.

The Commission was warranted in its apprehension by some abuses within the competitive service, but more by the violent play of politics in other areas, the example of which was not conducive to morale within the merit system. Secretary of the Treasury John G. Carlisle, said Roosevelt, was a "mean and underhanded spoilsman . . . viciously dangerous to good government. He has just capped the climax by driving one of the most noted scientific men of the country, Prof. Mendenhall, out of the Coast Survey by the way he has looted and allowed young Logan Carlisle to loot that office for pure spoils purposes."[50] Outright removals were paralleled by party and racial discrimination that was contrary to the spirit, if not the letter, of the Civil Service Act. The Commission reported in 1894 that the most common form of discrimination was to dismiss employees of one political faith for offenses which were allowed to pass unnoticed or with a slight reprimand when committed by employees of the opposite party.[51] In 1897 it gave evidence that the public printer demoted Democrats, and in the Pension Office lists were prepared showing the politics of employees; Democrats were dismissed accordingly. In the fiscal year ending June 30, 1898, there were 857 separations from the classified customs service, as compared with 333 in the previous year.[52] According to Commissioner Roosevelt both the War Department and the Interior, in reduction of force, "discriminated

[49] Report of the Special Committee of the National Civil Service Reform League . . . March 16, 1887, cited in Frank M. Stewart, *The National Civil Service Reform League*, p. 50. About the same proportion of removals prevailed in the departmental service in 1890; according to Roosevelt "a pretty good proof that the law is properly observed." Theodore Roosevelt, *Letters* (Morison ed.) I, 225 (June 11, 1890). While Attorney General (1893-95), Richard Olney wrote, "The rule of the Department, since my connection with it, has been not to ask for removals on political grounds." Henry James, *Richard Olney and His Public Service* (Boston: Houghton Mifflin Co., 1923), p. 26 (Dec. 12, 1894).

[50] Roosevelt, *Letters* (Morison ed.), I, 387-88 (June 25, 1894).

[51] U.S. Civil Service Commission, *Annual Report*, 1893-94, p. 20.

[52] Adelbert B. Sageser, *The First Two Decades of the Pendleton Act*, pp. 214-215.

a great deal because of politics, and still more because of color. In the War Department they have turned out about two-thirds of the young colored men who came in through our examinations during the past three or four years."[53]

In the unclassified service political removals were as much the rule after 1883 as before. In the first sixteen months of Cleveland's first term, 90 per cent of the presidential officers and 68 per cent of the unclassified employees of the Interior Department were removed. Nearly a clean sweep occurred among the fourth-class postmasters.[54] The majority report of the Senate investigating committee of 1888 declared that partisan changes had been made in the federal offices in a wholesale way; the Democratic minority replied in substance, cast out the beam in thine own eye.[55] The National Civil Service Reform League looked into the postmasters in 1890. Over 64 per cent of the presidential postmasters had been changed during the first year of the Harrison administration. Out of 356 cases of removal, reasons were given only in 47 instances. The League denounced removal on secret charges as "inquisitional in its character, and totally inconsistent with republican institutions and with our present civilization," and as encouraging falsehood and slander. Out of 437 cases, the postmaster removed or resigned was a Democrat in 427 instances. Among 513 new appointees, 510 were Republicans.[56]

The collector of internal revenue at Baltimore was more polite, and more candid, than many officers in authority. On May 11, 1887, he addressed the following letter to an unfortunate clerk.

To whom it may concern:
It affords me great pleasure to be able to certify to the fact that my intercourse with Mr. Lewis N. Rollins, former clerk of this office under Mr. John H. Sellman, formerly collector and my predecessor, was of the most pleasant and satisfactory character and such as to enable me to ascertain that he was a most conscientious and efficient officer, and a gentleman of the strictest integrity and honor.

He was requested to resign his position by me for no fault whatever, save that we differed politically, thus coming under the old rule that "to the victor belongs the spoils."

[53] Theodore Roosevelt, *Letters* (Morison ed.), I, 394 (August 14, 1894).
[54] Carl R. Fish, *The Civil Service and the Patronage*, p. 222.
[55] Senate Report 2373, 50th Cong., 1st sess., pp. 46-47 (Oct. 10, 1888).
[56] Frank M. Stewart, *The National Civil Service Reform League*, pp. 55-56.

I can commend Mr. Rollins with confidence to anyone who may desire the services of a faithful and efficient employé.

J. K. Roberts
Collector District of Maryland[57]

Whether executive power to remove subordinates in the competitive service should be restricted, and by what means was long a disputed point. The reform group was sensitive to the administrative responsibility of department heads and was reluctant to tie their hands in removing incompetent subordinates. Congress tended to take the same view. "Where a clerk is deemed by his immediate superior to be inefficient, it is clearly in the line of public policy that that clerk should be discharged, and there should be no impediments placed in the way of such a discharge except such as may be necessary to secure justice to the person removed."[58]

The view of many executive officers was expressed by Secretary of the Treasury George S. Boutwell. "It is essential to a proper administration," he wrote, "that the Secretary or the President should have the power of removal, and it should never be coupled with the duty of making a statement of the cause. Not infrequently a statement would be the occasion of scandal and of suffering by innocent parties."[59]

This position was taken also by President Grover Cleveland, who declined to approve a proposed rule requiring a statement of cause of removal to be filed in the departmental records. Cleveland found no authority in the Civil Service Act to sustain such a rule, and he also objected on principle. "If reasons are placed on file and are subject to examination the most violent disputes will be engendered . . . as to the truth and force of the causes alleged. If such reasons are not subject to examination it will immediately be claimed that they were suppressed because insufficient and insincere." He argued also that the discharged employee should not be unnecessarily handicapped in his search for other employment. He stated further that the proposed rule was based on the presumption of bad faith on the part of removing officers. "I am unwilling," he wrote, "to do by rule what

---

[57] Senate Report 2373, 50th Cong., 1st sess., Part 3, p. 116.
[58] Senate Report 659, 55th Cong., 2d sess., p. 7 (March 9, 1898).
[59] George S. Boutwell, *Reminiscences of Sixty Years in Public Affairs* (2 vols., New York: McClure, Phillips and Co., 1902), II, 135.

the law did not do, to wit, put officers of my own selection, in whom I have generally the utmost confidence ... in a hampered, suspected, and discredited position."[60]

The Civil Service Commission, nevertheless, consistently recommended a rule requiring a statement of cause for removal to be made a part of the departmental record. Commissioner Roosevelt argued in 1890 for a departmental hearing, and in 1891 for power in the Commission to investigate any charge of removal for political reasons.[61] In 1897 President McKinley amended the civil service rules to provide protection against unjust removal of classified employees, in the following language:

No removal shall be made from any position subject to competitive examination except for just cause and upon written charges filed with the head of the department or other appointing officer, and of which the accused shall have full notice and an opportunity to make defense.[62]

The Commission welcomed this rule as one of the most important orders since the enactment of the law. A similar rule had applied to letter carriers in 1894. In that year the percentage of removals was four; it fell in the immediately succeeding years to 3 per cent, 2.1 per cent, and 1.06 per cent.[63] Under the McKinley order some delinquent employees quickly sought to secure judicial review of official removal decisions, but the courts declined to take cognizance. On May 29, 1902, President Roosevelt issued an order clarifying the term "just cause." It was intended, he determined, to mean any cause (other than political or religious) which would promote the efficiency of the service, and did not require examination of witnesses or any trial or hearing.[64]

To complete the story, it may be added that the Lloyd-La Follette Act of 1912 wrote these and related provisions into law. Removal was required to be made only to promote the efficiency of the service; the employee was entitled to notice and charges, and a reasonable time for answering them in writing and submitting affidavits; no examination of witnesses or hearing was required, but the proceedings were made part of the departmental records. The Commission could

[60] House Report 4038, 51st Cong., 2d sess., p. 59.
[61] Ibid., pp. 74, 161.
[62] U.S. Civil Service Commission, Annual Report, 1896-97, p. 24.
[63] Ibid., p. 24.
[64] Ibid., 1901-1902, pp. 18-19.

ask for copies, but without right of hearing an appeal. Membership in certain civil service associations was declared not to constitute ground for removal.[65]

This enactment left authority in agency heads, subject to procedure designed to ensure orderly methods and protection against arbitrary and indefensible action by supervisors. It allowed no appeal to either the Civil Service Commission or the courts. It was a compromise between those who insisted upon "an open back door" and those who would have closed the door in varying degrees. On the whole it sustained both the views of most of the early civil service reformers and of most agency heads.

Where, then, did the public service stand in 1900 as compared with the unreformed service of 1880? So far as the competitive classified service was concerned, it was under an obligation, formally stated by Commissioner Roosevelt in 1893, to refrain from taking an active part in political management. Persons in the unclassified service were not to use their offices to control political movements, nor to cause public scandal by their activity, nor to neglect their public duties. Both branches of the service were declared free of coercion to pay party assessments, the collection of which by members of the public service or by any one in public buildings was forbidden. In 1897 it was ordered that removal should be made only for just cause and upon written charges with an opportunity to make a written reply.

Statutory enactments and executive orders laid legal foundations for the long struggle to achieve political neutrality and protection from party domination of the classified competitive service. The objective was fought by party managers and there was much evasion of the new standards. Gradually, however, by dint of strenuous work by the Civil Service Commission, notably when Theodore Roosevelt was one of its members, by constant pressure from the National Civil Service Reform League and friendly sections of the press, and by the emerging sense of security in the competitive service, the force of old habits diminished. A politically neutral public service was well in process of formation by 1900. It was to be notably strengthened by the succession of three Presidents committed to a new type of public service: Theodore Roosevelt, William Howard Taft, and Woodrow Wilson.

[65] 37 Stat. 539, sec. 6 (August 24, 1912).

CHAPTER SIXTEEN

The Emergence of a New
Personnel System

The establishment of the United States Civil Service Commission marked a new era in the growth of the federal personnel system. Although the Commission was not thinking in terms much beyond fighting spoils and protecting its own position, it was nevertheless compelled to initiate procedures that were gradually to form the core of a service-wide personnel program. That it was still embryonic did not destroy its significance.

There had been an elementary personnel system since the earliest days of the Republic. Prior to 1883 it comprised a statutory framework, a few presidential directives, and much responsibility in the heads of departments to work out their own practices. The statutory skeleton included the pay structure for the clerical staff, enacted in 1853 in conformity with earlier practice; the requirement of pass examinations for the departmental clerks, also enacted in 1853; an established workday; and a number of minor miscellaneous provisions. The pay structure was firm and controlled by the auditing officers; the character of the pass examinations was variable; and the enforcement of hours of work a departmental responsibility.

The President had great potential but relatively little actual influence on the system. He had constitutional authority to nominate a considerable number of officers, high and low, for Senate confirmation, but this was an operation that he could not modify. The most important recognition of his role was the legislation of 1871 authorizing him to make rules and regulations for the admission of persons into the civil service and to establish regulations for the conduct of public employees. This authority had been exercised by Grant, but had been suspended in the face of congressional opposition, although it remained on the statute book. The Pendleton Act again vested rule-making power in the President to implement the new civil service legislation. Presidents also had undoubted authority to advise and direct heads of departments as to employment matters, but there is scanty evidence that they did so. Secretaries were allowed to manage their own official affairs. Indeed, when President Hayes issued his instructions forbidding political assessments—presumably a directive to every department head—no one paid much attention.

Within the statutory framework the principal responsibility for the employment and management of subordinate staffs was vested in the heads of departments. By long-standing enactment the head of each department was authorized to prescribe regulations for the government of his department, the conduct of its officers and clerks, the distribution and performance of its business, and the custody, use, and preservation of its records, papers, and property.[1] The appointment of clerks, their assignment to duty, their transfer from office to office, their promotion, discipline, and removal were matters strictly within the range of departmental authority.

The Civil Service Act of 1883 introduced a new agency, external to the departments. In establishing the Civil Service Commission Congress did not, however, set up an independent organization, or one competing with the President. The Chief Executive was authorized to remove Commissioners, who served without term. The rules of the Commission required approval by the President, and throughout its history it has sought and taken the directions of the White House on policy matters. The Chief Executive thus remained the head of the personnel system, but was now endowed with a staff agency to assist him.

ENTRANCE EXAMINATIONS

From 1883 to 1901 the activity of the Civil Service Commission was directed primarily toward the examination and certification of applicants for admission to the federal classified service. Its authority in this field was a direct curtailment of the freedom of department heads to appoint whom they chose, although a restriction often welcomed as relief from political importunity.

[1] Revised Statutes, sec. 161.

The Commission gave two grades of examination for the ordinary departmental clerkships: the general examination and the limited examination. The former included nothing beyond the teaching of a good public school; the latter tested even more limited attainments, little except penmanship, capacity to spell ordinary words, and ability to apply the elementary rules of arithmetic. These examinations were held for clerical appointments in all the departments in Washington, and were the first evidence of recognition of a service-wide corps. Departmental examinations were offered for grades above ordinary clerkships in the State Department, Patent Office, Pension Office, Geological Survey, the Signal Office, and other establishments. The general clerical examination was supplemented for special appointments requiring a knowledge of law, medicine, stenography, typewriting, bookkeeping, and the modern languages. Questions appropriate to the various grades in the customhouses and post offices were prepared in Washington and administered in the field.[2]

The intellectual level of the early examinations was modest. The Commission was under constant attack as an agency for setting up a college-trained aristocracy. In fact the two basic examinations were firmly anchored to the common schools, as sample questions proved. In the general examination held in 1883 the following questions appeared.

Write below, at length, the names of fifteen States and fifteen cities of the Union.

Divide three-fourths of eight-ninths by one-seventh of three-fifths and subtract one-seventh from the quotient.

Give a definition as full as the space will allow of (1) a verb; (2) a noun; (3) an adverb; (4) an adjective; (5) a preposition; (6) a conjunction; and of (7) the phrase, "the grammar of the English language."

Write a letter, addressing it to the President and giving your views, as far as you are willing to express them, in regard to the duties and responsibilities of an officer in the public service which you seek to enter.

What is meant in our history, (1) by the Colonial period; (2) by the Continental Congress; (3) by the Declaration of Independence; (4) by the Emancipation Proclamation?[3]

The Commission deliberately based its general clerical examinations at this elementary level. In its first annual report the Com-

[2] U.S. Civil Service Commission, *Annual Report*, 1885-86, pp. 11-14.

[3] *Ibid.*, 1883-84, pp. 62-63. Subsequent annual reports reprinted sample questions year by year.

mission declared: "In none of these branches do the questions go further than is covered by the ordinary instruction in the common schools of the country." Of the limited test, less inclusive than the general examination, it reported: "The common-school education must have been exceedingly defective which does not enable one to pass this examination."[4] The Commission boldly defended the common school basis for the general and limited examinations, as being both adequate and democratic.

If any shall notice with regret that only common-school education is exacted for entering the public service at the higher grade, and that thus only a small direct reward is offered to academic and college learning, it may be remembered, on the other hand, that both by rewarding excellence in the common schools and by barring out corrupt influence from public office, learning of every grade, and good character and manly effort in every position are stimulated and strengthened. The common schools are the gates to the academies and the academies are the gates to the colleges.

It should always be a paramount object to keep the public service freely open to as many of the people as have the ability and information needed for doing its work. . . . And though the higher education is not necessary in order to gain admission to the public service, it will nevertheless prove its value in the mastery of the principles and methods of that service, and so gain higher consideration, and give increased power to those who possess it.[5]

The record of examinations for 1885–86 substantiated the predominance of the public school product. In the general examinations for this year, 7,138 candidates participated. Of these, 6,053 were from the public schools and 327 from business colleges, which, said the Commission, were more like high schools than colleges. The remainder, 758, claimed part college education.[6] "This," said the Commission, "is the answer to the often repeated charge that the merit system of office gives a monopoly to literary and college-bred men, and therefore favors an aristocracy."[7] The situation had not substantially changed in 1900. Analysis of 1,477 appointments in the classified competitive departmental service in Washington in the fiscal year 1900–1901 resulted in an estimate that not over 200

[4] *Ibid.*, pp. 20-21.
[5] *Ibid.*, p. 21.
[6] *Ibid.*, 1885-86, p. 8.
[7] *Ibid.*, p. 66.

appointments required more than a secondary school education, principally engineers (122) and physicians (41).

The first fundamental rule prescribed by the Pendleton Act required that examinations should be practical in their character and so far as possible should relate to matters which would fairly test relative capacity and fitness to discharge the duties of the service in which employment was sought.[8] The examinations offered by the Civil Service Commission for nearly forty years were readily defensible as "practical" and as related to the work to be done. The Commission, nevertheless, was subject to much criticism as to the practicality of its tests. In 1898 the chief examiner declared: "If one-tenth of the stories in circulation as to the questions that are asked in civil service examinations were true, I think the chief examiner and all of his 25 or 35 assistant examiners ought to be occupants of St. Elizabeth's [a hospital for the insane] instead of being allowed to go free."[9] Commissioner Roosevelt was a strong advocate of practical tests. Great was his disgust when he failed to secure agreement on an examination for cattle inspectors consisting of tests in brand reading, shooting, riding mean horses, and roping and throwing steers.[10]

The rule of practicality not only governed the character of the questions, it also tended to emphasize experience rather than education and thus to encourage high age limits to enable those with long experience to compete. At the close of the century the general age requirement for the departmental service was a minimum of twenty years, and no maximum. For the large block of postal employees, a minimum of eighteen and a maximum of forty-five was established, and for rural letter carriers, seventeen and fifty-five.[11] There was obviously no relation between school-leaving age and examination age.

In practice, however, the examinations tended to attract younger persons, with perhaps five to ten years experience after graduation. The average age of successful competitors in the general clerical examination of 1886–87 was 27.4; in that of bookkeeper, 33.2; and in that of customs examiners, 35.9. Postal clerks and carriers, however, averaged between 24 and 25 years of age.[12] These distributions were remarkably

---

[8] 22 Stat. 403, sec. 2 (Jan. 16, 1883).

[9] Senate Report 659, 55th Cong., 2d sess., p. 464 (Jan. 13, 1898).

[10] *Theodore Roosevelt: An Autobiography* (New York: Macmillan Co., 1913; 1920 printing, Charles Scribner's Sons), p. 143.

[11] U.S. Civil Service Commission, *Annual Report*, 1899-1900, p. 66.

[12] *Ibid.*, 1886-87, p. 33.

stable. Corresponding figures for 1895–96 showed the average age of the successful eligible for clerk copyist to be 28; for bookkeeper, 26; for postal clerks, 24; and for postal carriers, 26.[13] These figures are significant because they reveal that the government was attracting persons at an age when they still had their lifework before them. A career service was taking form behind the bulwark of competitive examinations and tenure.

The Commission had little reliable evidence concerning the quality of its examinations. It assumed that they eliminated the unfit and it had faith that the most competent earned the highest grades, a faith justified in part by the satisfaction of department and bureau heads with the eligible lists. A more sophisticated view was expressed by President Harrison: "The examination paper is not an infallible test of fitness for these clerical positions; but it is a better test than mere party service, and perhaps the best that can be devised."[14] It was a full generation before the art and science of test construction was introduced into the Civil Service Commission.

The Commission had no staff to supervise the examinations or to rate the papers, and depended upon employees detailed from the departments and field offices for this task. A single board did the work for the general and special clerical examinations in Washington; customs and post office boards operated in the large field establishments; and boards were appointed *ad hoc* for Patent Office examiners and other technical positions. Their members were carefully designated by the Civil Service Commission, "to secure gentlemen of candor, good judgment, and conscientiousness, united with a high order of intelligence and practical experience."[15]

The primary significance of the examination system was its role in

[13] *Ibid.*, 1895-96, at pp. 175, 176, 222, and 223 respectively.

[14] Benjamin Harrison, *This Country of Ours*, pp. 297-98.

[15] U.S. Civil Service Commission, *Annual Report, 1883-84*, p. 18. "Examinations of a technical or scientific character are held only when vacancies exist, and such examinations are announced through the newspapers. . . . The following is a list of such positions: Computer, botanist, chemist, astronomer, architectural draftsman, civil engineer, nautical expert, microscopist, ornithologist, editorial clerk, anatomist, climatologist, pomologist, entomologist, horticulturalist, vegetable pathologist, forestry clerk, photographer, librarian and bibliographer, chart corrector, cartographic draftsman, and mechanical engineer." U.S. Civil Service Commission, *Manuals and Schedules of Examinations*, I (1886-96), 11 (1895). Applicants for these positions were examined in the standard subjects, orthography, copying, letterwriting, arithmetic, and the elements of geography, history, and government, as well as their specialties.

replacing political and personal favoritism as the criterion for appointment to the government service. An important and direct corollary was to establish the democratic rule of equal right of all qualified citizens to demonstrate their fitness and ability for the public service irrespective of party affiliation. Another corollary was the recognition of tenure during good behavior instead of tenure dependent on the continued success of the party in power. Finally, the examination system laid the foundation for the concept of a government-wide public service in lieu of one in which employees were bound to a single department or field establishment. Many years were to pass before this view of the public service was generally held or put into operation, but here was its origin.

PROMOTIONAL EXAMINATIONS

The Civil Service Commission encountered relatively little resistance from the departments and the large field establishments to entrance examinations, despite some complaints that bright schoolboys outranked their more experienced elders.[16] Quite different was their reaction to an effort by the Commission to impose upon them an examination procedure for promotions. This episode, coming to a crisis in 1887, provided early evidence of a long-continued struggle for authority between the Commission and the operating agencies.

The Civil Service Act declared that no officer or clerk should be promoted in the classified service until he had passed an examination or been shown to be specially exempted from this requirement.[17] In its first annual report the Commission addressed itself to this field of potential activity.

The difference between the value of competitive examinations for admission and for promotion is plain enough. The applicant for original entrance to the service is a stranger to the head of the office and ignorant of its duties. But those who seek promotion are well known to the head of the bureau or office. . . . They are seeking places of authority where

[16] Cf. the collector of customs at Baltimore, "an undue proportion of those who passed with high averages are school teachers or very young men without business knowledge or experience." U.S. Civil Service Commission, *Annual Report,* 1886-87, p. 477; and the collector at San Francisco, "I am furnished . . . a set of young men, some of them yet in school or just graduated therefrom, and of school teachers, some of them poor ones at that. . . ." *Ibid.,* p. 481.

[17] 22 Stat. 403, sec. 7.

discretion, a sense of justice, facility in arranging and dispatching business, capacity for discipline and for command are not only the most essential qualifications, but are the most difficult of all to be tested by examinations.

Yet there are parts of the service in which examination for promotion may be of great advantage.

The principal causes of unjust promotions, in the absence of examinations, are (1) importunate solicitations and coercive influence from the outside; and (2) prejudice, favoritism, or corruption on the part of the appointing officers. We need not stop to inquire which class of these abuses is the most frequent or pernicious. . . .[18]

The Commission obviously believed it had a mission to perform. It made its first move in the New York customs district, which already had considerable experience.[19] Under authority of the act of 1871 the Treasury had instituted promotional examinations for subordinate personnel in this leading port. They were discontinued in 1875, but revived by Hayes on March 6, 1879. After 1883 they were administered by the local board of examiners appointed by the Civil Service Commission. Results were unsatisfactory, and late in 1886 the Commission took direct charge and, under authority of President Cleveland's order of January 4, 1887,[20] required all persons in the grade immediately below a pending vacancy to be examined, willy-nilly, and certified the whole list of eligibles to the collector.[21]

The Commission was pleased with the results.

The compulsory-examination feature of the regulations of 1887 has had a good effect. It has aroused into activity, mental and official, employés who, it may be stated without inexactness, were dormant in their places; has required them to exercise their minds in the acquisition of knowledge that is necessary to the competent discharge of their duties; and has incited them to interest in the affairs and functions of the offices in which they are serving. It has also discovered flagrant incompetency in some of the employés, and in others shameful ignorance of the duties of the places held by them and their unfitness in every way for the service they encumber. It has resulted in clearing out of the service at least some of this incompetency, ignorance, and unfitness.[22]

[18] U.S. Civil Service Commission, *Annual Report*, 1883-84, pp. 27-28.
[19] *Ibid.*, 1886-87, pp. 73 ff.
[20] Richardson, *Messages*, VIII, 572.
[21] U.S. Civil Service Commission, *Annual Report*, 1886-87, p. 83.
[22] *Ibid.*, p. 83.

Encouraged by this success, the Commission prevailed on President Cleveland to authorize it to make regulations for promotional examinations in the several departments, customhouses, and post offices.[23] Under this authority the Commission promulgated its regulations on the following day, May 6, 1887. They required a departmental examination board, compulsory examination of all persons in the class immediately below the vacancy, and an efficiency rating. The passing grade was set at 75 and the Commission certified the whole of the resulting register.[24]

Events demonstrated that the Commission had moved onto untenable ground. Although one promotional examination was held in the War Department, the Commission had to record that its other imperative duties prevented extension of the new system.[25] This admission told only part of the story, for the Commission encountered opposition from the departments and the customhouses. The character of this resistance is evident from the views of the collectors of customs, three of whom may speak for all. Leverett Saltonstall, collector at Boston, wrote: "Promotions here are made with great care. . . . I should regret extremely to be compelled to make them according to the result of examinations. Promotions are due to earnestness, zeal, and fidelity, which may not be shown as a result of competitive examinations."[26] The Baltimore collector, James B. Groome, informed the Commission that within his small force the principal clerks could best advise him which employees had the greatest claim for promotion on the ground of "clerical ability, industry, sobriety, courtesy of manner, pure morals, and length of service."[27]

Benjamin F. Jonas, collector at New Orleans, struck at the underlying problem. He declared his opposition "for the additional reason that the proposed regulations would be a further abridgment of the appointing power, already circumscribed, and in a great measure deprive the appointing officer of the means of rewarding by promotion deserving employés, of whose ability and qualifications he must be the best judge."[28]

[23] Richardson, *Messages*, VIII, 576 (May 5, 1887).
[24] U.S. Civil Service Commission, *Annual Report, 1886-87*, pp. 88-89.
[25] *Ibid.*, p. 91.
[26] *Ibid.*, p. 471.
[27] *Ibid.*, p. 475.
[28] *Ibid.*, p. 487.

The Commission made a second effort in 1896, with somewhat greater success. Cleveland now directed, in a revision of the civil service rules, that competitive tests should be established for promotion, "as far as practicable and useful"; authorized the Commission to negotiate with the departments on detailed plans; directed the department heads to promulgate agreed plans and gave the Commission a veto on any alterations; and empowered the Commission to designate agency promotion boards upon nomination of their heads.[29] The balance of authority over promotion procedure still remained in the departments, although they were now subject to heavier pressure from the Commission.

The issue of promotional examinations and of efficiency records was in the air, and many bureaus and offices were prepared to experiment. Subsequent to the order of May 6, 1896, the Commission negotiated comprehensive agreements with the Navy Department, Agriculture, and the Post Office, approved lesser arrangements with other agencies, and introduced a formal system for its own staff.[30] The role of the Commission was primarily to energize these agencies to develop their own plans; it could not impose a system upon them, nor could the President in fact go beyond the limits of what the departments thought practical and useful.

The nature of the new promotional system was well illustrated by the regulations approved for the Department of Agriculture.[31] In principle all vacancies above those of the lowest class were filled by promotion (unless by reinstatement, transfer, or reduction); a departmental board of promotion certified to the Secretary the names of the three persons in the class immediately below the vacancy with the highest efficiency records, provided they were not less than 85. The chief clerk of each bureau was made responsible for assigning efficiency ratings, on forms prescribed by the Commission after consultation with the Secretary. The ratings were used as the basis for all promotions, demotions, and continuations on the rolls of the Department. The Commission, however, reserved the right to require such further tests as it might deem necessary, and itself fixed the time for promotional examinations.

[29] Richardson, *Messages*, IX, 710 (May 6, 1896).
[30] U.S. Civil Service Commission, *Annual Report*, 1895-96, pp. 120-46.
[31] *Ibid.*, pp. 127-28 (Dec. 1, 1896).

Experience soon demonstrated two fatal faults in this procedure. The efficiency ratings proved unreliable, for reasons suggested below; and there was an absence of uniform clerical standards in the hierarchy of grades that made a rational system of promotion impossible to attain. The Commission formally recognized this handicap in 1902. ". . . before there can be a uniform system of promotion upon merit there must be a reclassification based upon the character of the work done."[32] This observation was so well-founded that the Commission in effect withdrew from the attempt to work out a consistent and controlled scheme of promotion procedures. It reported:

> . . . no further action has been taken by the Commission for the amendment of the promotion regulations. The matter has been left to each department to work out its own system, nominally under the regulations promulgated. There has, however, been a wide difference in the method of enforcing such regulations. In some of the departments they have been entirely ignored, while in others there has been either a partial or nominal compliance with the regulations. The result, however, shows that in most cases promotion regulations under existing conditions are far from satisfactory. . . .[33]

EFFICIENCY RECORDS

With his characteristic energy and confidence, Carl Schurz introduced one of the first formal efficiency records, if not the first, in the government service—in the Pension Office of the Interior Department. "We can ascertain," he wrote to E. L. Godkin in 1879, "with almost mathematical certainty the proportion of work done by each clerk in the Pension Office in point of quantity as well as quality, the number of claims disposed of and the accuracy of the work. . . . When the efficiency record is before me, those who have done the most and the best work are promoted, and those who have fallen behind are reduced. This system has proved to be a powerful stimulus, and the result is that almost every one in the Pension Office does his utmost."[34]

The initiative taken by Schurz was a lonely token of later, long-delayed developments. Indeed an efficiency rating system was

[32] *Ibid.*, 1901-1902, p. 23.
[33] *Ibid.*, 1901-1902, p. 22.
[34] Carl Schurz, *Speeches, Correspondence and Political Papers*, III, 490-91 (Dec. 7, 1879).

anomalous in a public service in which tenure depended primarily on partisan and personal connections. The case for an efficiency record made sense only after the enactment of the Pendleton Act in 1883. Discussion of such ratings began soon thereafter and earned presidential support from Benjamin Harrison in 1891.

The immediate objective was less to stimulate clerical exertion than to find a rational means of arranging promotion on the basis of merit and competence rather than on favoritism. Harrison informed Congress in his annual message of December 9, 1891, that he had directed the departments to establish an efficiency record in order to place the troublesome matter of promotions upon a just basis.[35] As already noted, this was the view also held by the Civil Service Commission.

In response to these directions, various projects were started by the departments and bureaus. They may be illustrated by a few examples. The Department of the Interior required each office and bureau head to keep a record of outstanding clerks and of incompetent clerks, noting the special traits of versatility, adaptability, scholastic requirements, and directed power.[36] The Weather Bureau kept a record of employee attendance, punctuality, deportment, and efficiency, and appointed a board to pass on disputes over these matters.[37] The Pension Office rated punctuality, attendance, industry, aptitude, accuracy, conduct, and ability.[38] In no two departments were the efficiency rating systems alike, nor did the Civil Service Commission have any responsibility for them.

It is clear, however, that the Commission was willing to move into this area of an emerging personnel system. The new promotional regulations issued by Cleveland on May 6, 1896, were soon followed by Commission regulations requiring each department to furnish it the office record of every applicant for promotion "from which the relative efficiency of competitors shall be ascertained." Although the context is not conclusive, apparently the Commission intended to perform this delicate task. It recognized, however, that the procedure

[35] Richardson, *Messages*, IX, 207 (Dec. 9, 1891); Executive Order of Dec. 4, 1891, *ibid.*, IX, 180.
[36] House Doc. 231, 54th Cong., 1st sess., p. 1; departmental order of April 23, 1894.
[37] Secretary of Agriculture, *Annual Report*, 1894, p. 82.
[38] Commissioner of Pensions, *Annual Report*, 1892, p. 13.

was hardly feasible at the moment and discreetly added a proviso that until such records were available, the efficiency rating could be omitted.[39]

The achievements of the following years were discouraging. The Commission took no further initiative, and the departmental systems soon began to show characteristic difficulties. At the close of the period, the Commission recorded substantial defeat, both for itself and the whole movement for efficiency records.

. . . . The elaborate system of efficiency ratings and records, based, as it necessarily must be, upon the individual opinion of the officer giving the marks, has become little more than the mathematically expressed opinion of such officer as to the relative standing of the clerks under his supervision. In nearly all cases the clerk at the head of the list receives a rating of 100, and the remainder of the list is graded by differences of two-tenths of 1 per cent in the standing of each clerk, the head of each division in the great majority of cases giving the highest ratings possible in order to put the clerks in his division ahead of or at least on an equal plane with the clerks of other divisions in the same bureau or department.[40]

Forces were at work on the process of rating clerks that Schurz did not foresee when he praised the almost mathematical certainty of his efficiency records, and that Harrison underrated when he founded a promotional system on them. The problem of consistency of ratings as between agencies hardly arose. Consistency among the bureaus of a single agency was a problem, and no means had been invented either within agencies or by the President and the Civil Service Commission to secure consistency or to curb interoffice competition. These early efforts to lay a firm cornerstone for this aspect of a well-rounded personnel system thus came to naught. The forms persisted even though their usefulness was frequently denied.

SALARY CLASSIFICATION

In another area the Civil Service Commission made greater progress in laying down service-wide standards, the salary classification of subordinate employees. The classes of departmental clerical employees in effect in 1883 were those established by Congress in 1853. A class one

[39] U.S. Civil Service Commission, *Annual Report, 1895-96*, p. 121 (June 22, 1896).
[40] *Ibid.*, 1901-1902, pp. 22-23.

clerk in 1853 was paid $900 a year; class two, $1,200; class three, $1,500; and class four, $1,800.[41] These classes were incorporated by reference in the Civil Service Act of 1883 and entrance to them was made subject to open competitive examination. From time to time the departments created new classes of positions, so that the original fourfold system was overlaid with a confusing variety of categories, whose examination status was often uncertain.

In its annual report for 1886–87, the Civil Service Commission declared that the several classifications existing in the departments were indefinite and unmethodical, and lacked the uniformity essential to an impartial and wise execution of the Civil Service Act and rules.[42] The Commission complained that as a consequence the civil service rules were one thing in one department and something else in another: a telegrapher could be appointed without examination in the Navy Department but had to be examined in War, due to different "class" assignments.[43]

The Commission accordingly recommended a new uniform departmental classification incorporating the four statutory classes, adding five others below the annual salary of $1,200, and one at the rate of $2,000 or higher. President Cleveland accepted this revision, which became effective in 1888.[44]

By this reform the Civil Service Commission achieved more than one objective. Its stated purpose was uniformity, but since the new classes fell under its jurisdiction, it also won a substantial extension of the merit system. "In this way," the Commission had declared in proposing the scheme, ". . . the clamorous demands for unclassified places, that now daily fill the ears of the appointing officers of those departments in which there are such places, would be hushed, and all persons seeking employment in the departmental service would thus be notified that influence had lost its power. . . ."[45] These classes, it will be understood, were based merely on salary levels and

[41] 10 Stat. 189, sec. 3 (March 3, 1853).
[42] U.S. Civil Service Commission, *Annual Report,* 1886-87, p. 116.
[43] *Ibid.,* p. 117.
[44] Richardson, *Messages,* VIII, 763 (March 21, 1888); U.S. Civil Service Commission, *Annual Report,* 1887-88, p. 42. This uniform grading of offices was in due course of time itself supplemented by exceptions; simplicity was hard to attain or protect.
[45] *Ibid.,* 1886-87, p. 119.

had no necessary relation to duties. They were, however, classes in the sense of the coverage of the Civil Service Act.

APPORTIONMENT

At one point the Civil Service Commission scored a notable victory, in enforcing the apportionment requirement of the Pendleton Act. By its terms appointments to the departments in Washington had to be apportioned among the states and territories upon the basis of their respective populations. This statutory provision confirmed an informal practice that began before the Civil War.[46] Procedure before 1883 was described in an illuminating passage in the second annual report of the Commission.

Under the old system a certain share of all the places was, with some rough measure of exactness, either by law or usage, assigned to a State, or to its members of Congress, and was by them, after a fashion, subdivided among the members or leaders of the party controlling the administration. This share or number was called the "quota" of that State. Every particular official belonging to that "quota" was known by name, and the member or leader who put in one of the "quota" was called the "influence." As soon as there was a vacancy in any one of these "quota" places, a competition arose between the various "influences" and applicants for filling it. That system has been superseded, but the theory of a "quota," with its mischievous and misleading consequences, still survives, though with diminishing effect. . . .[47]

The patronage quota was based upon a complex of feudal baronies, the exact distribution of places depending in some measure upon the balance of power within the state delegations.[48] There was no central point of control. The civil service apportionment system was based upon mathematics and was rigidly free from influence under the controlling authority of the Commission. Its success in maintaining due proportions was remarkable, although it never attained perfection.[49] Insofar as the basic grades of clerk and copyist were concerned,

---

[46] Leonard D. White, *The Jacksonians*, pp. 396-98.

[47] U.S. Civil Service Commission, *Annual Report*, 1884-85, pp. 18-19.

[48] The quota system applied only to the departmental service in Washington. Field offices had long been assigned to Senators and Congressmen of the dominant party, or to powerful political figures in the state organization. The apportionment rule did not apply to the field service and the influence of the politically powerful was not disturbed, except as subordinate posts were covered by the merit system.

[49] A full discussion of apportionment methods and limitations is found in U.S. Civil Service Commission, *Annual Report*, 1886-87, pp. 56-64.

the Commission made a near perfect record; it simply certified from eligibles who were residents of states in greatest arrears. The rule of merit was thus sacrificed to the rule of locality, but this was an exception decreed by Congress. In registers requiring special qualifications, however, such as stenographers and bookkeepers on the one hand, or scientists on the other, the Commission certified the eligibles standing highest from the whole country, except those from states and other jurisdictions already having a large excess. These were primarily the District of Columbia, Maryland, and Virginia.[50]

The Commission took pride in its ability to enforce the apportionment rule, and annually published a table showing exactly where each state stood. In 1893 it published also a revealing table demonstrating that its apportionment system was working much more effectively than that maintained informally for the unclassified patronage wing of the service. Of 3,881 merit system appointments, there were only 118 not in precise accord with the correct proportion of population of each state. Of 7,865 patronage appointments there were 3,185 in violation of the correct proportion.[51]

This element of the personnel system was thus well and firmly established during the formative years. It encountered no organized resistance, was in accord with congressional preference, and was administratively feasible.

THE "POLICING" FUNCTION OF THE COMMISSION

For obvious reasons the Civil Service Commission began and continued its career with a lively sense of its duty to enforce the Pendleton Act. It began operations with a background of many decades during which office was obtained by favor, not by qualifications, and old habits were strong. Constituents continued to look to their Congressmen for help. The pressure of office seekers on Presidents and Secretaries was great, and the Commission considered it an obligation to prevent even these high authorities from deviating from the law. Lesser ranks, such as postmasters and customs officials, were likely to be both more vulnerable and less resistant to pressures, and consequently required closer supervision. Moreover, the Commission recognized that its own moral position would be compromised by any

---

[50] *Ibid.*, 1890-91, p. 126.
[51] *Ibid.*, 1892-93, pp. 217-19. These figures incidentally reveal the relative strength of the merit and patronage branches of the federal service at this time.

neglect or defiance of the merit system. Commissioner Theodore Roosevelt was therefore justified when he declared that the first objective of the Commission was to enforce the law.

The Commission began this task at once by reading a lecture to Congressmen and their constituents. To break up "the old partisan and patronage mongering methods," it declared, applications for examination needed no appeal to influence or favor. " . . . nothing is more natural than that many of those wishing to be examined should begin by invoking such interposition, especially on the part of members of Congress. . . . under the new system no appeal to influence or official favor is needed, or can be useful to the applicant."[52] Congressmen generally were not unwilling to fall in with this doctrine; they were spared much annoyance and could better use their influence in the more numerous places outside the competitive examination system.

While the departments generally accepted the new civil service examinations, there were some problems of agency evasion. One of the most persistent was the appointment of persons as skilled laborers or workmen, positions outside the classified system, and then assigning them to work as clerks or copyists, positions for which competitive examinations were necessary. Presidents supported the Commission in outlawing this type of evasion, but it proved difficult to control. An executive order of June 29, 1888, sought to terminate the practice, but an investigation in 1894 disclosed that it was still alive. McKinley issued a new directive on May 29, 1899, prohibiting a person appointed as laborer or workman without examination from being assigned to clerical grades.[53] In minor but annoying degree, this evil was to persist.

The principal recourse of the Commission in its enforcement task was its wide authority to investigate, conferred by the Pendleton Act in these terms: "Said commission may make investigations concerning the facts, and may report upon all matters touching the enforcement and effects of said rules and regulations, and concerning the action of any examiner or board of examiners hereinafter provided for, and its own subordinates, and those in the public service, in

[52] *Ibid.*, 1884-85, pp. 14-15.
[53] *Ibid.*, 1898-99, pp. 102-103.

respect to the execution of this act."[54] In its annual report for 1886-87 the Commission disclosed some current cases.

The postmaster at Kansas City, Missouri, had nominated four letter carriers for confirmation by the First Assistant Postmaster General, Adlai E. Stevenson, stating that there was no board of examiners at his office and asking for appointment by noncompetitive examination. The Commission decided that the appointments would violate the civil service rules, and that any emergency at the post office was due to the negligence of the postmaster. Chief Examiner Lyman proceeded to Kansas City and discovered other persons employed in violation of the rules. The assistant attorney general for the post office was consulted and fully sustained the Commission. The Post Office Department yielded.[55]

An investigation of the Baltimore post office revealed a bothersome problem that escaped the power of the Commission to correct, and the Post Office Department at that time apparently was not anxious to cooperate. The postmaster, I. Parker Veazey, looked into the political affiliations of the eligibles certified to him by the Commission, appointed Democrats as such, and rejected Republicans as Republicans. He not only did not conceal his preferences; he stoutly defended them.[56] In a tart letter to the Commission he declared, "I take pride and pleasure in advising your honorable board that it is quite true, and I am glad to have been able to accomplish such gratifying results without affecting the efficiency of the postal service."[57] The Commission could only declare its intention of denouncing any violation of its rules.[58]

Most matters with reference to the conduct of agency staffs remained the responsibility of the agency itself and Commission demands for punishment for violations of the "spirit" of the civil service law were not certain of departmental acquiescence. The power to investigate was nevertheless important and its effects were cumulative. It played an important part in the progressive acceptance of the new merit system.

It remains to note that the Civil Service Commission gradually

[54] 22 Stat. 403, sec. 2 (4).
[55] U.S. Civil Service Commission, *Annual Report*, 1886-87, pp. 92-93.
[56] This illuminating case is reported in full, *ibid.*, pp. 313-27.
[57] *Ibid.*, p. 320.
[58] *Ibid.*, p. 327.

acquired additional "policing" authority by the revision of its rules and by agreements with the departments such as those for promotions. It was, indeed, by extension of the rules of the Commission, as authorized by the President, that the authority of the Commission expanded and its supervisory role was gradually emphasized. In the early years this trend was motivated by suspicion of political influence and favoritism, and by distrust of the departments; later it was concerned with the establishment of uniform government-wide standards for the employment and management of government employees.

Success thus attended the Civil Service Commission in its basic task, although frustration dogged its efforts elsewhere. Nevertheless it could not be denied in 1900 that within the old classification and pay structure still continued from 1853, a new personnel system was emerging, a system resting on the President's authority to make rules for the public service granted in 1871 and on the Pendleton Act of 1883.

At some points, such as examination, certification, and apportionment, the Commission had authority and a uniform system easily emerged. At others, the Commission could only investigate. It did investigate vigorously and by means of wide publicity of evasion and maladministration exerted a steady influence where it could not command. It fought political assessments by exposure and was only moderately successful; it fought evasion or violation of its rules and was more successful; it fought political discrimination among its eligibles with the only weapon it discovered that it possessed—publicity—and at the moment was defeated.

From another point of view these trends had broader significance. They contained the first institutional recognition of the President as the active head of the administrative system. They carried implicitly the idea that the congeries of departments and agencies in fact were part of a related whole, for which minimum standards of operation and common procedure could and should be devised. This concept was not publicly proclaimed at the time, but it was inherent in the government-wide civil service system and in the supervisory functions of the United States Civil Service Commission.

CHAPTER SEVENTEEN

Public Service Ethics

The Republican era opened in moral chaos. It remained sunk in moral degradation throughout Grant's two terms, during which members of Congress, high executive officials, and subordinate administrative agents were guilty of one dereliction after another. Improvement began with Hayes and was sustained by Garfield and Arthur. Cleveland did much, and the quality of presidential and Cabinet leadership during and after his administration helped restore the reputation of the government. In this long trend toward higher standards Washington preceded the states and cities, but all were bound together.

The deplorable levels of public and business morality from the 1860's into the 1880's were deprecated by reformers and journalists alike, but for years theirs were voices crying in the wilderness. Edwin L. Godkin wrote in 1868: "Another striking change which has occurred in the commercial world, and which is doing something to promote unscrupulousness, is what may be called the diminished value of character. . . . both here and in England the outer edge of the well-established and respectable circle of the commercial world swarms with adventurers whom no one knows, and to whom character is not necessary in order to do a considerable amount of business, and whom no number of failures seems to daunt or drive from the field. . . ."[1]

In 1884 a contributor to the *Century Magazine* deplored dishonesty in American life.

No feature of the present age is more displeasing to the moralist than the dishonesty that so widely prevails in commerce and politics. In what-

[1] E. L. Godkin, "Commercial Immorality and Political Corruption," *North American Review*, CVII (1868), 253-54.

ever direction we turn, this phenomenon meets our eye; and there is no branch of business, no department of government, and no class in society in which it does not appear. The forms of commercial dishonesty are almost endless in variety. . . .

If, now, we turn to politics, we find a similar or even a worse state of affairs there. Fraudulent contracts, sinister legislation, bought and paid for by those whom it benefits, trading of offices and votes, and all the various methods of robbing the public for the benefit of a few, have become so common among us as hardly to awaken surprise when exposed to the public view. There is, moreover, a close connection between the dishonest practices of politics and those of commerce, and collusions are constant between unscrupulous men in commercial business and equally unscrupulous men in public station. . . .[2]

Charles Francis Adams traced political corruption to an indefensible party system. "The single great end to which all reformers, whatever their private theories may be, must look is distinct enough; it is to overcome the tendency of our political system to corruption. All political systems, no doubt, have some tendency, greater or less, towards corruption. The peculiarity of ours is that it moves, and for fifty years has moved, in that direction with accelerating pace, and it has now arrived at a point where even the blindest patriots see that, unless the evil is checked, our political system must break down and some new experiment must be substituted in its place." He put the blame on the system of party organization, "bred in the gutter of New York politics," and adopted by the entire nation.[3]

THE MORAL SLUMP

The eight years of Grant's administration rocked with one scandal after another. Citizens defrauded the government in the acquisition of land and in claims for pensions; contractors supplying the army and navy were often venal; and unscrupulous lawyers levied toll on ignorant and defenseless Indians. Members of Congress were bribed

---

[2] "Dishonesty in Commerce and Politics," *Century Magazine*, XXVIII (1884), 463.
[3] Charles Francis Adams, Jr., "The 'Independents' in the Canvass," *North American Review*, CXXIII (1876), 461. There is no systematic study of the history of official morality in the United States, rewarding though such a presentation would be. The scandals of the Grant administration, which supply the background of these thirty years, are set out effectively in Allan Nevins, *Hamilton Fish: The Inner History of the Grant Administration*.

and disgraced. Cabinet officers were investigated and impeached. Subordinate officials and employees were revealed in outright betrayal of the public trust. Never had the Republic sunk to so low an estate of official morality.

The condition in the rank and file of many government offices has already been revealed in previous chapters. During the 1870's there was both incompetence and dishonesty in the large customhouses; discipline and integrity among the navy-yard labor forces were at a low ebb; the Indian service had been roundly condemned by Garfield; land agents connived at irregularities, and surveyors made fraudulent claims for work not performed. The story of betrayal of trust at some points, however, must be kept in perspective—the smaller customhouses were substantially untouched by the evils that flourished in New York or Philadelphia; most postmasters in cities large and small were entirely reliable; rascals among the accountable officers were gratifyingly few; the majority of the departmental clerks in Washington held high ethical standards and performed their duties faithfully.

The tone of the eight years of Grant's administration was nevertheless set by a small number of weak and unreliable persons holding seats in Congress and in high executive office. It was during these years that the most resounding scandals occurred, not only in Washington but in many states and cities. When the mighty wandered far from the paths of rectitude, it was not surprising that some of the lesser ranks followed their example. To a few of the scandals of these years we turn for brief review.

The Crédit Mobilier. This corporation, originally organized to finance railroad construction, fell into the control of a group of adventurers, including a member of Congress, Oakes Ames. The corporation was awarded a lucrative but fraudulent contract for the construction of a long section of the Union Pacific Railroad, the effect of which was to double the face value of its stock. Ames offered to sell shares of this stock to leading members of both the House and Senate at par value, for the purpose of protecting the interests of the railroad. "We want more friends in this Congress." The transactions were eventually exposed and a House investigation followed, resulting in the expulsion of two members of the House, Oakes Ames and James Brooks, the disgrace of Vice Presidents Colfax and Wilson, a recommendation in the Senate to expel James W. Patterson of New Hampshire, and a cloud on the reputation of Henry L. Dawes, James A. Garfield, and others.[4] The *Nation* of January 30, 1873, summarized the consequences as "total loss, one Senator; badly damaged, and not serviceable for future political use, two Vice-Presidents and eight Congressmen. The condition of Ames's reputation language is inadequate to describe."[5]

The case of the Secretary of War, William W. Belknap. Laxness or corruption in the award of Indian trading posts had been suspected for some time under General Belknap's administration of the War Department. A House committee took evidence in the winter of 1876 that revealed both.

Secretary Belknap's busybody wife, anxious for social display and needing income beyond her husband's salary, had secured from her husband a post tradership for a New York contractor, Caleb P. Marsh. The then incumbent of the post, John S. Evans, offered Marsh $12,000 a year to be let alone; Marsh accepted and agreed to give one half to Mrs. Belknap. Shortly after the first payment of $1,500 she died, but Belknap continued to receive the payments. Other favorites of the administration were also taking illegitimate profits, amounting to at least $100,000 a year.[6]

The outcome was sudden, dramatic, and symptomatic. The House Committee on Expenditures in the War Department found "at the very threshold of their investigations" uncontradicted evidence of Secretary Belknap's malfeasance in office and recommended that he be impeached.[7] One of Belknap's friends privately informed him of his impending fate, whereupon, before the committee could report, he dashed to the White House and presented his resignation. Grant accepted it "with great regret" without realizing, as he later confided to the Cabinet, that acceptance was not a matter of course.

Articles of impeachment were brought against Belknap despite his hasty resignation and his claim that as a private citizen impeachment proceedings would not lie against him. The Senate repudiated this

---

[4] House Report 77, 42d Cong., 3d sess. (Feb. 18, 1873); Senate Report 519, 42d Cong., 3d. sess. (Feb. 27, 1873).

[5] *Nation*, XVI, 65.

[6] The evidence is set forth in House Report 799, 44th Cong., 1st sess. (August 5, 1876).

[7] House Report 186, 44th Cong., 1st sess. (March 2, 1876), p. 1.

construction of the impeachment clause. When, however, the proceedings came to an end, Belknap was acquitted for lack of a two-thirds majority. On the fifth article (the most serious) thirty-seven Senators voted guilty, twenty-three not guilty for want of jurisdiction, and two more not guilty on the evidence. As to Belknap's moral guilt, there could be no doubt.[8]

The case of Attorney General George H. Williams. Williams was Attorney General from 1872 to 1875. In 1873 Grant nominated him as Chief Justice of the Supreme Court. A passage from the diary of Hamilton Fish tells the story of Williams' subsequent embarrassments. Fish was called to the White House by the President, who revealed that the nomination would probably fail for highly discreditable reasons.

. . . . He [President Grant] did not think that he (Williams) had done anything corrupt or illegal, but that there had been indiscreet things done. That Mrs. Williams had given orders for the purchase of an expensive carriage and liveries for two servants and that the expenses for those had been paid out of the contingent fund of the Department of Justice; as were also the wages of the two men who were employed as private servants. He manifested much regret at having learned this. . . . It was also alleged that Judge Williams had mingled his accounts with those of the Department, and that during the panic, when the banks were not paying private checks, it was said that the money for meeting the expenses of his house had been paid from the funds of the government; that he understood it had all been made good, but that this appropriation of government funds was unjustifiable. . . .[9]

Conkling reported the nomination favorably from the Judiciary Committee, but the Senate recommitted the matter and Grant shortly thereafter withdrew the nomination. Nevertheless the President allowed Williams to continue as Attorney General of the United States for another year and a half.

The case of the Secretary of the Navy, George M. Robeson. A House investigation of the Navy Department in 1876, colored no doubt by partisanship, nevertheless disclosed operations highly dishonorable to the Secretary, if not outright corrupt. When Robeson

---

[8] For impeachment proceedings, see *Congressional Record*, Vol. IV, Part 7, 44th Cong., 1st sess. (1876).

[9] Dec. 28, 1873. Quoted in Allan Nevins, *Hamilton Fish*, pp. 662-63.

took office in 1869 he had a small amount of property and a modest law practice. Once in office he formed a business connection with A. G. Cattell and Company of Philadelphia, a grain, feed, and flour commission firm. By reason of its connection with Robeson, the firm was enabled to levy percentages upon other contractors' engagements with the navy, always a heavy purchaser of flour and other supplies. Both the Cattells and Robeson grew rich. The House Committee proved through Robeson's bank books that between July 1, 1869, and April 4, 1876, he had deposited over $300,000 beyond his apparent income.[10]

The Democratic majority of the House committee thought impeachment was in order, but the disputed presidential election of 1876 foreclosed further proceedings. Godkin declared in the *Nation*: "we believe no man in his senses can read the evidence taken and doubt that a secret partnership existed between the Secretary and the Cattells, by virtue of which they levied toll on contracts and he levied toll on them."[11]

So far as the wasteful and extravagant operation of the navy yards was concerned, Robeson sought protection by alleging that he left all details to the bureau chiefs. The evidence contradicted him. The bureau chiefs sought excuse by trying to pass responsibility to the yard commandants. They declared that they had to obey orders, and could show repeated instances of gross mismanagement for political purposes due directly to the instructions of Robeson or the bureau heads. These offenses were less than high crimes and misdemeanors and could hardly lead to impeachment, but they revealed a sad state of official morality in eminent circles.

The Sanborn contracts. Since Hamilton's day in the Treasury the revenue laws had authorized informers to collect a moiety of delinquent customs and other revenue due the government. The Forty-second Congress repealed all laws providing such moieties for delinquent internal revenue taxes,[12] but a seemingly innocuous rider to an appropriation act empowered the Secretary of the Treasury to appoint

---

[10] House Report 784, 44th Cong., 1st sess., pp. 152-53 (July 25, 1876); majority opinion, pp. 1-161; minority opinion, pp. 163-219. The voluminous evidence is in House Misc. Doc. 170, 44th Cong., 1st sess. (1876).

[11] *Nation*, XXIII, 33 (July 20, 1876). Quoted in Allan Nevins, *Hamilton Fish*, p. 816.

[12] 17 Stat. 230, sec. 39 (June 6, 1872).

not more than three persons "to assist the proper officers of the government in discovering and collecting" money due the United States.[13] A bold scandal eventually developed from this rider, involving a protégé of Benjamin Butler, John D. Sanborn, Secretary of the Treasury William A. Richardson, and two of his high official associates.[14]

Despite the fact that Sanborn was already a special agent of the Treasury, he applied for and received appointment as one of the three assistants and secured a series of contracts to ferret out delinquent taxpayers. Successful on a small scale, he persuaded Secretary Richardson on July 7, 1873, to add to his contract the names of 592 railroad companies—a list taken from a railroad guide and including practically all the railroads in the United States. The law required Sanborn to make affidavit of personal knowledge of delinquency. Sanborn admitted some knowledge concerning not more than 150 of them, but nevertheless swore that all were delinquent.

The law specified that Sanborn's duties were *to assist* the regular internal revenue officers; the contract authorized Sanborn *to proceed to collect*, and the regular employees were directed to assist him. The theory of the law, as the House Ways and Means Committee declared, was thus completely reversed—a fact which the committee asserted, correctly enough, would demoralize the entire internal revenue force.[15]

The contract was a huge success for Sanborn. He collected $427,000 and received his moiety, $213,500. The House committee declared that most, if not all, of this huge sum "would have been collected by the Internal Revenue Bureau in the ordinary discharge of their duty."[16] Thus the contract in substance authorized a political favorite to require the assistance of the regular internal revenue staff in discovering delinquent taxpayers, then to substitute himself for the government officials in suit for recovery, all for the purpose of diverting one-half of the amount collected out of the Treasury into Sanborn's own pockets. The Commissioner of Internal Revenue made written protest

[13] 17 Stat. 61 at 69 (May 8, 1872).
[14] House Report 559, 43d Cong., 1st sess., p. 1 (May 4, 1874). See also House Ex. Doc. 132, 43d Cong., 1st sess. (Feb. 16, 1874) for a mass of documentary evidence.
[15] House Report 559, 43d Cong., 1st sess., p. 7.
[16] *Ibid.*, p. 6.

to the Secretary of the Treasury against this arrant trickery, but his letter remained unanswered.[17] The arrangements were concluded at the departmental level.

The House Committee on Ways and Means sought in vain to discover precisely who was to blame. Secretary Richardson testified, "I do not know the least thing about it any more than about ten thousand other things that are done in the different divisions of the Department. . . . I sign without reading."[18] The Assistant Secretary disclaimed any knowledge or recollection of his signature and said the papers were prepared by the solicitor. This officer testified that he had consulted with the Secretary or Assistant Secretary, that he had acted in obedience to the directions of his superiors, and that the contracts were well known to the Secretary and Assistant Secretary. The committee looked "with serious apprehension upon the apparent effort of these gentlemen to transfer the responsibility each from himself to the other."[19]

Although the report of the Committee on Ways and Means condemned the Sanborn transaction and severely criticized the principals, the committee found nothing to impeach their integrity or to demonstrate corrupt motives.[20] The Assistant Secretary, Frederick A. Sawyer, and the solicitor, E. C. Banfield, resigned. The fate of Secretary Richardson was astonishing and symptomatic; he was appointed a member of the Court of Claims. Godkin was struck dumb: "The transfer to the judicial bench of a person found guilty of the gross negligence and incapacity which Mr. Richardson has displayed in the Treasury needs no comment."[21]

The Whiskey Ring. The most dramatic and perhaps the most damaging evidence of official corruption during the Grant administration involved the evasion of internal revenue taxes on distilleries. Fraud had long been suspected, and protests by honest distillers against the unfair competition of the dishonest were known during the administration of President Johnson and the first term of President Grant. Shortly after the appointment of Benjamin H. Bristow as Secretary of the Treasury on June 4, 1874, he received private information that

[17] *Ibid.*, p. 5.
[18] *Ibid.*, p. 88 (March 31, 1874).
[19] *Ibid.*, p. 8.
[20] *Ibid.*, p. 8.
[21] *Nation*, XVIII, 355 (June 4, 1874).

offered him the opportunity to attack the Whiskey Ring. The events that followed were full of excitement, frustration, misunderstanding, and eventual triumph against evildoers but at the cost of Bristow's loss of the secretaryship.[22]

The Whiskey Ring included General John A. McDonald, collector of internal revenue in St. Louis (one of the principal centers), other collectors, notably in Chicago, Milwaukee, and San Francisco, subordinate personnel in considerable numbers, the chief clerk of the internal revenue division of the Treasury Department in Washington, and an unknown number of informants to the ring in Washington and elsewhere. It also included General Orville E. Babcock, President Grant's private secretary, who was subsequently indicted but who escaped conviction. So widely was the net of the ring flung that Bristow dared trust no one in the Department except the solicitor, Bluford Wilson.

The campaign to secure evidence of tax evasion was planned by Bristow and Wilson, initially with the aid of three private citizens of St. Louis and later with the help of departmental agents who were sent on apparently innocent missions to check railroad shipments—among others of whiskey. The ring became uneasy, but never penetrated the disguise under which Bristow's agents operated. The trap was sprung simultaneously in St. Louis, Chicago, and Milwaukee. At the end of the first day of seizures sixteen of the largest distilleries and sixteen rectifying houses were in the possession of the government; others were seized thereafter; and illegal shipments were taken into custody from Boston to Galveston.[23]

Indictments were served against 47 distillers, 60 rectifiers, 10 wholesale dealers, and 86 field agents of the internal revenue service ranging from collectors and deputy collectors to gaugers and storekeepers. All in all 230 persons were indicted, about 100 pleaded guilty, about 20 were convicted, and a dozen fled the country.[24]

These events were damaging enough, but equally disconcerting

[22] H. V. Boynton, "The Whiskey Ring," *North American Review*, CXXIII (1876), 280-327; Lucius E. Guese, "St. Louis and the Great Whiskey Ring," *Missouri Historical Review*, XXXVI (1941-42), 160-83. For testimony, see House Misc. Doc. 186, 44th Cong., 1st sess. (1876).

[23] H. V. Boynton, "The Whiskey Ring," *North American Review*, CXXIII (1876), 299.

[24] *Ibid.*, CXXIII, 300, 322.

were the apparent efforts to hamstring Bristow and to thwart the prosecutions. President Grant sustained Bristow until General Babcock's complicity was suspected, but then grew cool toward the proceedings, which were made to appear as a movement to strike at him through his secretary. Grant's mind was continuously poisoned against Bristow, who at one point saw no alternative but to resign in midstream. A forged telegram even made it appear that the President was being shadowed on a trip to St. Louis with Babcock, and set off an attempt to remove Solicitor Wilson.[25] At one point Grant himself determined to go to St. Louis to testify on behalf of Babcock, and actually did make a deposition in his favor. The weight of this deposition was influential in his acquittal. Babcock returned momentarily to the White House and received Grant's appointment as inspector of lighthouses, but his influence in national affairs had been destroyed.

Meanwhile Grant had become convinced that Bristow was strengthening his claim on the Republican nomination of 1876 by attacking the President through an innocent secretary, and determined to remove Bristow as soon as Babcock's trial was at an end. Formally Bristow resigned; actually Grant made it clear that he was no longer welcome in the Cabinet. Thus left the public stage a man of high character, moral strength, and unyielding courage. Bluford Wilson also went out, and so did many of the lesser persons who had been active in the prosecution of the Whiskey Ring. Punishment fell heavily upon this devoted group of men.

The fate of Secretary of the Treasury Richardson and of Secretary of the Treasury Bristow presented a melancholy contrast. Richardson, caught in dubious official operations, was rescued by a quasi-judicial appointment to the Court of Claims. Bristow, successfully fighting corruption in the revenue service, was forced into private life. "His reward," declared Godkin, "has been a practical isolation at Washington, the enmity of the whole political class, dastardly accusations of corruption in office, and a forced retirement at the very time when his honesty and good faith were most needed to protect the Treasury from being turned over to a corrupt gang of officeholders to keep themselves in power."[26]

[25] *Ibid.*, CXXIII, 307-308.
[26] *Nation*, XXII, 389 (June 22, 1876).

Treasury contingent funds. The public service began a long period of moral renovation with the reform of the New York customhouse in Hayes' administration, but recovery was slow. A Senate investigation of the Treasury contingent fund in 1881–82 revealed a mass of petty graft and of apparent conversion of public funds to the advantage of a committee seeking the nomination of John Sherman (then Secretary of the Treasury) for the presidency in 1880. Senator William B. Allison reported that stationery and other items had been furnished by the Treasury to the Sherman campaign committee in the amount of $502, for which vouchers were made out calling for fileholders. No fileholders nor any other article on these vouchers were received by the Treasury. Upon discovery, the amount was reimbursed.[27] In the early winter of 1880 gas fixtures were installed in the campaign committee rooms under cover of a requisition on the Treasury contingent fund for repairs. This amount was repaid after discovery. In the summer of 1880 a local druggist sold the Treasury Department three dozen bottles of Colgate's violet water paid for on a voucher calling for friction matches. Under the heading of an expenditure for ice, payment was made for 250 geranium plants. These were never delivered; in fact someone got 35 yards of evergreen, 6 wreaths, and a basket of cut flowers.[28] Three payments were made ostensibly for billiard cloth, but actually delivered were ulster overcoats for employees driving wagons.[29]

More damaging to Sherman's reputation were payments made by the Treasury for repairs and labor on his residence and for architectural drawings for his new house. Herman Blau relaid some of Sherman's carpets and was directed to bill the Treasury; James A. Rodbird put on weather strips, rehung sash, made horse troughs and hay mangers, and two bookshelves for the Secretary's basement, all on Treasury time.[30] A Treasury draftsman worked ten days during office hours on plans for Sherman's new house. Later he worked at night and on Sundays but with no other compensation than his regular pay.[31]

Sherman emphatically denied all knowledge of these encroach-

[27] Senate Report 265, 47th Cong., 1st sess., pp. ii-iii (March 15, 1882).
[28] *Ibid.*, p. iii.
[29] *Ibid.*, p. xi.
[30] *Ibid.*, p. xii.
[31] *Ibid.*, p. xiii.

ments on Treasury funds. The investigating committee admitted there was no testimony that he was aware of these payments "for his individual benefit."[32] The committee nevertheless noted "gross abuses and frauds perpetrated through false and fictitious vouchers,"[33] and set forth the duties of department heads and bureau chiefs. "It is absolutely necessary that the heads of the several departments and chiefs of bureaus shall exercise a constant supervision over the actions of all their subordinates, and make each one feel his personal responsibility for the faithful and honest discharge of every duty, and that his absolute personal integrity alone can secure his retention in the service. . . ."[34] These admonitions were richly deserved. Also needed was the kind of administrative assistance, then wanting, that would enable a department head to know what was taking place among his subordinates. Congress was laggard in providing the necessary, if only partial, administrative remedy to a moral problem.

The star route frauds. The star route frauds in the post office, occurring during Hayes' administration and exposed during Arthur's, gave evidence that unremitting caution was still essential.[35] They were reminiscent of the problems faced by the Post Office Department in the early years of Jackson's administration, involving collusion between postal officials and unscrupulous contractors.[36]

In the settled portions of the country the mails were carried by rail, steamboat, and messenger. In the western states and territories mail contracts (by stage, horseback riders, or otherwise) were awarded to the lowest bidders who would engage to carry the mail

[32] *Ibid.*, p. xvi.

[33] *Ibid.*, p. xxi.

[34] *Ibid.*, p. xx.

[35] The voluminous documents in the star route cases include: Testimony before the Committee on Appropriations in Relation to the Postal Star Service, House Misc. Doc. 31, 46th Cong., 2d sess. (March 25, 1880); Letter from the Postmaster General transmitting reports made by special agents . . . with reference to the star-route investigation, House Ex. Doc. 100, 48th Cong., 1st sess. (Feb. 21, 1884); Testimony Relating to the Star-Route Cases, House Misc. Doc. 38, Part 2, 48th Cong., 1st sess. (1884); Frauds in the Star-Route Mail Service, Report of the Committee on Expenditures in the Department of Justice, House Report 2165, 48th Cong., 1st sess. (July 3, 1884).

For secondary accounts see George F. Howe, *Chester A. Arthur*, ch. 16; Eugene Coleman Savidge, *Life of Benjamin Harris Brewster* (Philadelphia: J. B. Lippincott Co., 1891), pp. 112-72, *passim*; J. Martin Klotsche, "The Star Route Cases," *Mississippi Valley Historical Review*, XXII (1935-36), 407-18.

[36] Leonard D. White, *The Jacksonians*, pp. 253-63.

with "certainty, celerity, and security." These words were indicated on the clerks' registers by three stars, and the routes thus came to be known as star routes. Since the contracts were let for a four-year period it was natural that changes might be required in the interest of greater speed or more frequent delivery. The Post Office Department was accordingly vested with discretion to make extra allowances under certain circumstances and subject to safeguards, an authority which proved vulnerable in the 1870's.[37] Responsibility for contract changes was in the hands of Thomas J. Brady, Second Assistant Postmaster General, appointed by Grant in 1876 and continued through Hayes' administration and Garfield's brief term into Arthur's administration.

Hayes had not been decisive when in January 1880 the House Committee on Appropriations questioned the extravagant, if not fraudulent, acts of Brady.[38] The President appeared to regard the situation as one involving merely a dispute over restricted or liberal western mail facilities. He noted after he left the presidency that he had repeatedly called the attention of Postmaster General Key and his First Assistant Tyner to the matter, but that both saw in it only a controversy over policy. Hayes finally directed that no more increases should be allowed except by the Postmaster General after consideration by the President and the Cabinet. This raised the adjustments of contracts on remote mail routes to the highest political level—a solution, as Hayes declared, that should prevent crookedness, but at a heavy administrative cost in time of the President and Cabinet.[39]

Garfield quickly became aware of strange occurrences in the star route contracts and at once ordered an investigation. Brady and other subordinates were replaced and prosecutions were started. It appeared that in the western division of the post office alone, Brady had approved additional trips and greater "celerity," the effect of which was to increase original contract terms by about two million dollars a year.[40] P. H. Woodward, special investigator for Postmaster General Thomas L. James, reported by way of illustration the case of route No. 40,116 from Phoenix to Prescott, Arizona, which was twice

[37] Revised Statutes, secs. 3960-61.
[38] House Misc. Doc. 31, 46th Cong., 2d sess., p. 1.
[39] Rutherford B. Hayes, *Diary and Letters*, IV, 12-13 (May 3, 1881).
[40] House Report 2165, 48th Cong., 1st sess., pp. 2-3; Eugene C. Savidge, *Life of Benjamin H. Brewster*, pp. 123-24.

expedited at a change of compensation from $680 to $32,640.32 without readvertisement or competition; and route No. 32,024 from Las Vegas, New Mexico, to Vinita, where the annual compensation went from $6,330 up to $150,592.03.[41] Favored contractors offered impossibly low bids to freeze out competitors and then, once secure, proceeded to "improve" their service. An honest bidder was at an impossible disadvantage.

Conviction on charges of conspiracy to defraud the government proved impossible despite the confession, later repudiated, of one of the participants. The defense argued that the disputed increases of compensation were due (1) to those required by increase of population; (2) to those made in response to requests of influential members of Congress; and (3) to those allowed because of misinformation or mistaken, though honest, judgment. General William T. Sherman testified for the defense, explaining that the needs of the army on the frontier had required improvements in the mail. Senator Henry M. Teller testified that he had frequently urged better mail facilities for his constituents in Colorado. Amidst allegations of bribery of the jury, the trial came to an end in disagreement on September 11, 1882. A second trial from December 7, 1882, to June 14, 1883, with more charges of jury tampering, resulted in a verdict of "not guilty." Civil suits for restitution likewise failed.[42]

The United States marshals. The abuse of the Treasury contingent fund and the star route frauds were not the only evidence that old evils tended to persist. A shocking mass of corruption and extortion was revealed by the House Committee on Expenditures in the Department of Justice in 1884.[43] Marshals and their deputies, supervisors of elections, court commissioners, and others rendered false accounts on a huge scale, failed to report their fees, and in some cases conspired to arrest and harass innocent persons in order to increase their official income. Their crimes may be sufficiently exposed by quoting the report of the House committee.

. . . . The testimony before the committee clearly shows that utter inefficiency and criminal practices have prevailed in many parts of this

---

[41] *Ibid.*, pp. 132-33; House Report 2165, 48th Cong., 1st sess. pp. 5-6.
[42] *Ibid.*, pp. 13-14; George F. Howe, *Chester A. Arthur*, pp. 187-91.
[43] House Report 2164, 48th Cong., 1st sess. (July 3, 1884).

branch of the public service for many years past, and that the Government has been a heavy loser thereby.

. . . . The investigation reveals the wonderful unanimity with which these officers of almost every grade and in the several portions of the country have plundered the public Treasury by false, fraudulent, and fictitious charges. . . . They have charged for arrests that were not made; for travel that was not performed; for expenses that were not incurred; for guards that were not employed. They knowingly rendered false accounts against the Government; misappropriated public funds; became defaulters to the Government and to the courts; increased accounts after they were made up; made up accounts in the name of fictitious persons; arrested persons upon false charges worked up by themselves; extorted money from private citizens and in ways without number have swindled the Government and oppressed the people.[44]

The fiscal officers of the Department of Justice disallowed over $340,000 in the accounts of these field agents from 1882 to 1884. The House committee surmised that this was a small sum compared to total stealings. The committee's indignation was extreme: "We cannot expect the people to have an affection for the Government when, instead of having their rights and liberties protected by it, the most egregious wrongs are perpetrated upon them; and when the officers not only bring the public service into contempt, but actually convert the machinery of the courts of justice into an engine of oppression."[45]

RECOVERY

The misfeasance and corruption that flourished in the federal government during the Grant administration receded in later years. If comparison be made of ethical standards during McKinley's administration with those during Grant's, the change is marked and dramatic. Before McKinley's day, indeed, progress had been substantial. The transformation was gradual; no sharp transition occurred, and no outstanding events demonstrated the arrival of a new era. To close observers the direction of change was, however, readily perceptible, although progress was slow and victories were mixed with defeats.

What were the circumstances that favored moral reform in the

[44] *Ibid.*, p. 1.
[45] *Ibid.*, p. 6. The voluminous testimony in this case is in House Misc. Doc. 38, Part 1, 48th Cong., 1st sess. (1884).

federal administration? Those most fundamental were probably lost from sight and will remain undisclosed until a history of morality reveals the aspirations and standards of the people. It must be remembered that even in the years of the most rampant corruption, old Puritan ideals of conduct, although apparently submerged, prevailed among the masses of plain men and women. Honesty, reliability, and trustworthiness in dealings between man and man were the rule, crookedness was the exception. The churches did not waver in holding man's duty to his fellowman before him, and it may be asserted with justification that the loss of character, widespread though it was in business, politics, and government, never undermined the mores of the community. The basic ethical standards of the American people were untouched; most persons would have declared that it was wrong to steal from the public treasury, to give or to accept bribes, to deceive and to misrepresent. These basic standards were steadily opposed to skulduggery in public as well as private affairs.

The character of the Presidents following Grant was such as to encourage decency in government. Hayes was a deeply religious man of highest personal rectitude; in his Cabinet were men of integrity; their influence was steady if not spectacular, and in favor of honest performance of public duty. President Arthur may have lost renomination for a second term by his insistence on prosecuting some delinquent marshals. Cleveland was speaking for Hayes, Garfield, and Arthur as well as for himself and his successors when he declared that public office was a public trust. The advent of a reforming Democratic administration in 1885 after nearly a quarter century of one-party domination was itself a renovating influence.

Leadership in Congress slowly improved. Benjamin Butler disappeared with Grant.[46] The intended expulsion of Patterson from the Senate served notice that even in the depths of degradation discovery of corruption would reap its due and proper punishment. The evil influence of Senator Conkling ended early in Garfield's administration; the dubious influence of Blaine was diminished by his loss of the 1884 election. The quality of Congressmen and Senators depended, however, on the quality of the party system, election procedures, the integrity of state legislatures, and local leadership; these were hard to change, and progress was slow.

[46] Robert S. Holzman, *Stormy Ben Butler* (New York: Macmillan Co., 1954).

The reformers were in the forefront of the moral regeneration that slowly took place from the late 1870's to the 1890's. They were at best a small minority, but they were deeply stirred by the need for moral reconstruction of American democracy. They were based in New England and New York, as the Jacksonian ideas of democracy had been based in the Middle West. They were characterized by integrity, earnestness, intelligence, and determination. They could write and they could speak. They were in the line of moral succession from the antislavery advocates of the pre-Civil War period. Strong in their convictions, they faced the entrenched party system with demands for its purification and a higher standard of public morals.

Among the various wings of the reformers the civil service reform group was the earliest on the stage, and the first to gain substantial initial success.[47] The story has already been told, and it is sufficient here merely to relate civil service reform to the improvement of public service standards. The connection is an obvious one. Before 1883 a considerable proportion of the rank-and-file federal employees were political hacks, active in the small intrigues of the big city machines, well-informed concerning the corrupt practices that flourished in the winning of elections, disinterested in public office except as a livelihood, and expecting to hold their jobs only so long as their party, or faction, was predominant. There was little incentive to honest performance of official work; much inducement to do party work, pay party assessments, and carry out party obligations and orders.

The enactment of the civil service law built a wall around a steadily larger segment of the public service, access to which was on the basis of competence tested by open competitive examinations, continuance in which was contingent upon good work and good character. This wing of public office was protected in considerable measure from party obligation, and in its own interest gradually developed an ethical system that abjured neglect of the public interest, that bespoke a collective morale founded on a permanent work association, and that in some quarters, notably Agriculture, was permeated by ideals of professional conduct. From any point of view,

[47] See above, ch. 13.

civil service reform ranks high as a source of steady improvement in the standards of the government service.

Another wing of the reformers was attacking corruption and intimidation at the ballot box. Before the Civil War voting was generally viva voce; after the war it was by privately printed ballots publicly distributed, and so marked as to make secrecy difficult. Purchase of votes and intimidation of voters were common:

> . . . systematic organization for the purchase of votes, individually and in blocks, at the polls has become a recognized factor in the machinery of parties; . . . the number of voters who demand money compensation for their ballots has grown greater with each recurring election; . . . men of standing in the community have openly sold their votes at prices ranging from fifteen to thirty dollars; and . . . for securing the more disreputable elements—the "floaters," as they are termed—new two dollar bills have been scattered abroad with a prodigality that would seem incredible but for the magnitude of the object to be obtained.[48]

According to a Senate report in 1880, men were frequently marched or carried to the polls in their employers' carriages. They were then supplied with ballots, and sometimes compelled to hold their hands up with the ballots in them so that they could be watched until the ballots were safely deposited in the box.[49]

The Australian ballot provided the formal remedy for lack of secrecy and for open intimidation. This ballot, introduced on a state-wide basis in Massachusetts in 1888,[50] was printed officially, was distributed only in the polling place, and was marked in secrecy. Although it did not eliminate all corrupt practices in elections, it represented a major advance. The unprecedented use of money in the election of 1888 gave impetus to this reform. Between 1888 and 1892 thirty-two states and two territories adopted the Australian ballot, and by 1896 seven other states had followed this example.[51] Thus

[48] Quoted from James L. Gordon's address of July 2, 1890, in Eldon Cobb Evans, A History of the Australian Ballot System in the United States (Chicago: University of Chicago Press, 1917), p. 11.

[49] Senate Report 497, 46th Cong., 2d sess., p. 9 (April 19, 1880).

[50] Eldon C. Evans, History of the Australian Ballot System in the United States, p. 19.

[51] Ibid., p. 27. For a general review of the evolution of federal authority in elections, see Earl R. Sikes, State and Federal Corrupt-Practices Legislation (Durham, North Carolina: Duke University Press, 1928), ch. 6.

was laid another cornerstone for the reduction of corruption in public life.

A third wing of the reformers meanwhile was battling corruption in cities, whose government was described by James Bryce as the most conspicuous failure of the American commonwealth. Americans had been accustomed to the management of their rural communities and small towns, but the rapid growth of big cities, with large expenditures and emerging utility corporations, presented problems beyond their experience. The general relaxation of moral standards after the close of the Civil War had some of its worst consequences in New York, Philadelphia, Chicago, and other large cities. In 1890 Andrew D. White, former president of Cornell University, declared: "Without the slightest exaggeration we may assert that, with very few exceptions, the city governments of the United States are the worst in Christendom—the most expensive, the most inefficient, and the most corrupt."[52]

Even temporary success in the overthrow of a corrupt municipal gang was usually followed by a relapse from civic virtue. The Tweed Ring was dispersed in 1871, but Tammany was soon back again in the city hall.[53] The Gas Ring was overthrown in Philadelphia in 1887, but corruption could be discovered in the City of Brotherly Love in subsequent years. Most cities alternated between subjection to local bosses, occasional reform victories, and early loss again to the professional political rings.[54]

The municipal situation was exceedingly complex and from the point of view of the reformers uncompromisingly stubborn. Cities grew rapidly during the 1870's and 1880's. Numbers were swollen by newly arrived immigrants who proved ready recruits to the professional politicians. The "better elements" were too often indifferent to laxness in city affairs or were the complaisant beneficiaries. It was relatively easy, moreover, for a hardened machine to compel a reluctant businessman to "go along" by threat of annoyance through building or license inspectors, or by delaying municipal services.

[52] Andrew D. White, "The Government of American Cities," *Forum*, X (1890-91), 357.
[53] The unparalleled stealing in New York City by Tweed is recorded in Gustavus Myers, *The History of Tammany Hall* (New York: privately printed, 1901).
[54] Harold Zink, *City Bosses in the United States* (Durham, North Carolina: Duke University Press, 1930).

The prizes to be won in the era of streetcar franchises, gas and utility franchises, and other special privileges were enormous—so great that the machine could be bought by reckless businessmen for corrupt franchise bargains. The machine used its power over the little men as well by favors and threats. The New York Citizens' Association estimated in 1871 that Tweed could influence about half of New York City's 130,000 votes. A decade later it was estimated that the Philadelphia Gas Ring could control at least 20,000 votes.[55] Obviously the task of the municipal reformers was stupendous.

Slowly and with discouraging setbacks the cause of reform advanced. It took institutional form in local organizations of civic-minded persons, of which there were in 1894 more than eighty. The two most active—the City Club of New York and the Municipal League of Philadelphia—joined hands in 1894 to call the first National Conference for Good City Government. The object was to determine the best means of forwarding the cause of honest and intelligent municipal government and to unite the scattered forces fighting for better cities. Within a few months this Conference organized the National Municipal League, the outstanding center for improvement in the politics, administration, and morals of American cities for the next half century and more.

We may repeat that the moral quality of the federal government was dependent upon the ethical standards of cities and states, and the people thereof. State legislators elected Senators, party conventions nominated Presidents, voters elected Congressmen. Corruption in city government was bound up with the character of the local party organization and often proceeded directly from it. The same party organization comprised the local machine and played an important role in the state organization. It could make its voice felt in the halls of Congress and in the executive departments. Presidents, Senators, and Congressmen were dependent on party organizations for reelection; and they in turn drew much of their sustenance from the patronage and perquisites of their Washington representatives.

Civil service reform, ballot reform, and municipal reform had

[55] Noted in Frank Mann Stewart, *A Half Century of Municipal Reform: the History of the National Municipal League* (Berkeley: University of California Press, 1950), p. 9.

accomplished much, but had left substantially untouched the dubious connection between amoral business and utility corporations on the one hand and city and state governments on the other. Lincoln Steffens was still to write *The Shame of the Cities* and *The Struggle for Self-Government*. While there had been marked and salutary progress from Grant to McKinley, vigilance was still necessary.

CHAPTER EIGHTEEN

In Retrospect

A perceptive Rip Van Winkle who fell into slumber on the banks of the Potomac at the close of the Civil War and awoke at the close of the Spanish-American War would have remarked both the tenacity of tradition and the inevitability of change. The city was larger but still southern in atmosphere. The public buildings were more numerous but still reminiscent of the architectural style of earlier decades. The clerks also were more numerous, and the "female clerks" more in evidence, but the pattern of their character, wedded to an accustomed routine, faithful in the performance of their duties, necessarily parsimonious in their manner of life, would have been familiar. Horse-drawn vehicles still occupied the streets, but the pigs and chickens had been banished. More subtle were many of the changes that had occurred in the system of administration. Some transformations had become well established; others were in mid-course; some which were to be important were barely taking shape, a portent of things to come.

Before reviewing the two major institutional developments and some of their consequences—the presidency and civil service reform —it will be convenient to comment on a few of the underlying changes that were in motion. A new ideal of the standards of prose-cuting the public business was slowly gathering force; the great body of federal employees, which the Civil War and its aftermath had perforce based on the North and West, was again becoming national, not sectional, in character; the universality of the "clerk" and of handwritten manuscripts was yielding to the typewriter, while the tempo of action was speeded by the telephone.

GROUND SWELLS

Trend toward businesslike administration. The country was slowly moving from one broad ideal of the nature of its administrative system to another. For decades this ideal had been a system political in character, serving the interests of party at an admitted cost in competence and integrity, as well as, or often in preference to, the interests of good administration. This ideal was challenged and gradually subdued to the ideal of a "businesslike" government.

The ferment was more strenuously at work in municipal government than in the capital city, but it could be sensed in Washington as well as in New York. It was symbolized by the occasional appearance of businessmen at the heads of departments, such as John Wanamaker in the Post Office, William C. Whitney in the Navy, Stephen B. Elkins in War, and Ethan A. Hitchcock in Interior. It was implicit in the gradual extension of the merit system and in the demands of the merchant importers of New York for less politics and more attention to duty in the customhouse.

Bearing on the same tendency was the appointment of university faculty men to important government posts. As long as college and university curricula were based on classical studies, philosophy, and theology, the faculty were hardly prepared to serve in executive positions. As the newer disciplines of economics and statistics, political science, and the agricultural sciences found a place in the institutions of higher learning, specialists in these fields became useful in practical affairs.

Many of the larger institutions contributed faculty members to the public service, notably the state universities. Among these the University of Michigan was one of the most conspicuous.[1] The first chairman of the Interstate Commerce Commission, Thomas M. Cooley, was professor of history and dean of the School of Political Science at this institution and earlier had been a member of its law department. The chief statistician of the Commission, Henry C. Adams, had taught at Johns Hopkins and Cornell, and at the time of his appointment was professor of political economy at Michigan. James B. Angell, noted educator and president of the University of

[1] Earl D. Babst and Lewis G. Vander Velde, eds., *Michigan and the Cleveland Era* (Ann Arbor: University of Michigan Press, 1948).

Michigan, was appointed by both Republican and Democratic administrations to a series of important posts: minister to China (1880), Canadian Fisheries Commission (1887), chairman, Deep Waterways Commission (1896), and minister to Turkey (1897). Edwin Willits, president of Michigan Agricultural College and graduate of the University of Michigan, became Assistant Secretary of Agriculture in 1889.

The faculties of other universities were also called upon for government service, consulting or administrative. A rare early example of the scholar in politics who also rose to high administrative post was William Lyne Wilson, Postmaster General from 1895 to 1897. After service in the Confederate army, he was assistant professor of the ancient languages at Columbian College and eventually president of West Virginia University. He was a member of the House from 1883 to 1895, and in 1892 permanent chairman of the Democratic National Convention. He thus had impressive political as well as academic credentials. James Wilson, a member of the faculty of Iowa State College and Secretary of Agriculture under three Presidents, was another distinguished academician, equally successful in administration. John W. Foster, a member of the faculty of George Washington University, served as minister to Mexico, Russia, and Spain, and for a short period (1892–93) was Secretary of State. Many one-time faculty men were attracted to Washington for scientific research in such agencies as the Department of Agriculture and the Geological Survey; some of them took on administrative duties. Their appointment again was a symbol of the nonpolitical ideal.

The emerging concept of administration as properly businesslike rather than political in nature was still novel and was disputed in many quarters. Thus James S. Clarkson, Harrison's First Assistant Postmaster General, explained that the United States government was a political, not a business, machine.[2] It was indeed both, but its political character was receding, its business quality advancing.

Trend from a sectional to a national service. Prior to the Civil War the public service was drawn freely from all sections of the country, and southern influence was strong. Congressional interest in office had already introduced a form of apportionment in the 1850's, and in accordance with immemorial tradition local appointments of

[2] Dorothy G. Fowler, *The Cabinet Politician*, p. 214.

federal officials were confined to the locality. During the war many southern clerks and probably most southern officials withdrew from Washington. The service became northern and western. Prejudice against southerners remained strong after the war. The fourteenth amendment forbade the employment of former members of Congress or state officials who had given aid or comfort to enemies of the United States, until after civic rehabilitation. This was accomplished by a series of enactments applying to named persons and in 1872 by a general amnesty, with a few exceptions.[3]

On the higher levels the *de facto* southern proscription was tempered by Hayes' appointment of Postmaster General David McKendree Key, an ex-Confederate officer from Tennessee. Thereafter most Cabinets contained at least one representative from the Deep South and others from the border states.

Veterans' preference was a powerful factor in maintaining northern and western predominance in the public service. The thirty years after the Civil War were par excellence the generation of army officers in the middle and higher ranks,[4] and of the rank and file of the Grand Army of the Republic in the subordinate positions. The strength of the former lay in a sense of public gratitude and their active participation in politics; that of the latter in statutory preference as well. Promptly at the close of the war Congress for the first time required preference in civil office to persons honorably discharged from the military and naval service, if found to possess the necessary business capacity.[5]

Both Congress and Presidents saw to it that appointing officers did their duty to veterans. In 1882 the Senate ordered an investigation to discover whether the law had been faithfully executed—obviously suspecting that it had not.[6] The Civil Service Act of 1883 renewed

[3] Article XIV, sec. 3, of Amendments to the Constitution; 17 Stat. 142 (May 22, 1872).
[4] By way of example, note the middle range of Post Office Department executives in the 1890's: Captain James E. White, general superintendent, Railway Mail Service; Major R. D. S. Tyler, chief, Mail Equipment Division; Colonel Smith A. Whitfield, First Assistant Postmaster General; Major E. H. Shook, chief, Division of Post Office Supplies; Captain D. P. Liebhart, superintendent, Dead Letter Office; Colonel Luther Caldwell, chief, Bond Division. Marshall Cushing, *The Story of Our Post-Office*, pp. 70, 115, 165, 225, 275, 299.
[5] 13 Stat. 571 (March 3, 1865).
[6] Senate Report 780, 47th Cong., 1st sess. (July 3, 1882).

the enactment of 1865. In 1885 Cleveland wrote the New York collector of customs, "It is exceedingly important that the force of this law should be scrupulously regarded. Indeed, this *must* be done."[7] Departmental reports, however, justified the record of the appointing officers. In Treasury over 50 per cent of appointments from 1887 to 1882 were veterans, their widows, or orphans; in the War Department (1865–1882) more than 60 per cent; in Interior, about one-third. Other departments were less explicit, but all asserted their determination to favor the veterans.[8] The authority of the Grand Army of the Republic was the potent political sanction weighing upon all concerned.

The effect of this preference, from the point of view of the present analysis, was to enforce the regional character of the federal service. Veterans' preference was not enjoyed by the men in gray.

Party continued to play a role also in geographical dislocation. Except for Cleveland's eight years in the White House, the country was governed by the Republicans. There were few Republicans in the South and southern officeholders were often northerners or Negroes—members of the Republican organization. In the classified competitive service a reasonable balance was gradually achieved; in the rest of the service the disproportion persisted as Republican party control pushed into the twentieth century. It was in the North, too, that the business ideal flourished, and the Republican party was its home.

Trend from the age of the copy clerk to the dawn of the age of the technician. For a full century the characteristic figure in the rank and file was the person who sat at a desk and used a pen: the auditing clerks and the department copy clerks. Immense masses of handwritten accounts, letterbooks, and manuscripts accumulated in every agency, the product of painstaking, laborious, and usually excellent penmanship. Now began the transition to employees trained and skillful in the use of office machines, one of the earliest of which was the typewriter. By the 1890's the telephone was coming into use in government offices and a new class of employment came into existence, the telephone operator. The automobile mechanic was almost entirely a mark of the twentieth century. In the scientific

---

[7] Grover Cleveland, *Letters* (Nevins ed.), p. 91.
[8] Senate Report 780, 47th Cong., 1st sess., pp. 3-4.

agencies men skilled in instrumentation were the characteristic type. The geologist's hammer, the chemist's reagents, the plant pathologist's microscope became the marks of a new kind of public service.

Involved in these tendencies was another intimately related to them, the transition from a public service calling primarily for persons with a common school, academy, or high school education to one requiring college and professional training. In numbers they were a small minority, but in significance they loomed large. It cannot be said that the Civil Service Commission sought college or university men and women, apart from the scientific and technical fields; indeed it had to protect itself against allegations that it was building up an intellectual aristocracy. The task of keeping the machine in order was that of the chief clerks, who were formed by experience, not by study.

It is deeply to be regretted that it is impossible with the material at hand to do justice to the chief clerks, whose collective history began in 1789. Of them it could be said, to borrow the words of Secretary Jacob D. Cox, "An experienced clerk is a repository of the law, the history and the traditions of the department, and may often, by a word or suggestion, expose a fraud, which might otherwise escape unnoticed, indicate an important fact of which there is no record, or in a thousand ways save his superior from imposition or from a long and laborious investigation."[9]

The quality of the chief clerks was exemplified in the career of Robert S. Chew, chief clerk of the State Department, who was memorialized in 1874 by Congressman James B. Sener. "He . . . was forty years in the service of the State Department, serving with sixteen Secretaries of State, under twelve Presidents, and dying as he had lived, a most honest, faithful, and capable public servant, enjoying under all administrations the confidence of his superiors and the respect and esteem of all with whom he was brought into intercourse."[10]

One suspects that as a class chief clerks were meticulous, masters of detail, proud of their unique knowledge of forms and precedents, devoted to *status quo* and not inclined to innovation, quick to bend to the wishes of their immediate superiors but apt in blunting such

[9] Secretary of the Interior, *Annual Report*, 1869, p. xxv.
[10] *Congressional Record*, 43d Cong., 1st sess., p. 3132 (April 6, 1874).

policies as seemed to them in error. We may guess also that many of them were martinets, and we may be sure that as a group they were far from being partisans. Without continuity in their offices, Secretaries would indeed have been at a loss in the management of their departments.

THE PRESIDENCY

If now we turn to the institutional framework of the administrative system we note the gradual restoration of authority to the Chief Magistrate. The office had been nearly wrecked during Johnson's administration and from 1865 to 1877 the country in effect had been governed by a Senate oligarchy. Hayes challenged this small group and Garfield defeated it. Cleveland succeeded in securing the repeal of the Tenure of Office Act, the highwater mark of Senate pretensions. The Senate, however, remained powerful and no President argued during these years that he represented the people as truly as Congress.

As an executive the office of President was handicapped both by public expectations and by the absence of an administrative staff. It was not supposed that Presidents (or governors, and mayors for that matter) would take an active part in the management of the public business. So long as the departments ran smoothly and avoided serious congressional or public criticism they were generally left alone by the White House. Department heads were expected to keep Presidents informed and to warn them of impending trouble, but the responsibility of day-by-day affairs was theirs. Apart from the civil service system, indeed, there was almost no government-wide operation.

The executive staff to which a later age became accustomed was not even thought of. There were no administrative assistants, although Cleveland wished for one. There was no budget bureau. The Civil Service Commission was not understood to be a part of the executive office but (erroneously) an independent agency to police the departments. There was no agency directly serving the President to inquire, to report, and to advise. In the absence of such administrative aids he was necessarily barred from an active role in management. His mind was directed primarily to Congress, not to the executive departments.

CIVIL SERVICE REFORM

Without doubt the achievement of civil service reform in 1883 was a fundamental turning point in the history of the federal administrative system. Limited as was its initial application and bitter as was the hostility of the professional politicians, it was nevertheless the foundation on which the public service was to be built in succeeding decades. The government simply could not have supported the tasks that the country imposed upon it in the twentieth century without the stable, competent, and responsible public service which the Pendleton Act made possible.

Some of the consequences that were feared as a result of the merit system did not materialize. The friends of Jacksonian democracy discovered that an obnoxious officeholding class did not arise to vex them. The party managers learned that they could win elections with the patronage resources that remained at their command. The reformers learned that the merit system was not the wonder-working solution of all the problems of government. There was no transformation of the relations of the President to Congress, and of Congressmen to the White House and the executive departments.

One consequence, however, was quickly evident. The quality of the public service began a steady improvement. The quadrennial disruption was lessened in violence. The competence of the rank and file improved. Their loyalty to their work strengthened; to their party it diminished. The moral standards of the public offices improved, even if marred by some scandals.

Other corollaries of the merit system were not slow in emerging. Primary among these was the partial formation of a government-wide establishment in lieu of a loose collection of mutually independent departments and agencies. Before 1883 the only important element of a government-wide administrative system was found in the auditing offices. The settlement of accounts was presumably on the same principles, no matter what the department in which the expenditure occurred. The broad legal limits within which administration was confined were fixed by statute, such as the eight-hour day; and by the rulings of the Attorney General and the comptrollers. Most of the decisions of these offices, however, dealt with particulars, not with problems of a service-wide nature.

The civil service rules, to the contrary, were universal, so far as the classified competitive service was concerned. They were the same in every department, and in the field offices of every establishment. They were prescribed by the President, not by the Commission; they consequently had the highest authority and were a direct obligation upon every agency. They comprised the first major recognition both of a service-wide administrative system and of the President as the active head of that system.

The recognition of tenure for the classified competitive system raised in more acute form the problem of superannuation. Serious discussion of the plight of the aged clerk began in the decade following the Pendleton Act, but official opinion was hostile to pensions for civil employees. This element of a service-wide system was not to become effective until 1920.

The Civil Service Act also brought discussion of the proper line of demarcation between the subordinate nonpolitical employees and the directing personnel. McKinley's roll back of the classified competitive service doubtless had a strong political motivation, but it also was based upon a preliminary rational analysis of a basic distinction. Where "to draw the line," indeed, was a dimly understood problem for succeeding decades and first received an adequate analysis only in 1953.

A final consequence of the merit system was to lay the foundation for the organization of civil service employees. Without the guarantee of stable employment, organization even for beneficial objects was hardly worthwhile. The Pendleton Act also coincided with powerful labor movements in the industrial world and with a slowly changing climate of opinion, conducive to tolerating unions in some branches of the public service. Tenure was the essential element for the civil service union movement.

The Civil Service Act thus foreshadowed many emerging tendencies. Modest as were its early accomplishments, the merit system deserves to rank as one of the decisive administrative achievements of the period.

IMPROVEMENT IN MORAL STANDARDS

To obtain a proper perspective on the course of moral standards in the public service from Grant to McKinley it is necessary to assert at the outset that the vast majority of federal officials and employees were men and women of character, of whose integrity there could be no question. This had been the case during the rise and dominance of the patronage system before the Civil War and remained the case in the years of degradation after the war.

Riding on top of this solid mass of men of good will and honest devotion to duty, there was a layer of adventurers who had no hesitation in defrauding the public, stealing government funds, and shamefully abusing helpless government clients such as the Indians. Their number and audacity were greatest during Grant's administration, when even members of the Cabinet and of the President's official family were involved in dishonorable transactions. The official climate altered abruptly when Hayes became President, although unsuspected evil-doing continued in some quarters. The change in party control consequent upon Cleveland's election in 1884 was the occasion for a general housecleaning; Cleveland, indeed, had won success in large measure because the country believed him to be a stubbornly honest man.

The Civil Service Act was conducive to higher standards of official conduct. The rank and file, at least, had new motives for sobriety, attention to duty, and propriety in their departmental conduct. It became less important to seek political endorsement (at whatever price) as a condition of steady employment, and more important to earn a reputation for diligence and trustworthiness. Some breaks in the dykes did occur in civil service ranks, notably in the Post Office. The influence of the merit system was nevertheless pronounced in cultivating proper observance of official morality.

THIRTY YEARS OF INTELLECTUAL STAGNATION

Considering the state of administrative doctrine from 1870 to 1900, we must conclude that these were years of stagnation. Congress repeatedly investigated the public service, but its committee reports made no contributions to an understanding of the nature of administration. None of them approached the excellence of the 1842 report of the Gilmer Select Committee on Retrenchment.[11] Presidents had little to say beyond recommendations for particular reforms. None of them, so far as noted, offered a program suggestive

[11] House Report 741, 27th Cong., 2d sess. (May 23, 1842).

of an interest in the art of management as such. A department head occasionally evidenced an awareness of the administrative inadequacies of his own position and of the necessities of active management on his part, but none of them developed a systematic analysis of management at the departmental level.

What contributions there were to administrative doctrine came from outside government, from the pens of reformers and students of government. Only three of these were remembered by succeeding generations: Charles Francis Adams, whose masterly articles on the relation of the state to railroads and on the character of the public service were fundamental in character; Woodrow Wilson, whose single contribution in the *Political Science Quarterly* (1887) was the first recognition of the field of public administration as an object of study and a potential area of generalization; and Frank J. Goodnow, who published his *Comparative Administrative Law* in 1893. Reform was the dominant concern of the country, not the formulation of doctrine.

These writings, and others concerned with special problems, foreshadowed the emergence of a field of study and of systematic formulation. The latter was still a good quarter-century in the future; the former was recognized in a few institutions at the close of the century. Foremost among them was Columbia University where, under the leadership of Frank J. Goodnow, the study of administrative law and public administration was vigorously pursued.

The course of administrative history, after Grant, was one of recovery from the abuses of the Civil War and of the first twelve years thereafter. Hard battles were fought between Congress and the executive branch, between an older generation wedded to politics and a new generation emerging in an age of business, between reformers and skeptics. Although improvement was painfully slow, there was substantially no regression. A Potomac Rip Van Winkle, stirring into consciousness at the end of McKinley's first term, would have found relative satisfaction in the state of the administrative system. It was not yet fully prepared to tackle the emerging problems of the near future—colonial government, the regulation of business and banking, war administration, and a host of lesser responsibilities—but some essential foundations had been laid. Far-reaching transformations were to follow.

INDEX

Adams, Charles Francis, Jr., on laissez faire, 3-4; on parties and morality, 366

Adams, Henry, on Grant, 23-24; on presidency, 24-25, 26; on Congress, 52; on Treasury Department, 110

Adams, Henry C., 387

Adams, John Quincy, refuses to vote on roll call, 51

Administration, see Civil Service Commission, Congress, President, and entries under individual departments and offices

Administration and legislation, 68-70

Administrative careers, see careers

Administrative methods, congressional investigation of, 84-92

Administrative system, a general view, 1-3

Advance obligations, prohibition of, 59

Agency board system of examinations, 314-16

Agricultural experiment stations, 247-52

Agriculture, Department of, 232-56; Secretaries, 233-40; clientele, 240-42; and science, 243-46; animal industry regulation, 246-47; experiment stations, 247-52; overhead organization, 252-54; civil service reform in, 254-56

Alger, Russell A., Secretary of the War Department, on office seeking, 7; on failure of army administration, 150-51

Ames, Oakes, and railroad passes, 71; and Crédit Mobilier, 367-68

Angell, James B., 387-88

Animal Industry, Bureau of, 246-47

Appeals, in Patent Office, 228-30

Appellate functions of Congress, 73-84; on personnel, 73-74; on pensions, 74-78; on claims, 78-81; on patents, 81-84

Appointment policy and practice, office seeking, 5-8; Grant on, 24; Congress and, 26-27, 74; and Tenure

of Office Act, 29-31; senatorial courtesy, 31-35; and President, 95-97; in customhouses, 120-23; in navy yards, 171-74; in Indian service, 186-87, 191-92; in Pension Office, 211-12; in Patent Office, 224-25; in Agriculture, 243-45, 254-55; in Post Office, 268; under civil service system, 317-21; apportionment, 360-61

Apportionment, 360-61

Appropriations, and control of operations, 54-57

Appropriations, Committee on, 60-66

Army, military policy, 134; hostility to, 137-38; General Staff, 140-46; military bureaus, 143-44; War with Spain, 146-50; military administration, 150-53

Arnold, Matthew, quoted, vii

Arthur, Chester A., and New York customhouse, 33, 123; day as President, 104-105; Navy Department under, 159-60; signs Civil Service Act, 301

Assessments on officeholders, 332-40

Assistant Postmasters General, 263-65

Association of American Agricultural Colleges and Experiment Stations, 251-52

Atwater, Wilbur O., chief of the Office of Experiment Stations, 244; on experiment stations, 249-50

Audit, of experiment station funds, 250-51

Auditing, reorganization of in 1894, 112

Balances, reversion of, 59

Barron, Henry D., on compensation of government employees, 132

Beavers, George W., and corruption in Post Office, 272

Beck, James B., opposes civil service reform, 293

[397]